Australia, Britain, and Migration, 1915–1940

Studies in Australian History

Series editors:
Alan Gilbert, Patricia Grimshaw and Peter Spearritt

Steven Nicholas (ed.)   *Convict Workers*
Pamela Statham (ed.)   *The Origins of Australia's Capital Cities*
Jeffrey Grey   *A Military History of Australia*
Alastair Davidson   *The Invisible State*
James A. Gillespie   *The Price of Health*
David Neal   *The Rule of Law in a Penal Colony*
Sharon Morgan   *Land Settlement in Early Tasmania*
Audrey Oldfield   *Woman Suffrage in Australia*
Paula J. Byrne   *Criminal Law and Colonial Subject*
Peggy Brock   *Outback Ghettos*
Raelene Frances   *The Politics of Work*
Luke Trainor   *British Imperialism and Australian Nationalism*
Margaret Maynard   *Fashioned from Penury*
Dawn May   *Aboriginal Labour and the Cattle Industry*
Joy Damousi and Marilyn Lake (eds)   *Gender and War*

Australia, Britain, and Migration, 1915–1940

A Study of Desperate Hopes

Michael Roe

Department of History, University of Tasmania

Published by the Press Syndicate of the University of Cambridge
The Pitt Building, Trumpington Street, Cambridge CB2 1RP, UK
40 West 20th Street, New York, NY 10011–4211, USA
10 Stamford Road, Oakleigh, Victoria 3166, Australia

First published 1995

Printed in Hong Kong by Colorcraft

National Library of Australia cataloguing-in-publication data

Roe, Michael, 1931–.
Australia, Britain, and migration, 1915–1940: a study
of desperate hopes.
Bibliography.
Includes index.
1. Australia – Emigration and immigration – History – 20th
century. 2. Great Britain – Emigration and immigration –
History – 20th century. 3. Australia – Emigration and
immigration – Government policy. I. Title. (Series:
Studies in Australian history (Cambridge, England)).
325.2410994

Library of Congress cataloguing-in-publication data

Roe, Michael, 1931–.
Australia, Britain, and migration, 1915–1940: a study of
desperate hopes / Michael Roe.
(Studies in Australian history)
Includes bibliographical references and index.
1. Australia – Emigration and immigration – History – 20th century.
2. Great Britain – Emigration and immigration – History – 20th century.
3. British – Australia – History – 20th century. 4. Australia –
emigration and immigration – Government policy. I. Title.
II. Series.
JV9125.R64 1995
304.8'94041–dc20   94–45796

A catalogue record for this book is available from the British Library.

ISBN 0 521 46507 9 Hardback

Contents

For
Justin Roe

Illustrations

Tables

Acknowledgements

My first thanks must go to the University of Tasmania for continuing provision of an environment which makes possible the kind of scholarship whence this book proceeds. No less admirably has Cambridge University Press undertaken its role. Most funding has come from the University of Tasmania, but some also from the Australian Research Council.

Shane Roberts and Kati Thomson have laboured to translate my scribblings into legibility. Many students have had to bear side-effects of my commitment to this research, and two—Yvonne Furneaux-Young and Marie Ellison—have abetted it. Margot and Sophie Roe likewise have gone beyond familial duty through years of association with 'my migrants'. Among friends, let me proclaim Cyril and Joan Brackenbury, who both appear in these pages—he remembering Wembley, she (a migrant of both 1920s and 1950s) long sustaining our family.

Brooke Crutchley gave gracious permission for use of his father's papers. Librarians and archivists in two hemispheres have placed me ever deeper in their debt. This book is more one person's work than is commonly the present case, and yet stands dependent on boundless goodwill, effort, and sacrifice from others.

Abbreviations and Usages

CSIR   Council for Scientific and Industrial Research
CSIRO   Commonwealth Scientific and Industrial Research Organisation, the successor to CSIR
DMC   Development and Migration Commission
HMG   His Majesty's Government of the UK
ITB   Industrial Transference Board
NRF   National Relief Fund
OSC   Oversea Settlement Committee
OSD   Oversea Settlement Department
SOSBW   Society for the Oversea Settlement of British Women
YM(W)CA   Young Men's (Women's) Christian Association

'Australia House' refers to the offices of the Commonwealth in London, wherein was housed the bureaucracy dealing with migration.

'The Commonwealth' refers to the federal government of Australia, established in 1901 with the federation of the six then-existing colonies. The colonies then became known as States and retained extensive powers.

References to money and area remain in contemporary terms. For money these include occasional references to shillings (s.) and pence (d.), as well as pounds (£). There were 12 pennies in one shilling, and 20 shillings in one pound. Appropriate conversions for distance are 1 mile = 1.61 kilometre, and for area, 1 acre = 0.405 hectare.

Various usages define particular categories of assisted migrants. Nominees were those proposed by Australian residents (nominators). 'Selectees' were those recruited in Britain after State governments had specified (technically, requisitioned) desired numbers in particular categories of employment. Quotation marks are used throughout as to 'selectees' and their 'selection'.

The Agreement (capitalised) is the so-called 'Thirty-four Million Pounds Agreement' under which HMG subsidised particular schemes in Australia, more specifically described as 'undertakings'.

'Normal flow' migrants are those who presumably would have gone to Australia by whatever means, independent of the putative impact of the Agreement.

'Labor' is spelled thus only when referring to the pertinent Australian political force.

Introduction

This book sets out to narrate Australian migration policy between World War I and World War II especially as it involved both government and people of the United Kingdom. The central theme is that of two polities seeking maximum advantage for interests dominant in either place, with but little regard for each other or for the migrants themselves. Broadly, the British government wanted a high level of emigration, seeing redundancy of population and unemployment as threats to domestic stability. Australian policy as to immigration was sceptical, but generally there prevailed readiness to subsidise the movement of people who promised to supply Australian needs at modest cost and minimal trouble. From 1922, following the passage of HMG's Empire Settlement Act, this subsidy was complemented by Britain itself giving aid to migrants approved by Australian authorities. Further the Act provided for subsidy by HMG of developmental programmes in Australia which arguably increased capacity there to absorb migrants. Thus the way broadened for Australia to be cajoled or bribed into greater receptivity. All this adapted a fundamental of Australian history since 1788—reliance on British resources as stimuli to expansion.

One should not feel much surprise the two polities should have been resolute in pursuing their own immediate ends. Such is the task of all governments always. Yet the tensions and toughness which mark this story were indeed formidable. They modify, almost to extinction, any picture of Australian federal governments of these years, notably that led by S. M. Bruce, as being supine and obsequious before the mother country. Not that this is the first academic study to point thus. The work of Kosmos Tsokhas does so outstandingly, his major book proposing such an analysis in relation to the marketing of wool, while other papers extend into further areas, including migration. More general, but scarcely less potent continuity subsists with E. M. Andrews's study of Australian–British relations during World War I.

While governments were often mean and petty in their bargaining, some positive purpose lay in the background. Both polities were seeking to restore social economies sapped by the Great War and its aftermath. Bruce had very considerable abilities, as in a different if diminishing way had his precursor,

1

W. M. Hughes. The latter more enthusiastically upheld a vision for the future, yet Bruce had expansive hopes too. The most powerful British politicians of the day scarcely evoke such praise, yet the next rank—outstandingly but not only in the person of L. S. Amery—included some who truly believed in Empire and in the benefits which migration might bestow. That optimism extended to the fate of the migrants themselves. The following pages will show that some among these were reluctant to move, but on balance more affirmative attitudes were dominant. Thus, in various ways, did hope prevail. The structure of this book, most obviously its chapter-titles, is predicated upon the notion that migration indeed could serve political and human aspirations—but always with a sense of the desperation that prevailed at every level and which became stronger with time's passing.

While the book's main concern is the development of Australian policy and the consequent interaction of governments, there are some subsidiary stories of interest and importance. The place of migration in Britain's domestic politics has received little attention from the historians. It seems to deserve more: especially the strength of popular resistance to emigration, and the general debate on demographic matters. Australian scepticism about immigration is better known, but not all its intricacies and effects. There, too, demographic debate had some interesting passages. Political and administrative history is illuminated at various points, most deliberately in the work of the Development and Migration Commission, an exercise in modernist government. One of the Commission's roles was to mediate in the relationship between the government of the federal Commonwealth of Australia, and the various State governments. That continuing theme in twentieth-century Australian history obtrudes throughout.

The migrants' personal experience does too. However, the first eight chapters treat such matters only insofar as is necessary to explain the development of policy. The final two chapters reverse this emphasis and strive to give more than a mere flavour of the human dimension. To decide just which material should come earlier, which should be reserved, was extremely difficult: no two people, or any one person at different times, would make the same decision. The hope is that by the end some totality develops. Many a future monograph surely will expand the story of experience (as a couple have already).

While numbers were never so great as migrationists wanted, they still constitute a sizeable human shift. Nearly half-a-million beings enter our purview. To stress that point, statistical tables come immediately. They will be supplemented and modified—or even, in the way of statistics, be brought into occasional doubt—as the book proceeds, but throughout they serve as an essential base.

Table 1   Gross, net and assisted immigration to Australia, 1919–40

Year	a. Gross immi- gration from Britain	b. Gross immi- gration	c. Net British immi- gration	d. Net immi- gration	e. Immi- gration assisted by Australia	f. Immi- gration assisted by by HMG under Settlement Act
1919					245	
1920				27 606	9 059	
1921			17 630	17 525	14 682	
1922			34 729	40 157	24 258	5 611
1923			35 154	39 714	26 645	24 221
1924	19 572	30 974	35 734	46 069	25 036	23 645
1925	47 596	66 477	32 164	39 801	24 827	22 527
1926	42 219	59 664	38 482	44 783	31 260	32 689
1927	41 945	67 078	39 872	51 580	30 123	29 136
1928	31 149	48 233	24 746	30 054	22 394	20 603
1929	19 700	31 698	10 268	11 820	12 943	11 528
1930	8 369	17 537	–7 538	–8 530	2 683	1 978
1931	3 782	9 441	–6 640	–10 094	275	211
1932	3 493	9 868	–2 454	–2 997	175	188
1933	3 473	10 749	–134	214	72	117
1934	3 718	11 778	807	2 280	159	192
1935	3 688	12 608	–2 139	–289	100	89
1936	3 718	12 593	–1 080	1 497	9	
1937	4 672	16 294	–411	5 203	141	
1938	5 562	19 548	739	9 137	852	
1939	8 654	24 068	3 330	13 891	2 686	
1940	2 491	11 609				

Source:
   The main sources are statistics issued by Australian official agencies through the
   Demography Bulletin and *Labour Report*. Important figures as to HMG assistance
   are in *Report of the Oversea Settlement Committee, 1935–6* (Command 5200).
Notes:
1. Where no figures appear, it is because no official series provide them; such
   blanks do not necessarily mean zero.
2. Gross immigration columns *a* and *b* refer to people intending permanent
   residence, not all arrivals. Unfortunately columns *c* and *d* do not thus define
   immigration but result from subtracting all departures, for whatever reason, from
   all arrivals, likewise.
3. Column *a* refers to residents of the British Isles, including the Irish Free State,
   whereas column *c* applies to all citizens of the Empire/Commonwealth.
4. Most discrepancies between columns *e* and *f* result from Australia giving aid to
   various categories of nominees not assisted by HMG. The text describes these;
   most important were residents of the Irish Free State.
5. The figures in columns *a* and *b* for 1924 relate to the second half of that year.
   Only then, apparently, was this vital series established.
6. The statistics for inter-war migration have come under sophisticated demographic study by two scholars: Jupp, 'Factors Affecting … Australian Population',
   and Dryden, 'Australian Immigration'. Nevertheless, gaps and problems remain.

Table 2   Assisted immigration to Australia, by category, 1920–39

Year	Females among all assistees	All 'selectees'	Nominees	'Selected' domestics	'Selected' farmboys
1920	4 455				
1921	6 466				
1922	8 883	9 726	14 532	766	1 510
1923	8 744	15 367	11 278	1 013	3 500
1924	10 078	12 611	12 425	1 419	2 276
1925	9 766	10 131	14 696	1 268	2 409
1926	13 524	7 884	23 376	1 603	2 419
1927	13 880	7 409	30 123	1 897	2 318
1928	10 604	5 984	16 410	1 785	2 122
1929	6 179	3 762	12 943	1 243	1 318
1930	1 482			313	239
1931	164			29	7
1932	94				
1933	21				
1934	48				
1935	38				
1936	6				
1937	49				
1938	408				
1939	1 216				

Source:
  Drawn from material at AOT: PD55/8/36.
Note:
  Report ... of the Inter-Departmental Committee on Migration Policy (Command 4689) gives a total for 'selectees' 1922–31 of 58,574, very well below the above number. Perhaps the figure excluded dependants. The *Report* cited farm settlers as numbering 9125. Subtracting too the above totals of domestics (11,336) and farmboys (18,118), we are left with almost precisely 20,000, almost all of whom would have been adult male farmworkers.

Table 3   Requisitions by Australian States for 'selected' immigrants from Britain, by category, 1928

	Farmboys	*Adult Farmworkers*	*Domestics*
New South Wales	1 105	2 150	1 200
Victoria	480	830	600
Queensland	510		720
South Australia	125		240
Western Australia	172	2 150	480
Total	2 392	3 840	3 240

Source:
   As remarked later, there is but scant detail on the numbers of 'selectees' whom the States *sought* through requisitions. The major exception is in the 1928 annual *Report* of the Development and Migration Commission, *Commonwealth Parliamentary Papers,* 1929, vol. 2, pp. 28–9, when peaks had passed.
Notes:
1. Nearly all these farmboys had affiliation with one of the philanthropic groups interested in migration. While the names of some of these will convey little at this stage, details seem appropriate. In New South Wales, 960 requisitions were associated with the Dreadnought Trust, 25 with the Fellowship of the British Empire Exhibition and 120 with the Big Brother Movement; in Victoria, 300 with the Big Brother Movement and 180 with the Boy Scouts; in Queensland, 300 with the Church of England; in South Australia, 125 with the Big Brother Movement; in Western Australia, 100 with the Young Australia League and 72 with the Church of England.
2. In addition Victoria sought 80 farmers, with capital.

*   *   *

   The story which these statistics suggest and which this book pursues is a footnote to the truth that migration is fundamental to human experience. The history of Australia not only follows but embellishes that rule. The entry of Aboriginals into the continent traces to a past which research is pushing back to ever more distant times: an epic story, its detail will always remain in doubt. Since 1788 the potency of immigration has remained high, with several chapters of particular intensity.
   In establishing its first Australian colonies as convict gaols, Britain showed how government-imposed migration could help resolve problems in the metropolis. The brutality of that intent was the key to much else of the convict era. Yet in Australia some convicts found prosperity and many led decent lives. While convictism still proceeded (to 1853 in eastern Australia, 1868 in Western Australia) Britain began to assist the migration of other common people. The aim, just as much as with penal transportation, was to diminish social conflict arising from Britain's industrialisation. Most radicals within the working class scarified this policy, insisting that all Britons had a right to independence in their native land; to be pressured into going to colonies where convictism shaped social and political values, was a double-

dyed insult.[1] Yet a fair number of everyday Britons were ready to go to Australia, and a few radicals were among them. The archetype was Henry Parkes, active in the Birmingham Political Union in the early 1830s and on that base to build in Australia a political career of fantastic success. In the late 1840s Britain's radical press not merely abandoned hostility to Austral migration, but barracked for it. This switch was as remarkable as, say, the weakening of Chartism in revealing the ebb of British militance at mid-century.

Australia saw fierce debate as to both free and penal migration in the 1830s and 1840s. Concerning the former, complaints waxed that Britain was dumping alleged paupers and ne'er-do-wells, and they were to recur ninety years on.[2] Withal, most Australians agreed that redemption of their new home depended upon free migration. There remained scope for division as to who were desirable newcomers. The most famous upholders of free migration were J. D. Lang and Caroline Chisholm—one a Presbyterian cleric, the other a Catholic philanthropist. Lang alleged that Chisholm's activities aimed to Romanise Australia. This controversy also reverberated in later years.

Lang and Parkes became leaders of the movement against convict transportation. This developed into a crusade with many facets—political in its resistance to imperial dominance, ethical in its call for a morally elevated population, social-democratic in its demand that free workers be immune from convict competition. Arguably, no episode in Australian domestic history has had greater import. Population issues stood central in public discourse.

That proved less true in the later nineteenth century, but only by a margin. Relative prosperity at once quickened self-paid migration and diminished the involvement of governments. In Britain official assistance dwindled to nothing by the early 1870s. The several Australian colonies varied in their policies. Queensland was most enthusiastic. Especially in New South Wales workingmen feared lest immigration flood the labour market, and so fought against public monies subsidising newcomers.[3] Still more vehement and effective was hostility to entry of Chinese, largely curtailed by 1890. Recruiting of Pacific Islanders for labour mainly in Queensland sugar plantations aroused similar concern from the 1860s.

Securing of Australia against 'coloured' migrants had some place in the movement for inter-colonial Federation which culminated 1901. Ronald Norris has warned against its exaggeration,[4] however, and broader issues of migration scarcely appear in J. A. La Nauze's *Making of the Australian Constitution*. Still, 'immigration and emigration' appeared among pre-scribed federal powers. Exclusion of undesirable aliens—in effect, Asians and Pacific Islanders—was a major object of early Commonwealth legisla-tion. As very many future references will invoke, other immigration matters remained in constitutional limbo, the Commonwealth having ultimate power but the States jealously retaining their de facto control.

Strength was the passion of men and governments pre-1914, even more than usual. The new polity of Australia, operative from the century's first day, taught this lesson with appropriate fervour. Outstanding in this story was Alfred Deakin, Prime Minister for half the first decade. From at least 1905 Deakin included British immigration in his programme for a powerful Australia within a powerful Empire within powerful Anglo-Saxondom. All this comported with his leadership of Australia's brand of 'new' or 'progressive' liberalism. Deakin best expounded national-imperialism at the 1907 Colonial Conference in London, stressing defence issues and trade preference. Migration also arose at this Conference, via lobbying by British imperial activists who wanted their government to resume financial backing in its support. Only the Australian delegation showed enthusiasm in response.[5] Outside the Conference, Deakin found much communality with L. S. Amery. Talk arose of Deakin heading a grand crusade dedicated to their common cause.

Management of normal immigration yet remained with the several Australian States. Some modification dated from 1906 when a Premiers' Conference (that is, a meeting of State and Commonwealth leaders) agreed that the Commonwealth should sponsor relevant advertising in Britain. About this time, too, most States became more enthusiastic in granting migrants assistance. Partly for that reason, numbers boomed. The peak for net entry was about 92,000 in 1912: some 90 per cent were British, and about half assisted. The Premiers' Conference that year agreed on uniform maximum assistance—£6 for an adult, half the minimum fare. Recruitment was directed specifically at farmworkers and domestic servants, although most States also were ready to assist approved newcomers nominated by established residents.[6]

Meanwhile, the federal government continued its interest. Deakin was supplanted as Prime Minister in 1910 by Andrew Fisher and a ministry which, while having some doubts, proved more supportive of migration than any other Labor government in Australian experience until that of J. B. Chifley (1945–9). Fisher upheld migration at the 1911 Imperial Conference, whence arose a Dominions Royal Commission to ponder the issue. That year Attorney-General W. M. Hughes, dynamo of Fisher's government, prompted the Premiers to consider a broader policy. They responded by proposing at their 1912 meeting that the Commonwealth should subsidise 25,000 adult fares. Thereby the Premiers hoped to save State money, but even so it was remarkable for that group ever to foster federal assertion. Also in 1912 Commonwealth Parliament passed an Immigration Act which intensified medical testing of immigrants. This bespoke the eugenicist strain in current reform thought, notably strong in Hughes.

Further action came with another change in federal office in mid-1913, Joseph Cook then heading a Liberal government. The advertising campaign proposed from 1906 became reality. Costing £50,000 a year, it worked through cinema, press, lectures, and posters. The Commonwealth government developed its fledgling film unit through pertinent work. On a wall abutting the site on which Australia House soon arose was blazoned a migrant-seeking poster, said to be the biggest in London. High Commissioner (that is, quasi-ambassador) George Reid wrote lyrical on all this, but warned that migrants were becoming scarcer.[7] The federal government acted on the Premiers' resolution of 1912 and put aside £150,000 to subsidise migrant fares.[8]

CHAPTER ONE

The Great War's Impact

For migration, as so many other areas of life and policy, the Great War intensified elements already dynamic by 1914. An exemplar in the United Kingdom was belief in Empire settlement, not only as a solvent of Britain's domestic tensions but as a generator of race-power. Erstwhile servicemen became central in this debate: on one hand, they were a potential source of discontent which might wreck Britain if a safety-valve were not opened; on the other, they were martial heroes who deserved the chance, glorious as the migrationists esteemed it, to farm imperial frontiers.

The Royal Colonial Institute led enthusiasts for settlement. From 1912 the Institute's chairman was A. H. G. Grey, fourth Earl Grey. His uncle, third Earl, had been Under-Secretary of State for the Colonies, 1830–3, and Secretary, 1846–52. The older Grey generally upheld the notions of E. G. Wakefield as to how colonies might blend liberal institutions with conservative social structure, thereby remaining in happy union with the metropolis. In fact Australia's colonists had found much repugnant in the third Earl's policies, notably those on migration. His heir evidently saw no warning in that story. During the early War years, HMG resisted expansive notions as expounded by the Institute. The Colonial Office was almost as negative as Treasury, which was ever jealous for the public purse.

> Can we afford at the end of the war in addition to the capital required to repair the ravages, an enormous sum to effect a large settlement in the Dominions, and if so could it not be employed with as great advantage to the Empire at home?

The question was put by John Anderson, permanent Under-Secretary for the Colonies, in December 1914.[1] His words reveal how the Office saw metropolitan interests as its prime concern.

The Institute sustained the pressure. In January 1915 it presented to the Colonial Office a proposal from S. W. Copley, a man of large interests in Western Australia. Copley proposed to vest Lord Kitchener with 100,000 acres of farm land in Western Australia for the settlement of ex-servicemen, and himself was ready to loan £50,000 for its preparation. The Colonial

Office remained sceptical, and its letter to Australia on the matter struck no sparks.[2] However, politicians began conceding to the Institute: Colonial Secretary Andrew Bonar Law granted members an interview in late July 1915. It was suggested that the Institute sponsor H. Rider Haggard to go to Australia and there urge action. This idea won support from *The Times* and from J. W. Taverner, still in London after serving as Victoria's Agent-General (that is, representative in Britain), 1904–13.[3]

Haggard already knew Australia, having visited in 1913 as a member of the Dominions Royal Commission. His imperialism combined passion for country life with a sense of the mystic glory of the non-civilised world. In Haggard seethed that yearning for a new human consciousness, based in psyche and blood, which found so many expressions throughout early twentieth-century Europe. He spent April–May 1916 on his new mission. In 1925 he told Rudyard Kipling, 'I converted a hostile Australia to my views, and brought home offers that were worth millions—which were thrown away by our Government.'[4] Actually, Haggard provoked some criticism— from the Melbourne *Age* newspaper, ever suspicious lest imperial interests keep Australia a mere primary producer, and from trade unionists. Sir Ronald Munro Ferguson, Governor-General of Australia, described union hostility to migration as 'selfish, urban and short-sighted, arrogant to an almost inconceivable degree'. Yet overall, Munro Ferguson judged, Haggard did achieve 'a change in public sentiment'.[5]

Haggard's crucial discussions were with State Premiers. He thus secured a place for his crusade at the Premiers' Conference in May. It overlapped with two issues discussed at their 1915 Conference—immigration and, much more important, repatriation policies for Australia's own soldiers, especially their establishment as farmers. In his early talks, Haggard stressed to at least one Premier that the Colonial Institute 'did not wish to tempt men to leave the United Kingdom'; the aim was only that those committed to emigration remain within the Empire.[6] Most Premiers had promised that British servicemen would have the same treatment as locals, although their enthusiasm varied. Haggard had found the Labor Premiers of New South Wales (W. A. Holman) and Queensland (E. G. Theodore) toughest in negotiation, but at the May Conference Theodore spoke of making available a million acres, whereas Holman remained very cool. John Earle of Tasmania, also Labor, offered 300 orchard acres at once and a 'very much larger number ... if formal arrangements made with Imperial Government'.

Holman was further dissident. Whereas in 1912 he had urged the Com-monwealth to develop a migration policy, now he surmised 'that the emigration problem is an insoluble one'; Britain would not want to lose farmers to Australia, and urbanites were incapable of pioneering. Holman provoked some counter-insistence on the need for migrants, but won modification of a proposed motion. As revised, it still affirmed readiness to receive migrants. Haggard's Australian success helped push HMG towards favouring migration. A Reconstruction Committee was appointed to canvass departmental opinion. The Board of Trade was quite enthusiastic, the Colonial Office resistant. In September 1916 a circular went around the Empire, encouraging positive responses and foreshadowing a central migration authority; Western Australia and Victoria showed positive.[7] In December Walter Long replaced Law at the Colonial Office, strengthening commitment towards migration.

The issue came before the Australian Premiers again at their meeting in December 1916–January 1917. Since the previous conclave, Australia had entered upon its variant of the universal turmoil wreaked by the War. W. M. Hughes, Prime Minister of the Labor government since October 1915, proved Australia's counterpart of Lloyd George, Lenin, and Mussolini.[8] The most remarkable passage of his career came in March–July 1916, spent in Britain. There Hughes fought for Australian interests, yet with such imperial commitment that a movement arose to have him become a leader in Whitehall. Returned to Australia, Hughes determined that the nation must conscript troops for overseas service. This proposal divided the Labor movement and the community, most radical and Irish-Catholic elements being hostile. A plebiscite in October said 'no' to conscription, and subsequently Hughes and others, Holman and Earle among them, separated from Labor allegiance. Hughes formed a new government, excluding 'official' Labor (and in February 1917 another, combining non-Labor forces under the new label 'Nationalist').

Hughes introduced migration issues to the 1916–17 Conference. He spoke of having sought loan funds from Britain's Chancellor of the Exchequer, their intended purpose being settlement of Australian ex-soldiers on the land.[9] Hughes now told the Premiers that 'the British Government might be more inclined to advance money if the schemes included British soldiers'.[10] The opportunist tone told much. In the past Hughes had shared the suspicion lest migration cut wages: his eugenicism esteemed quality rather than quantity of population. But anyone concerned with defence, and apprehensive of Japan—as Hughes was, even before 1914—could not keep that divide absolute. If Australia's financial benefit also came into play, Hughes had to support immigration.

The Premiers were more reserved. In January they accepted equal treatment for British servicemen as landsettlers, but only if funding were available. Their discourse was grudging. Perhaps fear was at work lest Hughes use the Commonwealth's role in repatriating Australian servicemen to usurp State powers, especially over Crown lands. Into 1917 Governor-General Munro Ferguson became pessimistic as to Australian readiness to settle 'the British Tommy'.[11] Meanwhile, migration continued to surge in Whitehall. In March 1917 the Dominions Royal Commission reported, upholding the cause. The Imperial War Cabinet agreed that HMG should assist settlement 'under the British flag'. Walter Long appointed a committee to pursue this subject; members included Haggard and most Australian Agents-General, while its chairman, the second Lord Tennyson, was an erstwhile Governor-General of Australia (1902–3). Another committee-man was P. L. Gell, son of an Anglican cleric who had striven to bring Arnoldian culture to penal Van Diemen's Land. To the Tennyson committee Gell proposed an Empire Settlement Loan scheme, funded from Britain. The committee upheld that idea, as well as government subsidy of fares to imperial destinations for ex-servicepeople anxious so to venture.[12]

Some reaction against migration developed within British officialdom later in 1917. Important in this was appointment of Christopher Addison as Minister for Reconstruction. Addison's enthusiasm for settling returned men on the land in Britain pushed him against the migrationists. Complementary scepticism remained within the Colonial Office. Ideas of an Imperial Development Board, to fulfil one proposal of the Dominions Royal Commission, soon ran aground.[13] The key Colonial Office bureaucrat on migration matters was T. C. Macnaghten, a Tory gentleman. In mid-January 1918 he told his superior, Edward Harding, of Trafalgar Square being used for cinematic and other Australian publicity. 'A considerable crowd had gathered, and the whole thing was to my mind in result, a piece of emigration propaganda on a big scale.'[14] Macnaghten interpreted the move as a threat to Britain, facing a perilous future with manpower depleted by the War. Such views were widespread, but Macnaghten's call for official rebuke met no response from Harding: the time was wrong for trampling on Australia.

The forces surrounding migration impelled the Colonial Office to draft a Bill. 'The intention is to discourage emigration and keep it under proper control', wrote Macnaghten, repeating his concerns about British manpower.[15] Macnaghten was replying to Addison's concern lest the Bill *stimulate* migration; that he wrote thus indicates the situation's ambiguity. Macnaghten probably demonstrated its framers' greater intent. Certainly, the will prevailed to stop exploitation of migrants. Many clauses of the Bill addressed the business side of passenger transport. This was a most complex traffic, begetting a hierarchy of companies, brokers, agents. Scruples had withered in the scramble for lucre before 1914, with migrant-hungry governments bargaining for bodies.[16] An overlapping issue was deceptive propaganda. The Bill sought to control publicity issued by governments, as well as by shipping interests. All such matters were to come under a statutory authority, which Empire governments were to join. Its powers were to include encouragement of migration whithersoever it approved. So the measure tried to conciliate clashing interests. The result was to create general offence, as contenders feared lest their opponents be advantaged.

Parliamentary debate in early 1918 confirmed how volatile was the issue.[17] The most vigorous speakers were Leftists who saw the Bill as threatening forced migration; therefore they opposed it, as a denial of Everyman's right to decent life in his native land. R. L. Outhwaite—himself descended from Australian pioneers, and as a disciple of Henry George committed to land-settlement within Britain—alleged the government's intent to rid itself of 'objectionable characters' who, should they stay at home, might push for revolutionary change. He drew a parallel with the increase of convict transportation to Australia after Waterloo. Anyway, Outhwaite warned, Australia would not accept unemployed industrials from Britain, only those agricultural labourers whom the mother country herself much needed. The congruence between this thinking and that of the conservative bureaucrat, Macnaghten, was ironic and nice.

Lay criticism of the Bill was yet more damning. The shipping interest resisted its threat of intrusion. Various polities within the Empire prickled at the notion of their London representatives joining the proposed authority, and so becoming tools of the British government.[18] Australian Agents-General in Britain and State Ministers at home shared outrage at the Bill's purview extending to all migrant-publicity, so putting their worthy selves 'in the same category as unscrupulous rogues'.[19] These protestors, like the shipping interest, argued that the Bill would drive emigration outside the Empire. Its passage stalled.

The Imperial War Conference also debated the Bill, with dominant opinion coming close to that of, say, Macnaghten.[20] In mid-1918, however, Hughes returned to London, ever intent on securing British help to underpin Australia's post-war apotheosis as a nation still rich in primary production, but also in industrial skills and output. Hughes upbraided the War Conference for its coolness towards migration: 'after the war supposing you find a labour market in which tens of thousands or hundreds of thousands are looking for work, that will be no time to create an emigration policy'. On 5 November Hughes cabled his deputy:

Secret. Emigration. If we are to hold Australia and develop its tremendous resources we must have numerous population. The time is rapidly approaching—it is indeed at hand—when demobilisation of British Army will offer unique opportunity of securing right type of immigrant. The glorious exploits of our soldiers have given Australia magnificent and priceless advertisement. Tens of thousands of men in prime of life, who would make most desirable settlers on soil, and who will be disinclined to remain in Britain, will be soon released from army ... If we want to get men we must bestir ourselves immediately. What is wanted is concerted action, unified control this end, proper handling by States in Australia, and shipping facilities.[21]

Especially did Hughes call for integrating the States' 'six and feeble organisations' into one national migration office in Britain. He had ordered a further boost of display at Australia House. 'We must get men of right type and get them on the land and not in the great cities.'

Perhaps Hughes had foreknowledge of Walter Long's intent, realised in the following days, to appoint an inter-departmental emigration committee. It had powers like those promised to the authority which the now-becalmed Bill sought to have created. Evidently, Long himself wanted the new body to foster, rather than to limit, migration. The committee took some steps in this direction.[22] Early meetings considered emigration of the unemployed, and of single women. ('The superfluous woman' appeared to ruling-class Britons as a considerable threat to social cohesion.)[23] Australia loomed large in the committee's talk, but there was an ominous contrast between Hughes's ideal of the migrant and the committee's.

*   *   *

The government which Lloyd George formed at New Year, 1919, promised some hope for emigration. Two high priests of Empire-worship, Alfred Milner and L. S. Amery, became respectively Secretary and Under-Secretary at the Colonial Office. Amery proved the more potent, especially through his chairmanship of the government's emigration committee, which now became the Oversea Settlement Committee. Yet that name-change told an ambivalent story. Lloyd George himself was responsible, his argument stressing difference between 'settlement' within the Empire, and 'emigration' beyond it.[24] The Milner–Amery school was often to echo that point, but it seems that the Prime Minister felt misgivings about the process, however named, such as Addison and Outhwaite had voiced. The Emigration Bill shared the name-change to 'Oversea Settlement', but Lloyd George still disliked the measure, and it was not enacted.[25] The OSC never won legislative authority.

That did not matter too much: comprising representatives of pertinent departments and lay interests, the Committee operated for years. Its bureaucratic complement was the Oversea Settlement Department, headed by Macnaghten and situated within the Colonial Office. The OSC was never the mere creature of the migrationists. Treasury was represented, and its spokesman—especially but not alone—proved always ready to assert migration's expense and its potential to weaken Britain. Fainter, but still present, rang radical hostility to forced migration.

On 10 February 1919 Amery made a key submission to Cabinet. 'Development of the population and wealth of the whole British Empire is the key to the problem of post-war reconstruction' ran its theme;[26] to assist ex-servicepeople who wished to venture overseas was a demand of natural justice, complementary to this grand design. To quicken emigration was 'prudent as well as just', for demobilisation could entail social tensions. Yet even this statement was qualified, for example, by the remark that no certainty assured the success of veterans as Empire farmers; perhaps 'comrade settlements' might best organise their plantation. The statement accepted that general emigration could become 'inconveniently large', with British agriculture vulnerable to consequent harm. Accordingly, no reason prevailed for comprehensive state aid. Apart from ex-soldiers, the strongest case applied to children—girls as much as boys—and women. Amery invoked evidence that many females recently employed in war-work were ready to be domestics overseas but not at home; that is, they would not solve Britain's servant problem, and might foment problems of post-war adjustment.

Cabinet agreed to subsidise in full the Empire migration of ex-servicepeople and their families. The consent of the receiving governments (which meant, in Australian cases, of the respective Agents-General) would be requisite; entwined with this proviso was vague hope that work or farm-settlement would be available to newcomers. The scheme was initially to operate throughout 1920. The aftermath of the War further subsidised migration through the King's Fund for the disabled and, more important, the National Relief Fund. The OSD took the initiative in having NRF moneys used both to supplement ex-service migrants' resources and to assist other would-be migrants. Likewise, some of the King's Fund went to people who scarcely were war casualties, but did want to migrate.[27] The mechanics of the operation remain obscure. Local committees, organised by the Department of Labour's Employment Exchanges, vetted many applicants.

Among other early initiatives of the OSC, female emigration continued potent. Several older philanthropic bodies re-formed as the Society for the Oversea Settlement of British Women; it became an affiliate of the OSD, serviced by a salaried bureaucrat, Gladys S. Pott. Earlier in life Pott had worked against women's suffrage, an interesting complement to the notion of emigration as a check against militant feminism.[28] Immediately, the OSC planned to despatch missions of enquiry into possibilities for female-migration. To visit Australia were Dorothea Pughe Jones, of farming experience and during the war active in VAD work; and Lisbeth E. Simm, prominent in the National Amalgamated Union of Labour and wife of a 'Coalition Labour' Parliamentarian, in class-conscious eyes a dubious background. Meeting with the Agents-General before departure, the ladies were enjoined to make clear to Australia their realisation that domestic work must be the usual role of migrants, and that State approval was requisite for assisted migrants' entry. Yet the briefing had its positive note. 'They should give full information as to the new avenues of employment which women have followed in this country during the war, and make full enquiries as to the possibility of new openings in Australia for women of these types.'[29]

Milner wrote to Australian authorities, including Hughes, arguing that the Service Corps and Land Army promised to demobilise women 'of known capacity and superior education'.[30]

The Jones–Simm briefing occurred at one of the regular meetings where Amery met Empire representatives on 'settlement' business. The current Australian High Commissioner, Andrew Fisher, made little response on such matters, but the Agents-General were sympathetic. They were disposed to be so by the nature of their office: the development of migration policy promised to enhance their importance. C. G. Wade of New South Wales and J. D. Connolly of Western Australia best made the point.

Wade was colonial born and educated at Oxford. Returning home, he moved from law to conservative politics, being Premier 1907–10 and Agent from 1917. Wade proposed to Amery's committee in mid-1919 that the ex-service scheme extend to embrace civilians. 'His Government had authorised him to make a distinct offer to establish a permanent policy of settlement ... and to say that New South Wales was prepared to bear its share in any Dominion agreement.' W. A. Holman, still Premier, evidently had returned to his more positive view of migration. Wade spoke of American intrusion into Australia and its threat to imperial integrity. He developed his ideas in six lectures given at the University of London, duly published by the Clarendon Press. They recognised that hostility to migration prevailed in both hemispheres. In Australia it traced back to feeling against convicts; in Britain, it linked with fears of losing precious agricultural labour. Still, Wade insisted, the War had also shown how Australia and Britain could combine for mutual benefit. Demobilisation threatened to congest Britain's labour market, Wade continued, while Australia needed population, especially to secure defence. Might not HMG underwrite loans for Australian land-settlement, not only by soldiers but civilian emigrants too? Australia was not being profligate in calling for such help; the nation's growth had always relied on capital inflow.

Connolly was the son of an Irish Catholic labourer. Leaving his native Queensland, he made money and entered non-Labor politics in Western Australia's goldfields during the 1890s.[31] As a Minister, 1906–11, Connolly achieved considerable effect; immigration ranked high, conjoint with development of wheat-farming. His record pointed towards the Premiership, but that prize did not fall. Perhaps Connolly was the more determined to maximise the role of Agent-General, which he assumed in 1917. His enthusiasm for migration came to approach obsession and absurdity, yet had its logic. The pre-1914 growth of Western Australia seemed to establish its eminence as a field for Britannic expansion. One symbol was the location there from 1912 of the Pinjarra farm school, brainchild of K. O. Fairbridge. Born in South Africa, Fairbridge was an early (1908) Rhodes Scholar, and remains an archetype of that band. His ideal became to take children from British slums to imperial frontiers, and so exalt the race. Pinjarra won a mystique which outlasted Fairbridge's death in 1924: 'I think this is the finest institution for human regeneration that has ever existed,' Amery was to say.[32] Fairbridge returned from Pinjarra to Britain in 1919–20 to publicise his campaign, Western Australia giving him a stipend and an office in the Agent-General's building.

Connolly since 1917 had been developing his own variants of the farm-school concept.[33] The WA government, he proposed, might house the orphans of ex-servicepeople. Connolly was very conscious that such children, and war widows too, received 'liberal' pensions. That made them very attractive as immigrants. These families should be granted suburban lots in country towns, Connolly proposed to his home government, and/or the widows become farmers. He kept pushing these ideas during 1919–20, in the face of considerable resistance in Britain. Protestant and Catholic churches alike, he reported, were 'very much opposed' to migration of orphans in their care, 'especially those in receipt of pensions'.[34] Amery gave the same message, telling Connolly that there was

> strong feeling that the Home Government ought to be responsible for the care of widows and upbringing of the children of men who fell at the War, and that any attempt to encourage them to proceed overseas in large numbers would be met with strong opposition.[35]

Connolly stayed consistent in his avarice when Amery tried to persuade him to embrace older children. 'Many of them have become thoroughly demoralised by affluence', Connolly wrote home, and now were losing the war-time jobs which fed that sin.[36] On turning sixteen, moreover, they lost their pensions.

Other tensions between Connolly and government were minor but indicative. He alleged that the Pensions Office helped to thwart his efforts concerning widows and orphans, and also that Irish ex-servicemen were being encouraged to go to the USA although they would have preferred the Antipodes if subsidy offered. An internal minute within the OSD remarked that 'as to Ireland, we would of course prefer them within the Empire than in the US though, between ourselves, we can bear their loss better than that of our Protestant population'.[37] Meanwhile, Connolly had developed still more ambitious ideas. In February 1919 he proposed to the OSD that the Imperial and WA governments combine to settle on the land a thousand married ex-servicemen each year, for twelve years; London should provide loan money for the men's needs and also £1 million at 4 per cent for associated public works; Western Australia would grant land in 500–1000 acre blocks. Again dissident voices sounded, among them Connolly's own government.[38] Connolly nevertheless gained some support from

Macnaghten, by now ardent for 'settlement', and Milner. As Connolly told it, his own enthusiasm may have prompted Milner to achieve Cabinet approval of paying ex-servicepeople's fares.[39] However, Milner and his advisors jibbed at the more ambitious scheme: 'they feared an outcry if the bold statement went forth that they were inducing men and women to leave England'.[40] In following months, a thrust towards economy further doomed imperial backing for Connolly. Since May, however, the Premier back home had been James Mitchell, whose ideas followed his Agent's.

A private scheme similar to those of Wade and Connolly was Australian Farms Limited. This land-development company traced back to 1913 but burgeoned during the War.[41] In 1919–20 it sought investor-settlers among ex-servicemen. Among its backers were Victoria's Agent-General and many big names of Australian capitalism. Reportedly support also came from W. A. Watt, the able Treasurer in Hughes's government, who in early 1920 was visiting England. Australian Farms aimed at attracting ex-officer and public-school types. Imperialists enthused accordingly. Amery told Inchcape, Baron of shipping and finance, that the OSC had 'taken the extreme step of backing this Company officially'; a recent Governor of Victoria vouched its affinity with 'the Imperial school of thought in Australia which is engaged in combating the powerful Bolshevist and Sinn Fein elements'.[42] The NRF, the Ex-Officers' Association, and the Orient Shipping Line all subscribed handsomely.

Other Agents-General lacked the passion of Wade and Connolly, but still helped migration. To Amery they argued for Empire-wide fare equalisation, with its implied subsidy of voyagers to Australia. Related to this was distress at the rise in lower-class fares, now about double the pre-war figure. The shipping interest was seen as reaping undue gain from the current shortage of berths, which moreover delayed the flow of subsidised ex-servicepeople. The Agents urged continuation of the scheme, which in the end allowed approvals throughout 1921 and passage thereafter.

The Agents' support doubtless encouraged Empire-upholders in Whitehall, whose task was never easy. In a memorandum to Amery on 17 April 1920, Macnaghten neared hysteria. Americans were streaming into Canada, threatening its defection, and meanwhile,

> In Australia the situation is extremely difficult. The Labour Party ... has gone out of hand and under the control of Sinn Fein and Bolshevist elements whose whole purpose is anti-Imperial. ... The better elements in Australia are endeavouring to combat the tendencies referred to, and are anxious for settlers of the right type, both in order to raise the whole level of life in Australia and in order to safeguard the country by enlarging its population.[43]

Macnaghten accordingly wanted the Oversea Settlement Bill to become law. Amery and Milner agreed—but widespread misgivings about emigration still thwarted them. This made the prolonging of the ex-service scheme a notable victory. While Australian pressure helped that, more decisive was fear lest unemployed servicemen use their training in violence to disrupt society.[44]

Although enthusiastic about migration, the Agents found it a headache. Connolly's dynamism alienated his own earlier governments, and even after Mitchell came to office he complained of lack of co-operation. This was a general plaint among the Agents.[45] State governments had plenty to bother about, especially repatriation of their own soldiery. Agents were generally left to themselves in judging eligibility of ex-service migrants and in 1919–20 most applicants were approved, once through the British bureaucracies. Those taken to Australia under the scheme numbered over 37,500 (about half men and a quarter each women and children), 43.5 per cent of the imperial whole.[46] Numbers assisted by the NRF were much smaller and, not receiving strictly governmental bounty, further escaped bureaucratic nets. Still, the Agents would have had plenty of paperwork, the more as the pre-1914 machinery for assisted migration of nominees revived through 1920 in all States except Queensland and South Australia. Western Australia even subsidised some not nominated.[47]

The Commonwealth government did little about migration during 1919. Hughes's cable of November 1918 had prompted no decisive action. Immediately thereafter Hughes played his roles at the Versailles Peace Conference, most famously and relevantly in affirming Australia's defence needs against not only the enemies of 1914–18, but also Japan. He returned to Australia in August 1919, to remain Prime Minister for over three years, and a force for a generation—always upholding the ideal of a puissant Australia, but with decreasing focus and efficacy.

Migration issues had a small place at the Premiers' Conference of January 1919. Acting Prime Minister Watt invoked the 'imperative necessity' of Australians' assisting British comrades to become New World farmers. Watt urged that Western Australia and Queensland had most to offer. 'There is the question of finance involved', responded Queensland's Theodore.[48] Conference pondered the duties of Commonwealth and State governments in settling Australian ex-servicemen. This was already threatening to be expensive and tortuous, constricting fulfilment of the promises given to Haggard in 1916. In some States a few Britons came under local ex-service farm schemes, but at least Queensland told its Agent-General that imperial sources must provide funds before the State acted.[49] Federal Parliament noticed such issues in August.[50] Watt spoke of need for further discussions and the primacy of Australian soldiers' needs. The major initiative on immigration in that session was a Bill which tightened medical requirements and empowered prohibition or deportation of ex-enemy aliens and socio-political subversives. The Bill passed in 1920.

Early in that year, Connolly reported the rumour that part of Watt's mission to Britain was to organise concerted migrant policy. However, action came not in London but through further Premiers' Conferences. A paper prepared by the Commonwealth for a May meeting addressed 'immigration, including public works policy in regard thereto'.[51] The federal government should control assisted migration through a central body, 'with branches in each State, who would receive immigrants, maintain them until placed, and secure employment'. Overall, the paper affirmed, Australia could take large numbers—of 'the right type'. Stress was put on skilled workers, and their potential in hastening that industrialisation which federal governments had long encouraged via tariff Protection, a trend intensifying in these months as Minister for Trade, Walter Massy-Greene, prepared higher schedules. The paper affirmed the need also for domestics, youths, and farmworkers. Should private employment fail to absorb immigrant labour, then federal and State governments might finance 'reproductive' (in modern terms, cost-effective) public works.

All this accorded with the national-socialist vision that was characteristic of Hughes. Perhaps he hoped that the proposed authority would become a powerhouse of economic direction. Significant too was the paper's ignoring of nomination as a mode of migration. This suggested intent to draw from masses in Britain having no established tie with Australia. Thereby the paper had a radicalism never fulfilled. Likewise, Hughes's stress on industrial artisans as migrants was not echoed by future leaders.

A speech-draft among Hughes's papers probably dated from these weeks: 'A vigorous policy of immigration is I maintain the one simple and sure solution of our present difficulties. It would give us national safety. It would increase employment and multiply our individual and collective wealth.' The speech invoked White Australia and stressed that migration benefited all society, not just capitalists. Conversely, 'it may seem a little arbitrary for us to say to the British people that we will accept only of their best. But we have no alternative.'

In May 1920 the Premiers endorsed centralised control of assisted migration, albeit with fuzziness and log-rolling.[52] It appears that the Commonwealth did not distribute its position paper, and otherwise finessed. Nevertheless, Hughes's speeches were vigorous, postulating up to 200,000 entrants a year. Debate embraced defence issues, but not secondary industry. Final motions specified the 'primary object of the scheme to be the settlement of immigrants on the lands of Australia'. This echoed 1916, in a way, but Hughes agreed that, if British ex-servicemen were to receive the same preference as Australian, the funds must come from HMG. Finance also dominated talk about public works which might employ migrants. It was decided that individual States should parley with the Commonwealth, but Hughes avoided promises. Development of the

Murray River region and progress towards unifying Australia's rail gauges alone received his endorsement. Hughes bristled when Queensland representatives spoke of the State negotiating loans with British officials. 'I see no reason why their graciousness should stop at Queensland; if they lend you anything, I shall make their life fairly uncomfortable until they lend us something too.' Meanwhile, he warned, Queensland might find how tough were the masters of Britain's finance. The record tells nothing more about the Queensland move. The Premiers' Conference had further tensions. Contrary to the position paper, the Commonwealth now proposed that each State would determine how many migrants were to enter its borders. Hackles still rose. 'If men come to Australia you cannot stop them coming to New South Wales', responded J. T. Lang—(Labor) Treasurer there and supreme voice of State rights.

After the May meeting, federal authorities asked the States to clarify what lands they had available for migrant settlement, and what public, or even private enterprise, works might engage others.[53] Did they approve the nomination system? What facilities existed for reception and care of migrants; were there hostels to shelter children while parents sought work? The questionnaire also asked about resorts and attractions, recognising the tie between immigration and tourism.

In July the Premiers met again and confirmed the joint plan. They emphasised each State's right to determine the numbers and skills of its assisted migrants. A motion declared that the Commonwealth would assist with loans for approved land-settlement and for public works associated with immigration, and as to the latter Hughes again endorsed only the Murray River and railway gauge projects. All was somewhat confused.

The agreement on migration was publicised thus:

> The Commonwealth is to be responsible for the recruiting of immigrants abroad and for their transport to Australia, whilst the State Governments, on their part, are to advise the Commonwealth as to the numbers and classes of immigrants which they are prepared to receive. Briefly stated, the Commonwealth will select the immigrant according to the requirements of the State concerned and bring him to Australia; and on his arrival the State Government will assume the responsibility for placing him in employment or upon the land. Incidentally, the Commonwealth will undertake all publicity and propaganda in connexion with the encouragement of immigration.
>
> The Commonwealth Government will donate £12 towards the passages of approved settlers for Australia. Further assistance will be granted by way of loans in special cases. Under the joint scheme the immigrants entitled to part-paid fares are divided into two classes—'Assisted' immigrants and 'Nominated' immigrants. 'Assisted' immigrants are those who are originally recruited by the Commonwealth overseas. 'Nominated' immigrants are those nominated by persons resident in the Commonwealth, and the nominators, who must submit their

applications through the Officers in Charge of the State Immigration Offices in the various capital cities, are requested to undertake to look after their nominees upon arrival, and to see that they do not become a burden upon the State.[54]

Logically, the paragraphs should have come in reverse order. The inversion had its point, however, demonstrating assumptions that official policy would relate overwhelmingly to 'assisted' (later termed 'selected' or 'requisitioned') people. It was they whom the States would specify, and the Commonwealth actively recruit in Britain and supervise in Australia, while 'nominees' were the responsibility of their nominators and self-payers of themselves. Of course all migrants had to undergo health and other testing, as will appear especially in chapter 9.

Action followed agreement: Hughes took ministerial responsibility, and a Director of Migration and Settlement was appointed in London and a Commonwealth Superintendent of Immigration at home. Appointed to the former office was Percy Hunter. Born in 1876, he worked as a journalist before entering the NSW public service, heading its tourism and immigration office from 1906. Later Hunter set up as a migration agent in Britain, and in 1913 received joint appointment from New South Wales and Victoria apropos this work.[55] Furthermore, Hunter was an ancient mate of the Prime Minister's, and in 1919–20 served as an organiser for the Nationalist Party.

The Commonwealth Superintendent, H. S. Gullett, had also worked as a journalist and for migration before the War.[56] In his book *The Opportunity in Australia* (1914), migration propaganda took impressive form. Similar quality marked Gullett's war-time journalism, which led to major work with the *Official History of Australia in the War* and appointment (1920) as first director of the Australian War Museum. Gullett served on Hughes's staff at Versailles and shared the leader's view as to fragility of peace: a pamphlet, *Unguarded Australia* (1919), urged the consequent need for immigration.

The new mechanisms began to move. From about this time the OSD scheme for ex-servicepeople came under closer supervision from most Agents-General, with case-by-case nomination from Australia now being required. Consolidation of the States' staff in London into a Commonwealth entity jogged along, Western Australia for a while retaining right of specific approval of its migrants. From very early, Australia gave loans to help approved migrants meet their part of the fare. The pre-war pattern continued, whereby normally State requisitions were for male farmworkers (both adult and juvenile, from 15 years) and female domestics (normally from 18 to 35 years), while nominees proceeded under the aegis of relatives and friends already down-under. In Australia some friction developed when the Commonwealth sought to establish its own officers in the States, to supervise local handling of migration matters. The Commonwealth did not force itself against State resistance, and the plan collapsed during 1921.[57]

Meanwhile, Gullett built a modest office to handle the Commonwealth's specific responsibilities.

Discussion in late 1920 showed especially South Australia restive lest it be committed to *guarantee* employing all 'selected' entrants. Sparring resulted in a decision to speak of an 'offer'. Hughes was reluctant to concede even so much as that.

> Obviously you would not ask the Commonwealth to recruit workers for your State unless you were certain of being able to place them soon after arrival ... The desirable immigrant naturally looks for a definite assurance before he breaks up his home in the United Kingdom.[58]

Unusually for him, Hughes was being consistent. The decision to subsidise the fare at £12, about one-third of the minimum cost, followed debate on various alternatives, including total subsidy by the Commonwealth, either alone or by topping up each State's current contribution.[59]

Hughes had resisted hopes that the decisions of the 1920 Premiers' Conference might release ample Commonwealth-backed loan funds for the States, but still pressures rose. Queensland's Theodore urged upon the Prime Minister the potential of the Burnett River lands as a place for migrant farming—if capital were expended in preparing it.[60] Southward came a similar plan for using the Clarence River for irrigation and hydro-electric power.[61] The putative source of funds in this instance was the OSC. Premier John Storey of New South Wales failed the plan's backers and did not advance it while in Britain in early 1921. However, the episode retains interest as its chief begetter was E. C. G. Page, currently ascending towards federal leadership of the Country Party, the non-Labor farmers' group which waxed strong in these years.

*   *   *

While immigrant numbers to the end of 1920 were modest, the period witnessed developments that set a pattern for the future. Anger and frustration dominated the record, to a degree greater than reality warranted, but all the more significantly. Earlier references to Agents' tension with their home governments have hinted that these governments found problems in coping with the early post-war migrants, especially the subsidised ex-servicepeople. Archives of several States reinforce this theme.

Queensland, under the forceful Theodore, made no bones that its interest in British ex-servicemen lay in hope that they would entrain loan funds to assist development. That promise remained empty, but migrants kept on coming. Enough difficulties had resulted by mid-January 1920 for the government to call temporary halt. 'I shall at a future date send through you a claim on the Overseas Committee for the cost of maintaining their protégés at state expense, together with the cost of sending them back to England', went a follow-up letter from Premier to Agent.[62] Especially involved were W. H. Crawford and H. E. Whitlock; they will reappear.

South Australia's conservative government met problems similar to Queensland's. By the middle of 1920 the local bureaucrat in charge of immigrant matters, V. H. Ryan, was complaining that men were arriving with belief that jobs were guaranteed. Ryan tended to blame the Agent-General; the latter transferred all odium to the OSD while insisting that the State should continue with the scheme, as it was delivering high-calibre migrants.[63] Opposition (Labor) Leader John Gunn exhorted Parliament: 'I have no objection to people coming to this country but I do not want to see them coming under false pretences.'[64] If the government brought migrants, Gunn said, it should provide employment, desirably on public works.

Tasmanian bureaucrats also were vexed at migrants being given falsely optimistic accounts by the OSC. They tried to find jobs for newcomers, but often failed. The local Returned Servicemen's League liaised with Britain's United Service Fund to help some consequently distressed; there was recourse also to the NRF. One enormous file dealt with a family who caused endless problems, ending with deportation; 'The Island should not be regarded as a tip for human derelicts' affirmed a final minute. These files also tell the troubles of one Edward Brooker, yet he became a Minister (1939–48) and briefly Premier (1947–8).[65]

Behind the bureaucrats' minutes lay grassroots feeling. One indicator was a decision by Gullett and South Australian administrators 'to recommend that the use of the word "immigrant" should be discontinued if a suitable alternative could be substituted'.[66] This complemented Lloyd George's ban on 'emigration': across two hemispheres, that sound repelled. Mark Gosling, Labor Parliamentarian in New South Wales, spelled out why:

> my union, in order to get decent employment and conditions for its members, must get control of the industry, if possible. We cannot do it yet; therefore we cannot allow our industry to be flooded, and thus bring down our wages. We have to create, if possible, a scarcity of labour.[67]

Few might have been so articulate as Gosling; many would have agreed.

Antagonism to migration within Australia was one fundamental which this book relates. Stimulating that feeling, and situation, was HMG's readiness to use emigration for its own immediate ends, with little sensitivity for places of reception. Just as the extension of the ex-service scheme was a response to fears of rebellion by armed terrorists, so emigration of the unemployed in late 1920 embodied similar purpose, in softer mode. True, the OSC and the OSD had some sympathy for the Dominions' resistance to metropolitan cast-offs, and therefore they pushed for the NRF to subsidise people who truly wanted to migrate rather than to expel the workless from home. Significantly, however, the migrationists failed to win all this battle.[68] Likewise, the OSD, while accepting that Employment Exchanges be media of information about migration, strove to prevent coercion of the unemployed to follow that option, but with dubious effect.[69] The OSD itself encouraged use of the NRF to migrate pauper children, cast-offs though in a sense they were.[70]

More tensions developed as Britons who upheld an idealistic view of migration put pressure upon Australian authorities. One indicative occasion was Amery's meeting with the Agents-General, 29 October 1920. He insisted that in return for receiving fully subsidised ex-servicepeople, the Dominions must ensure they were 'welcomed, employed, and absorbed'. The Agents, unhappy in this squeeze, responded that arrivals must have *some* cash in hand, and that their medical certification had often proved faulty.[71] Another migrationist to express concern was one Christopher Turnor, in whom—as with Amery and Haggard—rural and race mystiques fused together. Turnor travelled through Australia in 1919–20. On return to Britain he won appointment to the OSC. Macnaghten reported Turnor telling:

> that the American Government have been looking round to find some suitable territory where food production can be very accelerated and are in touch with the Authorities in Australia with the view to obtaining permission to spend 50 million pounds sterling in developing land on that Continent. In Mr Turnor's opinion, the scheme, if carried through, would be disastrous to the Empire. The men who would be especially concerned would come from the Western states where in consequence of German and Irish propaganda, especially by the Irish priests, anti-British feeling is virulent.[72]

Turnor urged that the British government lend up to £10 million to Australia and other Dominions. Britain should appoint its own representatives in Australia to oversee this expenditure and the associated settlement of British ex-servicemen. Late in 1920 Turnor published a report on his travels. Generally, he felt, Australia was showing scant regard for its new migrants. James Mitchell of Western Australia was talking big, but had little idea of scientific settlement; seemingly the Premier wanted Britons to carve farms from the wilderness, with minimal aid. Official protests followed, but Turnor had made his point.[73]

Migrationists had more reason to deplore the ill-treatment of settlers because their opponents were ready to seize such data. When Amery moved for funds to sustain ex-service fares in March 1920, he spoke with fervour ('We are just at the beginning of development. Ours is the youngest Empire in the world'), but others responded very differently. Tories spoke of Empire as a place where ne'er-do-wells would sink or learn to swim; radicals insisted that government should develop Britain's own potential and thus meet ex-service demand for farm-life.[74] A few weeks later *John Bull* newspaper, continuing an anti-migration campaign begun before 1914, told of those two migrants to Queensland, Whitlock and Crawford. Both bore war-wounds, both had families. Their experiences in Queensland seem truly to have been miserable. Crawford's wife died in childbirth; Whitlock's suffered depression. In March, Whitlock sought repatriation from the Queensland government, half-threatening to expose his woes. Rebuffed, he and Crawford wrote to *John Bull*, which published just as Premier Theodore arrived in Britain, seeking loan funds. The Queensland government, the Agent-General, the OSD, all slanged each other. *John Bull* retracted some charges but maintained its general thrust. The Queensland government at last paid repatriation.[75]

Similar stories remained in popular circulation. Percy Hunter denigrated them as journalistic hyperbole, which was doubtless part-true but did not resolve the matter.[76] The resistance which met Connolly's several schemes partly derived from hostility to migration; this perhaps became sharpest among war-orphans' relatives who abhorred the possibility of losing that income to Australia.[77] At least one local committee appointed to minimise Britain's unemployment in 1920–1 questioned emigration as a solution.[78]

The OSD received further stories of anger and disillusion. From Melbourne there wrote an ex-service Scot:

> Why in God's name do we from the Motherland find such a well of prejudice against us. Chinamen are Chinamen here, Greeks are Greeks, Italians are Italians, but we from the Old Motherland are considered 'dirty pommies' and by no less than those who were recently 'pommies' themselves … Never have I seen (I mean the man in the street) such a lot of discontented people so steeped in dog in the manger tactics. All this great wide land only for the few who are in it.[79]

Having lost national insurance at home, this letter continued, newcomers had to pay much to local friendly societies. Housing was 'dreadful', with British ex-servicepeople being excluded from home loans available to their Australian peers. Bureaucrats at the OSD drafted and redrafted answers to Allen. A few files away, correspondence from an early Australian Farms settler showed that the company's propaganda had deceived. This presaged the grimness to be suffered by most connected with that venture. The OSC likewise heard from a migrant to Western Australia, 'farmers are not wanted here—only lumbermen and hewers'.[80] Complaints of the kind dominated a short-lived journal, *Austral-Briton*, launched by an association of British ex-servicemen in Australia.

Other straws blowing in the chill wind of migrant experience related to the voyage out. 'A feeling of enmity and some resentment' developed on at least one ship when some passengers found that others had received help from the NRF, while they had not.[81] More profound divisions were indicated by the OSC's *Report* for 1920. 'Third class passengers must realise that they will have to live for the whole period of their voyage at very close quarters with a number of fellow-travellers of very varied types.'[82] That sentence became a fixture in OSD literature.

The Jones–Simm mission on employment opportunities for women told further of tension and difficulty. Early reports in the Australian press stressed the mission's intent to uphold Land Army veterans as appropriate migrants. This was taken as intent that such women be employed as farmworkers. General obloquy resulted, part of extensive resistance to female migration. Unions were explicit in suspecting threats to wage-rates. The mission was told that local supply met demand for women teachers, clerks, typists, shop assistants. 'The fact that so many men of the Australian Imperial forces brought back brides also influenced the position, and raised doubts as to whether more women from the United Kingdom could be satisfactorily absorbed.'[83]

The enquirers told the OSD of these and other dilemmas. 'We have been besieged at all hours by people interested in the domestic problem', they wrote.[84] Undoubtedly, most of the besiegers were wealthy women looking for 'good' servants. Their avidity provoked criticism from officials and Labor politicians, people whom Mesdames Jones and Simm often crossed, yet the latter themselves criticised employers of domestics and their regime. 'The work is not easy or light in this climate, and the "status" is only higher because most girls here will not submit'. The commissioners urged that domestic work be made attractive, and so prompted a meeting in Sydney which endorsed a basic standard (a 56-hour working week; 'proper hygienic accommodation'; £1 per week for an adult 'general').[85] One suspects that at best the notion won lip-service from those avid mistresses, and at least one bureaucrat was hostile. Samuel Whitehead, key man in Victoria, told Mrs Simm that formalising conditions would further impede his persuading migrant girls to take jobs up-country. She bridled:

> I said, 'surely a girl will not be forced to take the most difficult of all the situations available'. Mr Whitehead said 'They must'. Then, when I looked very surprised, he said, 'Oh! of course if the British Government is paying, that would make a difference, but when we pay they must go where we send them'.[86]

The ladies heard many complaints from compatriots who had worked as Australian domestics.

Their consequent *Report* floated hope of women becoming owners of small farms or market gardens. Overwhelmingly, however, they stressed the social value of domestic service. The *Report* quoted a forecast of W. Jethro Brown, president of the Industrial Court of South Australia, that most Australians would cease to raise families were no such aid available:

> A scheme of wages which involved the abolition of the domestic help must involve the ultimate failure of the white races, and their gradual disappearance before the less sensitive, less educated, and less developed races of the tropical or semi-tropical areas.[87]

Both Brown and the commissioners knew that need for servants applied especially in country areas, so again race and ruralism meshed together.

The *Report* urged a lift in the status and conditions of domestic work. But was that a likely response from everyday Australians, desperate for a maid-of-all-work? Presumably Samuel Whitehead would have said not, but rather that most small farmers could pay only the barest wage. Brown argued to the same effect, in intellectual terms. Jones and Simm recognised this crunch when suggesting that the OSD appoint a representative in Australia to oversee migrant women's employment. The final sentence of their *Report* advised that 'intending migrants should be given to understand that while a great many people in Australia are in favour of immigration, there is also a considerable amount of opposition'.

While the ladies' mission had its genesis in the inclusion of ex-servicewomen in HMG's fare-subsidy scheme, their *Report* conflated those particular migrants with soldiers' wives, and entrants under State schemes. Separating out these groups seems impossible. One autobiographical fragment of this provenance tells of losing all capital in an orchard in north-east Tasmania; then taking a job at Cadburys' confectionery factory near Hobart; going next to Melbourne, where 'as in Tasmania, nobody seemed to look really kindly on a lady motor-driver'; but then matters turned better.[88] 'I can recommend this country to any ex-[service]member,' wrote another such, 'providing she has the average woman's idea of a domestic life.' These extracts were published in the *Imperial Colonist*, journal of the SOSBW and so biased towards flattering the story. Yet some of its reports were frank about troubles in early post-war Australia, with returned servicemen displacing many women from employment, and labour radicals militant.

By the end of 1920, the Great War had bestowed its legacy and established the moulds in which migration issues and experience were to remain through years ahead. The adventurers themselves were to suffer much, some desperately so. Popular feeling in Britain suspected and resented migration. Within the comfortable classes there, enthusiasm was fitful, and then usually directed to encourage movement of the commonalty, not themselves. In Australia, mirror-images prevailed. Labor interests, enmeshed with Irish Catholicism, looked askance at Empire and migration; they echoed that isolationism so potent in the contemporary world, and sustained feelings which had intensified in the latter years of the War. Bourgeois and Protestant sentiment was more sympathetic to migration, but still with much reservation. Doubts and qualms about migration also had play among politicians and bureaucrats. Yet hope remained in Britain that thereby social problems might moderate, and in Australia that cheap money might flow along with human movement. Various policy-makers acted to such ends. Increasingly erratic though he was, Prime Minister Hughes remained the most important.

CHAPTER TWO

The Whirl of Hughes: 1920–1923

Late in 1920 there arrived in Britain E. D. Millen, born in England in 1860 and by now member of the Australian Senate and of W. M. Hughes's government.[1] Therein he carried responsibility for soldier repatriation. Rich in political skills, Millen stood close to Hughes. His specific task on this sojourn was to attend a League of Nations meeting, there securing mandates for Australia over erstwhile German islands in the Pacific; Japan resented the move, which indeed signified Australian fears and suspicions towards it. Millen may have been instructed to assist Percy Hunter establish himself as Director of Migration and Settlement in London. Certainly the two had some liaison, although the office was not opened until 1 March 1921.

Meanwhile, Hughes showed that demographic concerns remained on his agenda. Meeting with the Premiers early in November 1920, he remarked 'there was a man called Griffiths Taylor who said this continent would take only 50 million people. I honestly believe New South Wales could take that many.'[2] So Hughes disposed of Thomas Griffith Taylor, the eminent geographer who calculated that economic constraints would make 20 million a likely Australian population by century's end.[3] No-one has done more than Hughes to shape Australian history; few have more sternly resisted rationality when it suited.

More important were developments in Britain. Late 1920 saw a sharp increase in unemployment. This weakened claims that post-war society might suffer such a shortfall of manpower as to make emigration danger-ous; rather, joblessness now became chronic, sometimes disastrous. Hughes had warned in 1918 that imperial migration policy should address such a situation, and now something like that proceeded.[4] The Ministry of Labour joined the OSD in leading these moves, with Trade and Health in support; Treasury remained ultra-sceptical, but it could not stem every tide. Cabinet's decision to continue the ex-service passage scheme through 1921 was one result of the crisis. Further, it appointed an Un-employment Committee which heeded migration. At meetings on 15 October and 5 November, L. S. Amery reported discussions with Millen and Hunter as to Australia taking 100,000 migrants a year.[5] How far the initiative was his, how far the Australians', remains opaque. In any case, little yet happened.

> The Committee was of opinion that having regard to the actual amount of unemployment in prospect it did not fall within their province to consider at this stage the question of State aided oversea settlement on a scale adequate to meet Australian requirements.

However, it agreed to grant £150,000, to continue into early 1921 the subsidy of emigration hitherto financed by the NRF. The Committee called upon the Colonial Office to consider broader migration plans.

Just as Australia's influence shaped these decisions, so it may have been in mind when Lord Milner spelled out to the Dominions in late November that expansion of migration would require their co-operation; HMG would not pay all costs indefinitely. Not only Treasury saw Australia as greedy to maximise every advantage. Hughes had often shown that skill. In February 1919 Amery noted Lloyd George's anger with the Australian (apropos post-war settlement in the Middle East):

> worked himself into quite a fine temper over the whole business, striding about and saying that Hughes was quite impossible and that he couldn't play fair with anyone, was a regular little cad, etc. I didn't venture to suggest that one of the difficulties in the case was a certain similarity in temperament between both little Welshmen.[6]

All distrusted each other.

The OSD had misgivings as to Cabinet's decisions of late 1920. T. C. Macnaghten feared lest blatant linking of migration with Britain's unemployment problems would prompt a destructive backlash.[7] Treasury was insisting that the £150,000 emergency grant be used to migrate only those destitute and unemployed, and this gave critics reason to allege that government was seeking to dump its problems abroad, continued Macnaghten; a Prime Ministerial statement on the issue had the same ill-effect. Without specific Cabinet approval, Macnaghten had phrased a cable to the Dominions on 21 December. It sought responses capable of

> initiating a large-scale policy of State-aided settlement within the Empire based on mutual co-operation. The objects in view would be to meet exceptional conditions which have arisen from the war, to distribute and use the population of Empire to the best advantage; to develop cultivation of the land and other natural resources and to ensure that the largest possible proportion of population likely to leave UK in near future should be attracted to the Dominions and available to strengthen and build up their national life, and not be diverted to foreign countries.[8]

Macnaghten hoped that herein lay the basis for grand policy.

Cables hummed during the following weeks. Hughes was exhorted by Milner, and himself exhorted Millen.[9] He stressed the need for Britain to 'facilitate' raising of Australian loans, and to share interest payments; in return, Australia would take more immigrants, promising them employment, and offering them the chance of becoming farmers on lands which loan money would open. All this revamped older tunes. In particular, averred Hughes, such loans would overcome the States' 'present cautious attitude about immigration'; money was much better spent thus, than in financing individual migrants. Millen built these ideas into a £20 million loan proposal, with British and Commonwealth governments each paying half interest; the money would provide infrastructure for between 20,000 and 25,000 migrant farms. The assumption always was that the farmer be a family-head.

Millen made some show at consulting the Agents-General, but a meeting with them was tense. Afterwards Edward Lucas of South Australia asked home whether he was *really* expected to hand over all his migration responsibilities to Percy Hunter. Lucas warned that costs would rise under Hunter, whom he implied to be an adventurer. Adelaide duly responded that the State had accepted Commonwealth leadership, but that Hughes had been told there must be no exaggerated guarantees of migrant employment.[10] Western Australia looked even harder at Millen's activities. Agent Connolly spoke to Premier Mitchell of his own 'several' protests to the Colonial Office concerning infringement of States' rights by the Commonwealth, and alleged that the Office strengthened such centralism in its preference for dealing with just one government.[11]

Whitehall was planning too. Macnaghten wrote a paper which further agonised over unemployment. Of course migration would relieve the problem, he admitted, but that should not rank as a major priority, and if stressed would offend Dominion susceptibilities. More fundamental issues of world-power were at stake. Britain had allowed Canada's population to become increasingly foreign in origin, and as for Australia:

> The present political conditions, the extreme attitude of labour, and the revolutionary propaganda which are active in parts of the country appear to be largely due to the fact that His Majesty's Government has never in recent years concerned itself with the selection of settlers for that country. Meanwhile other powerful influences have been at work. There is evidence that for the past 50 years Roman influence has been exerted to introduce a large Roman Catholic element. There has probably been active recruiting in Ireland … The result is that a large part of the population is of low Irish origin, disloyal, Sinn Fein and even Bolshevist.[12]

Macnaghten was realist enough to call for HMG to insist that, as a condition of its subsiding migration, Dominions maintain their current spending in that cause. His phrasing hinted at Dominion duplicity, with Australia surely cast as lead.

Austen Chamberlain (Chancellor of the Exchequer), Stanley Baldwin (President, Board of Trade), and T. J. MacNamara (Minister for Labour) joined Millen and Amery in discussing Millen's scheme. Chamberlain was hostile, his own judgments enhancing Treasury's. 'Capitalists are afraid of Australian finance', he affirmed, invoking E. G. Theodore's recent clash with British lenders. It was dangerous for HMG to guarantee another polity's loans and to commit itself to developmental plans so financed. Contra Hughes, Chamberlain much preferred subsidising individual migrants. 'If we provide the men free, it is up to the Dominions to do the rest'; his concern was to ensure that British largesse resulted in emigration, at once. The Dominions must not be offered temptation to take money now, and migrants never. Subsequently Chamberlain stiffened his opposition to developmental loans. He foresaw that their grant would require supervision by Treasury, yet protocol inhibited such participation in Dominion affairs.[13]

Nevertheless, various Dominion representatives met in late January–early February 1921 to discuss migration. Millen advanced his proposals, much more emphatic than any others. Amery responded with a variant which heeded Chamberlain's dissent. The new idea was that HMG should make available £2 million annually for Empire schemes. Half of this sum would subsidise—part by loans, part outright—fares and other passage costs; half would finance landsettlers through a £300 grant each. Amery's ideas found acceptance; Treasury minuted the Dominions 'expressing appreciation (if not surprise) at the generosity'.[14] Expectation ran that the matter would advance at the Imperial Conference planned for mid-year.

In following weeks, action again came from Connolly. In March 1920 he had spoken as if there were many prospective emigrants with around £5000 capital.[15] Now he proposed to settle, under Western Australia's Act for its own veterans, some 20,000 British ex-officers.[16] Thus Connolly pursued his hope of injecting bourgeois virtue into the colonial bloodstream. (He was also meditating a public-schoolboy scheme.) Yet Connolly's chief supporters and potential subsidisers of the 20,000 were HMG's Ministry of Labour, and controllers of the NRF and of the emergency employment grant, who insisted that anyone they helped should be unemployed, which scarcely comported with the bourgeois ideal.

Connolly's scheme became embroiled in hostilities between the Commonwealth and States on one hand, Treasury and other British offices on the other. Hunter objected to being bypassed. A relevant letter was one of the earliest to show that his office designated itself an agency of the 'Government of Australia',[17] a centralist usage otherwise unknown until the early 1970s, and even then angering upholders of States' rights. The OSD, wanting the WA scheme to advance, disparaged Hunter, stressing the States' constitutional power over land. (So Connolly's charge that the Colonial Office favoured the Commonwealth was impugned.) Treasury, sceptical of Connolly's as of all such ideas, was ready to use the tension between the Commonwealth and the States as a reason for delay. Its officials moulded further bullets: Cabinet had advised caution until Imperial Conference; the enthusiasm of a few Ministers did not over-ride fiscal truths; 'the Colonial Office really cannot be such fools' as to suppose otherwise.[18] Connolly's scheme stalled, the Ministry of Labour lost its enthusiasm, potential applicants dwindled.

In early 1921, Hughes received a briefing on migration matters. H. S. Gullett, now in office as Superintendent of Immigration, beseeched the Prime Minister to allow him to fulfil plans for an organisation devoted to migrant welfare. That step Gullett saw as crucial in making immigration a great supra-party policy, ranking 'with White Australia, Defence, and Protection'. There duly appeared the New Settlers' League, further discussed in chapter 10. Gullett generally urged Hughes to stir migrant action, specifying Queensland.[19] That State had firmed its earlier proposal, now asking for a £2 million loan from the Commonwealth which might build railroads in the Burnett valley, and so prepare it for farming. Gullett was asked to advise; his report, published in May, was favourable.[20] He hoped that railway-building would provide work for immigrants, whose performance should determine their right, if ex-servicemen, to ballot for a farm. Overall, Gullett proposed, half of all farms should go to Australians, half to Britons. They should be well-accoutred, with nearby butter factories to process their output, and well-planned townships to stimulate social life. Hughes let the matter ride, provoking criticism. In federal Parliament T. J. Ryan, erstwhile Premier of Queensland, indicated that in 1916–17 he (Ryan) had spoken of the Burnett valley to Rider Haggard, and that HMG had indicated readiness to finance railways there.[21]

While Hughes sometimes blew cold, other decisions were more positive. At the outset of the Commonwealth–States scheme the assumption evidently prevailed that only UK Britons would receive aid, but from April 1921 nomination and fare-grants were open also to residents of France, Belgium, Switzerland, Italy, Norway, Sweden, Denmark, Holland, Poland, Finland (all of whom had to go to London for checking), the USA and other Dominions (who would receive a fare-rebate on arrival, should testing then be satisfactory). While most States had presumably aided a few aliens in the past, this was a more explicit policy than any precursor. In July 1922 Hughes was to ask London to check on Continental migration so as to approve numbers only in accord with present ratios in Australia. French were excluded from this restriction, and Italians very much included. Yet Hughes currently had a good word even for the latter; they were already the butt of much ill-feeling in Australia and during the decade were to become more so, with Hughes to the fore.[22]

Meanwhile, both Hunter and Millen assured Hughes that the plan put forward by Amery at the January–February meeting promised at least as much as the Australian scheme.[23] Hunter forecast that it could benefit Australia by £2.5 million over the next five years, 'besides being of considerable value politically'. That is, Hunter implied, garnering cheap British money would win votes. This notion may well have become dominant in Hughes's mind. Both Millen and Hunter urged him to get Amery's promises fulfilled at the Imperial Conference.

Hughes reached London on 9 June, and two days later Hunter prepared a memorandum.[24] Australia's security, it insisted, required its population soon to rise by ten millions, to which immigration must contribute 80,000 to 100,000 annually. Present reality fell much below that, with neither New South Wales nor Queensland taking any 'selectees'. Hunter argued that massive developmental works 'would probably extinguish the unemployment problem at present existing in Australia and a great deal of the objection to the immediate introduction of new people would disappear'. Depots accommodating up to a thousand migrants should give training for rural labour. 'Away from the cities and out of the sight of political agitators … it would not matter whether they found work speedily or not.' Hunter stressed that British opinion was ripe for co-operative policies. The OSD likewise primed Hughes for an active role at Conference.[25]

In fact, migration took low priority there. Hughes fought for Australian security primarily in terms of controlling Japanese naval power; also he frustrated J. C. Smuts's efforts to formalise British–Dominion relations, fearing lest such moves would prevent Australia from putting pressure on London when national interests so demanded. Some discussion on migration did take place.[26] Hughes spoke of Australia having capacity to take a thousand farmer-migrants annually; he stressed the need for loan-credit. The Conference called for HMG to advance such schemes.

The next few months saw most initiative come from the OSD. Its current situation was especially ambiguous. In February the ageing Milner had resigned as Secretary for the Colonies, to be replaced not by Amery but Winston Churchill—as dry on economic matters as Austen Chamberlain, and having little empathy for the Empire of settlement, least for Australia. Nor did Amery continue as Colonial Under-Secretary, instead going to that rank in Admiralty. Yet he continued important in migration matters. In June he warned Cabinet that the USA threatened both Canada and Australia, making planned migration 'the only constructive policy of defence which can, in the long run, maintain the existence of the British Empire'.[27] Amery remained chairman of the OSC and the inspiration behind the OSD. As these bodies strove in later 1921 to maintain migrationist momentum, some distance grew between them and the Colonial Office establishment.

Nevertheless, their activities were effective.[28] From September the OSD gained support from all major departments, except Treasury, in upholding

relatively lavish expenditure on migration. Especially important was backing from Alfred Mond, Minister for Health and chairman of the Cabinet
Unemployment Committee. On 19 October, Prime Minister Lloyd George
told the Commons that his government would guarantee Dominion loans,
provided they mitigated British unemployment. Doubtless that emphasis
bothered Macnaghten, but he rode with it. Perhaps at his initiative, a late
October meeting took place between the OSD and Hunter and other
Australian representatives; it insisted that funds must flow if immigration
were to continue.[29] Thus the Millen proposals of January returned to vogue.
Hughes and Hunter may have agreed in June–July that after all Millen's
scheme was preferable to the Amery compromise. Certainly Macnaghten
cited Hughes (at the Imperial Conference) when advising in late October
that Millen's proposals become policy.[30]

Hughes continued to receive stimuli towards a Millenarian stance.[31]
Gullett sustained argument for Commonwealth subsidy of 'properly
controlled reproductive works in the States', saying as Hunter had that this
would invigorate the economy and make massive immigration viable in
both political and fiscal terms. Gullett proposed a Commonwealth
Agricultural Bank to underwrite pioneering.[32] Hughes returned to Australia
and in late October a Premiers' Conference again confronted immigration,
settlement, and funding. State sensitivities on these matters had continued.
On 24 August 1921, London's *Morning Post* reported Hughes as declaring:

> Now that we have obtained the assent of the States to hand over to the
> Commonwealth the control of immigration we have got rid of the old conflict of
> authority and diversity of policies in that respect, but we still have to secure the
> control of the required areas of land necessary for settlement ... We are, however,
> hopeful of overcoming that difficulty, as we overcame the other.[33]

This was madness, seeming to confirm the States' suspicions that Commonwealth interest in migration cloaked aims of usurping power over Crown
land. Connolly's report of the episode to Mitchell made that point. Like
feeling permeated the Premiers' discussion in October of related issues,
especially soldier settlement.[34] Hughes claimed that the States were abusing
the Commonwealth's generosity in helping finance that policy; the
justifiable response ran that the Commonwealth had coerced the States into
ill-founded moves. Yet Hughes now spoke of adding 50,000 migrants a
year—10,000 farmers with families. The Commonwealth, he said, would
advance loan funds for this, and in return claim oversight to ensure that the
money was used to prepare suitable land. Hughes intimated that Queensland's Theodore was likely, if unchecked, to use the money and eschew the
migrants: the same point that some Britons made against Australia at large.
Further, Hughes averred that British capital would flow only if immigration

were guaranteed. The Premiers declared resistance to Commonwealth control over such matters; however, they were prepared to accept particular obligations, in return for Commonwealth help with financing.

Gullett was probably more disappointed with this outcome than Hughes. Before the Premiers' Conference he had urged that, unless the States became more active, the Commonwealth should take complete control of immigration. Hughes, for all his bluster, had not dared to do so. Later, Gullett again warned that the States were likely to use developmental money without taking migrants. The Commonwealth must prevent that, and insist on effective spending of the funds that it advanced.[35]

Hughes made the best of the Premiers' Conference. A cable to Whitehall on 24 November asserted that it opened the way for

> the inauguration of a great developmental policy for the building of railways, roads, the clearing of forests or bush, water conservation or irrigation. Immigrants coming out under the scheme would be guaranteed employment in constructing such railways ... etc. and then given the opportunity to select land upon which he and his family could settle.[36]

All this justified £50 million worth of loans over the next five years, said Hughes, proposing that the British government pay half the interest during that period. He stressed that Britain suffered from chronic over-population and that doles could never solve its social problems. The cable made a stir, Treasury's men springing to opposition.[37] R. G. Hawtrey reiterated that war deaths had reduced Britain's manpower, which might be further impaired by recent low birth-rates. The current depression resulted from credit contraction rather than excessive labour supply, continued Hawtrey; the main effect of the latter was to cut wages and that, went the clear implication, was no bad thing.

Other misgivings blunted Hughes's initiative. The Colonial Office elite saw his scheme as ultra-unorthodox, and so did much opinion on the OSC. Especially influential was Oscar Thompson, a shipping magnate. The Committee asked Thompson to write Millen concerning its doubts. Thompson was forthright, citing 'a feeling here that Australia wants money from us so that they can go on paying inflated wages and a fear that they mean to develop Home Manufactures, building up such a Tariff that Trade between them and the UK will decrease'. He argued that migration should foster primary production. While the Washington Treaty (whereby the UK, the USA and Japan recently had agreed to stabilise their navies at current relative strengths) promised stability over the next decade, after that time

> Great Britain will not have the power to guarantee Australia immunity from attack and the only hope to secure comparative safety is for Australia to go ahead during the next ten years so that their weakness will no longer invite attack.

The question had become less that of immigration than whether or not 'to lose the Country'. Thompson urged that Hughes invite a commission from Britain to advise Australia on migration and economic policy.[38]

Thompson sympathised with Hughes's political problem in overcoming the odium attached to immigration. Amery likewise saw that a generous developmental scheme, involving migrants only as farmers and outback workers, was essential if Australian Labor were to be conciliated.[39] His own reply to Hughes was still wary.[40] The Treasury critique of the Millen approach had its point, Amery conceded: State governments might spend pertinent moneys to secure political ends and employ supporters, without heeding immigration. In proposing a solution, Amery referred to Milner's government of South Africa, when fear prevailed lest Boers deceive British settlers. 'A Land Settlement Board or Commission', above the political battle, had met the case there and could do so again: on it might sit representatives of the States, the Commonwealth, and Britain.

Hughes would have had doubts about that, and the Premiers too. However, this did not bother Amery. His letter reminded Hughes of Treasury's opposition to sharing loans, rather than aiding individual settlers. He stressed that HMG wanted to see its people employed on Australian public works and farms, although recognising that this could not exclude Australians. Amery further hoped that Australia would take some women and juveniles, and provide training facilities for all. He looked forward to developmental works resulting in contracts for British suppliers. To make the scheme surge, ships carrying migrants should brim with cargo, consequent upon Australia giving greater tariff preferences to British goods, or at least diminishing those granted the USA.

While presumably dubious about Hughes's good faith, Amery remained committed to securing money and legislation which would give sinew to the talk of 1921. Likewise Alfred Mond stayed in resolute support. Late in December Amery proposed to Cabinet that it set aside £5 million annually to finance migration schemes.[41] He thereby conceived the Empire Settlement Act. Meanwhile, Hughes's plans prompted discussions within the Board of Trade.[42] The Board's bureaucrats knew how sluggish Australia's economy was, and believed that immigration threatened to cause further problems there. Worse, data showed that much produce from Australia's farms already glutted the world market: Amery was wrong in postulating a food shortage which Empire co-operation must relieve. While demographic redistribution promised to assuage Britain's social problems and strengthen Australia's defence, economic realities did not favour such processes. In particular, they blighted prospects for farm development—which Amery, Hughes, and most migrationists saw as the necessary complement to their policies.

Such matters did not inhibit Hughes. After the October–November Premiers' Conference, he had written to Premiers, asking for schemes supportive of the immigration policy then discussed. An answer came quickly from Mitchell of Western Australia.[43] He and Connolly had kept frenetic in these matters, notwithstanding the failure of the officer-settlement programme. The public-schoolboy plan still lived, and so too did long-cherished hopes of winning British favour for massive settlement in the Kimberley region of their vast State; as well, they had proposed in October schemes for settling 2000 unemployed Britons.[44] The response of Theodore of Queensland was to propose the Burnett valley scheme again. More benignly received by Hughes were the ideas of J. H. Carruthers, long an active non-Labor politician in New South Wales. Another upholder of racial-rural Empire mythology, Carruthers since 1919 had led a campaign to establish 'A Million Farms' in New South Wales, with British money and men the essential factors. Hughes backed Carruthers and his movement. The OSD had also heeded Carruthers's notions, finding them of interest but too grandiose.[45]

The Premiers met again in January 1922, with immigration having its usual turgid debate. Gullett was present, answering critics of the current system and urging more vigour in State activity under its terms. Hughes expostulated that only Western Australia had given a proper response to his call for projects, and there followed another brush with Theodore, who wanted the talk to end and the flow of money to begin. Rhetoric nevertheless continued to be Hughes's chief weapon: he invoked his mid-1921 talks with Amery and Churchill, and the encouragement he was receiving from a British Parliamentary group of Tory imperialists.[46]

Late in February came the bombshell of Gullett's resignation as Superintendent of Immigration. In successive statements he accused Hughes of talking big about immigration, yet doing little. Even the Millen plan of January 1921 was claimed by Gullett as his own idea. Gullett pointed to Hughes's rejection of the Burnett valley scheme as a gross example of party politics suborning national policies. While Britain stood ready and anxious to help, continued the indictment, Hughes had shillyshallied—even at the Imperial Conference. In his office, memoranda went unread, letters unsigned for weeks; he had no interest in boosting migrant numbers, independent of the development schemes; concerning entry of domestics he had been hostile, affirming that Australian women should attend their homes.[47] Hughes answered Gullett in bravura style, showing flaws in the latter's record too. Gullett's critique surely carried much truth. Yet it made only a little impact: Hughes had faced many a crisis in his career. Perhaps one effect appeared in March, when he sought information twice from Whitehall about progress on migration matters, and told of political embarrassment caused by delay.[48] Soon came the reply that the Empire Settlement Bill was in final stage of drafting. Amery and the OSC had carried the day.

Various British officials discussed the Bill. One interesting statement came from the War Office representative on the OSC, Colonel L. H. R. Pope Hennessy. He echoed the usual point about a well-populated Australia being important for imperial defence, but went further:

> a scheme which will enable large numbers of unemployed ex-servicemen to emigrate to Australia under favourable conditions, will do much to reconcile that numerous section of the population which is now discontented and distrustful, both of the Government and of the Army. Incidentally, it will help recruiting if ex-soldiers are assisted on a large scale to start new lives in the Colonies.[49]

Winston Churchill's thoughts showed his disregard for the settlement Empire:

> the alternative to this expenditure is an equivalent or greater expenditure on dole and relief works, and whereas in the latter case the burden falls entirely ... upon this country, in the former we shall at least be getting pound for pound from the Dominions.[50]

This was written to Robert Horne, currently Chancellor and chairman of a Cabinet sub-committee pondering the Bill. Officers from the Treasury led the critics. Otto Niemeyer and M. F. Headlam vied in lamenting that HMG should become involved in Australian public finance, so careless and spendthrift. They warned that the outcome would be either HMG's capitulation to Australian extravagances or effort to control them, with resultant friction. India and other Dominions would be tempted to follow the Australian example. These monitions bothered Horne little, nor did the Geddes Committee, currently imposing economies, smother the Bill. However, the annual expenditure ceiling was set not at the £5 million sought by Amery, but £1.5 million in 1922 and £3 million for fourteen years thereafter.

The Bill's other provisions were simple. The Secretary of State could arrange schemes jointly with Empire governments or public or private authorities. They could provide for direct migration of UK residents in terms of fares, training, and establishment costs—or, more ambitiously, for development, normally oriented towards farm expansion. Treasury was to approve all schemes, and the maximal British contribution in any instance was half. That could be by grant or loan, or (by implication) interest-sharing. Moving the Bill's second reading on 26 April, Amery extolled vital, self-sustaining Britaindom. His devotion to higher trade preferences throughout the Empire became explicit. There was some Dominion opposition to migration, Amery agreed, but largely from industrial workers. Hence the Dominions had stressed land development, which Amery hoped would absorb about two-thirds of the moneys available; he believed £3 million a year would soon prove 'quite inadequate'. Happily, Australia's Treasurer, S. M. Bruce, had indicated readiness to spend £5 million on complementary activity.

Labor's leading speaker, J. R. Clynes, did not oppose the Bill, but made obvious points about Dominion resistance to migration, the prime importance of Europe in Britain's trade, and grassroots opposition to the measure for boosting Dominion, as against domestic, farming. Josiah Wedgwood, free-thinking disciple of Henry George, was more acrid: in contradiction to the promises of the recent past, he averred, 'now it is not this country but Western Australia and the valley of the Darling that is going to be made fit for heroes ... at our expense'. On 3 May relevant Estimates came before the House, prompting radical Labourites to express the spleen against emigration that Clynes had rationalised and suppressed.

Even before the Bill became law, Amery experienced its potential for arousing strife. Western Australia was the locus. Hughes had used Mitchell's current plan to stir London, and then Sir James himself had gone thither. 'Mitchell is incredibly inarticulate and incoherent in exposition,' recorded Amery, 'but I believe the scheme is really a sound one and I should think he had a good business head in action.'[51] On 3 April a cable to Hughes proposed that both Commonwealth and British governments pay one-third interest for five years on loan moneys for Mitchell's scheme, and suggested this as a model for the future. Thereupon Hughes attacked Whitehall for dealing with Western Australia direct, rather than giving the Commonwealth a decisive part in negotiations.[52] Hughes repeated that the States could not be trusted, and might use the funds for short-term political advantage. Only if the Commonwealth had a central role could it stop such abuses. 'There is not one Australia but very many', Hughes insisted. This might appear a strange argument in support of centralist power, but Hughes presumably sought to present the Commonwealth as distilling various and fluid components of the national interest, while the States were rigid and archaic.

To Hughes's critics, his stand could mean only to diminish the States and their power over Crown land. Amery himself had long doubted Hughes, and Gullett's resignation must have strengthened such feeling. Moreover, Amery seems to have feared that if commitments were organised through federal government, the States might not see themselves as bound by them, and so a change in federal government might cancel all arrangements. Interwoven with such issues was the distribution of constitutional powers between the Commonwealth and the States. The States' authority over Crown land seemingly strengthened Amery's view, but the 'Dominions' group within the Colonial Office argued for salience of the Commonwealth, and saw Amery as devious and wrong in preferring to negotiate with States. Treasury sided for once with Amery, seeing more chance of holding the

States to effective account. The 'Dominions' view prevailed with the Secretary for the Colonies: 'Mr Churchill has intimated that he doesn't mind a bit in what form agreements are drawn up as long as Mr Hughes is not aggrieved', ran one minute. That outcome angered Premier Mitchell, who therefore postponed approving the scheme affecting his State, under debate all this while. More perturbation resulted in Whitehall. At last Mitchell signed, but later complained to Hughes that the document included material of which he was unaware. Maybe Mitchell alluded to a clause specifying that HMG would pay through the Commonwealth. That proviso was crucial in placating Hughes.[53]

All this delayed the approval of the WA agreement until 9 February 1923. Working within the Settlement Act, it embodied a plan to run over five years. The State was to take at least 75,000 migrants (men, women, and children), employ males on farmwork, and from them select 6000 for settlement on farms. All was to happen in the State's southwestern region. Continuing established local practice, a structure of co-operative or 'group' activity would prevail. Each migrant farmer was to receive help with land preparation; the land was free, but preparation costs were accounted as debt, which should not exceed £1000 and was payable over thirty years. Finance was to come from loans amounting to £6 million raised by the Australian government; for the first five years of each loan, the latter and HMG each would pay one-third of the interest.[54] In retrospect, the whole scheme appears fantastic. How could it have ignored such matters as the appropriate ratio of breadwinners among the 75,000 migrants, let alone assume the capacity of one region to take about 20,000 workers, many with families, and to provide 6000 farms at so modest a cost? Yet such misgivings appear not to have bothered even Treasury, let alone the OSD. Christopher Turnor maintained his critique of WA methods and estimates, foretelling the future all too well.[55]

Similar agreements were made in 1922–3 with Victoria and New South Wales.[56] Procedural complexities continued vast. In consequence of Hughes's insistence on federal primacy, the two States first treated with the Commonwealth, and then the Commonwealth with HMG. In both cases, however, the respective Premiers (H. S. W. Lawson of Victoria and G. W. Fuller of New South Wales) went to Britain and engaged in further negotiations. Australia's new Prime Minister from February 1923 was S. M. Bruce; their action caused him the same kind of annoyance as Hughes had expressed vis-à-vis Western Australia. Each State strove to secure preferential terms. At one stage, Hughes encouraged Fuller to do the best for himself; overall, however, the Commonwealth called for equal treatment. The basic principle of one-third interest-sharing prevailed throughout. Victoria committed itself to 2000 migrant farmers within eighteen months, and another 8000 in due course; New South Wales more closely followed the WA model. While Victoria seems to have won the best deal, Lawson affirmed that Britain had secured a bargain, the cost of establishing farms being what it was.[57] Promises to assist migrants in preparing their land followed a common pattern.

The NSW scheme descended from Carruthers's 'Million Farms' chimera, and otherwise offered interest in its history. A letter from Hughes to Fuller, June 1922, showed the Prime Minister explicit in accepting migration only as a complement of national growth:

> It is to be distinctly understood that the Commonwealth Government's policy in this connection applies to the settlement of immigrants on the land. The introduction of immigrants for whom no such provision is made can only be approved by the Commonwealth if some great public works policy is in progress which will be the means of absorbing not only our own unemployed, but affords opportunities for immigrants.[58]

For his part, Fuller insisted that the proposed development, largely in irrigation areas, required changes in Britain's trade policy:

> It would be but a poor policy in the end if this State should spend millions to develop large areas of its lands, and to induce British settlers upon such lands, only to find that Great Britain allowed such settlers to endure ruin simply because Greeks, Turks, Egyptians and other foreigners monopolised an open market in Great Britain.[59]

Fuller ensured that the Commonwealth–New South Wales agreement committed the former to act on marketing. In London, the Ministry of Agriculture remarked that this could reinforce British farmers' complaint that the Settlement Act threatened themselves.[60]

While these agreements were the most visible Australian aftermath of the Settlement Act, in everyday terms it had more effect in granting assistance to rank-and-file migrants.[61] As told above, the joint Commonwealth–State scheme meant that currently Australia was giving to approved migrants (both nominated and 'selected') a grant of one-third of the shipping companies' special minimum fare for migrants; this fare stood at £36 in 1922, but the next year was to drop to £33. Australia continued making loans to some migrants, enabling them to meet the fare-deficit. A key Australia House bureaucrat, M. L. Shepherd, commented that such loans were advanced 'only … when we are absolutely certain that we cannot get the migrant without it'.[62] Yet Shepherd also averred that very few potential migrants (he might have been speaking only of 'selectees', this being a constant source of ambiguity) were able to provide the outstanding two-thirds of the fare. He added that for this reason some State requisitions were not being filled, so implying that loans were not always given, even when they would have secured a body. (Extraordinarily, details are rare as to requisitions for this or any other period.)

The Settlement Act changed the situation, somewhat. The Act provided for HMG to assist with fares, and consequent negotiations achieved an Assisted Passage Agreement in July. The dominant theme within this story was the OSD's urging of Australia to be generous in subsidising fares, to little effect. According to J. D. Connolly, the OSD was anxious to grant up to 40 per cent of fares, with Australia matching.[63] Instead the total grant remained normally one-third, equally shared. Thus the effect was to halve Australia's outlay, with no attendant obligation to take more migrants. Winston Churchill had got it diametrically wrong! Likewise, Australia rejected a British proposal for a higher level of subsidy for women.[64]

As to loans, a complementary situation prevailed. The Passage Agreement provided that the two governments share in these, and that they might cover not only the fare-deficit but medical-inspection fees and landing money. Australian officialdom had grudged such largesse. Percy Hunter cabled home:

> OSC and officials rather inclined to molly coddle migrants and being amateurs in business are very susceptible of influence by cranks ... if we give way on that they will soon spring something else ... It will pay Great Britain abundantly to find the money if it is really necessary as people of this class are clearly being maintained out of unemployment dole and the rates.[65]

Hunter wanted HMG to pay a big share of migrant-funding, but the passage may have meant more. It hints that he believed sufficient migrants with some basic means would offer—and that Australia had little reason to entice others with loans.

From the British side, all pressure was towards maximising loans. 'Lack of means should not act as a barrier to those who are otherwise suitable and willing to proceed overseas as land workers', went an OSD memorandum.[66] The Ministry of Labour was even more emphatic, citing the utter poverty of many applicants.[67] In July or August Hughes recalled Hunter to Australia (where he helped prepare the State agreements). This probably smoothed matters, as his next-in-command at Australia House, J. T. Barnes, was easier in granting loans, at least for 'selectees'. Some reciprocal laxity developed on the enforcement of the Agreement's means test (£250 for singles, £500 for marrieds). Australia House, hoping thus to lure moneyed people, bargained hard on this point.[68]

Treasury remained troubled and troublesome. As early as 3 April, Frank Skevington, its representative on the OSC, urged the development of guidelines for projects under the Settlement Act. 'What the Treasury is especially concerned to guard against is that any voted moneys should go to the Dominions without our receiving an immediate quid pro quo in the shape of inhabitants of this country being migrated to Australia etc.' [69] Conversely, it argued for a strict means test on recipients of assisted fares.[70] Treasury also probed the possibility of refusing aid where the potential migrant, such as agricultural labourers, might be a loss to Britain.[71] Skevington welcomed Australia's reluctance to give loans to the destitute, seeing that as 'a very effective safeguard against waste of public funds'.[72] While crucial in administering the Settlement Act, Treasury rejected its central tenets.

This ambivalence caused an early storm.[73] Late in 1922 Skevington put to Treasury's solicitors a case for very narrow interpretation of the Act, denying that it legitimated defrayal of the Fairbridge school's housing and maintenance costs. Macnaghten was appalled: 'is it sound or even sane policy to destroy the best piece of pioneering in child migration since Dr Barnardo?' (Thomas Barnado's work for emigrating waifs had become a by-word.) Relations with both Western Australia and the Commonwealth would suffer; Treasury's recalcitrance was making the OSD's situation impossible and corroding the Settlement Act. Macnaghten threatened resignation of the OSC. 'For the umpteenth time' went a Treasury minute. Its chieftains muttered that the Colonial Office should control the OSD 'in a much more real way', but that department was 'notoriously susceptible to Dominion pressure', and so Treasury must hold the line. The matter went to the Crown Law Officers, who plumped for a generous interpretation. Perhaps Treasury found that easier to accept because already evidence was gathering that, contrary to OSD hopes and its own fears, applications under the Act were proving modest.

While Treasury grudged, the Ministry of Labour pushed the other way.[74] Recognising the Dominions' hostility to having unemployed men dumped upon them, Labour yet argued that Britain's problem warranted appeal to the Dominions. The OSD remained lukewarm, while Treasury remarked that 'although we have unemployment peculiarly in mind, there is nothing to be gained by telling the Dominions so'.[75] A consequent letter from Churchill to Hughes, 22 July 1922, took a careful path. Ignoring (as did so much commentary) migration-by-nomination, the letter accepted that only landwork was appropriate for adult male migrants. It stressed that Australia should become much more receptive to females—in their normal, although not exclusive, role of domestic service—and children. All migrants, Churchill continued, would benefit from training; that should be provided, and generally a positive welcome given newcomers.[76] Between the lines lurked much disappointment at Australia's performance in these respects. Canada certainly took more children and gave better reception. Nothing indicates that Hughes heeded Churchill's letter.

That complemented heightening worry in Britain as to migrants' troubles. The OSD and the OSC made plain this concern. J. T. Barnes of Australia House responded with churlish obduracy. He minimised Australia's duties both to ex-servicepeople for whom HMG had paid full fare and to nominees; 'the persons who have nominated them take full responsibility, either for their employment or sustenance'. Macnaghten's continuing protest achieved merely an undertaking that the States would be asked to keep a more careful eye on the nomination process; the Australians further remarked that the burden of debt on many migrants resulted from HMG's policy of liberalising fare-loans.[77] Meeting in November, the OSC agreed that Britain should establish a migrant-welfare agency in Australia, even though that might encourage grievance-mongers and bedevil local bureaucrats.[78] Discussion prompted the idea of sending out a commission of enquiry into migrant conditions in Australia. The Ministry of Labour was especially emphatic, taking the cue from its head— that super-bureaucrat of inter-war years, Horace J. Wilson. Under this pressure, the OSC and OSD proposed that Wilson's ministry organise such a mission; yet they advised that its role be concealed lest it stir Dominion fears of destitute-dumping. Macnaghten urged that the enquiry pursue decent after-care. 'They have got to convince the Australian authorities that public opinion here will not be satisfied unless ... every new settler who reaches Australia has a chance of happy and successful settlement.'[79] Just a hundred years earlier a British commissioner of enquiry, J. T. Bigge, had advised how to make the Australian colonies more effectively serve the needs of imperial capitalism. Parallels between the centuries ran close.

The plan to send the proposed delegation appeared in a Cabinet paper of January 1923, which spoke of OSC concerns, doubtless concerning migrant welfare, too delicate to reveal in its annual *Report*.[80] The document was presented by the Duke of Devonshire, Secretary for the Colonies since Andrew Bonar Law had become Prime Minister in October; Amery then had almost won the position of Secretary for the Colonies but instead became Admiralty Secretary. Devonshire besought the new government to heed the concerns of the OSC. He invoked the political situation in Australia. A general election in mid-December had strengthened the Country Party and so weakened its enemy, Hughes. The upshot was that Hughes left office in February, his last action on migration being to begrudge appointment of HMG's delegation.[81] Replacing him was a coalition of Nationalist and Country parties, led by S. M. Bruce and E. C. G. Page.

Devonshire's paper argued for a total emigrant flow of up to 700,000 annually. A salient aim must be to move Britain's under-employed onto land in Australia, 'where the necessity for development and population is most acute from an Imperial and strategic, as well as from a Dominion point of view'. True, the Labor party there resented migration; in response, HMG's delegation was to include James Wignall, a respected Labour parliament-arian who sat on the OSC. Devonshire hoped that the delegation might so burnish emigration that henceforth many would volunteer who needed no state aid. Appointed head of the mission was William Windham, one of the Ministry of Labour's key men. His team set sail early in 1923, a time of much action on migration. Much of this anticipated an Imperial Conference which Law had first mooted in November 1922. Amery ensured that settlement stood high on its agenda.[82] Planned at first for April, the Conference actually met in October–November. It proved a fateful occasion, notably for and through Bruce of Australia.

CHAPTER THREE

S. M. Bruce and Empire: 1923–1925

The change of Australian government in February 1923 caused little shift of policy in imperial matters. Australia continued to respect the British heritage and both to serve and to use British power. The new Prime Minister came from a family which had prospered through importing British goods; he had gone to Cambridge and excelled in sport, coaching the university crew 1911–14.[1] A successful man of Anglo-Australian business, Bruce had joined the British Army, fought at Gallipoli, won the Military Cross. His future critics—most effectively, Labor politician F. G. Anstey, himself an immigrant—were to scoff at Bruce 'as an agent of imperial ascendancy.'[2] That image conveys only a partial truth. Bruce believed in Britaindom and was ready to engage in imperialist rhetoric. Yet in so doing he acted with calculation and conceit, aiming to direct imperial resources much as he had those Cambridge rowers. His purpose was to create a potent and integrated Australia, altogether capitalist and somewhat corporative. Bruce's pertinent abilities probably were most substantial of all Australian Prime Ministers', but still not sufficient to fulfil that aim.

On reporting the accession of the new ministry to Whitehall, the Governor-General, Lord Forster, remarked it to be the first altogether native-born.[3] No policy was more likely than migration to be affected by the Austral birth of Cabinet: for natives, characteristically, the migrant is different, and not quite equal. Bruce was even more likely than Hughes to value migration only insofar as it furthered Australian purposes. In November 1921 he had quizzed the migration vote, suggesting that this was a dubious way of spending loan money.[4]

From early days in office, Bruce attended to the forthcoming Imperial Conference. He resisted Whitehall's suggestion that economic issues be separately discussed. Such matters, Bruce affirmed, were integral to 'defence and welfare of, and migration within, the Empire'. Hughes had foreshadowed this approach. HMG accepted: the general and economic Conferences fused. Bruce also echoed Hughes in foreshadowing intent to seek preference for Australian produce in British markets.[5] This touched a sensitive nerve. While moving a little towards 'safeguarding' (that is, Pro-

tection) and even towards imperial preference, post-war British governments generally upheld free trade. Bonar Law had pledged his government
against fiscal change.

Bruce met the Premiers in May–June, and migration found its usual
place.[6] The three State schemes received notice, together with the need for
welcoming migrants and training some in farmwork. One novelty lay in
Bruce's advocacy of extended nomination, urging that church and regional
groups as well as individuals thus might benefit both themselves and the
general good. 'If the whole of our operations could be conducted under this
... ideal form of migration ... it would undoubtedly prove advantageous.'
Percy Hunter had remained in Australia, and possibly influenced thinking
along these lines. Yet the general issue of migration soon became subord-
inated to plans for development, The Commonwealth estimated that entries
would reach 50,000 in the next year. That was as many as the economy
allowed, but not enough. Accordingly, 'there should be an Australia wide
stocktaking of our resources', assessing the capital and labour requisite to
'successful development'. While the government's design stressed land-
settlement, with complementary 'railways, roads, conservation schemes and
other works', there was also reference to secondary industries. The States
should do the stocktaking, and then the Commonwealth propose action.

The sole Labor Premier was Queensland's Theodore, and he proved the
sternest critic of these proposals. High unemployment made it 'lunacy' to
encourage migrants; Hughes (with Hunter in attendance) had played
political games with migration during the recent election campaign, but
achieved nothing in the matter; internal movement brought migrants to
Queensland in sizeable numbers, but no imperial largesse resulted. New
South Wales echoed Theodore on the last point, and Bruce agreed that the
nation's total intake should be salient. He also concurred with H. N.
Barwell (South Australia) that the State agreements were awry in giving
centrality to establishing migrants as farmers; pioneering was better done
by locals.

The Premiers' Conference accepted Bruce's plans. Little follow-up
occurred; despite Barwell's argument, one letter asked the States to tell
Australia House of land which might attract migrants with capital.[7] Bruce
was very busy in mid-year, prior to departing for London. On 24 July he
spoke to Parliament about his mission, giving some heed to migration but
much more to marketing. He had forced this item onto the agenda, Bruce
affirmed, stressing Australia's role as buyer of British goods, and forecasting
Britain's abandonment of free trade. He spoke of possibilities for HMG
to subsidise developmental works throughout the Empire, provided that
requisite materials came from Britain. (This plan was fathered by Philip
Lloyd-Greame, President of the Board of Trade, and almost as ardent an
imperialist as Amery; its history was similar to that of the Settlement Act,

especially in arousing Treasury's wrath.)[8] On 26 July, Bruce provided in his Budget for loans up to £5 million under the Settlement Act; the aim would be 'to produce a reciprocal and proportionate development of primary and secondary industries'.

Lloyd-Greame's proposals were part of a surge of interest by the Board of Trade in migration matters. In late 1922 HMG's Senior Trade Commissioner in Australia, S. W. B. McGregor, argued that the answer to Australia's current economic sluggishness lay in fostering secondary industries, which (he believed) would in due course attract more migrants than were presently coming.[9] Similar ideas appeared in London's *Financial Times*, 26 May 1923. Old OSC and OSD hands saw all this as repeating fallacies which Australian Protectionists had long maintained. 'The policy of the OSC must be the conversion of industrialists [i.e. industrial workers] into landworkers', affirmed T. C. Macnaghten. Yet McGregor's essay may have impinged on Albert Buckley, who from March to October was chairman of the OSC as Parliamentary Secretary for Overseas Trade. Speaking in the Commons on 10 May, Buckley admitted that many disappointments beset the imperial idealism which he and others had cherished in the War's immediate aftermath. Yet, he claimed, the Settlement Act still promised some hope. A paper that Buckley presented to Cabinet a few weeks later advanced what would become a basic OSD argument. Historically, Buckley proposed, migration had accompanied economic buoyancy. That buoyancy did not now prevail, 'and I cannot but feel that we are endeavouring to force a movement against the natural economic tendencies of the moment'.[10] Buckley developed his theme in relation to Australia, citing such matters as reluctance or inability there to pay farmworkers enough to sustain a migrant family, and Premier Fuller's warnings that the New South Wales scheme offered no quick and certain success.

Buckley proposed that the OSD amalgamate with Overseas Trade. Macnaghten answered that such shuffling would undermine confidence; anyway, the virtue of the OSD lay in its commitment to the Dominions, and that would be smirched by a move implying that HMG cared for them only as trading partners.[11] Macnaghten would have been happier with Buckley's proposal to develop training-camps where unemployed men could learn skills to win them Australian 'selection' as farmworkers.[12] The matter had arisen at the recent Premiers' Conference, and the OSD hoped that on returning to Britain (which he did in July), Hunter would offer plans for such units in Australia.

In fact his ideas ranged wider, revamping those of Millen and Hughes. As developed, Hunter's plan was for Australia and HMG to share interest on loans to £70 million over a ten-year period, through which Australia would take a million assisted immigrants. The latter would receive nothing beyond fare-subsidy, and such intricate detail as had permeated the State schemes must be eschewed. The Commonwealth should transfer moneys to the States at 1 per cent.[13] Presumably Hunter saw the Commonwealth as directing a process like that foreshadowed at the Premiers' Conference. Despatching the scheme to Bruce en route from Australia, Hunter claimed support from Buckley, and urged intransigence. 'The unemployment troubles of England do not diminish sensibly and immense sums are being spent in poor relief and unemployment pay.' Bruce must expect protests against the Commonwealth reaping 1 per cent from the States and HMG nothing—'but the objectives would be waived if the Prime Minister makes it clear that he will not agree to any other arrangement'. Hunter disparaged the State agreements; 'attempts to place people from overseas on farms can only succeed under conditions which are too onerous financially to be practical'. Presumably he rationalised his own part in shaping the State schemes in that they gained something, for a while.

The Australian indeed had found a sympathetic listener in Buckley. To Treasury, he affirmed Hunter's view that earlier planning had stressed *settlement* rather than *development*; the latter, Buckley agreed, offered much more migrant-absorption.[14] He concurred too that negotiations should be with the Commonwealth, not the States. Buckley admitted that Hunter had offended HMG's stand in proposing that interest payments be 'a contribution, and not an advance', and that purchase of materials for loan-funded projects not necessarily occur in Britain, but even on these points he allowed sense. Buckley recognised that immigration carried political odour, especially among radicals and Irish, in Australia; in response he could only repeat that while some 80 per cent of emigrants were unemployed, the Settlement Act aimed not to dump such people but to increase wealth, Empire-wide. (Perhaps Buckley spoiled his case by giving a figure which applied to 'selectees' rather than all migrants.)

Other thinking within the OSC and OSD also tended Hunter's way, with more reservations.[15] Macnaghten and Oscar Thompson foresaw that Treasury would resist his ideas, and that there need be specified particular schemes and resulting capacity to absorb migrants. Macnaghten harped on the intricacy of Australian procedures as regards 'selection'; he was particularly unhappy at States' refusal to accept industrial workers even when available agriculturalists did not fill farmwork requisitions. Notwithstanding such plaints, negotiation with Hunter advanced, even when John Sanderson, a London-based Australian of big finance and shipping interests whom Bruce had selected as an advisor at the Imperial Conference, warned that the latter might disdain Hunter's plan. The negotiations verged on conspiratorial, with Hunter a sort of double-agent; his plan was readied for submission to the Conference by HMG, rather than Bruce. Macnaghten wrote to Hunter as 'my dear Percy' and told William Clark, his counterpart at Overseas Trade, that 'Oscar Thompson and I are old acquaintances even frie· ls of Hunter.' 'Hunter is a bit of a mystery to me', came the reply.[16]

'I should prefer myself', Clark added, 'not to show Hunter the quotation from Windham as to the Australians not being pressed to take a single man more than they ask for, since we do not want to make them a present of Windham's support should they be out to go unduly slow.' The Windham Delegation was sending home a dispirited message to HMG. Probably Hunter knew that, but (contradicting his own advice to Bruce) he joined British bureaucrats in pre-Conference discussions. These raised OSD hopes that Australia would become more responsive, quickening procedures at Australia House, broadening qualification for 'selection', regularising numbers in 'selection' quotas, and allowing higher fare-subsidies especially for female and juvenile migration. These discussions also mooted Britain establishing an office in Australia to attend to migrant matters.

Treasury maintained a pre-Conference rage.[17] Its major target was Lloyd-Greame's scheme, especially vis-à-vis Australia. Few documents can be more extraordinary than that consequently prepared by Treasury in mid-year. 'Arrival of Australia as a Mendicant (or as a Burglar)' went its heading. Figures showed that Australia's population in 1898 was 3,600,000 and its debt £164 million; now the figures were respectively 5,400,000 and £314 million; government meanwhile had changed from 'Liberal' to 'Socialist'. Otto Niemeyer ensured that the statement went to Stanley Baldwin, Chancellor of the Exchequer under Bonar Law from October 1922 to May 1923 and thereafter Prime Minister. As well, Niemeyer prepared a memorandum which berated Australian over-borrowing and lauded Baldwin's cooling of Lloyd-Greame's readiness to negotiate with Bruce. Baldwin evidently had remarked that the settling of this matter before the Conference might reduce HMG's power in bargaining for greater Dominion assistance as to defence.

Writing to L. Cuthbertson, now Treasury's representative on the OSC, his colleague M. F. Headlam commented that while Canada was taking little British money under the Settlement Act, its migration intake was much the same as ever-costly Australia's. Such data impugned assisted migration and should modify administration of the Settlement Act. 'I trust therefore that the scheme adumbrated by Mr Hunter for developing Australia at the expense of the United Kingdom will be at once turned down.'[18] Headlam inveighed against HMG establishing representation in any Dominion, because it might prompt migrants to make claims against their native land. 'Our line should be that an emigrant is an Australian or a Canadian the moment he lands in Australia or Canada and that we must not and cannot share any further responsibility.'

Bruce was joined for the last leg of his voyage by Sanderson and F. L. McDougall.[19] Of upper-bourgeois English birth (1884), McDougall had settled as a fruitgrower in South Australia before joining the Australian Imperial Force. After the War he became involved in the politics of his industry. That meant securing British markets. McDougall returned to Britain on this mission in late 1922. Before leaving Australia he met Bruce, and the two agreed that work must begin to persuade HMG to grant preferential tariffs. Arrived in London, McDougall became skilled in lobbying and saw the impending Imperial Conference as a grand opportunity. In June he urged that it establish an 'Empire Economic Commission' which might ponder 'the problem of making the Empire as self-contained as possible for essential supplies in case of war'.[20]

Also assisting Bruce was Senator R. V. Wilson, a minor member of his ministry, having oversight of health and immigration, and involved in Australia's preparations for the Empire Exhibition planned for 1924.[21] McDougall was soon to call Wilson 'shit' and generally he appears just another politician, confirming McDougall's judgment that Cabinet was 'extraordinarily incompetent'.[22] McDougall's own recruitment indicated Bruce's desire to strengthen Australia's delegation. Bruce was to reminisce that on the voyage he pondered this question. Consequently, his story went, he cabled Lord Milner, who gave staunch support.[23] Amery's diaries show that he and Bruce kept constant touch.[24]

Whatever his advisors' role, Bruce performed at a peak in Britain, 1923–4. The clichés tell that he advanced an Empire-integrated policy based on 'men, money, and markets'. That phrase might mislead. Bruce gave overwhelming emphasis to markets, some to money, while that accorded men was significant chiefly for its relative diminution. Never was migration more obviously a pawn in the power game.

The early sessions of the Conference stressed diplomatic issues. Lord Curzon, Secretary for Foreign Affairs, probed the world's problems, painting France in blackest colours; chaos prevailed in China, Persia, Spain; the USA was none too certain an ally. Bruce, arriving late, did not hear Curzon, but speaking on 8 and 11 October remarked that while the Secretary's subject matter was interesting, he had failed to propose counter-policies. Bruce wanted a powerful and cohesive Empire, committed to the League of Nations. Beyond that, HMG must curb its involvement in Europe's endless troubles, at which Australia now looked askance:

> We are advancing very fast ... Our people think a very great deal. They are imbibing doctrines which are certainly not going to encourage them to take part enthusiastically in wars in the future. The doctrines I am referring to now are not doctrines of Bolshevism, the doctrine of paralysing Socialism or anything of that sort. I mean doctrines that nobody can complain about. They are sincere. They are perfectly honest and possibly they may be right; they are doctrines that many people hold today, that wars are wrong and that the masses of the people have the right not to be thrust into war.[25]

Bruce was warning that Britain could not rely on automatic support from Australia should it again enter upon war.

Between his two speeches on diplomacy, Bruce had given another, famed for expounding 'men, money, and markets'. It suggested what Britain must do to secure Australia's loyalty. 'The paramount question is that of markets.' That had been overlooked in the past, in complement to glib assumption that the key to growth was migration. Again a little hyperbole mixed with much truth:

> We do not plead that we are guiltless—we have gone ahead, we have talked migration, we have brought people in, we have held up alluring pictures of what we could do, and now, to some extent, we are reaping the harvest.[26]

Bruce cited fruit grown in the Murray valley by ex-servicemen (he cheated in implying that all were Britons) as illustrating the need for protected markets. Survival of such farmers was a national issue, he continued, impelled by defence and destiny. If HMG refused help, then Australia must look elsewhere; Bruce affirmed that 'during the last few years … we have had many requests that we should enter into arrangements with different countries'. (Indeed an Italian proposal somewhat like the Settlement Act had been rejected by Bruce's ministry in July.)[27] For Australia so to move must slash British exports. Bruce proposed that Britain consider imposing duties on food and raw materials. Producer subsidies, import licensing, building of reserves through a National Purchase Corporation were all called into support; as Bruce said, such policies had had widespread effect in the War, and many nations were adapting them to the tense and jealous present.

During the Conference HMG declared its readiness to increase imperial preference through duties on foreign produce—intensifying those on dried fruits and wine; creating new ones on canned fish and fruit, honey, apples, fruit juices; keeping present imposts on sugar and tobacco. It proposed formation of an Imperial Economic Committee to foster mutual ties. Bruce, liaising with Amery, protested exclusion of meat and wheat. A sub-committee reported against his more ambitious proposals (as to price stabilisation, import licences, and stockpiling), and the Conference rejected his motions on preference.[28] Bruce had failed. It was his desperate hope to have aspired to unite Empire at this time when Canada, the Irish Free State, and South Africa all pulled in the opposite direction.

Meanwhile the Lloyd-Greame proposals for Empire development had received endorsement: HMG would pay up to 75 per cent of interest on loan moneys spent in Britain on materials to be used on works in the borrowing polity.[29] Whereas Canada disparaged this scheme by asserting that its national priorities were now altogether with manufactures, Bruce claimed to be 'extraordinarily interested'.[30] He cabled homeward asking Australian Premiers to develop pertinent proposals, and simultaneously urged them to prepare works schemes which could employ migrants.[31] As will appear, he hoped that these would be subsidised under the Settlement Act.

Bruce gave migration a little more notice during the Conference. He attended a session at which Buckley posed the crucial problem: HMG was bothering about migration only because of economic slump, yet that very despond doomed such efforts.[32] Especially disastrous was stagnation in receiving countries, for stories of migrant failure provided grist for 'certain extreme elements' at home, and their propaganda was very effective. Buckley admitted that migration fell far below hopes. Even Australia, comparatively active, was taking less than half the OSD target; and nothing like the annual £3 million available under the Settlement Act was being spent. Amery likewise bemoaned that emigration was meeting much resistance from do-gooders, when in truth 'Empire development is only social reform writ large.' Bruce asserted the superiority of migration by nomination, and proposed further encouraging recent arrivals to nominate others in their wake.

Bruce sent Wilson as his representative to a sub-committee which specifically pondered migration.[33] Its chief Australian reference was to praise group-settlement, on the WA model, as an aid to migrant adjustment. That sentiment was echoed in the OSC *Report* for 1923, which also applauded Australia for subsidising nominees, done otherwise only by New Zealand. The *Report* affirmed need for years of 'scientific' groundwork before migration policies could grip. A gulf lay between this equivocation and the hopes which the OSC and OSD held before the Conference.

While Bruce failed to carry the Conference, he might have influenced Baldwin to go to the polls in early December 1923, on a Protectionist platform. The details of this decision remain mysterious, but it must have teased Baldwin throughout the Conference. In the campaign, Baldwin's opponents made much of the danger of his policy causing higher prices, especially for food. The government suffered defeat, and in January gave way to a minority Labour administration, led by J. Ramsay MacDonald. The British electorate had been even more forthright than the Imperial Conference in rejecting Brucean notions.

During and after the Conference, Bruce spoke on various public platforms.[34] He urged the inevitability of Britain adopting trade preference in order to meet problems of over-population. Certainly, went his message, 'Australia cannot absorb the unemployed of Britain' without guarantee of export markets. As at the Conference, Bruce invoked pressures driving Australia to look beyond a free-trade Britain for commercial partners. His sternest public words addressed HMG's failure to sustain appropriate defence expenditure. In semi-private, it appears, Bruce directed 'party' animus against free-trade Liberalism.[35] An upholder of that cause was Earl Beauchamp, former Governor of New South Wales. Bewailing the Australian's 'crude tariff propaganda', Beauchamp affirmed that 'Mr Bruce, more than anything else, was the indirect cause of the General Election'. In its aftermath Bruce met leading Labour Parliamentarians. All went well, and McDougall mused 'that there is ever so much more chance of getting Labour with us than getting the damned Liberals an inch our way'.[36] McDougall had long hoped for alliance with such as J. R. Clynes and Arthur Henderson.

On 24 January Bruce at last did something positive about migration, and conferred with Macnaghten, Oscar Thompson, and G. F. Plant (also of the OSD). He spoke of 'big development schemes' in the way which Millen, Hughes and Hunter had hewed, and which pervaded his own cables to Australian Premiers in mid-October.

> Mr Bruce hoped that if development schemes of that kind were put forward with a view to absorbing stated numbers of new settlers from this country, it would be possible for the British Government to co-operate under the Empire Settlement Act without requiring any guarantee that the new settlers could be placed on farms of their own'.[37]

His auditors' response was neutral. They could scarcely but feel that Bruce had disdained migration over the past weeks, and was now turning to it only because all his brighter hopes had collapsed. This surely was the matter's truth. In retrospect the rest of Bruce's Premiership appears a succession of efforts to meet problems which only an imperial *Zollverein* could have solved—and 1923 showed that a political impossibility. Having failed as to markets, Bruce turned to men and money. They offered semblance of hope, but no true basis for success.

During his talk with the OSC and OSD people, Bruce referred to particularities of several Australian States. During 1923 the three State agreements had wound their way to signature. Beyond that, the main noise about migration still came from Western Australia. Its Agent-General Connolly remained hyperactive, irritating the OSC and OSD, and provoking Christopher Turnor to further criticism. Connolly, cherishing hopes for a railway from Geraldton to Wyndham, protested 'against he or the Committee questioning the right of my Government to say how when or where any settlement should take place in Western Australia'.[38] The Agent turned to the Ministry of Labour in seeking subsidies for mass emigration. 'Why does he try to embroil our Ministers in wild cat projects?' cried Macnaghten.[39] The same file implied that Premier Mitchell had lost trust in Connolly, who soon gave way to H. P. Colebatch, a closer friend of Mitchell's.[40] They proposed another grand enterprise involving £10 million

'If W.A. can't spend the loan promised under the existing agreement at any more rapid rate, how is she to spend another ten millions?' asked Plant, and the idea withered.[41]

*   *   *

Back in Australia, Bruce did his best to rebuild. During March several despatches reproached MacDonald for withholding the preferences offered by HMG at the Conference, and for failing to establish an Imperial Economic Committee. Bruce also protested Labour's resolve not to fortify Singapore.[42] On 27 March, Australia's House of Representatives debated the Imperial Conference. A motion sought endorsement of Bruce's Singapore strategy as well as of his economic policies. This faced the Labor Opposition with either criticising their British comrades or appearing neglectful of defence. Only the Labor leader, Matthew Charlton, spoke at length. He upheld MacDonald's policy 'not to create a Singapore naval base, and thus menace Japan and Holland'. So the traditionally anti-imperial force in Australian politics rallied to HMG! Charlton scored few points as to the Conference's rejection of Bruce's economic programme.

The Prime Minister alluded little to defence. He made what he could of Conference moves towards economic co-operation, and affirmed that their expansion alone gave hope for prosperity in either Britain or Australia. The former's troubles traced back to pre-war years, proceeded the argument; Germany and the USA by then had shown their industrial puissance, while Britain's labour unrest in 1913–14 warned of intractable social problems. Bruce repudiated any trespassing into British domestic politics. He said nothing about migration. A complementary debate occurred in the Commons in June when Baldwin moved such new and increased duties as HMG had offered at the Conference.[43] His speech went like that of Bruce's to the Australian Parliament. Confirming McDougall's analysis, some support came from Labour whereas Liberal speakers were resolute for *laissez-faire*. The crucial vote went 272–278 against Baldwin. Perhaps as a makeweight, the government now did move towards establishing the Imperial Economic Committee.[44]

Meanwhile, broader imperial ideas survived. Most obviously signifying this in 1924 was the Empire Exhibition at Wembley; the weather was terrible, and other difficulties prevailed, but something like the Exhibition's purpose held true. In government, Labour's Secretary for Overseas Trade, William Lunn, proved to have ideas similar to Albert Buckley's. Chairman of the OSC throughout Labour's term (to November), Lunn pursued negotiations with Australia which led to the so-called 'Thirty-four Million Pounds Agreement'.

Ultimately signed on 8 April 1925, the Agreement was a sub-set of the Settlement Act, but it owed much also to Lloyd-Greame's 1923 proposals which took form as the Trade Facilities Act, 1924. Under the Agreement, Australia pledged with HMG in assisting development and settlement, always through the States. The latter were to submit for approval (by both Commonwealth and HMG) pertinent 'undertakings'. These could embrace not only land purchase and subsidy of farmers, but also public works—roads, railways, bridges, irrigation, hydro-electricity, afforestation—and even 'sugar mills, butter factories and similar enterprises'. Several clauses bound Australian authorities to ensure decent conditions for migrants, who as employees must have status equal with Australians. Provision was made for reception and training depots. So far as nominees were concerned, welfare responsibility was to lie more with nominators than government.

Britain was to pay the Commonwealth £130,000 for every £750,000 advanced to the States for 'undertakings', with variation if the interest rate differed from the supposed 5 per cent; States were to pay no more than 2 per cent for the first five years nor 2.5 per cent for the second. (The Settlement Act being due to expire in 1936, the Agreement fitted that time-span.) Under clause 5, the States were to take one assisted migrant for each £75 of loan money received for financing developmental works, and 37.5 per cent of all such migrants were to be members of family groups without personal capital. Different scales would apply under clause 6, which dealt with loans to be spent on creating new farms: £1000 was allowed for each such farm and on at least half of these the pertinent State had to achieve 'satisfactory' settlement of a migrant family, averaging five members and without capital. All migrants concerned must have departed Britain since 1 June 1922. A British representative in Australia would monitor all such details, and stocktaking would take place after three, six, and ten years. The Agreement envisaged that the three established State schemes would adopt these new terms; the resulting commitment covered loans up to £14 million. A ceiling of £20 million was put on further loans. HMG's direct pay-out was limited to £7.083 million—a fair sum, but far from that which the Agreement's nickname seemed to promise.[45]

Discussions on the Agreement had interesting passages. When they began in April 1924, Senator Wilson was still in Britain. Earlier he would have been a party to Australia's reluctant approval of modest increases in joint subsidy of under-age fares.[46] As against that concession, Wilson withstood OSD pressure for Australia to contribute to training centres in Britain for would-be emigrants; evidently he feared lest such become conduits for dumping unemployables, and/or that graduates might give themselves airs inimical to employers' expectations in rural Australia.[47] After Wilson left, Hunter continued the Agreement negotiations, but more crucial became E. G. Theodore, who so regularly had criticised Commonwealth policies. Now he was in Britain restoring relations with financiers, and having considerable success. Theodore and Lunn also found affinity.[48] The

Premier spoke of settling many farmers in Queensland, 2000 on the Burnett, were moneys available; he scorned the three State agreements of 1922–3, his prescription being for HMG and the Commonwealth to pay all interest over the 25-year term of requisite loans. Theodore made no promise that all these farmers would be migrants. What mattered that to Britain, so long as migrants were absorbed according to an agreed scale? In arguing thus, Theodore was following the line already cast by Bruce.

Lunn's central purpose was to assist poor families to emigrate and ideally become farmers. He believed the Agreement-in-embryo to be truly generous towards Australia. So did Labour's Colonial Secretary, J. H. Thomas, although the latter saw it also as compensation for Australia's being denied preferential duties, whereas Lunn inclined to view Australians as selfish in withholding their land from others. Within the Colonial Office and the OSD, the Agreement had more questioning than might have been anticipated. William Bankes Amery, an OSD accountant, declared that 'if Australia is to be colonised, something much more heroic is required',[49] while another Colonial Office man, J. F. N. Green, remarked:

> Our present system is to induce them to take people by lending them capital at a rate of interest attractively low to begin with. (This will lead to a hell of a row in time, but that is not my affair.) But we do not want to insist too loudly on this, as a lot of Australians declare that the result is that production is skimmed to provide interest to be spent in England, and talk of 'pawning Australia'.[50]

A new Australian government might reverse current policies, Green continued. Macnaghten had more racking doubts. Perturbed by stories of Australia ill-treating migrants, he saw its obduracy over the Agreement's detail as a characteristic 'try-on'. 'That they think they can squeeze so much out of us, rather suggests that they think we are trying to dump our surplusage and unemployed upon them, and will not realise it is quite as much to their own as to our advantage to make this policy successful.'[51]

For Niemeyer and most of his colleagues in Treasury, the situation told yet louder of Australian greed. 'Emigration is an excellent thing for the uninhabited receiving state,' Niemeyer opined; 'it may be a good thing for the actual emigrant, but it is not so clear that it is for the emitting country.' These views did not prevail unanimously, Niemeyer agreed, but 'if there is anything in them at all there is no need for us to pay through the nose in order to populate Australia with our more enterprising spirits'. Cuthbertson, Treasury's man on the OSC, likewise now spoke of 'the Australians who are disposed to wave the Union Jack and put their hands in our pockets at the same time'.[52] These departmental views had full backing from Labour's Chancellor, Philip Snowden. As Australian demands for modification continued into 1925, Treasury attitudes ranged from scorn

('Oliver, I see, is again asking for more') to abnegation of responsibility for the Agreement.[53]

Yet Macnaghten, rather than Treasury, grasped the import of the Agreement as to Australia's commitment on assisted-migrant numbers. Early cables from Australia to Hunter told of readiness to take a million in the decade. Hard-head Percy had himself once thought of that number; in the event he strove to have a figure set at 200,000 in the next eight years, finally accepting 450,000 in ten. The Agreement endorsed this last figure, on the basis that one migrant would go for about every £75 of loan money expended *and that the present rate of nominated migration continue independent of that.* The British hope-cum-assumption was that expenditure under the Agreement would very much increase requisitioning by the States for 'selected' migrants to be employed in work generated by 'undertakings'. This was not explicit in the Agreement, and so, as Macnaghten realised, the way opened for Australia to meet its responsibilities by counting *all* assisted migrants, including nominees.[54] Moreover Hunter succeeded in having the migrant-count (which determined how much 'credit' was earned) backdated to the signing of the Agreement, rather than from time of loan issue.

Hunter fought on other fronts.[55] Debate as to the extent and form of HMG's payment ran on and on, Australia's hope being for half-interest over ten years. Winning inclusion of hydro-electricity works, sugar mills, and butter factories took sizeable effort; likewise, resisting pressure that Australia necessarily buy materials for 'undertakings' in Britain. Australia also strove, but vainly, for deferral of all stocktaking until 1935–6, and for HMG to float the loans and bear related costs. The Commonwealth won a point in that the Agreement prohibited direct State negotiations with HMG; it failed to secure power to arrange 'undertakings' independent of the government of the State involved, should the Australian constitution permit.

Public opinion in Australia knew of the Agreement's progress, and Bruce referred to it in Parliamentary debate, 9 September 1924. He upheld need for migration, chiefly in justifying retention of Australia against the world's hungry and dispossessed. The Agreement, he said:

> contemplates that settlement on the land shall be open to the native-born just as much as to the migrants from overseas. I believe that when it is in full operation we shall see happen here what has already taken place in America—the native-born becoming the pioneers to open up the country and the migrants not actually going out on the land in the first place but gradually becoming absorbed.

Yet Bruce remained defensive about the Agreement. Messages to London urged quick resolution to save political embarrassment. A final chapter of negotiations awaited the New Year, prompted by Bruce himself, acting in consequence of political pressure. Australian Labor parties gained much ground through the mid-1920s; they took office in Tasmania from October 1923, South Australia and Western Australia from April 1924, and Victoria from July 1924 (if only until November). Bruce discussed the draft Agreement with the Premiers early in 1925.[56] They insisted that the Agreement spell out a capacity directly to subsidise new land-settlement; the current draft, it seems more emphatically than did earlier ones, concentrated upon associated public works and infrastructure. Theodore led the charge in favour of farm-creation. Urging HMG to comply, Bruce argued that new land schemes were likely to be scant, as their cost to States would remain high. He suggested that Labor leaders could and would accept only a scheme guised as promoting land-settlement, as distinct from stressing migrant intake—but (Bruce continued) the latter would come, once Agreement moneys flowed.[57]

The aspect of Bruce's consequent proposal which most bothered Whitehall was failure to specify that migrants must own some of the consequent farms. As Macnaghten put it, a tough government could 'manipulate in favour of Australians ... to make our migrants mere "hewers of wood and drawers of water" '.[58] While OSD officials professed that Bruce surely could not have meant to exclude migrants altogether,[59] such a purpose was consonant with his argument as to native-born being pioneers of agriculture. Anyway, he probably thought it worth a try, perhaps encouraged by the fact that Amery was Colonial Secretary in Baldwin's new government. (From mid-1925 that Secretaryship also embraced the new Dominions Office.) Counter-forces in Whitehall were too strong for that and so clause 6 took form, specifying 50 per cent allocation of farms to migrants. Its implication was to diminish Australia's responsibility for absorption (£1000 so expended required but one family, whereas otherwise the number was at least thirteen individuals); this was perceived, but not as yet pursued.

Even as amended, the Agreement thrilled neither the Premiers nor Australian opinion. In June the super-isolationist J. T. Lang became Premier of New South Wales and for the next two years Labor held government in all States except Victoria. Meetings with State leaders in mid-1925 were very grumpy, with Queensland threatening to break the migration compact.[60] Formal affiliation to the Agreement by the States was slow; by January 1926 five said yes, New South Wales never doing so throughout Lang's term. Contrary to original expectations, these approvals proceeded without legislative endorsement. Governments brought the issue to debate only in Tasmania and Western Australia. Nor did the Agreement come before federal Parliament, full-formal. Migration was indeed a tender issue.

Around the time of the Agreement's signature, Australia made a rare move towards sharing more generous fare-subsidy: the outcome would be for children under 12 to travel free, domestics, youths (17–18), and family-parents to pay £11; 12–16-year-olds £5 10s.; other adults £16 10s. The OSD was quick to agree, and made a vain effort at having virtually all adults travel for £11.[61] Migration must not become *too* cheap, remained the Australian line. Late in 1924 Bruce had submitted to continuous pressure from public opinion and State governments (Labor and not) and made some show of restricting entry of southern Europeans.[62] In mid-1925 a new Act increased pertinent powers, and at about that time, too, all fare-subsidy of non-Britons ceased.[63]

The OSD kept to its general work. Macnaghten was keynote speaker at an upbeat symposium at Wembley on 'settlement and migration'.[64] He developed a theme becoming central in OSD publicity—that contemporary policy followed the ideals of E. G. Wakefield in seeking decent, family-oriented migrants rather than shovelling out paupers. Amery and Clynes spoke to complementary effect. Halford Mackinder, pioneer of geopolitical studies, remarked pressures making for industrialisation in the Dominions, but stayed confident that while Britain's market for 'coarse' manufactures might diminish, it could long recoup through expanded demand for sophisticated wares. True to its Wakefieldian commitment, the OSD continued to resist the Ministry of Labour's pragmatism. Macnaghten expunged from the 1923 OSC *Report* a paragraph submitted from Labour's Overseas Employment Branch. 'Those who want to pick holes in our policy overseas', he wrote, 'would simply say that our Report shows definitely that the Government here tried to force 25,709 unemployed on the Australian Authorities, and that, in fact, 6,714 of these were put through.'[65] There must be greater British sensitivity to public opinion in the Dominions, Macnaghten continued. Such attitudes surely caused the Windham Delegation to tread carefully in reporting the migrant troubles they had found in Australia.[66]

Two other episodes well illustrate current complexities. Early in 1924 the Minister for Labour, Thomas Shaw, a unionist by background, felt affront in his officers assisting 'selection' for Australia of building-trades artisans, when such were in demand at home. As the OSD had long bewailed Australian resistance to 'select' any but farmworkers, Shaw ran against policy. Bureaucrats told Shaw that Australia House would resent their stopping the artisans 'while Australia was willing to take substantial numbers of unskilled workers who appeared to be a burden to this country under present conditions'.[67] This was scarcely true, but the artisans went. The second indicative incident arose later, in the Ministry of Health under Conservative Neville Chamberlain. Some miners in South Wales had agreed to offer to Australia, grudgingly: 'to put it mildly there is no great enthusiasm for emigration among these men, so long as they can get even meagre means of livelihood from public funds in this country'. However, Australia House refused them, and so provoked the local department head:

If we are to sit quietly in face of the admitted surplusage of population we shall in effect be admitting what our friends the Socialists are preaching in South Wales that the Capitalistic System has failed ... The Dominions should be made to realise that this is not merely, or even primarily, a domestic question, but an imperial question of first importance.[68]

Chamberlain sent the memorandum to Amery. The OSD negotiated not only with Australian authorities, but those of Canada and New Zealand also; nowhere did they place the miners.

The Agreement gave hope of resolving such dilemmas. None cherished that hope more than Amery. In his new office he had much potential to advance it, although Winston Churchill was now Chancellor of the Exchequer and ultra-supportive of the money-parers within Treasury. In mid-1925 a Commons debate on migration saw several members, including the Empire Tory, Henry Kinloch-Cooke, and J. H. Thomas, bemoaning the paltry effect of the Settlement Act (in 1923–24 Estimates provided for spending £1.206 million of the possible £3 million but the actuality was £456,000) and castigating the Dominions for blocking migrants. Amery countered, invoking 'men, money, markets'.[69] Perhaps he and Bruce could yet save Britaindom.

CHAPTER FOUR

The Modest Zenith of Hope: 1925–1926

S. M. Bruce's government won well at a general election in November 1925, and this proved harbinger of the next months of his term. The economy stood on a plateau of moderate boom; one result was to foster that optimism which the OSD currently saw as crucial to vigorous migration, and pertinent statistics conformed. Bruce now moved to reconstruct the Council for Scientific and Industrial Research[1] and to establish the Development and Migration Commission. These he saw as supreme engines for creating efficient, rational, corporative state-capitalism. Through the two agencies, disinterested experts would pursue the general good, free from the corruptions of everyday politics. Bruce was too much a realist to ignore the many problems besetting his Australia, but politicians even more than the rest of humanity must maintain hope and here lay its bastions for him.

The 1925 electoral campaign followed convention. The government made much of law-and-order, especially in relation to industrial troubles in the shipping industry. Bruce sought endorsement for his efforts to deport two radical leaders, born in Ireland and Holland respectively; the statutory basis for the deportation (ultimately declared invalid by the High Court) rested on the Immigration Act passed a few months previously, and at this point the government presumably benefited from that anti-migrationism which Labor so often deployed against it. A symbol of the latter story lay in R. V. Wilson losing his place in the Senate (although that did not take effect until July 1926). Bruce must have pondered deeply when deciding how much emphasis his campaign should give the Agreement. His policy speech boosted it as 'the greatest step forward that has ever been taken in the solution of populating and developing Australia'.[2] The government stressed attachment to King and Empire.

Victorious, Bruce could turn to putting reality into his rhetoric. Several forces conduced to establishing a body (in the event, the DMC) which would be independent of politics and link migration with overall economic policy. While the electorate evidently was not repelled by the Agreement, support of immigration always remained a likely count against any government; one reason for voters favouring Labor at State polls and non-Labor federally probably lay in State governments having enough control over migration to check any Commonwealth enthusiasm in the matter. Such patterns made this an issue ripe for depoliticising, and more abstract considerations rendered immigration appropriate for aloof and expert scrutiny. Amidst W. M. Hughes's posturings lay a sense of migration's relationship with the whole national economy. William Lunn's contribution to the Agreement had included a suggestion that Australia establish an 'Advisory Board' to consider proposed schemes, especially their capacity to absorb migrants.[3] Early in 1925 Sir Hugh Denison—an Australian potent in business, the press, and imperial loyalism—argued that migration become altogether a federal issue, under an autonomous Board.[4] No doubt Denison, a close associate of Bruce and about to become Trade Commissioner in New York, spoke for many of his type. He figured often in the homeward letters to the Prime Minister of R. G. Casey, Australia's liaison man in Whitehall. Casey himself in mid-1925 had proposed that Bruce establish a body similar to Britain's Committee of Civil Research, 'like a Permanent Royal Commission', bringing bureaucrats and experts together to consider national development, including migration.[5]

The federal immigration bureaucracy had never been strong, H. S. Gullett's clash with Hughes and consequent departure having a crippling effect. His successor as Superintendent of Immigration, L. J. Hurley, had served governments with sufficient distinction to win a CMG in 1918. Ill-health diminished him thereafter. His office had only about a dozen tenured employees, their business to mediate between the States and the migration office in London, check on debts due from immigrants, and liaise with groups concerned with migrant welfare. A complicating factor from mid-1925 was Percy Hunter's return to Australia. Presumably this was to enable him to advise on policy, especially in relation to the Agreement, but he resigned as Director of Immigration at the year's turn. Meanwhile he had again become a butt for Labor denigration in Parliament. 'For mendacity I have never met his equal' affirmed a trustworthy judge.[6]

Later 1925 also saw the arrival of the British Government Representative for Migration in Australia, appointed in terms of the Agreement. He was William Bankes Amery, that accountant with the OSD. Bankes Amery had a naivety which distanced him from the Whitehall norm; Casey found him 'a good quiet type'.[7] Earlier in 1925 he went against T. C. Macnaghten in favouring an 'Empire Migration Corporation' whereby private enterprise would take over such business from government,[8] and also argued for HMG to push for emigration of skilled labour in rejection of 'the assumption that the Dominions are always to be mainly providers of "raw material" and foodstuffs and that Great Britain is always to supply *all* forms of industrial products'.[9] Presumably Bankes Amery took the job as Representative with high expectations, the outcome providing its own species of migrant disillusion. Meanwhile, his letters told much of Bruce's policy-shaping and of the broader Australian context.

In the first of these, 28 August 1925, Bankes Amery reported that Bruce was so anxious to promote the Agreement that he induced the Representative to appear in a cinema film.[10] The Prime Minister was already planning the appointment of a board to supervise the Agreement. Less amenable to the Englishman was 'the appalling language used by Ministers & everyone; it is worse here than in Australia House itself'. Most serious was Bankes Amery's repugnance towards Hunter, whom he reported as meddlesome, indolent, and sordid; the man was hospitable enough, but Bankes Amery found little pleasure in listening to dirty jokes or meeting half-world impresarios. R. V. Wilson and Percy Deane, secretary of the Prime Minister's Department (and truly an over-sharp operator),[11] further illustrated the mediocrity of Australia's public figures. Back in London, Macnaghten and Lord Clarendon, currently chairman of the OSC, lamented this situation, the latter opining 'that if the right type of public school boys could be induced to migrate in sufficient quantities they will—if they make good, as a proportion of them should—enter public life and so raise the whole tone'.[12]

Especially irksome to Bankes Amery was official contempt for anyone who heeded migrant welfare. His own happiest contacts were with the few Australians who did so care. One of them, Sir Robert Anderson, warned that officialdom resented appointment of a Representative. As to other spokesmen for imperial migration, Bankes Amery made a different point. All sorts of people ground axes of personal interest, he reported: even the prestigious Sir Edward Mitchell's enthusiasm for migrant land-settlement in Gippsland might have sprung from his owning land there.[13] Other 'big' interests converged on Bankes Amery. On one hand local Tories hoped that he would abort what they saw as the gross extravagance of State governments. 'I feel that I shall require the financial ability of a Rothschild and all the qualities of the Archangel Gabriel if I am to comply with many of the requests which are being showered on me in unofficial circles.' There were also proposals that HMG should subsidise schemes under the aegis of pastoral companies. John Garvan, chairman of the Commonwealth Bank, advised rather that HMG should colonise a tract of Australian land.

Bankes Amery was much concerned that current schemes mired settler-farmers in debt. Within weeks of his arrival, he expressed doubt as to whether any more migrants should be put at risk of that fate. He worried at Bruce speaking as if the Agreement might extend beyond its original sums; his own inclination remained to give governments less, and boost voluntary work for migration. Perhaps the situation would right itself if indeed 'the federal people could establish a Central Immigration Authority', independent of politicians. Bankes Amery's ideal for its head was John Monash, that war-hero whom many saw as Australia's saviour.

Into the new year, job-speculation included Hunter's succession in London. Hurley fretted for it. There was a suggestion that Wilson, on the expiry of his term as Senator in July, should take this post and combine it with a supercharged Trade Commissionership. Macnaghten blanched at this version of subordinating migration to economic bargaining—beyond which, 'I formed an unfavourable impression of Senator Wilson'.[14] Bankes Amery reported that Wilson was also being mooted as possible head of the proposed migration Commission, as too was John Butters, pioneer of hydro-electricity in Tasmania and currently preparing the Australian Capital Territory for its destiny.

Bankes Amery would have liked H. S. Gullett, now a Nationalist Parliamentarian, to fill the London post, but recognised that was unlikely on political grounds. However, he reported that Gullett had rapport with Bruce and attributed to him a radical change in the projected Commission's structure.[15] The prime intent was always for the Commission to check 'undertakings' submitted under the Agreement, but whereas at first the notion was for a permanent chairman assisted from case to case by two experts from the State concerned, the plan then altered to a larger permanent body with broader functions. Early in 1926 Cabinet pondered an 'Immigration Board' and agreed that H. W. Gepp should be invited to lead it. Subsequent Cabinet references spoke of the 'Migration and Development Commission', but when enabling legislation came before Parliament the two functions had reversed order.[16] The Commission's role ranged well beyond migration: it could pursue virtually any matter of economic import, either on its own initiative or at the government's request. Development of new industries had particular emphasis.

Moving the Bill, Bruce declared his purpose to lift Australia's population to a level that world opinion would either respect or fear, while integrating that process with planned economic expansion and thus maintaining living standards. Bruce repeated that recent immigrants rarely made good farmers, and claimed to have scoffed in 1923 at opinion in Britain which proposed to settle that country's jobless on Australian land. He professed hope that the Commission would assist State regimes:

> They, like all governments, are subjected to a great deal of political pressure, and sometimes might have difficulty in refusing to forward to the Federal Government a scheme submitted by influential persons. But the Commonwealth cannot be satisfactorily developed on that basis. There must be a thorough and impartial examination of every scheme before it is approved.[17]

No 'undertaking' could proceed, Bruce emphasised, without the Commission's approval.

Bruce surely believed that State expenditure verged on profligacy, and anyway the Commonwealth had long hankered to overview loan policy nation-wide. That had been a major element in the States' antagonism to Hughes. Since 1923 the so-called Loan Council had provided for some degree of co-ordination. However, until 1929 the Council lacked mandatory power and general clout.[18] Conceivably, Bruce hoped that the DMC would establish a model for the Council to follow. Anyway, it would check such massive expenditure as had occurred on soldier and other settlement schemes. Further, Bruce doubtless wished to impress the London money market with Australia's heightening responsibility, perhaps even to gain favour with Treasury. During mid-1925 that office had imposed an embargo lasting several months on Australian loan-raising in London. Otto Niemeyer felt no qualms in pushing Australia towards American interests, but the Board of Trade disagreed; 'you know how extremely important the Dominion markets are to us'.[19] Meanwhile Bruce's London-based friend, John Sanderson, told the OSD of his belief that the Commonwealth government 'would welcome the OSC's veto on any schemes [i.e. 'undertakings'] which were merely political'.[20]

In the federal Parliament, debate on the DMC Bill followed predictable lines. Labor's opposition to immigration was often veiled, sometimes explicit. More consistent was the thrust that the Agreement had been a good bargain for Britain, tying Australia into debtor-subordination, and restricting development of its own secondary industry while abasing itself as a labour dump:

> Is Australia expected to take as immigrants the victims of the capitalist system of Great Britain? The maintenance of those persons should be a charge upon the capitalists of the old Country and not upon Australia. If the British working people are not wise enough to alter their social conditions they must suffer for it; but we should be foolish if we permitted similar conditions to be perpetuated in Australia.[21]

Parallels between assisted migrants of this era and convicts of a century before received notice. Labor's anti-imperialism extended also into *Realpolitik*, Francis Brennan insisting that Australia faced no threat from Japan, or anywhere else, save through association with Britain. W. M. Hughes responded:

> It is useless to speak as if this were a mere question of ethics. We speak of peaceful penetration but how did we get possession of Australia? Where are now the legitimate owners of this country? Most of them have disappeared from the face of the earth. We are here by the grace of God and the arm of strength.

That was as close as Aboriginal Australia ever came to the migration debate.

Hughes detested Bruce, but now gave him more support than did any member of the ministry. Gullett upheld migration, but even he declared the

Agreement a doubtful deal. Bruce heeded criticisms that the Bill gave the Commission excessive freedom from ministerial and parliamentary oversight, and amendments followed. There remained hostility to Bruce's penchant for government by commission and to Chairman Gepp's salary of £5000. Withal, the measure became law, and in the following weeks the Commission took form. Its base was in Melbourne, still serving as the federal capital.

H. W. Gepp had many qualifications for leadership.[22] Born in Adelaide in 1877, he had built an outstanding career as metallurgical engineer, strong in practical achievement but always receptive to academic learning and insights. From 1907 he worked in Australia's most remarkable mining city, Broken Hill, overseeing plant which extracted concentrates from tailings. His employers were Australia's surpassing entrepreneurs, the Baillieu group. The War opened enormous opportunities for the Australian metal industry, enhanced when HMG determined that the Empire must develop a top-class zinc refinery. Accordingly, the Baillieus' Electrolytic Zinc Company established a plant at Risdon, in southern Tasmania, with Gepp as its manager. Work began in New Year 1916–17:

> Six years later, Risdon was producing some 100 tons of zinc each day. The works had been built during troubled times, from the bare earth, in an isolated place lacking a supportive infra-structure. That what happened did happen proved it could happen; but the historian might not be absurd in suggesting that the achievement at Risdon went close to a miracle, or at least defied the probabilities of logic.

One factor contributing to Risdon's productivity was Gepp's success in industrial relations. From his Broken Hill days he upheld welfare capitalism, and Electrolytic Zinc provided services in health, housing, insurance, recreation, and education as well as a degree of worker participation in management. At least by Australian standards, this comprised an epic story.

Gepp hoped that the Risdon plant would diversify into many chemico-metallurgical products. He served on Tasmania's State Development Board, formed by J. A. Lyons's Labor government, originally to develop schemes which might benefit from the Imperial 'Trade Facility' funds hovering in 1923–24; the Board was later hailed as anticipating the DMC. Gepp himself put money into developing an essential oils industry in Tasmania. He became a hobby farmer and propagandist for scientific agriculture. Another role was that of an Australian Commissioner at Wembley in 1924. While in Britain he arranged a visit to Australia by Sir Frank Heath, secretary of HMG's Department of Scientific and Industrial Research. This in turn determined the structuring of Australia's CSIR. Probably Bruce considered Gepp for a leading role with that body, but instead decided to link his genius with the DMC.

Gepp's success had its shadows. One of his daughters has presented herself as crushed by his egotist insensitivity.[23] Yet Gepp's own letters and those of his business associates show a man living on his nerves, with almost manic-depressive variation. Electrolytic Zinc archives tell not only of this situation, and concern at its effect, but also of Gepp over-spending both on the technical side and on welfare schemes.[24] From this perspective he showed much the same weaknesses as the DMC was supposed to correct in State governments. 'He had us in the clouds too long', once wrote W. L. Baillieu, chairman of Electrolytic Zinc.[25] Probably the Prime Minister knew only part of Gepp's story. The truth remains that he had chosen a big man to lead the DMC.

One aspect of Gepp's background received strangely little comment. Electrolytic Zinc depended for its early economic viability on contracts for purchasing its produce to which HMG had committed itself during the War. In peace these proved a heavy charge. The contracts were modified in the early 1920s but continued 'a feature of unique strength to the Company', as Baillieu reported in December 1921. British public opinion railed at the zinc contracts, angry questions recurring in Parliament; in 1929 a ministerial statement estimated HMG's net loss at £3.9 million.[26] Here was a supreme example of Australia milking the mother country, and on that nutriment Gepp's fame had fed. Was Bruce taunting his British counterparts in elevating Gepp to imperial statesmanship? At Wembley he had bargained toughly for Australian interests.

Another of Australia's Wembley Commissioners, C. S. Nathan, became Vice-Chairman of the DMC. Born in Melbourne, the young Nathan moved to Perth and there prospered as businessman and civic leader. He had interests in development, notably of Australia's north-west. Politically, Nathan was well to the Right, in 1925 helping establish the Western Australian Consultative Council, which financed the local Nationalist Party.[27] An academic described Nathan in 1926 as believing himself to have 'a heaven-sent capacity to manage anything … a super-commercial gentleman of the buying-and-selling variety with a congenital tendency to butt in'.[28]

Balancing the politics of the DMC, and stressing the role of the small States, was the appointment of John Gunn, who thereby forsook being Labor Premier of South Australia.[29] Gunn had proved a successful and able politician, notably in reconciling urban and rural interests. He shared the usual Labor disdain for immigration, although his animus went against Italians rather than Britons.[30] No radical, Gunn alienated some Labor support by being equivocal about the 44-hour working week and supporting Bruce's efforts to establish a federal monopoly over industrial arbitration. One account reports Gunn as a close friend of future Labor Prime Minister, J. H. Scullin, and influenced by him to join the DMC.[31] The fourth Commissioner, E. P. Fleming, had long and distinguished service in the NSW bureaucracy; land-settlement, railways, and migration had all come under his purview. Fleming's particular role with the DMC was to be overview of migration issues. Power-structures became very clouded. The Commonwealth migration office moved under the DMC, with Hurley's position especially ambiguous. The Commission owed responsibility in migration matters to the relevant Minister (Thomas Paterson succeeding Wilson), but otherwise had a special relationship with the Prime Minister, who often deputed that to Senator G. F. Pearce.

*　　　*　　　*

While establishment of the DMC wended along, a few proposals under the Agreement received approval from both Australian and British authorities. Western Australia bulked largest in this story, especially in consequence of the 1922 State scheme being adapted to finance 2031 group-settlement farms. New thinking addressed another 300 dairy farms, and water-supply schemes for three group-settlement areas. Victorian authorisations comprised £1000 each for 335 farms developed under that State's 1922 agreement, and £541,000 for a new scheme at Maffra–Sale, Gippsland. Various further projects went into the pipeline.[32] These matters provided a staple of Bankes Amery's continuing reports, although his pen's greater value was in telling the fate of migrants already arrived, especially farmers in Western Australia and Victoria. His perturbation with farmers' debt-load continued to increase, although in a different way between the two States.

While numbers were smaller in Victoria, there throbbed the greater pain.[33] Enquiries by Bankes Amery and his assistant, E. W. M. Wood, found a grim situation. A particular goad was that Britons had been put on farms deserted by Australians. Already one victim had expressed himself in an angry pamphlet. On 21 June, Bankes Amery cabled London about Victorian affairs: 'inadequate supervision … gross delay … majority of settlers lost all capital and faced with bankruptcy'. All must have rankled more as the OSD had long protested Victoria's demand that potential settlers own considerable capital. Even without waiting for the report which detailed Bankes Amery's charges ('appalling, distressing, heart-breaking' were some of its adjectives),[34] the OSD halted the London end of the Victorian scheme. The matter became public knowledge. Sir George Fairbairn, Victoria's Agent-General, fulminated. That was nothing to the row between Bankes Amery and Victorian bureaucrats. Chief antagonist was William McIver, Director of the Closer Settlement Board, and currently amidst storms arising from agonies of soldier settlement.[35]

The Representative had somewhat happier but still tortuous relations with Western Australia. They centred on the group-settlement scheme.

Soon after accession of Philip Collier's Labor government in April 1924, it appointed a Royal Commission into that story. The Commission told of mammoth expense for disappointing return, and of much human stress. A few months later Bankes Amery wrote his own account of group-settlement. It was quite laudatory; introducing it as a Command paper, L. S. Amery affirmed that 'in spite of certain imperfections … these settlements stand out in my opinion as one of the most remarkable experiments in the history of colonisation'.[36] Apart from the debt problem, Bankes Amery called attention to the need for effective marketing of produce and for better provision of religion and education. He recognised that the communal approach to pioneering had failed—individuals spent their energies on their own farms, while some 'shirkers' had exploited the provision of guaranteed employment. His estimate was that about one-third of 1900 assisted migrant settlers had abandoned their blocks, fewer than among Australian counterparts. While his unpublished comments had some sharper barbs, Bankes Amery's perspective differed from that of locals, who as taxpayers were bearing the blown-out costs of the scheme. He judged the State's bureaucrats much superior to their eastern colleagues and also praised W. C. Angwin, Minister in charge, though putting him well below Collier.[37]

There remained other worries in the West. It disturbed Bankes Amery to see railways passing through great tracts, left vacant by their owners or lessees, awaiting escalation of land values; the State's Legislative Council forbade compulsory acquisition. Projected applications under the Agreement for further railways seemed germane less to advancing settlement than to winning votes of such landholders.[38] The spectre threatened that Britain's taxpayers might be enriching Australian sharpsters. How far should he assert himself on such issues? agonised the Representative. Hunter warned against intrusion: 'as in London his attitude is what business is it of yours so long as they take the people'. The OSD meditated this, and concluded that Hunter's counsel was right.[39] Bankes Amery simmered, in June 1926 suggesting that HMG take unilateral action in pursuit of Western Australian colonisation.[40] He had already so argued as to Queensland, where officials were 'hopeless', and 'red raggers' among Labor back-benchers negated whatever goodwill Premier W. N. Gillies might have.[41] Bankes Amery did not explain how unilateral colonisation might proceed; it is boggling enough that he could conceive it at all.

The Representative's contact with New South Wales was ambiguous. Premier Lang seemed affable. Bankes Amery met with Cabinet and flattered himself on scoring well, although here too he judged backbench Laborites to threaten malign influence.[42] In fact, the State continued to abstain from the Agreement and in mid-year restricted migrant-nomination to blood relatives of nominators.[43] Meanwhile, Bankes Amery reported his apparent success, only to meet a chill response from the usually good-natured Hurley. At issue was how pro-active the Representative should be, and where his responsibilities lay. The OSD pondered the matter, and the related one of Bankes Amery's role as against the DMC. The upshot was little more than again to advise tact and caution.

Bankes Amery's enquiries in New South Wales included the fate of the (very few) volunteers for that State's land scheme. As in Victoria, to the OSD's further chagrin, they had been selected on condition of having capital, and none had yet been found a farm. The Representative found that local bureaucrats 'have by no means the same ideas in regard to the necessity for close supervision and the general shepherding of the migrants which the OSC have formed'.[44] An even more hapless sub-set of migrants were farmworkers in Victoria. Bankes Amery spent a 'sleepless night' on receiving evidence of their distress;[45] an aggravating thought might have been that the nastiest migrant stories came from the one non-Labor state.

Juvenile migration received Bankes Amery's heed. Few extra-family children came to Australia, but a Barnardo support group in Sydney complemented the work of Fairbridge in the West. Bankes Amery met with its leaders as with other migrationists, notably Richard Linton, a Melbourne businessman-philanthropist, freemason and conservative politician. In 1924 Linton founded the Big Brother Movement, members of which undertook to care for migrant farmboys. Linton told Bankes Amery that no-one, from Bruce down, gave proper support. He alleged that Australia House was deliberately sabotaging him by sending inferior boys, such as could not well be invited into Big Brother homes. Bankes Amery felt that Linton might be exaggerating, 'although I well know the hostility of Australia House to private organisations'. Anyway, he himself wrote thither, affirming the virtues of 'the Public Schools of England', and he warned the OSD that 'migration continued on the present basis may eventually give to one political party an overwhelming majority, a position which should not be lost sight of from an Empire point of view'.[46] Macnaghten had said similar things a few years earlier, but now OSD comment spurned the Representative's remarks, stressing that all experience showed that the comfortable classes disdained emigration.

A trip to Tasmania showed Bankes Amery's amiability. He found Premier Lyons 'a very decent fellow', who would strive to act on the Agreement. An enthusiast in the cause was the Conservator of Forests, L. G. Irby, long-time advocate of a scheme for establishing 'plantation homes' throughout Tasmania, devoted to raising softwood pines and employing British boy-power on Fairbridge lines. Bankes Amery recognised Tasmania's perennial economic problems. He commended Governor Sir James O'Grady, appointed by Ramsay MacDonald and the first Labor man to hold gubernatorial office anywhere in the Empire. R. V. Wilson, a fellow passenger on the return trip, declared Tasmanians feckless beyond redemption, but Bankes Amery abjured such pessimism. An OSD minute went otherwise— 'as long ago as 1822 Governor Sorell found the few inhabitants lethargic and indolent'.[47]

The Representative sought other cheer in mid-1926. He declared Paterson a welcome change from Wilson: 'we are in fact in clover with a sympathetic Minister and with Hunter gone'.[48] Thomas Paterson, born in Britain in 1882 and migrating in 1908, was supportive in the row between Bankes Amery and the Victorian government. Hurley's subordinate, H. F. Farrands, was another to win the Representative's favour, while Gepp was 'a real wonder, full of imagination and force'.[49]

In May 1926 a Premiers' meeting received a position paper from the Commonwealth which affirmed that 'the unsatisfactory position of Migration in recent years, which cannot be allowed to continue, is the strongest evidence of the need for Commonwealth assistance on a generous scale and in accordance with a well-balanced plan'.[50] The issue received little specific attention. However, in August, preparing for his role as Bruce's advisor at the 1926 Imperial Conference, Gepp chaired a meeting of the Commissioners, State bureaucrats, and Bankes Amery. The purpose was to discuss migration and the Agreement, partly so as to indicate amendments which might be sought in London.[51] The States' main thrust was that the £1000 'credit' for each farm was far too niggard; costs went much beyond that. They also fretted at the Agreement requiring five as the average size of a settler's family, rebuffing Bankes Amery's pleas that farmers benefited from large families and that children made the best migrants. Likewise the States called for liberal interpretation of the 'without capital' requirement. The matter of 'satisfactory' settlement raised similar, but even harder problems.

During debate on the £1000-a-farm issue, Bankes Amery repeated his lament as to settler debt-load. This prompted McIver and his fellow Victorian bureaucrat, William Cattanach, to vehement anger; they evidently suspected that HMG was trying to force reduction of such debt, and, claiming to speak for public opinion, scorned any special provision for assisting migrants onto farms when Australians were being frustrated in that desire. Gepp pushed for the States to encourage farmers to build decent habitations for their employees. Bankes Amery urged bureaucrats to work harder at finding jobs for newcomers, and there was talk of general invigoration of migrant welfare services. All rang pretty hollow, yet provoked reaction. Victoria's pertinent Minister, Alfred Downward, affirmed that 'a good many criminals have entered the country in addition to many persons physically unfit'. When Bankes Amery urged encouragement of locals to nominate likely migrants, both Hurley and Gepp spoke of difficulties in coping with present numbers. Various speakers indicated problems with understanding the Agreement. There was reason for some puzzlement, but the delegates' homework had been patchy. Gepp himself proved less than master of requisite detail. As so often happens at conferences, the ultimate motions appeared more positive than the preceding discussions. They supported initiatives for rural housing, for example, and the establishment of a vast register of rural employment opportunity.

*　　*　　*

This meeting rounded off the Australian background to the Imperial Conference, but as ever our story has to comprehend both hemispheres. Many links joined them, above all Bankes Amery's despatches. The Representative's position vis-à-vis the States on one hand, and the DMC on the other; interpretation of such matters as 'satisfactory' settlement and settlers 'without capital': these issues ever bothered the OSD. Its bureaucrats early feared that, despite Bruce's words, a high proportion of Agreement proposals might relate to direct land-settlement, rather than public works, and so diminish the number of migrants Australia would be obliged to receive per British pound.[52] Likewise when the question arose anew of easing the means test for fare-subsidy, the OSD saw that concessions could further erode HMG's wish that genuinely poor people become landsettlers; Australia might argue that everyone so subsidised met the 'without capital' criterion.[53]

Such disquiets indicated continuing belief within British circles that Australia, along with the other Dominions, was trying little to attract and welcome migrants. Bankes Amery provided plenty of data to that end, and other voices contributed to the chorus. A near-Australphobe pair were Lord and Lady Burnham, he having chaired the 1925 meeting of the Empire Press Union held in Melbourne; Burnham was on terms with Stanley Baldwin, which deepened the situation.[54] The current Governor-General, Lord Stonehaven, declaimed to L. S. Amery that 'Bolshevism masquerading as the "Trade Union Movement" and "White Australia" … are withholding not merely from Australia, but from the Empire, precious resources.'[55] Reports of local negligence towards recently-arrived domestics in Western Australia caused temporary suspension of further sailings in mid-1926, coincident with similar action as to Victorian farmers.[56]

The number of assisted migrants peaked in the mid-decade, but more because of swelling nominations than because of requisition by State governments. British policy-makers still gave the latter centrality; as remarked, the Agreement had embodied this disposition because the British hoped that public works thereby funded would employ 'selected' labour. This strengthened the OSD's sensitivity that early proposals under the Agreement were aimed more at farm-settlement than at public works.

With the Agreement giving little promise of lifting numbers, British migrationists had more reason to ponder their strategies preceding the Imperial Conference.

Early in 1926 the OSC meditated spending £100,000 on further subsidising fares to Australia and New Zealand.[57] This followed reduction in the assisted fare to Canada, which drew a jealous reaction from Australia House, perhaps now a little more enthusiastic for migration than during Hunter's tenure. Baldwin declared that current economies forbade the OSC scheme. Macnaghten lamented this, his current mood tending to assertion rather than apathy. In a memorandum of 17 February he speculated as to 'whether we ought to suggest or threaten any change in the present Empire Settlement policy of HMG'.[58] Macnaghten and Secretary Amery appear to have sought to outflank Baldwin. In March, Amery proposed to Bruce that their governments subsidise shipping companies to cut fares;[59] thus self-funded emigration would be easier, and (although Amery did not spell this out) migrants would be freer from the odium and restrictions currently besetting those who sought Australia's fare-subsidy. The idea was to resound time and again henceforth, always to founder on the Australian fear of opened floodgates.

A few weeks later, Amery thought of forming an Empire-wide body, perhaps structured like the Imperial Economic Committee, which might lift migration to a higher plane.[60] OSD bureaucrats stressed the unreality of such proposals, as Macnaghten had already done when Sir Robert Greig, chairman of the Board of Agriculture for Scotland, urged that 100,000 unemployed youths be conscripted annually to serve in a 'Development Army' for the Dominions.[61] Schemes such as Greig's were occasionally aired in Parliament, notably by the maverick F. E. Guest;[62] his name-sake, L. Haden Guest, sat on the opposite benches, but joined in Empire-mystique migrationism.[63] Others from either side of the Commons criticised the Dominions, Australia especially, for thwarting decent Britons in wish to migrate. In the last financial year only £395,000 was expended under the Settlement Act. Amery kept up his rhetoric, and promised to strive for lower fares at the Imperial Conference.

Baldwin's intervention against the earlier fare-subsidy scheme probably symbolised that he had soured against Australia. The chief cause may have been memory of his 1923 electoral defeat. Further animus developed when Bruce alleged tardiness and ill-faith in HMG's establishment of the Empire Marketing Board, charged with spending up to £1 million annually to foster sales of Empire produce and so compensate for loss of those preferential duties promised in 1923. Bruce objected that the Board had little of the autonomous power originally envisaged, but instead had become an inter-Departmental agency under Treasury control.[64] His cable caused a stir. 'Winston quite intractable', Amery wrote in his diary of Chancellor Churchill at the next Cabinet meeting; 'nothing but nonsense about Bruce cadging, trying to squeeze the last drop of our blood, etc. It really is a disaster that Stanley put him at the Exchequer where he intensifies all the "little England-ism" of the Treasury.'[65] Baldwin advised a stern reply to Bruce. Amery argued otherwise, and the final response minimised 'Treasury or other departmental control'.

Treasury never relaxed its antipathy to Empire projects. In June 1926 Niemeyer wrote a paper attacking the Agreement. 'It was a delicate matter for HMG to take the initiative in pressing on Australia ... a matter of considerable domestic controversy', he wrote, establishing common cause with those Australians who bewailed public works programmes which elevated wages, increased costs of production, and so hampered export prices and sales.[66] Niemeyer and other Treasury officials pointed to the failure of the Trade Facilities Act as showing the absurdity of imperial involvement in such policies—which nevertheless, they expostulated, Amery was encouraging delegates to pursue at the forthcoming Con-ference.[67] In October, Treasury received a confidential critique of Australian spending by Sir Frederick Waley, true-blue tycoon. 'It is this Labor extrava-gance which Amery's schemes are directed to supporting', Niemeyer told Churchill. The latter refrained from publishing Waley's words only when told that protocol forbade.[68]

A less contemptuous, but still chiding attitude to the Dominions pervaded the report of an 'Inter-Departmental committee appointed to consider the effect on migration of schemes of social insurance'.[69] The committee upbraided disposition abroad to scorn recipients of relief: 'unemployment is the result, not of lack of resourcefulness but of prolonged trade depression'. Wrong-mindedness on this point, the committee sugges-ted, may have led the Dominions to apply excessive standards, especially of physical fitness, in approving migrants; consequent rejections caused ill-feeling within Britain which itself damaged imperial relations. The committee argued that immigration, far from threatening standards in the receiving community, rather was a precondition for agricultural and industrial development there. It admitted that Britain's relatively generous insurance and pensions probably did diminish interest in migration, and found no easy solutions to that. To give unemployed emigrants a lump sum on departure would encourage Dominions' feeling that they were being used as dumps; such sensitivity, and other considerations, made it repugnant to threaten to withdraw the dole from unemployed who did not volunteer to emigrate. Administrative difficulties prevented making pay-ments abroad under Britain's current welfare schemes. The best hope was for other members of the Empire to establish comparable programmes (currently Queensland alone had done so), and establish reciprocity. Training unemployed people for Dominion work should proceed. The

Imperial Conference ought consider such matters. The committee noticed other hurdles to emigration. Current conditions made juveniles' earnings crucial in many a family budget, reinforcing sentimental hostility to youngsters departing. Not that there was much emigrant enthusiasm, even among youths in their late teens. Dominion requirements of experience in domestic work for 'selected' girls were very stultifying. Lively knowledge prevailed in Britain of economic problems overseas, and also of the disdain often accorded immigrants. Most of the committee's references appear to have borne especially on Australia.

Serving on this committee was a bright young man from the Ministry of Labour, C. W. G. Eady. A member also of the OSC, Eady dominated pre-Conference discussions within the bureaucracy through mid-1926. His thinking hinted at the distinction of a career which saw him sitting with J. M. Keynes in shaping the post-1945 monetary world.[70] Yet Eady's arguments were not altogether coherent; their ambiguity proved how dense were problems involved.

Eady, closer to Treasury ideas than to earlier thinking in the OSD and his own department, diminished Britain's need for emigration. Industrial nations, he insisted, had great resilience and capacity. Eady reiterated that it was the Dominions who were in need—specifically of labour, to solve problems of under-development. Especially should they welcome skilled workers to build secondary industries, as indicators warned of a likely slump in world prices for primary output, boding catastrophe for Australia. Yet Britain had little to gain from artisan emigration: 'it would suit this country better if Australia and Canada filled up with hard working Continentals and thus increased their purchasing power in the home industrial market'. But strategy and sentiment denied that kind of scenario, at least for Australia. Eady granted too that a case prevailed for emigration of miners and other victims of 'black spots' in the British economy. (Australia's reluctance to 'select' miners as agricultural workers caused particular distress within the Board of Trade in this year of general strike.)[71]

Eady argued for HMG to be tougher with the Dominions, disabusing them of any belief that they held a strong bargaining hand as potential migrant-acceptors. Rather they should be told that self-interest required them to take more migrants. At the same time, he was scornful of government-managed migration and its consequent 'politicisation'; the issue, he said, thus became one of factional debate, stimulating labour interests in Australia to mobilise hostility to immigration. In Britain, too, politicising of assistance spread its taint; one result was that most emigrants to Canada paid their own way, as even did a 'surprisingly high' number to Australia. Eady offered no remedy for the politicising of migration, but his arguments implied rejection of the Settlement Act. Other migrationist thinking in Britain, even Amery's proposals as to subsidising the shipping lines and establishing an imperial council, tended likewise. The exasperation which Australia provoked at the OSD pushed its officers the same way, as became apparent in Macnaghten's talk of threatening the Dominions with a change in policy.

The OSD's briefing papers for the Imperial Conference were appropriate.[72] 'The time is right for a bolder policy', went their theme. More Britons were offering for migration than the Dominions were taking. Perhaps the latter would be readier than before to approve training in Britain of industrial workers for rural life overseas. The load of debt suffered by migrant landsettlers might be reduced by governments doing all preparation; co-operative organising had promise further to ease the problems suffered by these people. Welfare facilities in the Dominions should expand, especially to comprehend self-paying migrants. A confidential paper addressing Australian issues deepened the after-care debate by citing recent suicides among farmboys; the Big Brother Movement offered a response to avert such tragedy. The paper spoke further of ill-feeling in Britain when migrant volunteers were rejected on health grounds; medical standards appeared to fluctuate with Australia's current need for 'selected' people, or so it was argued. As a result, steadiness of requisitions was the more compelling. Attention was drawn to current indications that the British labour movement possibly was becoming more sympathetic to migration.[73]

The Imperial Conference of 1926 had its chief importance in defining Dominion status; on other issues, discussion lacked the depth of 1923. Such deprecation applies to Bruce's role. His major speech concentrated on explaining that his 1923 call for 'men, money, markets' had not intended radical change in Britain's fisc. Yet some steel glinted. Britain's trading position continued in decline, Bruce stressed, and HMG bore blame. Australia's trade with the USA was increasing much faster than with Britain. 'The real fundamental thing that will revolutionise the whole situation is for great development to be going on in the Dominions and for their absorptive power to be increased.'[74]

'Settlement' had its own sub-committee, Gepp leading an Australian team. Opening its work, Clarendon praised the DMC, and Gepp expanded on Bruce's words: 'The dominating factor in the matter of populating Australia is the absorptive power of that country; this power has well defined limits which can be enlarged only by the provision of financial assistance from overseas.'[75] The DMC would ensure effective spending of that assistance. 'National will', 'national efficiency', 'national standard of living' were all invoked, and arrayed against 'haphazard and controlled migration from overseas', of which Australians were properly suspicious. Gepp granted the need for population increase but stressed that at every point of the DMC's charter, 'development takes precedence of migration'.

The sub-committee's proceedings were otherwise humdrum. Britons raised migrant debt-load, lack of welfare services especially in country districts, need for reciprocity in pensions, various aspects of administration which put off potential migrants, and the case for training camps. As to the last, Gepp angered Treasury's Cuthbertson by insisting that HMG should bear total expenses, while suggesting that Australia was generous in taking Britons at all. 'If Australia were to adopt a purely economic view of the problem of rural settlement, she would encourage the emigration of peasant peoples from northern Europe.' Eady, member of the sub-committee, might have been interested to hear that; he affirmed several of the British concerns indicated above, but did not present his view that it was the Dominions, rather than Britain, who were suppliants vis-à-vis migration. The chief such hint came from Clarendon, who remarked that Britain's declining birth-rate might well diminish available settlers henceforth.

Gepp's most remarkable work in Britain was to negotiate with the OSD and Treasury for favourable amendments to the Agreement.[76] Chief among them was increase from £1000 to £1500 for loan moneys allowed for each new farm; the Australians sought £2000 but Gepp reported the result happily, adding 'this, incidentally, lessens the obligation of a state in regard to the number of migrants to be absorbed under the Agreement'. Another coup decreased the required average size of a farmer family to four. The rubric 'families without capital' was to embrace all who received assisted fares, and the means test rose to £1500 for a married couple, plus £200 per child; for singles the ceiling stayed at £750. Britain henceforth would share costs of medical examination of all would-be assisted migrants, and pay rail fares to embarkation points. As against these and some other (small) gains, Australia lost its renewed attempt to persuade HMG to raise the loans for Agreement moneys. Britain also reaffirmed that migrants must get half all farms created under the Agreement. Gepp undertook to improve matters as to requisition and other processes of emigration. While the Dominions still refused subsidies for training camps for men, Australia agreed to contribute part of the funds for an establishment at Market Harborough where girls might qualify for 'selection' as domestics. Henceforth, moreover, domestics' fares would receive a complete, joint subsidy. Otherwise Australia shunned hints 'that the British Authorities rather favoured a more or less all-round reduction in assisted passage rate'. This must have especially galled British bureaucrats who remembered Australia House's recent jealousy of further subsidies for Canadian fares.

Another amendment increased from £130,000 to £150,000 HMG's contribution for every £750,000 advanced under the Agreement, but this was in return for concessions at other stages of accounting. Gepp reported that the original calculation of £7.083 million as HMG's maximum contribution had been found wrong, and would be amended. It never was:

perhaps because even for contemporary accountants, let alone latter-day historians, the sums were all too complex; perhaps because politicians decided it was too embarrassing to admit error.

Gepp's hyperactivity ranged elsewhere. He met with voluntary enthusiasts for emigration, and urged co-operation upon them. The Big Brother Movement had a London wing and Gepp soothed tensions that had developed between it and Australia House. Yet Gepp never became a migrationist in the Amery or OSD mode. Late in December he prepared notes concerning the DMC's future. They accepted a case for increasing nominee migrants, but said nothing about 'selectees' or the Agreement. Gepp's whole stress was upon new production in Australia. Immigration should attract wealthy entrepreneurs to assist such work. Further, 'young Britishers with money and inclination' might be trained on Australian station-farms under DMC auspices. The idea was like one pursued by an OSC sub-committee the previous year, producing small result.[77] If he knew about that, Gepp bothered not, instead meditating how his scheme would break with the past. 'Go to the Minister and say, our activities have been migration of paupers; ... it costs us we do not know what, say £1,000 to £2,000 to settle a family in Australia.' Clearly, Gepp judged this to have been largely waste. He approved changes that made migrant-testing more stringent still, against the apparent spirit of his earlier assurances.

Gepp attended two other Conference sub-committees—Forestry and Research —and the latter evoked enthusiasm:

> It demonstrates the final emergence of the British Empire from the stage of empiricism, and marks a new era. It says to the world that the British Empire realises that research means economic development and this in turn means balance of trade and population and continuation of the Empire as the controlling force in the evolution and balance of the civilised world.

Outside the Conference, Gepp had much contact with governmental and academic research centres, usually involved with primary production of Australian relevance. The role of science in Australia's development engrossed two hours' talk with the Prince of Wales.[78] That event was reported in a letter to Nathan ('Dear CSN') in which Gepp presented himself as taking most initiatives in discussions with Whitehall. British staff work he then disparaged; his later memory presented the bureaucrats more happily, but still 'Baldwin as PM left one cold' and Churchill's talents were muffled. Indeed, the period saw the 'nadir [of] British imperialism'.[79]

Bruce probably felt that way at the time. Speaking on 1776 to an American Chamber of Commerce luncheon, he averred that Australians 'had we then existed, would have ranged ourselves at the side of the American colonists'.[80] Meeting with Baldwin just before departing home,

Bruce urged his counterpart to take imperial matters seriously. If he did not, the Labour Party would. (Not only the OSD, but also F. L. McDougall, now in Australia House, still cherished such hopes; nevertheless, Labour remained suspicious, especially of Australian migration policies.) 'He was I think impressed,' Bruce wrote of Baldwin, 'and the present government will probably try to show a little initiative on Empire questions, although I have grave doubts whether they have the ability to do anything very useful.' Bruce pursued other matters. In common with much Australian opinion, he held that HMG, under influence of Treasury and especially Niemeyer, was extortionate as to Australian interest payments on war loans. Revelation of Britain's profiteering in this matter threatened much 'undesirability', Bruce told Baldwin, also raising Churchill's reluctance to fund the Imperial War Graves Commission. 'I told him frankly that I did not think Churchill was quite sane on the subject.'

Sometimes Bruce donned a different style. To the Empire Parliamentary Union he fantasised that Australia could take 250,000 emigrants a year, provided that plenty of capital flowed in and the DMC directed its use. Flourishing secondary industry would enhance, not impede, Australia's imperial role. Rapid growth was an imperative for his country, Bruce insisted; it could not be content with such rates as prevailed elsewhere. Yet, he continued, although he had advanced such arguments at home, invoking strategic dangers and the effect of the USA's new immigration policies in deflecting European interest towards Australia, support of assisted migration remained a political debit there. To illustrate the subject's dilemmas, that much-respected spokeswoman of moderate Labour, Margaret Bondfield, then spoke of widespread feeling that Dominions were trying to grab Britain's best, spurning the mass.

Bruce little impressed Treasury. It saw his readiness to offer 6 per cent for Agreement loans as confirming that Australia's 'financial policy is as bad as is alleged and there is all the more reason for limiting our assistance'.[81] Gepp seems to have made a more favourable impression on Treasury. Some months later, Governor-General Stonehaven reported Gepp's account of his Conference role:

> He had been successful in stimulating in Great Britain interest in Australia, and in removing some misapprehensions and misgivings which had hitherto prevailed about Australian prospects and Australian finance. He did not attempt to defend some aspects of the financial policies of the States or of the Commonwealth.[82]

The obvious reason for Treasury's accepting most Agreement modifications sought by Gepp is that such assurances won trust.

That was a big achievement. More could scarcely have been gained, and so the Imperial Conference added to Bruce's ascendance at mid-decade. Yet we have seen that even he and Gepp had their doubts as to migration matters. Events that had been happening in Australia meanwhile, and were later to intensify, gave yet more reason for misgiving.

CHAPTER FIVE

Ambiguities: 1926–1927

The longer I stay here the more I become fearful that HMG is incurring a serious responsibility in encouraging people to come to a country which from all available indications is heading for financial disaster. Many thinking Australians consider that such a disaster would be a blessing in disguise as it might bring the country to its senses. But such a disaster would temporarily bring untold hardship to the people we are encouraging to invest their all in the country.[1]

So William Bankes Amery, meditating a recent report from Australia's Tariff Board, wrote home in mid-October 1926. At about the same time, two other informed Britons passed judgment on Australia. One was J. S. R. McLeod, also an OSD bureaucrat, who had come to Australia (once his residence) with a touring group of public-schoolboys. McLeod took a more sanguine view of Australia, especially its receptivity to migrants, than did most of his ilk. Even he, however, saw the ultra-Protectionist Minister for Customs, H. E. Pratten, as Bruce's 'evil genius'.[2] The other commentator was the Marquis of Salisbury, Lord Privy Seal, who had led Britain's delegation to the 1926 meeting of the Empire Parliamentary Association. His consequent essay is the most impressive of all Tory critiques of inter-war Australia, well expounding those ambiguities which are our theme and which underlay Bankes Amery's outburst.

The Marquis found much hedonist materialism in Australia, and with it 'an overwhelming national and individual optimism'. Deficient were religious feeling and social duty, conspicuously among the 'well-to-do'. Filling this spiritual vacuum was a monarchist loyalty stronger than in Britain itself. Yet this complemented rather than diminished national patriotism, especially through awareness that White Australia needed armed support from the mother country. Salisbury diagnosed social forces behind Australia's federalism:

It is a striking circumstance that the same voters who will return to power a Nationalist Federal Prime Minister to look after Imperial relations on patriotic lines, and who will return what we would call a Conservative Local Authority to keep down the burden of local taxes, will maintain a Labour State Government in office as being best qualified to look after the wages and conditions of the working man.[3]

Although this exaggerated the role of State governments, Salisbury was acute. He stressed how introverted was Labor thinking, but recognised that autarky had its logic. Australian enthusiasm for Protection fulfilled itself across an ever-broader range, geared to supplying home demand rather than to fostering production for the world market. Hence prevailed no desire for skilled workers, which might impel migration.

> The point is not that Australian policy as a whole is against immigration—on the contrary, many Australians are very keen for it, and in a mild way, probably a large majority are in favour of it—but in practice, in present circumstances, it is held by those who run Labour policy and control Labour Governments that migration is up against their theory as to the best way to maintain their beloved standard of living.

Salisbury otherwise followed the Anglo-Tory critique of Australia. Governments, especially of Labor States, borrowed excessively. Only Western Australia had sinking funds, 'a most significant illustration of the financial methods which are fashionable in Australia'. The Loan Council lacked muscle and the DMC promised no surer effect. Bruce's key Ministers, E. C. G. Page and G. F. Pearce, had confirmed to him, said Salisbury, that Protection and high wages threatened doom, yet also that the electorate demanded both. Herbert Brookes, of the Tariff Board, intimated that its current *Report* (which had aroused Bankes Amery's fears) had met Bruce's desire that the Board signal Australia's economic dilemmas. Premier William McCormack of Queensland showed that some Labor men saw the situation correctly: 'like many other responsible persons, he actually looks for bad times in Australia as the only condition through which an exit for their false position can be found'. Salisbury averred 'in deep confidence' that Commonwealth leaders were hoping for the presently constituted States to disintegrate, as 'it would be easier for them to deal *en maître* with smaller States'.

The attitudes which Salisbury lamented went even deeper than he allowed. L. J. Hurley, no radical republican, judged the Empire Parliamentarians to be obsessed with land-settlement's part in migration. That complemented what Hurley saw as British selfishness in wanting to deny secondary industry to Australia. Further, it ignored the centrality in immigration of the nominee, 'who is invited to come to the Commonwealth by his satisfied relative or friend and for whom neither the Commonwealth or State Government has any responsibility by way of reception or future welfare'.

Hurley prepared a speech which Senator Pearce delivered to the Parliamentarians; it intimated that so long as Australia received plenty of capital, immigration would look after itself, and that the DMC's role was to ensure that truth.[4]

The Commission had met first on 19 August, and continued in Gepp's absence.[5] Vice-Chairman Nathan dominated accordingly. That he had taken the Vice-Chairmanship only for a limited term, and without salary, perhaps sharpened his assertiveness. Gepp's return in mid-February modified the situation, and the following consideration of the DMC's early work, relating mainly to Agreement projects, runs into the latter period.

The Vice-Chairman had many causes for disquiet.[6] The federal immigration office impressed him as little as it had Bankes Amery. Hurley's ill-health continued; Gunn also suffered indisposition. Nathan found that apart from Bruce, federal Ministers ignored the DMC and its potential for creative policy-making. HMG's Treasury became a more positive adversary. In retrospect this might seem inevitable. Treasury had washed its hands of the Agreement in early 1925; for a while the OSD not merely hoped but believed that it would not challenge 'undertakings' approved by the Representative in Australia.[7] Gepp gave State bureaucrats this message at their August 1926 meeting. Events soon ran contrary. Perhaps Treasury accepted Gepp's proposals for amending the Agreement because of its confidence in retaining veto powers. Anyway, the Office soon affirmed itself. 'It is true that we now know very much more about the Development Commission from Mr Gepp', wrote doughty Cuthbertson in December, 'but we do not know the individual Commissioners as we know him, and he has not yet conveyed to them the atmosphere he has sensed over here.'[8] Cuthbertson served on an OSC sub-committee which vetted all Agreement proposals. Furthermore, to enforce the stringencies of the 1926 Budget, there functioned an expenditure committee of HMG's Cabinet, and Agreement matters came also under its purview.

Early in the New Year, Secretary Amery and Chancellor Churchill battled in Cabinet over the £3 million annual funding for the Settlement Act. H. E. Fass, another Treasury chief, upheld his Minister's attempt to curtail that sum:

> Overseas settlement … takes our best men and leaves us the ne'er-do-wells, the aged and the deficient. And the Empire Marketing Board seems to be going to any length to get rid of their money. While this country is bearing the burden of defending the Empire, I would submit that £2m. a year is as much as we can afford for developing it.[9]

Pursuing the argument, Churchill invoked Salisbury's paper as depicting Australia's likely doom, and besought Cabinet to ponder the fate of emigrants it had encouraged to go there. Perversely, he also remarked that the more HMG subsidised migration, the more departures shrank. Niemeyer noted that Churchill exaggerated Salisbury's pessimism, but agreed as to Australia's predicament: 'in these circumstances it is doubtful friendship to force undue "development" expenditure upon her'.[10] About this time, Niemeyer shifted to the Bank of England —a happy move for Australia, F. L. McDougall wrote Gepp, but not distant enough.[11]

Victorian land-settlement already gave the DMC its biggest headaches. Nathan mediated between Bankes Amery and State bureaucrats, generally supporting the latter and pressuring the Representative not to despatch further anathema on the situation.[12] The OSC relaxed its embargo on landsettlers, despite continuing anger at Victoria's insistence on volunteers having capital. Victoria then doubled the requirement to £400! One memorandum said such money was required so that newcomers could survive without the settling-in wages which originally had been promised them; another indicated that some subsistence was paid, but not openly as wages since popular feeling repudiated such favouritism to migrants.[13]

Victoria proposed further schemes, and thickened the brew. Near-incredibly, the State appears to have read the original Agreement to offer £1000 'credit' for *every* migrant settled on the land, rather than for each family on a new farm.[14] Proposals to settle fifty-odd farmers at Childers, south Gippsland, extended turbulence as the Victorians insisted that the challenges of the region would defeat any migrant; hence they disputed the Agreement rule that at least half the farms in each project go to Britons. Whitehall resisted in turn, and cables flew back and forth. Nathan lectured Bankes Amery as to the crisis that might result if this, the first 'undertaking' vetted by the DMC, suffered rejection; Victoria might lead other States out of the Agreement. The Representative duly pleaded for flexibility from HMG. Against Treasury's resistance, a compromise transferred the scheme to the Agreement's 'public works' clause, so avoiding the half-share issue.[15]

The Vice-Chairman hankered to shoot the messenger, insisting that 'complete disruption and abandonment' must follow if the Representative ('he has but little discretion and not enough to do') continued to report every Australian detail to Whitehall.[16] Nathan prepared guidelines. Bankes Amery should not report homewards on migrant problems, or engage in public discussion of migration policies, until both the DMC and State authorities had probed them, nor comment on any Agreement proposal until the DMC had endorsed it.[17] These restraints henceforth applied, more or less.

Bankes Amery believed that his agitation had saved some migrants from being dumped on derelict dairy farms,[18] but the general situation remained grim. In May the OSD reimposed its embargo on Victoria recruiting farmers. Nathan upbraided the Representative, again threatening the Agreement's collapse. Bankes Amery insisted that migrants' troubles could not be hidden.[19] Tension renewed soon afterwards when he and Victoria's Governor, Lord Somers, together publicised concern over migrant welfare.[20] Especially distressing Somers was the plight of former Indian Army officers, lured by Australian Farms Limited, now shamefully bankrupt. Perhaps Nathan's continuing outrage was a little synthetic. Three other Victorian schemes were as yet deferred by the DMC. One (at Beech Forest), estimated to cost £1 million, largely comprised abandoned farms; speculators were hoping to profit, and Nathan himself judged the government's proposals a grab for cheap money. Public bruiting of the proposal caused the land-price to increase, and so the DMCs hesitated.[21]

Western Australia continued large in migration matters. Its farm scheme presented many puzzles, especially how the Agreement modified the State pact of 1922–3. The latter was more demanding, notably in that *all* farms thereunder were to go to migrants. Bankes Amery argued for the easier terms. Treasury was aghast. 'I do not cease to be astonished at the letters that come through from Bankes Amery', wrote Cuthbertson, outraged at 'a barefaced attempt to fleece the British government'.[22] In fact Bankes Amery had been critical enough, warning that Western Australia planned to deny migrants better farms and that in Australia the promises of one government were likely to be broken by its successors. The State's current plans for a 'new' scheme in fact embraced already-attempted farms. This bothered the OSD, but still that office blasted Treasury's rigour. The 1922–3 pact, went an OSD minute, had been 'an impossibly bad bargain for Western Australia … we cannot work the Empire Settlement Act in the spirit of Act IV of the Merchant of Venice'.[23] The situation as to WA land development remained grotesquely confused. Treasury lost its point as to maintaining a strict interpretation based on the 1922–3 rules. Nevertheless the State's proposals went on hold—the consequence, Bankes Amery later said, of himself and Gepp imposing restraint and research.

Treasury longer denied funding for certain railway works in the West.[24] These had been finished about a year before the claim was made. Cuthbertson reacted predictably, sounding his anxieties about the Commissioners other than Gepp, and declaring that the latter had questioned his colleagues' procedures in the matter. Cuthbertson insisted that the Agreement was for *new* development, and then started another round of complexity as to whether 1922–3 or 1925 rules prevailed. Coincidentally Nathan complained about Bankes Amery's 'obsession' that moneys be used for *new* development.[25] Yet while the Representative earned that obloquy, despatches from home about the railways were also distressing:

> I am finding myself so often in disagreement with the OSD … that I am wondering whether I have completely lost touch with the British point of view.

I do not think I have ... I prefer to think that as a result of my residence here I can see both points of view.[26]

Bankes Amery may have underestimated support the OSD was giving him against Treasury. At least Treasury provided the Representative and the Commission with a common enemy. Oscar Thompson, currently in Australia, told L. S. Amery of the latter's anger at intervention from that quarter.[27]

The DMC visited Western Australia in November 1926 and Nathan recorded its work.[28] Both politicians and bureaucrats were wary of this instrument of federal government, he wrote, but most would respond to sympathetic co-operation. He was probably over-confident at that point, yet acute in diagnosing the 'ludicrous position' resulting from hostilities internal to the State bureaucracy. Thus roads were built with scant reference to farmers' needs, or to any other plan. Nathan also bemoaned that the State should be pushing railways into the hinterland when good land nearer Perth stood idle, speculation and vote-seeking again being at work. The State's chief forester made his profession's usual plaint about promiscuous conversion of forest lands to farming. Nathan acknowledged the economic and personal costs of group-settlement, often resulting from 'lack of human judgment in throwing raw Migrants into country, in which even experienced Australians would have baulked', yet concluded that national advance required such processes. He and Banks Amery agreed that immigrants, perhaps from the Hebrides, might settle a fishing village on the south coast.

South Australia offered a few small proposals, most importantly for reticulation on the Tod River.[29] It was not an altogether new work, Bankes Amery reported; it should open virgin farmland, but he could not say how much. He advised dubious approval. Nathan attacked him for seeking unrealistic standards of governmental 'probity' in the matter, and Cuthbertson again upbraided his slackness. Approval did proceed.

The Representative declared himself overworked and fatigued.[30] He suggested that the OSD send out as his superior a 'commercial magnate', to match Nathan. The latter, Bankes Amery remarked, was affable enough in private, but with fellow Commissioners sought 'to impress with his cleverness and with his refusal to give way'. Hurley joked that such was Nathan's 'liverish' nature, and told Bankes Amery not to fret. He was further hurt at being denied a place of dignity during the visit in May 1927 of the Duke and Duchess of York. (The OSD attributed this slight to Australia's understandable contempt of its own public servants.) A different bother for Bankes Amery arose from rumours that a Melbourne businessman, T. M. Burke, was organising substantial Italian Catholic immigration; the Italian government, went the story, was subsidising the purchase of land for the newcomers to settle. If Italy, why not HMG, the Representative wondered. Here his thinking again had some accord with the Commissioners'. They had already disdained Italian immigration, and met an official enquiry from the Netherlands about movement thence by declaring that to be a matter for the States.[31]

Minor DMC approvals by mid-1927 included another farm 'undertaking' in Victoria, an afforestation programme in South Australia, various farm-services (rail, road, water) in Western Australia; about as many items again were 'deferred' or 'under consideration'.[32] But the DMC had never been meant to deal only with such specifics. From the outset, other issues came within its reference. High among these was the economic quandary of Tasmania.

With other small States, Tasmania could and vehemently did claim that federal policies (Protection, criteria-based wage levels, restraints on inter-state shipping) comprised its root problem. In 1926 the federal government appointed one N. C. Lockyer to report on the State's position. The Common-wealth then determined that special financial aid should be made available, and the DMC was asked to advise on the most effective spending of this. Nathan visited the island in September 1926, lauding the State Development Advisory Board as a simulacrum of the DMC itself. In response, Acting Premier J. A. Guy rejoiced that 'the closer and more systematic application of science and economics to questions relating to the administration and the development of the State is about to materialise'.[33] The DMC duly appointed various investigators—W. J. Rose, a businessman-accountant associated with Baillieu enterprises; G. F. Finlay, a Cambridge Ph.D. in agriculture; and R. R. Pennefather, also an agricultural scientist and on the Commission's staff. Finlay, who was part-subsidised by CSIR (although its head, A. C. D. Rivett, told of him being 'dangerous and unreliable scientifically'), produced a massive report on the island's primary industries, while Rose embarked on a more cogent one as to the general economic situation.[34] The DMC advised first and foremost considerable extension of the State's Department of Agriculture. A research division should be established, to include 'entomologist, farm engineer, apiarist, agricultural economist, home economist (female), seed testers'. An extension service would preach science and efficiency to practising farmers. That gospel should soon extend:

> Generally, it may be said that all phases of production, transport, and marketing are found to be capable of improvement by systematic work by experts in each department of activity. The enquiry so far made by the Commission has entered into the questions of agriculture, markets, extension of co-operative action among producers, finance, timber, industry, mining, fisheries, manufacture, transport (external and internal) and the tourist traffic.[35]

Even while in Britain, Gepp urged such work along. On meeting an enthusiastic young plant scientist, Alexander Nelson of Edinburgh, he saw a likely man for Tasmania.[36]

The Chairman himself was dominant in preparing a DMC *Report* on the future of goldmining, specifically at Kalgoorlie and Gwalia, Western Australia. Amalgamation, rationalisation, purposeful investment, techno-logical innovation, cost-pruning—all came into play.[37] Seemingly, Gepp was ready to coerce pertinent businesses into action. Gunn told Nathan that 'the Prime Minister expressed himself very strongly on the methods that had been adopted by the mining companies'; however if the crunch came, Gunn continued, no doubt government would bail the industry.[38] The report angered the companies, and a fog descends on the further story.

The DMC's homage to science and expertise led towards bonding with economic theorists. Australia came to boast a number of such in the 1920s, academics to the fore. D. B. Copland, most vocal among them, had called in 1924 for his peers and government to forge a constructive amity.[39] This indeed developed, yet with at least apparent paradox. Early in the 1920s W. M. Hughes had scoffed at T. G. Taylor's strictures on Australia's demographic potential; the Bruce government followed Hughesian concepts, yet Taylor-like beliefs pervaded the economists' thought.[40] Their scepticism applied to migration and even to 'development'. One perceptive academic, J. B. Brigden, had criticised the Settlement Act and the impetus given by easily-garnered capital to short-term exploitation of resources, at posterity's cost.[41]

Despite this, an alliance formed between the DMC and the economists. One specific impulse was the Bruce government's concern, referred to the DMC, to minimise fluctuations in employment. This in turn related to the agenda of a current Royal Commission on National Insurance. As remarked, Gepp broached pertinent discussion, apropos rural labour, with State bureaucrats in August 1926. That month the DMC surveyed the issue more broadly, Gunn proposing 'that to more effectively regulate employment public works should be so planned as to provide regular, steady employment'.[42] The matter continued under review, everyone knowing that while unemployment prevailed, immigration must suffer odium.[43] Broader ventures into economica were discussed. G. L. Wood, Copland's associate at the University of Melbourne, told the DMC of relevant academic work: by himself on population, E. O. G. Shann on land settlement, Brigden on wages and labour relations.[44] The DMC learned also of the plans of two federal bureaucrats, statistician C. H. Wickens and tax-commissioner Robert Ewing, to develop a 'prosperity index', which would reveal 'the Australian individual net income'.[45]

Many other issues came before the DMC and received notice in its first *Report*, covering the period to mid-1927. Synopsis best comprehends such material:[46]

- *Geophysical Prospecting.* Among all Gepp's enthusiasms, prospecting ranked top. This mode of 'seeing underground', it was hoped, would reveal vast mineral wealth in Australia, and artesian water too. Much negotiation secured agreement that the Empire Marketing Board half-subsidise an Australian survey by a British team.[47]
- *Dried and Canned Fruits.* Investigations were proceeding into each, the former more advanced. It was probing the efficacy of irrigation and other water-supply matters, and as well 'the cost and methods of production, processing, transport, marketing, finance and other matters'.
- *Fisheries.* The DMC organised a major conference to review this industry, long beset by difficulties of co-ordination. The conference called for the establishment of laboratories, and for various modes of regulation. The DMC affirmed the industry's promise greatly to reduce the £1.7 million currently spent on fish imports. The notion of attracting 'many skilled British fishermen' to Australia was the sole reference to immigration in these chapters of the *Report.*
- *Tobacco.* The British-Australian Tobacco Company had undertaken to join with governments in subsidising research into tobacco-growing. Gepp was chairing an executive committee, its first task to find a chief investigator.
- *Mechanical Transport.* Gepp and many others were hyper-conscious of Australian distance, and of the need to resolve its tyranny. Giant trucks with six wheels, or caterpillar-tracks, might roll across the expanses of inland Australia; producer gas could cut fuel prices. In London Gepp had garnered relevant data (from the War Office), and he headed an initiatory committee, succeeded in June 1927 by an all-States body under Major John Northcott.
- *Fuel Production* followed from the above. Charcoal offered the best immediate hope for innovation, but shale oil and coal had promise too. New fuels would demand modified engines. 'The huge volume' of imports made action urgent.
- *Forestry, Timber, and Paper.* The Tasmanian enquiry had broached relevant matters, and South Australia also was much interested.
- *Textile Technical College.* Geelong had been selected as the site for the college, based on the Gordon Institute, where 'instruction might be imparted in such technical matters as scouring, cording and spinning, weaving, dyeing, finishing'.
- *Rural Housing* remained a matter of high priority. The DMC believed that appropriate provision could be decisive in establishing a secure and satisfied rural workforce. Discussions had pondered the problems of financing and managing such schemes.
- *Other Industries.* The *Report* gave separate paragraphs to 'cider and apple brandy' and 'potato products'. Then followed a grab-bag heading:

'institution of new industries in Australia'. The Murrumbidgee Irrigation Area was hailed for promising to supply Australia's demand for rice. A list followed of the import values for thirty other commodities. Beyond those already cited were cotton, hides, cars, metals, oils, nuts, dairy products, even 'sausage casings'. All offered as targets for Australian assertion.

- *Tourist Traffic* received considerable attention. The Orient Line was willing to co-operate, while within Australia the DMC hoped to build upon the scintillating example of the chief of Victoria's Railways, H. W. Clapp.[48] Especially the *Report* looked forward to 'tours to enable young men, who have just left public schools or universities, to see something of the life and prospects of Australia with a view to becoming residents of the Commonwealth'. The DMC managed the government's long-established interest in propagandist cinema: the mighty abilities of Raymond Longford, Lotte Lyell, and Arthur Higgins had been employed in work for Wembley, and that story continued.[49] A successor Empire Exhibition was being planned, under DMC auspices, for Sydney probably in 1931.
- *Simplified Practice*, otherwise 'industrial standardisation', also had been probed at the Imperial Conference. The promise of this tactic to eliminate waste gave it much clout. Yet another arena for engineers to bestride, it came under Gepp's patronage, and the Australian Commonwealth Association of Simplified Practice had been established.

The DMC became sizeable. Staff numbers reached the mid-eighties, including thirty-seven on migration work (with ninety-nine more at Australia House). As well, seven specialists, on secondment, were advising on specific issues. By current standards the Commission was an expert, even elitist, corps.[50] Rose and Finlay of Tasmania typified the seconded advisors (the former praising the latter to Gepp as 'a patriotic Australian ... his only desire to get into harness in your team'),[51] while Pennefather was among some seven or eight graduates to find permanent employment. T. R. Adam had degrees in both Arts and Law. E. N. Robinson, while not a graduate, had much experience in agricultural education and journalism. One DMC career-bureaucrat was J. F. Murphy, who became Controller of Food during World War II and Chairman of the Australian Wool Board thereafter. Keith Officer, Dermot Casey and Julian Simpson were three young men of distinction in terms of both background and future career who approached Nathan as to employment early in the DMC's history, so recognising its potential as a superior branch of Australian bureaucracy.[52] Their association was nugatory, however. The other staffers' morale may have suffered from Gepp's public declaration in July 1927 as to his 'longing for some of the senior men of the Staff of the company with which I have previously been associated'.[53]

Gepp spoke thus at the outset of a grand tour of Queensland, meant to acquaint him with the State's pastoral resources. While in Brisbane, Gepp had a series of meetings; their record discloses his thought, flaws and all. Perhaps the exchange of greatest revelation was with A. F. Partridge, head of the State's Water and Irrigation Commission.[54] Partridge was now chief barracker for an old cause, farm settlement in the Dawson valley. Gepp, accompanied by E. N. Robinson, acted as devil's advocate. 'Irrigation', he affirmed of general Australian experience, 'has resulted in a number of terrible financial calamities … it is generally the third crop of people who have made the profits'; the Murray River story was black, and the Goulburn's little happier:

> We have been skimming the cream off the continent and doing it in a slapdash way. We are just now realising that we are a competing nation with other nations in the world, and that our surplus products have to be sold on the markets of the world … It comes down to markets every time under our artificial conditions of industrial life.

The last phrase hit at Protective tariffs and arbitrated wages; Gepp could sing in Tory chorus.

The market dilemma applied especially to cotton, he judged. As for tobacco, his committee should find how Australian-grown leaf might be better cured but that might take five years. (Gepp became fond of invoking a quinquennial path to paradise, in this following diverse international models.) Maize, lambs, dairy produce, all had problems. Diversification seemed well in theory, but he had found from running his son's farm that the ordinary farmer could not deploy multiple skills: 'the mentality of the average person is so much lower than that of the specialist that they have crashed every time'. Probing indicated that Partridge's hypothetical farmer had 'perhaps a couple of boys', for whom he allowed no wages. E. N. Robinson stressed the likely variability of soil types within the valley. In spite of all, Gepp held out some hope—if there were a five-year plan! Bankes Amery was more enthusiastic.[55]

Gepp also expressed doubts when talking to managers of the British Australian Cotton Association. 'Do you think the people of Australia are going to continue indefinitely supporting the sugar industry?' he demanded, fending requests for similar aid to cotton. His respondents suggested that such logic would leave Australians with nothing to do. 'We will have to become more efficient', the Chairman answered. (Later he softened, perhaps on learning that Hugh Denison and the Baillieus were backing the Association.) Representatives of the meat industry likewise heard as to the absurdity of enlarging their output without diminishing costs. However, Gepp professed himself ready to help, in words extraordinary from head of an agency active in committee-creation: 'A committee of one is the only committee worth having; you show me the man in this industry and I will get behind him.' No such mitigation appeared in Gepp's analysis of some of the State's mining interests. Allegedly the miscreants paid excessive profits while letting their plant decay, and then called for doles. 'That is what Kalgoorlie did and they got very angry with us when we told them so.' The government geologist applauded the DMC's work for geophysical prospecting, but warned about popular hostility to expertise: recently one ignoramus had 'made £100,000 through pure luck' and ever since, his disastrous word had ruled the local district.

Gepp sometimes took a positive stance. To the Chamber of Manufactures he cited Electrolytic Zinc's achievement in Tasmania as showing that management could gain the workers' trust and inspire them to strive for maximal production. Queensland's fisheries won his acclaim. When the chairman of the Forestry Board baulked at planning an Agreement 'undertaking' because he presumed that it must entail using new immigrants on the work, Gepp assured him such was not so. (He had said the same to Victoria's new Premier earlier, keeping within the Agreement's strict letter but contradicting what the OSD still believed to be an implicit understanding.)[56]

With all that done in Brisbane, Gepp set out on his outback tour. In retrospect that probably seemed halcyon: for the rest of the year, as indeed for the rest of its history, the DMC was increasingly beset by problems. Gepp's personality played its part. 'I should rather like to stress one point to you', wrote McDougall to Bruce after farewelling the Chairman from London; 'I feel that he has so active a mind and so much enthusiasm that there is a quite real danger of his overdoing things to the detriment not only to his health but perhaps even to the work of the Commission.'[57] Presumably the Imperial Conference had accentuated obsessive elements in Gepp's nature; his autobiographer-daughter whom, aged eighteen, he had taken as his unpaid secretary, recalled the period as critical in her own psychic distress. In early June, McDougall told Bruce he was 'extremely sorry' to have heard from Australia that Gepp's nerves continued troublesome; his references thereafter indicated judgment that the DMC never came good. In July H. F. Farrands of the DMC told Whitehall that Gepp's labours in Britain had impaired him.[58]

Tension developed between Gepp and Nathan. The latter's own ego waxed healthy, and his dominance of the Commission during Gepp's absence made for further difficulty. The WA gold *Report* proved the first major problem, Nathan being annoyed that Gepp had usurped the matter and then prepared an incoherent document.[59] More fundamental issues arose concerning Western Australia's railway proposals. Gepp argued, wrote Nathan, for 'consideration of such things as proximity to other railway systems, cost of operation and an examination of more advanced methods in relation to transport'. Nathan judged Gepp's 'Overlord' approach to demand an unrealistic apparatus of enquiry. The Chairman's Queensland trip provoked further censure from his deputy, who wanted action on various current enquiries, and reform of the immigration office. All the while hovered Nathan's own future relationship with the Commission and appointment of a successor Vice-Chairman. Gepp procrastinated, save in promoting Farrands over Hurley.

Nathan and Bruce discussed these matters in mid-June, and on 31 October the Prime Minister interviewed the Commissioners seriatim.[60] Nathan told that Gepp had blocked himself from retaining effective association with the DMC. The two men had best part, determined the Prime Minister; Nathan was big, but not enough to subordinate himself. Then the Chairman:

> I pointed out to G that there was the possibility that he might be spreading himself too much in different directions, and not be getting down to definite and concrete issues. I reminded him of the conversation I had with him before leaving London, when I asked him to put on paper the practical results that would flow from the activities that he was inaugurating, and that I had never had that statement ...
>
> I told G that he was the horse we were backing, and that he could go ahead in confidence that the Government was behind him, and that if ever we felt that we could not back him I would tell him quite clearly and definitely.

Gunn and Fleming confirmed that DMC staff to some extent divided between the two chieftains, with themselves as stabilisers. At year's end both Fleming and Nathan departed the Commission, the former to enjoy (until his death in October 1928) the super-salaried post of Sydney's city commissioner, and the latter a knighthood.

While these troubles appear not to have become public, the DMC was always vulnerable. Labor parliamentarians most importantly made that point. The Commission had an impossible task, argued E. G. Theodore (now a member of the House of Representatives), and was being used by government as 'a more or less effective way of shelving its responsibilities'.[61] A radical was more emphatic in denouncing 'the stupid and rascally practice of carrying on government by commission'; the DMC was doing little, costing too much, 'roaming and romancing around Australia'. Another critic was H. S. Gullett, who declared horror lest his own espousal of an independent migration body might have prompted this money-eating machine. Like others, Gullett remarked that the DMC was encroaching on the Tariff Board, and subverting Protection. Bruce got only a little support in defending the DMC. Two backbench Senators were the most forthright. Those closer to power and to the electorate kept quiet.

Wrangling with the States continued. Victoria saw the advent in May of E. J. Hogan's ministry; despite being Labor, it won Gepp's welcome.[62] That signified how crass was its precursor, and perhaps Gepp's desperate search for friends. Events soon modified his hopes. The situation of Victoria's migrant farmers remained dismal, and debate descended into further acrimony in December when bureaucrats cancelled the leases of four such people who had publicly protested their plight.[63] Meanwhile E. N. Robinson had joined Bankes Amery as a target of William McIver's anger at outside interference—although Robinson found Victorian land management fair enough, and himself affirmed that recent migrants should not go onto farms.[64] Gepp, with much naivety, proposed comprehensive devaluation of Victorian land so as to reduce settlement costs; G. F. Finlay, himself no ultra-realist, pointed out 'how much capital is advanced on loan securities', based on current values.[65]

Finlay played a crucial role when the DMC blocked Queensland's proposals for the Dawson River area. While not totally hostile, he remarked soil deficiency, water salinity, pests, and so on. The Queenslanders had spent much on irrigation, said Finlay, in districts unsuited to that use. Projected farm sizes were too small. There was no 'carefully thought out plan' either for the marketing of produce or for the development of sociable communities.[66] South Australia also told a negative tale. From late 1926 a committee of departmental leaders considered submissions under the Agreement, but there was always hesitation lest the State commit itself to absorbing excessive numbers of migrants. A few schemes were advanced but, following discussions with Gunn, they were abandoned in early 1928.[67]

The DMC's relation with Tasmania intensified. Finlay and Rose pursued enquiries, the latter becoming mordant. The DMC retained the services of P. E. Keam—a gentleman-farmer from northern Tasmania, intelligent, good-natured, ardent for technology and progress, although but moderately successful on his own land.[68] Keam's task was to liaise with the Tasmanian government. Gepp himself strove to build upon his marvels at Electrolytic Zinc to become saviour of the island-State. The supreme document is a manifesto prepared by Gepp, probably with Rose's help, in October 1927. It argued for co-operative principles on a grand scale:

Let us endeavour to visualise the operation of these general principles in Tasmania. First, we have a system of rural and developmental finance through a banking institution operating in this direction under a Government guarantee and working with an advisory Board of Directors nominated by the State Government, and upon whose recommendations advances for developmental and co-operative purposes shall be made. The profits for trading business will be credited to the Government account, and losses and expenses debited. The Tasmanian Government have, it is suggested, under this scheme, a high-class man with a small staff, acting as full-time economic advisers, as permanent

Chairman of the State Development Board, and as Development Commissioner for Tasmania, reporting direct to Cabinet through the Premier. This official is in full touch with Heads of all Departments, and through the State Development Board, with the leading citizens of Tasmania, and through the State Advisory Boards and other organisations such as the Agricultural Bureaux, with the various industries of the State. He is charged with the responsibility of giving the necessary lead and assistance in the foundation of, for instance, new co-operative organisations. He consults with the above State instrumentalities on the one hand and with the Development and Migration Commission on the other, and prepares reports and recommendations for the consideration perhaps primarily of the State Advisory Board of any particular industry, and secondly of the State Development Board or a sub-committee thereof, and finally forwards, under instructions, to the Premier, a recommendation to Cabinet perhaps dealing with the question of a Government Guarantee for a particular co-operative project, setting out in this report a reasoned argument in detail.

It is suggested that the Tasmanian Parliament have passed a Bill giving the Government authority to provide these financial guarantees …[69]

And so fantasy continued.

Already the DMC had sponsored an extraordinary essay in co-operation in Tasmania. Its author was L. R. Macgregor, Director of Queensland's Producers' Association. Macgregor proposed massive compulsory organisation of major primary industries, and declared his readiness to supervise the foundation of the new structure. The Queenslander's dynamism compelled local politicians. Gepp and Premier Lyons had a sticky exchange, the Chairman assailing coercive elements in Macgregor's scheme.[70] The latter went home and told his Premier that the DMC was power-hungry, hostile to the States.[71] Gepp, he thought, might crib his ideas. The episode wins not one of the half-million words in Macgregor's autobiography, *British Imperialism. Memories and Reflections*.

Macgregor criticised a fundamental of DMC's Tasmanian policy— fostering co-operation and improved farm-practice through *voluntary* action. To this end it had backed a farmers' movement to establish 'Agricultural Bureaux', which Gepp had sponsored even before he left Electrolytic Zinc. Macgregor believed that such methods took too long. Certainly they had to combat powerful inertia; voluntary co-operation more easily arises from affluence than from the survival-battle long besetting most Tasmanian farmers. Keam himself affirmed the unpopularity of co-operatives in Tasmania.[72] The DMC's first attempt to implement its concept, the Tasmanian Egg Company, floundered deeply during late 1927.[73] At that time a more promising aspect of the Commission's Tasmanian initiatives was imminent expansion of the Agriculture Department, from the New Year to have Alexander Nelson as superintendent of research. Also the DMC subsidised efforts to identify new farm land. One or other Commission experts reviewed possibilities of improved farm output, timber and tourism initiatives as well. Gepp hoped for extended mining, remarking that the Baillieus might take as low as 8 per cent profit in such ventures.[74] The geophysical project could help there, although more specific to Tasmania was a proposed topographical survey, to amass data for all primary industry.

Secondary enterprise had more appeal for Tasmania's Labor ministry, and this threatened tension. Gepp even rejected the cardinal doctrine that cheapness of Tasmanian hydro-electricity offered a potent lure to industry.[75] Worse followed. For many months the State had negotiated with Italian interests to establish an artificial silk industry, but an enabling Bill failed by one vote in the Legislative Council after W. J. Rose had questioned its cost-analysis. As some compensation, the Chairman continued efforts to get a special deal for Tasmania under the Agreement, a matter of vast but sterile discussion.

Premier Lyons stayed pretty true to Gepp and the DMC, personal friendship playing its part.[76] The Hobart *Mercury* likewise found more to praise than blame in the Commission, welcoming its campaign against 'bonusing' inefficiency and its stress on intra-industry co-operation: 'this is the essence of the very great plan adopted by Signor Mussolini in reorganising the whole industrial machinery of Italy'.[77] At 1927's end Keam claimed the support not only of Lyons but also ('despite some gibes') of Opposition Leader Walter Lee. Everyday farmers, meanwhile, 'are at that stage of thought when they are critical and asking questions. My interpretation of this is that this is just a phase through which the movement is passing, and is indicative of interest rather than hostility.' Being the Commission's man in Tasmania was no sinecure.

*   *   *

The States cared enough about the Agreement to insist that Gepp's hard-won amendments were retrospective, and this delayed formal assent throughout 1927.[78] They disdained granting of free passage to domestics, seeing the likely result as the arrival of yet more 'girls' who would flout commitment to work in that role, and so pressure the general labour market.[79] More negative still, the latter months of 1927 saw a lessening, down to 150 per month, of requisitions for 'selected' men.[80] M. L. Shepherd, returning from his stint as secretary at Australia House, upbraided the States for this. Gepp defended the States,[81] an opportune ploy which implied his own disinterest in migration numbers. Further moves from Britain for reciprocity in social services evoked no Australian answer in 1927, a negation in early 1928.[82] During 1927 Senator Pearce travelled in Britain and on return circulated a memorandum seeking ways to boost migration.

Commissioner Fleming replied that to find migrants a job which could sustain a family was difficult; putting them on farms had a sorry history; and to encourage investment in small businesses was likewise fraught, as Australians crowded that sector.[83]

Late in 1927 the London migration office abandoned its self-designation as an agency of the 'Government of Australia', this resulting from a States' protest led by J. T. Lang and perhaps symbolising weakened resolve.[84] Migration statistics generally were declining. The office continued through the year without a head, although about to arrive was C. H. E. Manning, a gallant soldier and Perth businessman; Nathan had recommended him, citing Mrs Manning's splendid work for migrant welfare, but the government first tried F. C. Govers, an outstanding NSW bureaucrat.[85]

Previous references have shown that as Treasury resumed its crusade against emigration, and especially against Australian projects, the OSD objected. That situation continued, but the OSD maintained its own discontents with Australia. As early as 5 May, T. C. Macnaghten told Gepp of his regret that no big schemes were coming along: 'it is difficult to answer Members of Parliament and others who write … to complain that their constituents who want to settle on the land in Australia, are not afforded the opportunity to do so'.[86] The letter showed Macnaghten's invincible Britocentrism, and his yearning for land-settlement clashed with lessons of both past and immediately future events. An anti-Australian shift was perhaps strengthened by the accession to the OSC chairmanship of S. J. Fraser, fourteenth Baron Lovat. Charismatic and aristocratic, famed in warcraft, forestry and Empire-building, Lovat minimised the difficulties of migration. 'Everything that I have seen up to date confirms me in the belief that the local official whether at Australia House or in Australia, stuffed up with his own importance, is … the hindrance to settlement on generous lines', he declaimed.[87] Macnaghten was always vulnerable to influence from a dominant personality, and Lovat was that. Maybe it is otiose to invoke personality and sufficient to emphasise, as Bankes Amery did to the DMC,[88] that HMG had determined to secure more emigration, especially of miners, in return for its settlement expenditure. Anyway, Treasury now took yet tougher stance. This was well revealed in a paper briefing Secretary Amery for the imperial odyssey he undertook in late 1927.[89]

Amery had asked whether fulfilment of the Agreement did not entail Australia accepting 450,000 assisted immigrants over the decade. To pose this question suggested discontent with Australian performance. Treasury told him what the careful reader of these pages already knows: the strict answer was 'no'; the figure of 450,000 derived from the notion that one migrant would go for each £75 of loan moneys extended under clause 5 of the Agreement, *all being additional to the flow already prevailing in 1925*; further, this had not been specified in the Agreement, and the more ample terms as to moneys advanced under clause 6 for land-settlement further reduced Australia's obligation. Treasury stressed that the land-settlement clause had been inserted and specification of the 450,000 abandoned because of Bruce's intervention in February 1925:

> It will be seen, to put the matter bluntly, that Mr Bruce, in effect, asked that the Agreement should be camouflaged so as to appear 'one entirely for land settlement' and should not specifically mention large numbers of settlers. He clearly explained his reason for this request, viz., that for political reasons Labour Premiers, whilst favouring the Agreement, could only subscribe to it as a land settlement proposition ...
>
> At that time Mr Amery and his advisors undoubtedly inferred, perhaps rather more than Mr Bruce's message justified, that there would, in fact, be very little land settlement under the Agreement.

The inference was fair: Bruce *had* given that impression. In reality, as Treasury now stressed and exaggerated, clause 6 schemes had kept coming. While the strict answer to the 450,000 query therefore was 'no', continued Treasury's document, 'morally' the opposite applied: the whole pre-Agreement debate, on either side, had assumed 450,000 as the target. As to this there is no scintilla of doubt.

Treasury urged that Amery should make no further concessions while in Australia. The concurrence of Lovat and Macnaghten in this was cited (but not its mode of achievement). Every effort should strive to diminish clause 6 schemes, and emphasis be put upon the Agreement's provision for scrutiny of 'undertakings' after three years. News of this tougher policy went to Bankes Amery and Australian authorities.[90] The Representative had been in constant joust with Australian perfidy. To his mind clause 6 'undertakings' still made better sense than those based on public works because the latter received funding from credit amassed by nominated immigrants, and so did nothing directly to impel further movement:

> Not a single State Government of Australia has raised a finger since the agreement was signed to encourage migration. Not one single avenue has been opened up. Scarcely one Clause 5 scheme has been approved which would not have been gone on with Australian money had there been no agreement. New South Wales which is anti-agreement got about half the total migrants in 1926 thus proving that nomination will go on whether there is an agreement or not.[91]

These criticisms were as penetrating as Treasury's. As noted, Gepp himself had encouraged disregard of the understanding that recent immigrants should work on Agreement projects. The Victorians, affirmed Bankes

Amery, had calculated to ensure that the State already had received sufficient migrants before submitting their schemes. As for the DMC, members were venturing around Australia, leaving a power vacuum at the centre. A brighter note was Manning's appointment; 'a fine type of man, much superior to some we know', but maybe lacking the strength 'to keep Barnes in order'.

The Representative's next letter spoke of influential opinion characterising Gepp as always having conjured with big ideas but rarely effecting them. Nathan was leaving the Commission in disgust. Better scrap the Agreement in favour of reducing fares, Bankes Amery argued, 'provided it was accompanied by a complete abandonment of the present State government control of migration and by a drastic overhaul of alluring literature, films, etc'.[92] Yet after meeting with Gepp in mid-September, Bankes Amery reported sympathetically. He told that Whitehall's move against clause 6 schemes distressed the Australian, who had striven to uphold his assurances in London, and now saw himself betrayed. Amery endorsed the argument; 'it is unfortunate that a man of such sterling qualities and high character as Gepp should have begun to have even a remote suspicion of the good faith of the British government'. The Representative relayed Gepp's theme that it must take years for the DMC to cleanse and energise Australia. More immediately, Bankes Amery struggled with immigrant distress and destitution. He found that £15,000 sent years before from the National Relief Fund to Western Australia remained largely in government coffers.[93]

Perhaps L. S. Amery read some of this commentary as he voyaged across the globe. His party included senior OSD man G. G. Whiskard, and Gervas Huxley, chief publicist for the Empire Marketing Board. McDougall told Bruce of the two respectively being 'quite able, but perhaps rather heavily affected by the Dominions Office atmosphere' and 'an extremely pleasant fellow'.[94] Both of them, and Amery too, left records of their journey.[95]

The party made its Western Australian landfall on 10 October. The following days were the happiest of the Australian tour. While not blind to the rigours suffered by many migrant farmers, the visitors found much optimism and achievement. Huxley showed that imperial idealism still vibrated:

> The romance of all the pioneering work that I have seen in the past few days has filled me with a sense of exultation, and my heart has been singing a paean in praise of the triumph of man and his works, of the victory of field and furrow, of fence and plough, of all things man-made and finite over the wild and boundless disorder of Nature.

A visit to the Fairbridge school deepened this enthusiasm, sustained also by meeting C. G. Latham, a migrant (as a child in 1890) who had triumphed as a farmer and was now pursuing a fine political career.[96] That Latham, a non-

Labor man, should enjoy official dignity reflected the moderation of the State's Labor government; the visitors noticed that most political animus was directed against Commonwealth policies, especially Protection. Joining the party in Western Australia were Bankes Amery and Nathan. The former now told Whiskard that Nathan was better to deal with than hot-and-cold Gepp. Nathan spoke of the desirability of a grand WA scheme, and Premier Philip Collier showed amenable. The Britons agreed that only some such coup could give the Agreement meaning; currently in Western Australia it was financing merely a few miles of railway, benefiting farms owned generally by old Aussies.

The wheatlands of South Australia withered in drought. The State's politicians were a poor lot, as bad as any being the (non-Labor) Premier, R. L. Butler. Some Ministers were better, so too Opposition Leader L. L. Hill; even so, Whiskard now remarked that 'in dealing with the State Governments in Australia one is dealing with a body little if at all superior to the small Town Council at home'. He thought Australia's system of triennial parliaments contributed much to the awful vote-consciousness of politicians. Dialogue with such men and their bureaucrats became very onerous. And ahead lay Victoria! McIver, with whom Bankes Amery had patched a reconciliation, seemed not too bad: 'rather of the Sergeant Major type', thought Whiskard, 'stupid, a bit obstinate but ... capable of being managed'. A couple of migrant farmers praised the Victorian government highly. They had served in the ranks; Whiskard and Huxley agreed that it was ex-temporary-officer-types, wanting much bounty for little effort, who led the dissidents among Victorian immigrants. Yet the visitors suffered nativist bile. 'Two and a half hours' talk with Ministers chiefly on migration; all of them fairly sticky and one old boy, Prendergast, convinced that all migrants were criminals or paupers.' So wrote Amery. Whiskard cited another of the Labor ministry, J. P. Jones, as one 'who seemed to touch bottom in the direction of complete parochialism and general incompetency'.

Sandwiched within the Victorian sojourn was Tasmania. The visitors enjoyed its England-like charm. They followed Bankes Amery in applauding Governor O'Grady and Premier Lyons. Gepp and Minister Thomas Paterson were now accompanying the party; Whiskard enjoyed hearing the latter denounce tariffs as sustaining Australia's uneconomic industries and wage-levels. The Britons sympathised with Tasmanian complaints that they were victims of federal policy (Australia, alone in the world, commented Whiskard, saw freight by sea more expensive than by land), but were put off by local yearning for industrialisation. At Government House, 'after-dinner discussion on Tasmania's problems consisted mainly of feeble-minded vapourings about secondary industry with a fine disregard for economics'. Premier Lyons proposed to Bankes Amery that the Agreement underwrite the artificial silk industry so long proposed.[97] When this was reported back to London, majority opinion within the OSD scorned the idea—why assist a concern which would get Protection from Australian tariffs and compete with Courtaulds'? Whiskard, by now himself in Britain, responded that Australian secondary industry must grow, that Tasmania had particular advantages in this instance, and that desirably Britons should direct the process. (Italian entrepreneurs remained active in Tasmanian discussions about silk.) Bankes Amery seems to have felt much the same.

Although Amery's party met Bruce in Melbourne, their major conference with him and the DMC occurred in Canberra, now in its first months as the national capital. The Britons presented the points made in the Treasury document of mid-year. They urged a check on clause 6 schemes, and proclaimed Australia's obligation to take close to 450,000 assisted migrants were the Agreement to be fulfilled. They were more enthusiastic, however, in urging that Australia develop big public works programmes rather than use Agreement moneys on minor items. Amery also sought increased immigration by both nomination and requisition.

The Australians defended themselves, Nathan rejecting commitment to 450,000 migrants and Gepp saying that the States simply could not absorb so many. Both stressed that 'normal flow' migrants qualified the States for Agreement funds. The Australians proposed also that the nation's intake should count overall, rather than each State having to meet its own quota; the point was that separate quotas handicapped smaller States, which attracted even fewer 'normal flow' migrants than their proportion of population. (Bruce did allow that the present quota arrangement had the advantage that 'we can keep the whip over the States'.) Gunn, drawing from his studies of fruit-growing, stressed how Australian expansion of such kind demanded market-preference from Britain. Treasury came under heavy fire, notably from Bruce:

> I have no doubt Mr Amery that if your department and the Overseas Settlement Committee ever becomes a power in the land, so that you will be able to stand up to the British Treasurer, the agreement will be carried out in a spirit of decency and co-operation; but if the matter remains with the British Treasurer throughout the whole piece it will be a Jew's bargain to the last ditch.[98]

Did Nathan wince?

Conversations proceeded, and memoranda evolved. They proposed a more systematic Australian approach, and offered possible guides for approval of clause 6 schemes. Maybe they would be acceptable if in conjunction with clause 5 schemes; maybe there could be a 50:50 ratio overall, with understanding that all clause 6 operations be in Western Australia, South Australia, and Queensland. Perhaps the Britons were paying mere lip-service to Treasury's principles: upholders of Ameryesque faith had to empathise with the direct settlement envisaged by clause 6. The Western Australian discussions had exemplified this rule. More generally, the delegation appears to have been sympathetic to Australian viewpoints. Huxley became surer of Bruce's 'ability and force of character, which put him head and shoulders above anyone I had met in Australia'. To Whiskard, Bruce spoke of Australia's 'tariff madness'. Gepp stressed the intractability of Australia's economic sluggishness; only gold rushes had dynamised Australian population growth in the past, and only something like that could do so now.[99]

The Canberra meetings may have been emptier for Amery than his juniors. Writing to Baldwin he scarcely mentioned them, emphasising instead defeat in October of J. T. Lang's government in New South Wales.[100] The delight this aroused in other Labor leaders, wrote Amery, proved their good sense; most 'were very decent fellows' and more able administrators than their opponents. True, Labor and much public opinion clung to fallacies about protecting secondary industry and arbitrating wages. Bruce promised to defy these ills. 'His hands would be immensely strengthened in that direction if we could make any advance in preference on our side', wrote Amery, still fighting battles of 1923. Almost simultaneously Governor-General Stonehaven wrote to Whitehall bemoaning Australia's mediocrity and its denial of economic truths. Immigration remained a party-political issue, he warned.[101]

In Sydney the Governor's secretary told the visitors that Lang was of doubtful sanity. The new Premier, T. R. Bavin, they found able but negative. In Queensland, Premier McCormack won plaudits almost as admiring as those accorded Bruce. 'It was hoped by the federal authorities that he would bring back sane Government to Queensland after the Socialist excesses of Theodore', wrote Huxley. Queensland had grandeur, but also heat, distance, and surpassing barbarism of civic behaviour. The group struggled back to Sydney. Whiskard had a last round of talks with Gepp— domineering and difficult, but potent in his sincerity.[102] On 18 November the party embarked for New Zealand. Huxley summed Australia:

> While it had been a depressing experience to find that a loud-voiced, brash arrogance, and an utter lack of culture or appreciation of any non-material values seemed to characterise nearly all the Australians I had met, those unendearing qualities had, for me, been outweighed by the attraction of the refreshing vitality, the sturdy independence and open hospitality that I had found to be equally characteristic.

During the mission's final days in Australia, the DMC had met with NSW authorities.[103] Earlier in the year Lang had probed to see if the Agreement offered benefit; now Bavin foreshadowed thorough commitment. At these meetings Gepp dwelt further on minerals, proposing that the Agreement could fund works which might enable processing of low-grade ores on established fields. Bankes Amery and Gunn doubted the legitimacy of such 'undertakings'. Gepp spoke also of his desire that each State establish a committee for liaison with the DMC, and which might develop comprehensive five-year planning; the Ameryites had affirmed that magic span.

While the Amery party proved often sympathetic to Australia, other Britons continued sceptical. Surveying reports of the Australian discussions, Macnaghten concluded:

> Instead of showing eagerness to meet us and exploring all means of increasing the flow of migrants, Australia is trying to limit its commitment ... For this attitude neither Mr Bruce nor Mr Gepp is to blame ... The trouble is that the state Governments have not risen to the bait of the Loan Agreement.[104]

Macnaghten doubtless drafted the annual OSC *Report*.[105] It reprimanded Australia especially for diminishing 'selected' labourers, and more generally for reluctance to accept that immigration was no drag but a boost to economic growth. The *Report* pointed to scope for industrial development in Australia and hoped that urban migrants would assist that fulfilment. It noted sluggishness in the British desire for emigration, becoming ambivalent in explanation: on one hand, trade depression suffocated adventurous enthusiasm; on the other, 'improvement in social conditions' and especially state-funded welfare had also worked as checks. Among proposed remedies there reappeared the idea of increased subsidy of all fares, through the unilateral action of HMG.

That issue had arisen too in the major Parliamentary debate on migration in 1927.[106] Before the Commons was a motion proposed by Anthony Eden, who had visited Australia with the 1925 Press Union. Eden exhorted the House, declaring Whiggish *laissez-faire* to have ended in imperial as other realms; he praised the DMC and suggested that Britain develop a complementary body, more forceful than the OSC. Eden showed, as did Whiskard and Huxley later in the year, that goodwill and optimism still had some play.

Through Confusion to Doom: 1928–1929

Those gleams of optimism and goodwill might somehow have upheld effective immigration, had not economic torpor in general and unemployment more particularly continued to beset both Britain and Australia. Instead, our story becomes one of ever more complex disaster. The following account is most at fault in imposing a greater degree of order than truly prevailed. Only one thing is certain: the validity of our chapter title.

Early on, Britain's economic situation was grimmer, and its politicians more vigorous in responding. In Cabinet, Churchill and Neville Chamberlain strongly favoured reducing taxes, while Amery continued ardent for tariff revision and imperial integration. Baldwin sat in the middle. Early in 1928 government appointed an Industrial Transference Board, its task to suggest how unemployed labour could be prompted to search for jobs, at home and abroad. The ITB's chairman was N. F. W. Fisher, head of the Treasury—not so active a critic of Australia as some of his officers, but hostile to feather-bedding the Empire. 'Warren Fisher is out definitely to smash the Empire Marketing Board', Amery had noted in July 1927.[1] That C. W. G. Eady was secretary to Fisher's enquiry confirmed that Australian attitudes would gain little heed before it.

Amery and the OSD had generally marginalised ultra-Tory imperialism, but now it became more vocal. Chief spokesman was A. A. Somerville, for thirty-seven years a master at Eton before entering Parliament in 1922. Early in 1928 Somerville introduced a Bill providing for HMG to embark on massive training schemes for the unemployed; as appropriate, it should purchase tracts of imperial land where trainees might fulfil their vocation. In charge would be a board comprising 'men of energy, ability and wide vision'; in Australian matters this body should liaise with the DMC. Somerville praised both the latter and Bruce, while castigating trade unions for imposing their dire hostility to migrants on Australia, while yet it relied on the Royal Navy for protection from Asia.[2] Cabinet merely determined not to oppose Somerville's Bill at its second reading,[3] but in debate Amery showed more enthusiasm than that. While remarking Dominion suspicions of training schemes as a British ploy for dumping unemployables, he

stressed the need for imperial economic dynamism. Among other Conservative supporters were Anthony Eden and Sir Newton Moore (once
Agent-General for Western Australia) who respectively deplored timidity in
the OSD and red-tapery at Australia House. William Lunn was an
Opposition voice in favour, although he approved the current situation
overall, praising Gepp especially. A very different view came from the
notable Labour Parliamentarian John Wheatley. He repudiated the Bill's
whole thrust: 'What is really in the minds of the Conservatives—there are
various minds—is not so much Empire settlement as the disposal of our
Empire proletariat.' The measure, said Wheatley, would tax the worker in
order to fund training intended to result in him being 'deported from his
native land'. Wheatley called for cultivation of land at home, ignoring the
Bill's provision for some such outcome. Off it went to a committee.

Meanwhile, Amery urged Cabinet to take a positive approach to the Bill.[4]
T. C. Macnaghten reported that the clerk of the Commons had told him that
majority sentiment there 'is determined that something shall be done to
promote Empire Settlement'; unemployment doubtless impelled this view
(Macnaghten said the clerk said), but the journeying of the Empire
Parliamentary Association had fostered a more abstract commitment.[5]
Macnaghten believed that Somerville's Bill was too open-ended as to costs.
Amery proposed amendments to cover this weakness. They went to
Cabinet, there suffering hostility and postponement until the ITB reported.
Amery's political efficacy, never great, was diminishing; F. L. McDougall
so reported to Bruce around this time.[6] The Bill never returned from
committee.

Although the ITB *Report* did not appear until early July, its gist had
formed weeks earlier. The Board was less interested in Australia than in
Canada, where since 1926 Prime Minister W. L. Mackenzie King had
responded to migration proposals with unwonted alacrity; Amery believed
that Canada promised the best results of his imperial tour.[7] Nevertheless, the
Board studied the Australian situation. Late in February Macnaghten told
Eady, 'it is really not a review of the Agreement which is wanted but a
revision of the spirit in which it is regarded, not indeed by Mr Bruce and the
DMC, but by the State Governments and population generally'.[8] In April the
Board floated an interim report.[9] It spoke of 'the deplorable facts' as to
diminution of emigrants from Britain to the major Dominions, the more
drastic when compared with the current movement of Continentals thither
and with British statistics pre-1914. The Board intended to recommend
training, much as Somerville had proposed, and to secure reduction of
fares—that oft-mooted ploy to boost migration without recourse to
Dominions' subsidy, so inhibiting their supervisory rights. Muscles should
flex:

Insistence (if necessary by threatening to withdraw the £34m agreement with Australia) that added traffic secured by these measures shall not be used to reduce settlement under the ES Act below—*at the least*—to the average immigration to Australia and Canada respectively during the past five years.

'A really suitable officer' should attend to the matter in either Dominion. It beggars belief that as of 1928 intelligent men should write or even think in such terms. Macnaghten's response hinted at that, while confirming the OSC's agreement 'that none of the Dominions is playing the game in connection with Empire Settlement'. Amery remarked to Baldwin on the ITB's presumption, but was ready to use its arguments to win Cabinet backing for his own variant of Somerville's proposals.

The polished ITB *Report* was less 'insistent' than foreshadowed in April, but assertive enough.[10] Small farming at home could not accommodate Britain's unemployed, opined early paragraphs; 'forest holdings' promised only a little more. So migration mattered much: 'This does not mean that we associate emigration and unemployment in the sense we are concerned to ask the Dominions to share our industrial difficulties. We do not. There is no question here of dumping unemployables.' The Board denounced the 'calumny', prevalent in the Dominions, that recipients of the dole were irredeemable 'vagrants and loafers'; rather, they were transient victims of fluctuating circumstance. Likewise the Board spurned 'the silly parrot cry about our national decadence'. In truth there prevailed, now as in the past, 'the same quality; the same endurance; the same cheerful adaptability; the same stirring in the blood of a call to adventure'. True to this spirit, many more Britons were ready to emigrate than the Dominions would receive. The Board slammed the administrative complexities imposed by the latter. Politics added their venom: 'every failure, every accident is intensified, the hundreds and thousands of successes are passed over in silence'. Meanwhile Continentals took their opportunity: distorting reality, the Board found a figure of 22,000 such entrants to Australia in 1927.

The *Report* specified as first priority government action to secure lower passage rates; 'we take it, of course, for granted that any increase in migration outside the provisions of the Empire Settlement Act would not be used as an argument for reducing the numbers accepted by the Dominions under the Act'. It dismissed the OSC's thesis that migration had choked because of economic gloom, Empire-wide. In fact, went its counter-argument, current economic reality conduced to migration from Britain, the Dominions being much more prosperous. The promiscuity of these generalisations is gross, made more odious by Fisher's Treasury colleagues, and Eady himself, long having painted a very different scenario for the Australian economy. The prize for perfidy had returned to Whitehall!

The *Report* prompted various Britons to vent outrage at Dominion, and especially Australian, restrictiveness on migration. To the fore was that proverbial voice of gloom, the Dean of St Paul's, W. R. Inge.[11] 'Tyranny of labour', 'dog in the manger': such clichés rolled towards the claim that 'an underpopulated country has no right to exclude migrants—that is, if they are white'. In the Commons, Baldwin bewailed that their present attitude dishonoured the Dominions' fine history.[12] Somerville-type Tories pressed their case against ingrate colonists. Amery rode with the swell, telling of his hopes to negotiate with shipping companies for fare reduction, 'not to the assisted special migrant, but to the ordinary man who wants to get a ticket out to go overseas without any unnecessary Government formalities or any sense of dependence on public assistance'. Macnaghten felt such humiliation at the *Report*'s scorn of his office that he sought escape, although not until August 1929 did he become Administrator of St Kitts, with G. G. Whiskard succeeding him as OSD head.

McDougall's enormous correspondence with Bruce had scant references to migration but foreshadowing the *Report* he wrote:

> It seems clear to me that schemes for the transference of men, either within the United Kingdom or for overseas settlement, are rather hopeless and that we should all be well advised to talk less and less about the redistribution of population and more and more about the importance of development. If we can once persuade the people of this country that it is to their direct economic advantage to throw all the energy, capital and brains that they can spare from internal affairs into the development of the most promising parts of the Empire from a development point of view, then we shall automatically achieve the transference of population which is making such dreadfully slow progress while we think in terms of migration rather than of development. This I know is your own point of view.[13]

McDougall and like-minded friends in the Conservative Party joked about the ITB's ignorance of Dominion status; he made that point to Amery, and prompted John Buchan to reprove the Board in *The Times*.

Back in February, Bruce had received data about the ITB from Australia's current High Commissioner, Sir Granville Ryrie.[14] This intimated Fisher's readiness to support big-scale funding should Australia make land available for migrant settlement. Doubtless Bruce quashed that, maybe hardening animus in Fisher. On 26 July the Prime Minister assailed the *Report*, insisting 'that Australia was not prepared to transfer from Great Britain the problems of unemployment that had been found impossible of solution, nor was Australia prepared to undermine the standard of its national health by lowering the standards required of migrants'.[15] Gepp likewise issued a condemnatory statement. Undoubtedly both men believed what they said, although equally political and popular hostility to the *Report* ('scandalised indignation', one characterisation went)[16] left no alternative but to respond thus. Bruce went on, as McDougall had prompted, to urge that Britain might well save dole expenditure by investing further in Australian development.

HMG took some action in terms of the ITB's advice. A migration committee of Cabinet met under Amery's leadership, although more than ever he saw Britain's need as revised tariffs rather than emigration. The committee concentrated on Canada. The transatlantic fare was subsidised down to £10, available on loan; all funding came from HMG, and so proceeded outside the Settlement Act. This boosted migration in the immediate future, although not to the level of Amery's hopes. From mid-1928 the OSD began negotiations with shipping lines for a subsidised £10 fare to Australia.[17] The Australian government appears not to have been told of these moves, which at one level is extraordinary. But it is understandable in light of Bruce's response to the ITB; and of an earlier Australian negative to renewed proposals that migrant youths pay nothing towards their fare.[18] Now too, Australia spelled out that reciprocity in social welfare payments posed impossible administrative problems.[19] HMG prepared a Bill in 1928–9 to allow emigrants to claim British unemployment relief. This failed, but (under the Pensions Act, 1929) from 1 January 1930 widows', orphans', and age pensions became payable to emigrants qualified when departing Britain; furthermore, emigrants could maintain qualifying contributions to British welfare funds.

*   *   *

The current economic malaise had its complementary effect in Australia. One result was for migration numbers to decline; more authentic statistics than the ITB's showed that throughout Australia in May 1928 British departures exceeded arrivals by 294, while Continental Europeans had a plus of 66.[20] Anti-migration feeling fed on the latter datum.[21] Meanwhile, the DMC intensified its checking of Agreement proposals. Perhaps this very restrictiveness deepened the stagnation. Writing in August 1929, HMG's current Senior Trade Commissioner in Australia, R. W. Dalton, argued that over the previous two years federal government agencies had worked in deflationary ways, for good reason but inevitably to stultifying effect.[22] Outside the DMC, specific acts of such deflation seem modest: Australian borrowing continued to rise until early 1929.[23] For ill or good, the DMC was uniquely diligent among the 'economic disciplines' which Bruce had set to work. That was recognised by W. K. Hancock, who coined the phrase in his acute and influential book, *Australia*, then being written. Hancock's analysis of his homeland harmonised with Empire idealism: he was a Rhodes Scholar and Fellow of All Souls.

Gepp was as bemused by the economic dilemma of the time as anyone. In July he wrote that 'the worst phase of our business depression has, I think, passed'.[24] Yet within a fortnight Gepp hazarded 'that the troubles of Tasmania and South Australia are not necessarily peculiar to those States, but are symptomatic, presumably indications of a general malaise'.[25] Such confusion must have weakened his leadership of the DMC. That might have been more apparent because the new Vice-Chairman, W. P. Devereux, previously an executive with the Australian Mercantile Land and Finance Company, played but a modest role. Fleming's successor, specifically in overseeing migration, was E. J. Mulvany, a career bureaucrat who forsook the secretaryship of the Department of Markets, so avoiding transfer to Canberra.

An influence deepening Gepp's worries may have been that of the academic economists. Commenting on a draft of the DMC's first *Report*, D. B. Copland had exhorted Gepp to stress the difficulties of migrant absorption, and to insist that Australian production of any item was viable only if its labour component was modest and economic; that way the Commission would help in 'reversing the present tendency to give assistance to all and sundry who can claim to produce a few goods at some appalling cost'.[26] Soon afterwards Bruce appointed Copland and other economists to advise on the Australian tariff, and their answer inexorably pursued such themes. Congruent notions dominated two scholarly symposia published in 1928, *Studies in Australian Affairs* and *The Peopling of Australia*.[27] G. L. Wood and J. B. Brigden contributed to the latter, Brigden emphasising his disdain of immigration. Gepp applauded *The Peopling of Australia*: 'for the first time, in book form at any rate, some of our most vital problems have been treated from the scientific and commonsense point of view'.[28] His hypothesis as to South Australia and Tasmania blazing a downhill track for the nation to follow had the flavour of Brigden. Within the Commission, the Chairman encouraged appropriate research by T. R. Adam: 'Lines of equal habitability (isoiketes) are drawn on a map of the world. Using the present European populations as a criterion of reasonable saturation it is shown that the isoiketes may be translated into isopleths of future population.'[29] Such science was likely to be dismal.

The outstanding 1927 exemplar of the DMC's stringency was its stalling of the Dawson project in Queensland, and reverberations continued into the new year.[30] A. F. Partridge fulminated that the DMC's argument would require proof based upon years of trial, whereas the Agreement predicated immediate pioneering. He alleged further that the verdict derived from the failure of migrant and soldier settlement schemes elsewhere in Australia. The Commission offered a more modest proposal, and Devereux journeyed north in July, to find Premier McCormack recalcitrant.[31] While indicating his misgivings about Partridge (Devereux reported), McCormack denounced

Bruce's 'political' use of the episode; the Prime Minister had cited the DMC's stand as a paragon of judgment. Queensland might well withdraw from the Agreement, came the threat.

Perhaps that was just a routine ploy; anyway, at length emerged an alternative plan, to fund an agricultural survey in Queensland.[32] Neither the OSD nor, of course, Treasury were enthusiastic. Predictably, they criticised the proposal as altogether *preliminary* to settlement, rather than *being* settlement. William Bankes Amery nevertheless had concurred, so interference from Whitehall was the more repugnant in DMC eyes. Gepp cabled the OSD:

Our objective is to make a very necessary gesture to Queensland under the £34m Agreement without delay ... in view of cabled summary of the report of the Industrial Transference Board which has developed considerable Press publicity and to a certain extent an attack upon the D&M Commission. Our deferment of the Dawson Valley scheme aggravated by the publication of the Report of the ITB may lead the Queensland Government to play strong anti-migration card in connection with the forthcoming Federal and state elections.

Gepp's cable moved the OSD to talk with Treasury. C. H. E. Manning, now in office at Australia House, acted through Horace Wilson, ever more potent at the Ministry of Labour. Wilson's intervention, Manning believed, achieved Treasury's approval. Coincidentally, Bruce cabled his agent in Whitehall, R. G. Casey, and he saw Churchill. HMG succumbed, Casey told Bruce, 'but with rather a bad grace, as they considered that they should not have been pressed about it'.[33] All this for £30,000, funding an alternative to something which would have cost much more! The tale twisted further. Showing its contempt for the DMC, the Queensland government went alone with the Dawson scheme. In 1933 a committee reported that Partridge's 'sublime optimism and enthusiasm' had led to an expenditure of over £1 million, more than £8000 per farm, and nearly all had failed.[34]

The episode which W. K. Hancock selected for illustrating the DMC's 'economic discipline' concerned a railway in Victoria's north-west (precisely, from Nowingi to Millewa South, Mallee district).[35] The Commission preferred to develop road networks, and it believed economic rationality required Victoria and South Australia to co-operate in servicing boarder areas such as this. A Victorian bureaucrats' committee saw force in the latter point, but the State government pushed ahead. To meet another DMC objection, it had an officer estimate wheat output from the farms to be served, and then distorted his advice, so favouring the project. The DMC called attention to this 'error'; the government persisted. Gepp urged that costing must recognise the man-years of labour required to prepare the land for farming, and wondered 'what was the use of any country undertaking a scheme which would possibly not pay the interest on the expenditure involved'.[36] Bureaucrats replied that if such thinking prevailed, no young nation would ever grow. Next the DMC expressed shock-horror at the shallowness of the Victorians' research and called for postponement to allow study of

> all influencing factors such as rainfall, soil productivity, the effect of high winds, particularly in early spring, the cheapest and best form of water supply, improvements in the methods of destruction of mallee suckers, the provision of increased mechanical power for farm operations, the most economic farm unit, and the improvement of pastures and the growth of fodder crops.[37]

Bruce lauded this episode as further showing the DMC's virtue. The Victorian government, as had Queensland with the Dawson, funded the scheme itself.

Western Australia continued to offer its hopes and agonies. Another railway project ('Ejanding northwards') came along.[38] 'We have had very considerable trouble in getting the real facts and estimates', wrote Gepp to Senator (now Sir George) Pearce, 'as it would appear that close consideration in this direction has never been given to any of the railway propositions in Western Australia.' The WA government calculated wheat freight at less than a farthing per ton mile. That fantasy depended on excluding depreciation and interest payment for rolling stock. Politics forbade the DMC to demand revolution in Western Australia's accounts, so the nonsense had to stand. E. N. Robinson, the Commission's pertinent expert, jeered also at the optimism of the State's Department of Agriculture; were the district to fulfil departmental projections, he wrote, 'it will be the most remarkable settlement in not only Western Australia ... but in the whole of the world'. Despite all, £400,000 was advanced. Western Australia failed, however, in trying to have boosted an earlier advance for a group-settlement railway, so as to meet its increasing costs. One of these was interest on the loan itself, computed not at the 1 per cent actually being charged the State, but at 5^1/$_2$ per cent, which the local Treasury estimated as ultimate cost.

More grandiose plans still simmered in the West.[39] As 1927 closed, long-pondered ideas for revamping the 1922–3 State agreement clarified; this prompted submission for 700 farms, which would bring the total to 3031. As well there arose during 1928 proposals for 3500 more, under clause 5 of the 1925 Agreement. Migrants would be requisitioned for employment on the associated works, just as HMG always wanted. The DMC had fostered these suggestions and put the proposal before HMG, 'pointing out that this was the first real effort by a State to substantially increase its absorption of migrants, and to make it clear that the State was undertaking a very big task and was deserving of sympathetic consideration'. C. S. Nathan was briefed to argue the case in London on his prospective trip thither.[40] T. C. Macnaghten noted that elements in the Westralians' thinking were 'fantastic'. Still the OSD was approving. It strove to ease Western Australia's commitment to absorb migrants, by discounting its deficit against the surplus of wealthier States; Treasury squashed that, but even there a little goodwill glimmered.

Gepp was at his most variable apropos the WA scheme. In mid-1927, we have seen, he urged restraint, whereas by April the next year he rejoiced to Oscar Thompson 'that the State Government had been "big" enough to look ahead'.[41] His enthusiasm then cooled again, perhaps because of short-comings revealed by the Ejanding railway enquiries. The new proposals were put on hold, pending more research. In London, meanwhile, Nathan believed himself to have secured Treasury's ear. He wrote to Gepp:

> I was vain enough to believe that my association with your Commission and my intimate knowledge of the Migration Agreement might have been of some little value in influencing the Chancellor and even perhaps if necessary Cabinet's view-point, particularly at a period when, owing to unemployment, Treasury's policy must conform to National necessities.[42]

The deferral of action countered all this, Nathan growled; he turned to proposals, virtually independent of the DMC, for developing his State's northern reaches.

The Commission's *Report* for 1928 justified deferring the 3500-farm scheme.[43] Should predictions come true, it said, this venture would produce 12,000,000 bushels of wheat each year and carry one million sheep.

> Obviously in a project of such magnitude and importance, ... dealing with country where settlement possibilities are but imperfectly known, it is essential that a searching investigation should be made of all the factors making for its success—the land, the rainfall, water conservation, and transportation.

The Agreement was funding that enquiry. It included consideration of terms under which land would become available, the Commission being anxious 'to prevent speculation in land values; to promote rapid development; and to ensure that, from the sale of land, a sinking fund will be established to liquidate various items of capital expenditure'. Had there been a tribunal for probing un-Australian activity, it must have indicted the DMC.

While the Western Australian proposals touched sublimity, South Australian works of 1928–9 invited ridicule.[44] The afforestation project attracted Whitehall's criticism since the State did not requisition for any migrants who might work thereon. In response, three men were sought. They had, however, to be trained. 'The idea that a miner—who has used the pick all his life—will require three months training, is to my mind absolutely crazy', declaimed Macnaghten. In any case, Australia House had much travail finding volunteers, largely because South Australia demanded up to £70 landing money; two were found and withdrew; two more appeared, but then the proposal aborted. The Tod River waterworks meanwhile won praise in the DMC *Report* as serving 'a large and courageous land settlement project already well advanced'.[45] Simultaneously a committee of the South Australian Parliament was finding that its catchment could not fill the reservoir, and that mains had been built before due enquiry, 'but with four small exceptions they have either been commenced or completed, and it is too late now'.[46] Gepp and Gunn battled on to improve the State, especially its south-east. They were told that many farmers wanted to keep their land as pasture, rather than pay 'betterment taxes' consequent upon government spending upon it. Those farmers would launch appeals against such imposts, and probably win. 'Is it possible then that no appeals should be allowed?' asked Gepp. 'It is very doubtful indeed that such an Act would go through Parliament' came the answer.[47]

Accession in New South Wales of the government led by T. R. Bavin—that Nationalist of intellectual and moral force, if scant charisma—promised joy for the DMC, but proved ambiguous. In March 1928 the State at last signed the Agreement, and soon offered proposals. One of them, the Wyangala Dam on the Lachlan River, had credentials that muted even Treasury's snarls.[48] A committee of bureaucrats promised to achieve liaison such as the DMC ever sought, but rarely found. Yet that was about that. Bankes Amery had grumbled at New South Wales's prospective admission into the Agreement, noting that this wealthy State already had plenty of 'normal flow' migrants to its potential credit and so would qualify for cheap money without any need to boost numbers.[49] Truly no hint wafted of requisitions for migrants to build Wyangala. Further railway proposals dematerialised. Enquiries into the hydro-electric potential of the Clarence River left the DMC cold, while NSW bureaucrats became as restive as others under cross-examination from the Commonwealth and Whitehall. Bavin agreed with the Commission's insistence that landholders who profited from Agreement works should pay higher taxes, but 'he was particularly desirous that the Commission, in its report, should not allude to the matter, as it might be interpreted that the Commonwealth, in making the loan, was dictating terms and thereby infringing State Rights'.[50]

The Commission always pursued general enquiries into Australia's socio-economic affairs. The tone of some of this activity was positive, even optimistic, but the stronger thrust was otherwise. Several projects, while coming to fulfilment over an extended span, are best considered *en bloc*. Their message was to offer the usual master-class remedies of harder work, for fewer people, at less pay.

A report on dried vine fruits attacked the proliferation of small packing sheds, especially in South Australia; fewer units should achieve higher and homogenous quality.[51] A growers' organisation ought oversee the industry, especially marketing. An expert from the USA might advise on factory design and equipment. A crunch came with recommendation that for the time being, no more plantings should occur. At a conference in July 1928 growers writhed at this restrictionism.[52] Nor did the co-operative ideal win their favour. Wasn't competition the necessary game? Yes, responded Gepp, but competition by a national unified industry, meeting a global challenge. Some rationalisation of sheds did follow, mostly in South Australia. Similar but larger issues prevailed as to canned fruits (apricots, peaches, pears).[53] The USA dominated British markets, went the Commission's plaint; everywhere competition was fierce. Perhaps an Imperial Conference might secure preference. Anyway, a board of management must apply itself to retrieving the industry's 'present deplorable condition', the outcome of corruption through governmental subsidy. Proprietory companies had been guaranteed monopoly over the domestic market, and grown slack. Plantings had occurred without due care for soil survey and like matters. These fruit enquiries bore especially on the Murray–Murrumbidgee valley. The Commission became central in Bruce's efforts to meet this region's problems, and well defined them:

> There is no area in which the potentialities for development are so great, nor are greater opportunities to be found elsewhere for the absorption of additional settlers; yet development has now reached a stage where it is difficult in view of marketing and other problems, to determine the lines upon which future development should proceed.

Accordingly, the Commission oversaw the Murray River Advisory Committee, which embraced a medley of State and federal agencies. It pondered many dilemmas, ramifying as the economy worsened and experience taught that irrigation could destroy environments as easily as enrich them.[54]

The Commission's interest in gold reached its peak with an enquiry of mid-1928.[55] A more committed tone was apparent than in relation to fruit industries, doubtless reflecting Gepp's belief that minerals remained essential to Australian solvency. By its nature, gold could not be protected by tariffs, went the argument; to uphold its own logic, the Commission should have endorsed this independence as a desirable norm. Instead it was used to support a case for government help—by reducing taxation, or providing springboard loans, or exempting necessary machinery from customs duty. The report proposed that government release the industry from codes of industrial relations, so as to allow field-by-field variants in the cause of efficiency. Some onus for improvement was put on management, Kalgoorlie being cited as an anti-model.

These empirical enquiries had their counterpart in a *Report on Unemployment and Business Stability in Australia,* mainly the work of F. J. Murphy.[56] In complement ran an analysis of the business cycle by D. B. Copland. Their message was that experts should study the situation and give warning of downswings, and that policy-makers should minimise them. The most obvious way to that end was for governments to juggle expenditure on public works. Bankers also should strive to smooth fluctuations, most obviously those consequent upon movements in exchange rates. The manufacturers' task was to offer diversified, attractive products: only at this point did the *Report* stress consumption, although W. J. Rose offered an in-house critique along that line.

The *Report* advised the sophisticated training of industrial labour and the development of State government employment bureaus: acknowledgement here went to the thinking of the current Royal Commission on National Insurance. Immigration was seen as possibly boosting employment. The *Report* made a little stir. 'A platitude is no less a platitude because it is delivered in resounding language by a gentleman on a high salary', sneered Melbourne's Tory *Argus,*[57] and employer interests were sceptical. Bigwigs of Australia's Commonwealth Bank protested that such intervention as Copland enjoined was impossible, short of turning the institution into a full central reserve bank. That would be good, said Copland. Bruce thought the *Report's* ideas were 'sound' if 'somewhat ahead of the time'.[58] He clutched the straw anyway, calling on Premiers to establish further agencies:

> Perhaps it is not too much to say that the Industrial Stability Committees, if properly organised and efficiently conducted, will become the central organisation to deal with the problem of unemployment on a uniform basis throughout the Commonwealth. Possibly the best form of Committee would be one composed of the leaders of industry, representing employers and employees, and permanent officers to represent Government and Civic Authorities, who would attend regular meetings as delegates and lay down lines of policy and programmes of investigation for execution by the staff.[59]

Hogan of Victoria was the only Premier directly to oppose this corporative statesmanship. Elsewhere, tentative moves were made. Employer resistance continued, despite Prime Ministerial heavying.

This episode overlapped with another Brucean ploy: to establish an economic research office. Gepp responded with a justifiable claim that the DMC already so served,[60] but Bruce, like many politicians, preferred a plenitude of advisors. Debate took place as to the location of the office. Gepp reiterated that his Commission did economic work, but he came to think that an elite corps, attached to the Prime Minister's Department and forming the nucleus of a Senior Civil Service, might well address broader policies. Other DMC commentary agreed: able research economists should pursue 'a united effort to gain for Australia a position of eminence in the industrial world'. All this cohered with Bruce's appointment of economists to report on the tariff, and also to foster round-table industrial discussions. An Act of early 1929 established the economics bureau, much as Gepp proposed, but it never was to function. Had it done so, the director might have been J. B. Brigden, whom in August 1928 Bruce extolled: 'Of all the so-called economists with whom I have come in touch I am inclined to think that Brigden ... has the best and most practical mind.' Yet Brigden had been advancing the most acute contemporary questioning of over-capitalised Australian 'development' and of assisted migration.[61]

Migration and the DMC continued to attract critics, above all those who wished to make party-political points. On 23 February 1928 Matthew Charlton, in his last weeks as leader of the Labor Opposition, moved Parliamentary censure against the government's 'failure to adequately protect Australian industries and to limit migration to the nation's ability to absorb new arrivals'. He stressed that the Commonwealth had power over migration, giving it potential to direct the economy; yet that potential had gone for nothing. The DMC talked much and achieved little. Britons and Continentals were 'largely responsible' for the nation's unemployment. Labor speakers reiterated those themes. Bruce made the obvious answers, even affirming a positive link between migration and employment. Appointing boards of enquiry was no cause for shame, continued Bruce; had it prevailed earlier, Australia would have saved much. The DMC's work on fruit-growing best made that point. As for the Commission's critics:

> Cannot they see that they are thus opposing the whole policy of visualising future development, deciding upon a definite policy to be adopted, securing the co-operation of the States with the Commonwealth, and ensuring that developmental schemes shall be of real benefit to the country and increase its absorptive capacity?

Charlton's motion failed, but such rhetoric as his strengthened through the rest of the Commission's life. It provided more material for (always hostile) Parliamentary questions to Bruce than did any other issue; the cost of expert staff was a particular goad. The Prime Minister used all his tough-bluffery in response.

The Premiers' Conference of June 1928 saw variants on these themes.[62] Hogan brought migration under discussion, citing grievous unemployment in Victoria. He called for curtailment of assisted migration and cessation of all alien entry. Most of his fellows spoke in support. The Premiers invited

Bruce to discuss the issue. His speech, presented in camera, referred especially to Europeans' entry, arguing that the international community and the League of Nations were likely to attach increasing importance to free population movement. The matter belonged to that struggle for economic equilibrium on which all hopes for world peace must rest. 'We in Australia, if we antagonised the white races as we have already antagonised the coloured races, might then find ourselves without a friend'; Britain, most importantly, would resist any such policy as Hogan advocated.[63] Then Bruce feinted and told of his government's efforts to moderate European inflow. He had stressed to the Italian Consul-General Australians' pride in their British blood. 'I was sure a national aspiration such as this would appeal to no-one in the world more greatly than it would to his Excellency Signor Mussolini, with his own great national aspirations in regard to the Italian people.' As for unemployment, Italians in Australia markedly avoided that fate. Nevertheless, Bruce agreed to tighten quotas on European entry—while himself continuing publicly to scorn this xenophobia. He was happier in urging the Premiers to fulfil the business-stability proposals.

Notable among other critics of the DMC was Alexander Hay, chieftain of a NSW pastoral family. In late 1928 Hay propounded to the OSD another upper-class migration scheme. This aimed to train aspirants in sheep-station management, with the rich pastoral firm of Dalgety ready to provide finance. 'The only fear I've got is that Mr Gepp ... may block such an organisation unless he controls it', wrote Hay; 'the public is very fed up with him and his expensive department ... he has an expensive staff at work, no results to date.'[64]

Bruce went to the polls in November 1928. His staff sought advice from the DMC as to one proposal, virgin and entire, that it had fostered. The nearest to an answer was the Wyangala Dam in New South Wales, but even there final endorsement had yet to arrive from HMG.[65] Even so, Nationalist publicity-writers proposed DMC material for their *Speakers' Handbook*, but then the Commission demanded the passages be cleansed of 'party' calculation.[66] In the event, the DMC took small place in Bruce's armoury, a sharp contrast to 1925. Rather, critics used migration and the Commission to harry the government. It lost several seats, but remained in office.

*   *   *

Australian relations with the OSC and OSD were at some points more cordial in the later 1920s than earlier. The Amery–Whiskard–Huxley venture helped that process along, as did the arrival at Australia House of Manning. Despite all tensions and disillusion with the Dominions, the OSC *Report* for 1928 sustained an idealist view of migration: E. G. Wakefield had been right

Bruce's Army: Labor electoral propaganda, 1928. (National Library of Australia: Theodore Papers, MS 7222; reproduced by permission.)

in giving first heed to colonies' intrinsic welfare rather than seeking 'the solution of immediate problems created by the redundancy of labour in this country'.[67] This *Report* also endorsed redistribution of secondary industry throughout the Empire according to integrated and rational plan. This idea was to gain increasing, even tedious, vogue.

In mid-year the OSD put to Treasury a proposal, hatched between the DMC and Whiskard in late 1927. It provided that if HMG's Australian Representative approved any 'undertaking' within the Agreement, it should have virtual guarantee of approval; in other words, there should prevail what most parties originally assumed to be intended practice.[68] Treasury refused, scorning 'this extraordinary document, typical of Dominions Office "statesmanship" '. Another fruit of the Australian tripping of late 1927 was a proposal that all States prepare five-year plans for their Agreement activities. This idea had originated with the DMC, but by its desire was promulgated by the OSD so as to give the Commission a whip with which to hurry the States. The proposal formed part of a memorandum of August 1928 which also conveyed that Treasury approval remained necessary for 'undertakings', and that HMG still believed Australia bound to take 450,000 migrants in the decade, should all Agreement money be taken up. This memorandum presumably prompted the Commission's subsequent call on the States to rationalise and streamline their developmental programmes under a potent Director, but otherwise had little impact.[69]

All the while, Amery and the OSD toyed with amending the Settlement Act, and/or subsidising fares so as to reduce interference in passenger movement by Australian regulations.[70] Oscar Thompson was involved, hoping to cut down-payments to £5. Thompson was in touch with Gepp, who in November declared that such a scheme was impossible, as the States would 'bitterly oppose any suggestion of bringing into this country a large number of people without means'. Gepp's riposte was that HMG should abandon its means test for the fare-subsidy. This received some consideration in Whitehall. It overlapped with pondering of a Tasmanian proposal whereby the State planned to advance loans for fares, up to first-class, for people of means. The Tasmanians hoped that its beneficiaries would be exempt from usual health checks on assisted migrants, but the Commonwealth affirmed that it would give its subsidy only after full scrutiny. That decision diminished the OSD's interest. The Tasmanians passed their Act, which after much effort attracted six families, most to suffer antipodean tragi-comedy.[71]

Underlying all this was an intensified Australian restiveness at migration. That most traditional of Governors, Lord Gowrie of South Australia, advised HMG in December 1928 that movement be discouraged.[72] An interesting exchange took place at this time when the DMC (not until then!) became aware that posters, printed by the OSD and distributed throughout Britain, summonsed to Australia 'men for the land; women for the home', with 'employment guaranteed; good wages; plenty of opportunity'.[73] Cables went to Manning, asking that such optimism be muted. Gepp urged that boys rather than men be targeted. 'The Home authorities were very emphatic in their opinion that such action would cause grave comment at this end', came Manning's response. Gepp continued emphatic, but the only change was to have 'plenty of opportunity' replaced with 'good prospects'.

Pervasive negativism vis-à-vis migration continued to anger Bankes Amery as he dealt with Australian officialdom. He made the charge against Gepp himself in September 1927.[74] Thereafter the Representative's despatches were most interesting for further detailing the miseries of migrant farmers in Victoria.[75] By early 1928 he was disbursing up to £25 apiece to those in distress: 'Are they to starve? We cannot escape responsibility, because we encouraged the Victorian settlers to come out and so far as I know we have taken no effective steps to enforce the Agreement.'[76] The reference was to the Agreement's clauses as to 'satisfactory' settlement. Bankes Amery now urged Gepp to action, who in turn sought Bruce's approval of token relief. 'The Prime Minister was much concerned about the situation, but thought he could not risk trouble with the Victorian government by sanctioning the proposal.' Governor Somers continued his involvement, arranging for the *Argus* newspaper to publicise the issue.

Settlers became increasingly vehement in protest. A leader was P. A. O. Gray, whom with several others the Victorian government had moved to evict. Gepp 'fought like a tiger' on Gray's behalf, Bankes Amery reported, but perhaps that only steeled the dissident in his anger.[77] Another of like resolve was P. R. Nightingale, more impressive than Gray, and capable of fierce prose:

> Are the first settlers mere cannon fodder then, to be thrown into the battle and when their money and their hopes are gone, sacrificed that others may succeed? If that is the case it is a most heartless swindle, yet everything points to that.[78]

Indeed it did. Nightingale spoke as leader of a branch (at Murrabit, northern Victoria) of an Overseas Settlers Association, which evolved at this time.

The fate of erstwhile Indian Army officers settled by Australian Farms Limited had become notorious enough to prompt an official enquiry in mid-1928.[79] Bankes Amery thought the majority report was far too gentle with both government and company; the fact that the chairman submitted a minority statement, much more abrasive, supported his claim. E. W. M. Wood, the Representative's assistant, made further investigation and stressed that government had coerced Australian Farms to take land which the State had bought at excessive cost. This burden passed to the farmers. The company had failed to make due preparations, and misled prospective

Publicity or propaganda? (Australian Archives: 434/1; 49/3/21685; reproduced by permission of the Department of Immigration and Ethnic Affairs.)

buyers. Meanwhile the chief recruiter, H. A. Currie, flourished as a grazier-sportsman-politician; he later served in non-Labor governments, and won a knighthood.[80]

There were further wrangles over Victoria's Agreement 'undertakings'. The Nowingi railroad story has been told. More modest and sensible proposals concerned road building in the Mallee and Gippsland. While the proposals were being considered, Premier Hogan declared opposition to virtually all assisted migration. Bankes Amery thought that must abort the road negotiations. Gepp urged him to relent, stressing how desperate was unemployment in Victoria. The Representative succumbed, with grumbles as to the Agreement securing nought for the British taxpayer; 'moreover all our plans are in danger of subsequent fanciful legislation which will neutralise past efforts'.[81] Commissioner Mulvany spent much time in later 1928 striving to untangle the State's land schemes. The Victorians were told that they had 'received advances considerably in excess of the amount which your Government is entitled to claim'. Their response was to claim more. Relations between Commonwealth and the State worsened, Bruce and Hogan disputing on DMC and migration matters.[82]

On 11 September arrived in Western Australia Bankes Amery's successor as Representative, E. T. Crutchley. As diarist and autobiographer, Crutchley endears himself to the historian, and by other criteria too probably had greater substance than his precursor. Crutchley reminisced that Bankes Amery was disgruntled by the OSD's failure to support himself, as against both Treasury and Australians.[83] The newcomer did not repeat such complaints. However, he was never to bond with Commissioner Mulvany, who met him in the West. 'A queer, nervous fellow', the Englishman found his counterpart; 'a typical civil servant'.[84] Austral-Irish to the core, in the service forty years, Mulvany personified a style opposite to Crutchley's, accented by their common-but-so-different Catholicism. Mulvany's views on migration probably followed, say, E. J. Hogan's.

Crutchley's fellow first-class voyagers had disparaged British migrants. His initial engagement at Perth was with an ostensibly pro-migrant body—where, remarkably and (he found) offensively, the tirade continued. Yet Crutchley's own first report, of a WA group-settlement, remarked that too many Britons preferred wage-labour to their own farms, and that even farmers showed improvidence: few kept gardens and three had bought pianolas at vast time-payment debt. He judged that migrants who deserved to would struggle through, and sympathised with Westralians' concern at the enormous settlement costs their taxes were defraying.[85] Crutchley traversed the continent by Christmas. In Queensland he met Catholic Archbishop James Duhig, to be told that Britain was emigrating criminals. Queensland bureaucrats grouched at federal direction on migration matters; the NSW committee formed by Bavin was much more promising.

Crutchley discussed with the DMC proposals for subsidised fares outside the Settlement Act. Just possible, came the answer, if recipients had capital.

On 20 December Crutchley met with the British Empire Mission, another of those imperial enquiries which crowded the decade. The Mission arrived in Australia only a few days after Crutchley. 'The Big Four', as colloquialism went, were Sir Arthur Duckham, chemical engineer and cousin of F. L. McDougall, who hoped that Duckham might convert his intimate, Winston Churchill, to sympathy for Australia;[86] Hugo Hirst, managing director of General Electric, and active in the Empire Industries Association; D. O. Malcolm, director of the British South Africa company; and Ernest Clark, previously head of Treasury in Northern Ireland, now in business. Liaising with them was Frank Skevington of HMG's Treasury (and its member-elect on the OSC); he was to have formed a two-man delegation with Lord Lovat, but came alone when the latter's health failed. The Mission brought in train some twenty-five aides, servants, and relations. The size of the party prompted H. F. Farrands to advise that the usual request for State governments to help with costs would probably suffer 'a most unfavourable reception'.[87] The Empire Marketing Board was the chief subsidiser of the mission.[88]

The venture's history dated back to late 1926 when Gepp, still in Britain, had proposed to Amery and Lord Clarendon 'that a Committee appointed by the British Government should visit Australia to confer with the DMC, and later with the Federal Cabinet, on the development of Australia in relation to the readjustment of the white population of the Empire on an economic basis'.[89] Bruce endorsed the idea, his pertinent cable stressing the current interest of American investors in Australia. Australia could go the way of Canada, he said, towards an economy 'financed with American money and controlled by Americans. This can only be countered by visits of really first class people.'[90] That surely meant that Bruce hoped to use the Mission to strengthen Australia's status on the London borrowing market.[91] More specifically, according to Trade Commissioner Dalton, Bruce was ready to have the Mission probe Australia's tariff structure 'and be much influenced in modification of policy' thereby. How Bruce's opponents would have seized upon that! E. G. Theodore blasted the Mission as 'a reflection on the capacity of Australians; ... a declaration of incompetence on the part of Ministers ... savouring of burlesque'.[92]

Again HMG's Treasury took a stand complementary to that of Bruce's domestic critics. At first it forecast difficulty in finding good men for the Mission, and indeed not one of the cohort first considered eventually went.[93] Treasury's objections went further.

It is going to be extremely difficult for them, having regard to the condition of labour politics in Australia, to give the advice which they ought to give (vide, for instance, Lord Salisbury's recent note), without becoming a source of controversy.

So said Otto Niemeyer. Months later, British bureaucrats agonised whether Hugo Hirst's German roots should preclude his candidature. 'This mission is not popular in labour and other circles in Australia, which hold that all the necessary thinking can be done by Australian natives', wrote Lovat's secretary; 'and it is conceivable that Sir Hugo's origins might be made the subject of comment.'

Canberra's perspective went otherwise. 'We have got rid of the Duke', wrote Bruce to McDougall on 21 May 1927 about the scarce-completed triumph of the York visit, and then turned to the Mission. 'The main point is to get these people out here, and educate them a little, so that they will in time be able to educate the right people in Britain.' In the following months Bruce's enthusiasm waned, even towards apprehension: 'we will have to keep them away from some of those people who cannot speak about Australia without damning it'.[94] During the summer of 1928 McDougall applied himself to giving the Big Four a '*dynamic*' view of Australia.[95] As they approached landfall, Bruce followed suit, writing to Duckham that indeed Australia had applied tariffs beyond economic rationality, but (yes, Sir Arthur) opinion was changing.[96] To McDougall, Bruce confessed that political pressure for tariffs was irresistible. Schedules were still rising, just as were overseas loans.[97] The Prime Minister pursued with Duckham the notion of rationalising secondary industry between Britain and Australia, citing iron and steel.

The DMC's position paper for the Mission duly addressed tariffs.[98] Their harm, went the tortuous argument, had been to foster workshops which swarmed in backyard anarchy. 'This mischievous profusion of small and marginal plants will best be checked by reorganisation of industries, possibly in the form of a financial organisation, from the top downwards.' The Commission's reports on the fruit and gold industries were cited as offering models for such action. 'The type of settler most likely to increase Australia's prosperity comes on his own initiative attracted by the opportunities and standards of life created by the inhabitants themselves', went the paper's brief remark on migration. The meaning was that the Commission did not much like the current situation. Further, it declared, public opinion would not allow over-rapid development (scan, through big migration schemes) which might threaten living standards. In difficult juxtaposition, it made the further claim that 'the period of easy living is definitely passing. Haphazard methods will no longer provide for the growing needs of the community.'

The Mission came to altogether predictable conclusions, saying much the same as had other Establishment Britons through recent years, with a sugar coating.[99] Public debt was too heavy, developmental money often misspent on unrewarding adventures. Deflation was 'the course of wisdom'. The DMC and CSIR were showing the way to happier practice. Migration languished because of economic despond in general and lesser public expenditure. (The Mission did not ask whether deflation would not intensify this situation.) The Agreement suffered many difficulties: its nature encouraged 'schemes not fully matured', worthy though the DMC had been in counter-effect. It might be amended so that the 'developing' States did not have to absorb so many migrants, and it should subsidise scientific investigation as to more intensive land use via agriculture and dairying. Nothing would be achieved, however, unless production costs diminished. Tariffs and the wage-arbitration system therefore demanded radical revision. The Mission met unionists who had been as emphatic as employers in criticising present structures of arbitration; judicial and government involvement therein should be minimised. (Bruce had hopes that the Mission would encourage a more 'co-operative' approach among unionists, and initiated meetings to this end.)[100] There followed more specific advice on various aspects of public policy. Ought not the Directors of the Commonwealth Bank, on its proposed transition to a Reserve Bank, be appointed by non-government agencies? The civil service should have a 'cadre' of more highly-qualified men: CSIR and DMC should grow, so too the economics bureau. Pastoralists might be assured of greater security over their leaseholds, and transport should be co-ordinated to reduce public expenditure and losses.

Even this lukewarmth was contrived. Pollyanna McDougall applauded that *any* report appeared in print, as rumours about the Mission's first reactions led him to suppose that Bruce might avoid that outcome.[101] Malcolm, supported by Skevington, would have terminated the Agreement save for one last enquiry into intensive farming, whereas the others decided to be more 'political'.[102] In discussion, Crutchley had denounced the Agreement's failure; he countered Gepp's rhetoric as to the need for 'the long view' by insisting on HMG's wish to see migrants absorbed, and he became angry when Gepp refused point-blank to ease the entry of unemployed miners. Skevington endorsed Gepp's 'long view', presumably because it implied little immediate demand for funds. Yet otherwise his Treasury-style modified, so that Crutchley judged him to be attaining some sympathy for the Australian situation. The Representative suggested that this might duly ease relations between the OSD and Treasury—although as Crutchley had lost faith with the Agreement, there appears paradox in his so hoping. Anyway, Skevington never softened much. He did not like the notion of encouraging Australian butter production, for example, being appalled that such largesse should go to an industry already subsidised by government.[103] He judged that such immigration as had occurred was achieved only by 'reckless' borrowing; like Crutchley he believed the WA group-settlers to have been spoonfed, luxuriating in gramophones, pianos, cars and holidays.[104] Australia's triennial elections and the reliance of its politicians on Parliamentary salaries meant that 'all Governments have their ear continually to the ground and policies are shaped to popular feeling however unsound'. Bruce half-recognised Australia's crisis, but still it worsened. 'Unhealthy position will very likely as in 1893 lead to crash which may not be long delayed.'

Whitehall discussed these matters as they came to hand.[105] Macnaghten scoffed at Skevington's shock-horror, saying that the OSD and OSC long had known all such things, and would have said many of them in the OSC 1927 *Report* had not discretion prevailed. Perhaps that hit at L. S. Amery, but Macnaghten agreed with his boss in rejecting the Malcolm–Skevington proposal for shutting the Agreement. However, when the final report arrived, Macnaghten waxed apocalyptic. Fired by an interview with John Sanderson, he invoked a likely sequence for Australia of 'deflation … unemployment … civil commotion … redness in the sky'. Treasury's reactions were blander. Cuthbertson thought the document essentially sound, but too generous with its 'whitewash', which might strengthen an Australian case for further borrowing; any move to extend the Agreement to subsidise research into farming must be resisted.

Gepp and Bruce both wrote of the Mission with apparent acclaim. The former upheld it as promising to broadcast true understanding, always grasped by 'a minute proportion of the population', of Australia's post-war economic dilemma.[106] Bruce concurred, especially when writing to McDougall.[107] His letters of thanks to the Missionaries might appear altogether froth and form,[108] were not events of later 1929 to suggest that their work indeed had shaped his own thinking. Bruce may even have believed that Duckham and Hirst had influenced labour opinion.

*   *   *

The Mission was one of many events pertinent to our story, overlapping and zigzagging, confounding confusion. Such chaos was appropriate to months in which world capitalism staggered towards doom, but it presents difficulty for the order-seeking analyst. It prevails most of all in respect to the DMC's story, which continued central and indicative.

As already illustrated, this record had positive aspects. Even when modifying some developments or aborting others, the Commission and its staff could and did feel that they were working for a longer, more positive good. Gepp himself every so often spoke in optimistic, if inconsistent ways. Scores of fat files in the Australian Archives tell of continuing enquiries into many potential stimuli for the national economy. All this was evident in the Commission's *Report* for 1928.[109] A foreword proclaimed the DMC's credo:

Efficiency and success in industry, whether primary or secondary, largely depend upon the elimination of waste—the object of scientific and economic research and of business management in every progressive country. Waste does not lie entirely in processes or methods of production. It obtains in a specially grave form and to a lamentable degree in neglect of the sources of production— in the relative unproductiveness of assets like the lands, for the improvement of which the public has shouldered heavy obligations.

The improvement of soils and pastures and of herds and flocks, the eradication of pests and diseases, the economic application of mechanical power, the perfection of farm management, the determination of the extent and nature of the most economic farm unit, the utilisation of by-products, the economic application of the principle of fodder conservation, the establishment of secondary industries utilising agricultural products and by-products, the introduction of first-class systems of marketing—advances like these give a new productive value to land and offer inducements for bringing it under intense cultivation. Knowledge of progressive movements can be sought both at home and abroad, and turned to account with reasonable promptitude.

The remedy for ineffective use of the most valuable sections of the public estate is not to be found in the immediate application of some specific or panacea. It is to be sought, rather, in the adoption of a consistent public policy, vitalised by Commonwealth and State departments and instrumentalities responsible for all possible assistance in promoting the country's progress. It is necessary to awaken public intelligence to the gravity of the situation and to create a stern driving force of public opinion. Government agencies, public bodies and many progressive land-owners in Australia are already studying the latest advances in land development. They are keeping an open mind for new ideas and are disseminating information that will demonstrate the means by which enterprise can be profitably extended.

The *Report* invoked the Empire Mission's arguments to like effect, especially regarding intensive agriculture. 'The remarkable absence of unbalanced criticism' as to the Mission was hailed as showing a maturity in Australian public opinion which justified 'quiet optimism' for the future. Articulation of Commonwealth–State planning and the advance of research, scientific and economic, further upheld such hope. That the DMC had authorised relatively few schemes resulted from its application of properly objective criteria.

Yet the *Report* recognised big problems. The War had killed 60,000 of Australia's 'best manhood', disrupted world and Empire trade, imposed a cruel financial debt. Continuing crisis was the inexorable result. 'Obviously the first duty of the country is to find satisfactory and profitable employment for its own people', continued an affirmation which told much of the DMC's attitude to migration, while also stressing the need for capital: some £750 investment was necessary to sustain each new job, and on present demography 38,000 '*extra* breadwinners' were entering the workforce annually.

The *Report* called for minimising luxuries so that money might be available to create employment, but not only luxuries appeared in a list of goods proposed for import-replacement. Of primary industries, fruits, tobacco, fishing, paper, and mining received the same kind of comment as in other DMC statements. Possible use as fuel of the (very high) wastage in timber processing linked with general advocacy of motorised transport, a subject under continuing review from John Northcott's committee. The Commission sponsored the Australian National Travel Organisation and envisaged great boosting:

> Here we have a land wherein there are riches almost beyond imagination. Soil, climate and rainfall combine for remarkable productivity. Here we have a New World, possessing a tourist appeal principally because it is Australian with a heritage of sunshine and beauty unlike that of other countries. Here is a land which we can confidently recommend to the investor, the investor-settler, and the tourist.

What a contrast to the sombre economicism of the mainstream *Report* and to most other aspects of the DMC story.

Saddest among these was the Commission's work in Tasmania. Reconstitution of the State Development Advisory Board as an advisory committee to the DMC, and appointment of P. J. Perry as Director of Development (who devised Tasmania's major effort to generate migration, giving fare-loans to wealthier people) gave a little promise that the island might become a model of modern political economy. That chimera soon shattered.

The most eventful scenario occurred within the State's Department of Agriculture, whither the DMC had vested its warmest hopes and committed most federal money.[110] The Department's troubles dated back at least to 1926 when F. E. Ward, Tasmanian by background but immediately from New Zealand, was appointed Director, which step itself antagonised some older members. This was nothing to the feeling that developed when the Department was expanded, as advised by the DMC. It will be remembered that from New Year 1928 Alexander Nelson headed research work. Nelson took his office seriously, and expected solid funding. Tension developed between his group—generally newcomers, comparatively well-paid and prestigious—and the 'extension' staff whose task (also much esteemed by the DMC) was to take science to the farmers. In the consequent power-battle, Ward sided with the extension staff. Nelson, after much buffeting, resigned in August 1929. The current Minister, Walter Lee (Lyons had been succeeded as Premier by J. C. McPhee in June 1928), responded by dismissing Nelson, but uproar forced an enquiry which praised the latter's work. Nelson went back to Edinburgh, remarkably unembittered. Tensions continued to rack the Agriculture Department. Through it all there probably percolated some stimulus to improve farm practice.

The Agricultural Bureaux became tangled in these matters. It appears that, under G. F. Finlay's direction, they did arouse hope, even enthusiasm, among rank-and-file farmers. For some reason, however, the Bureaux organisation was established outside the Department. Finlay and Ward became hostile, the former obsessive in his plans for the Bureaux and paranoid as to criticism.[111] The DMC recalled him to Melbourne in mid-1928. Under new leadership the Bureaux had modest effect through the years ahead.[112] That achievement did not extend to developing co-operative marketing schemes such as the DMC cherished. Legislation proposed in summer 1927–8 never became statute. The scheme concerning eggs fell into ever-deeper mire; a similar plan for fat lambs also failed. Tasmanian farmers would not co-operate as the DMC believed they should.

The Commission's involvement with Tasmanian forestry had a similar pattern.[113] Here the central figure was Conservator Irby, a man of much enthusiasm but dubious judgment, both traits evident in his scheme for putting migrant boys into plantation homes. Irby antagonised various people—many timber millers, and farm-boosters who disliked being told that forestry was a better use for much land. The DMC set up an industry organisation among the millers, and planned to revamp the Department; chief advisor was C. E. Lane-Poole, Commonwealth Inspector-General of forests. While he and Gepp plotted to minimise Irby's defects, the Conservator was sacked, in April 1928, for alleged sexual association with boys.[114] His plantation scheme indeed had a homo-erotic strain, but Irby's friends rallied and their agitation prompted the man first chosen as his successor to withdraw.[115] The Forestry Department long remained very modest. Meanwhile, the timber industry proved as recalcitrant as the farmers in refusing to conform to the Commission model.

Tasmanian expenditure on public transport more than conformed to the national pattern abominated by the DMC: railway debt still lay heavy, while demand for roads forced much further spending.[116] The Commission appointed its usual enquiry-by-experts, who urged that the State establish a powerful Transport Board, free from duress. Again the outcome was different, with the McPhee government going its vote-winning, parochial way. Gepp and Senator Pearce shook their fists in vain.

The Commission pursued other local enquiries into various branches of the fruit industry, into minerals, into dairying, fishing and pig-raising—but to no happier result.[117] A nice touch came from the scientist who conducted the geophysical mining survey in Tasmania: 'I doubt that we shall have any startling finds to report; the old-fashioned prospector seems to have done his work very completely.'[118] A fisheries project had interest inasmuch as its backers hoped to get support under the Agreement in return for employing sixty skilled migrant-fishermen.[119] It had some fantasy, but nothing as to that advanced by an erstwhile employee of Gepp's at Electrolytic Zinc. He proposed formation of an elite group who would bend their genius to uplifting the nation, and receive formal honour in reward. Its initial project should be

> a complete road-making train, the front of which will break up existing worn-out roads, while from its rear new complete roads will extend … It will operate at the rate of one mile per day and will not interrupt traffic because a continuous road will be provided over the top.[120]

Gepp, whose building of Electrolytic Zinc had made him a Tasmanian hero, now suffered ridicule, notably from the *Mercury* newspaper and the Hobart Chamber of Commerce. He was presented as exercising 'Dictatorship'; his Tasmanian supporters, allegedly strong in the island's wicked north, were 'Federal temporisers'.[121] Former federal minister and political adventurer J. A. Jensen declared the Commission 'one of the worst things that had happened to Tasmania'.[122] The local Parliament heard such comment from others. In March 1929 J. A. Lyons supported Premier McPhee in seeking yet further aid from the Commonwealth: 'they had sent experts over to advise us, but their advice had not remedied our troubles'.[123] The Prime Minister's refusal cited the Tasmanian failure to do as the DMC recommended on transport.

Western Australia also told troubles, as the DMC still side-tracked the plan for 3500 more farms. Gepp had become very critical of government and bureaucracy there; most galling was the failure to take legislative action to check speculation in land designated for settlement schemes. Rather, such speculation had been encouraged.[124] Also contributing to the Commission's decision was a report by an agricultural scientist, L. J. H. Teakle, who stressed salinity of soils in the projected area.[125] So resounded the message that the Commission could see little way ahead for Australia.

Migration matters ran parallel. Requisitions especially of men fell further, intensifying the general decline in numbers. Economies reduced staff at Australia House. Director Manning could scarcely protest: in July 1928 he said in public that 'the best plan, I think, is to take migration out of the hands of Governments'.[126] Eight months later the DMC advised further reduction of entry.[127] Whitehall complemented this malaise. Treasury stayed as hostile to Australia as ever. The OSD havered, awaiting new approaches on lines advised by the Empire Mission, but in April–May 1929 it told Crutchley to discourage Agreement activity.[128] Accession of Labour to government in June strengthened the restrictive thrust. Philip Snowden, Chancellor again, had just written an article for *John Bull* with the question-begging title, 'Is the Empire Bleeding Britain?'[129] Sidney Webb (Lord Passfield) had more sympathy for Empire and migration than that, but scarcely filled Amery's place as Colonial/Dominions Secretary. The new OSC Chairman, A. A. Ponsonby (of Grey descent), spoke of reducing fares to Australia and reconstituting the OSC as a statutory body, but nothing developed.[130]

Inert though the DMC itself was becoming, Crutchley yet argued that the deepening negativism of HMG's policy went close to bad faith vis-à-vis Australia,[131] and Bankes Amery also spoke thus on his return to the OSD. He did not make much way, reported Manning.[132] When the Audit and Exchequer Office enquired, in apparent innocence, as to some Agreement schemes, Bankes Amery advised to 'tell them quite frankly that for political reasons, we shall never be able to get our money back again'.[133] His statement affirmed that Australia had provided little of the documentation required under the Agreement. While the ex-Representative had learned to accept such behaviour, it reinforced Australia's critics in Whitehall. 'The sooner the crash comes the better for Australia', wrote Skevington in July, 'for the longer things are allowed to drift the greater will be the dislocation.'[134] When Crutchley wrote of an 'undertaking' whereby the Agreement might fund more fruit-growing in the Murray region, dedicated to the British market, the OSC responded that the Australians knew the scheme would be rejected, and wanted it thus, so as to deflect any charge from Britain as to lethargy in attracting migrants.[135] Whitehall now accepted that Australia offered little to farmer or farmworker. One of Macnaghten's last memoranda pondered why this should be, when Continentals so often succeeded.

> I suppose the answer is that these foreigners go from a low civilisation to a higher, bad to better prospects; our people, on the other hand, go from the amenities of an industrial and old civilisation to a rough life which requires immense effort.[136]

What British initiative survived as to emigration had passed to an inter-departmental body, the Overseas Development and Migration Committee. (How deliberately that title followed the DMC is unknown.) The Committee boosted a scheme advanced by J. R. J. Passmore, a Ministry of Labour man who had visited Australia in late 1927.[137] Aiming at grand private-enterprise land colonisation in Western Australia, Passmore echoed various ideas of the preceding decade. Most recently such notions had emitted from James Mitchell of Western Australia, Josiah Wedgood (very surprisingly), and D. H. Drummond, a Minister in the NSW government. Italians and Greeks, averred Drummond, were prospering in Australia through chain migration, financed by ethnic communality.[138] Whiskard also advanced ideas akin to Passmore's. Further backing came from Passmore's boss, Horace Wilson, who in April had protested to Gepp at the near-cessation of Australian requisitions for men, after his department had expensively trained them.[139] Treasury opposed the Passmore scheme, nor were all in the OSD enthusiastic. A working-party comprising Bankes Amery, Whiskard and Eady surveyed possibilities.[140] Whiskard, especially through studying the success of Cadburys' confectionery plant in Tasmania, joined those calling for Britain to share industrialisation with Australia.[141] Arthur Duckham, who with other Mission members struggled, against dominant investor opinion, to improve Austral–British relations, said the same, most interestingly to Baldwin.[142] Even the Board of Trade presented a sympathetic minute on these lines to Cabinet.[143]

Crutchley's despatches and diary of 1929 generally chanted doom. The DMC's coldness towards migration was central to this. When Crutchley reported HMG's disposition further to tighten the Agreement, he met anger from the Commissioners and rudeness from Pearce: 'evidently a British Government Representative can do anything he likes so long as he doesn't represent the views of the B.G!' Crutchley thus suffered from both sides as he delivered messages. From May, Gepp's chief commitment was membership of a Royal Commission into the coal industry—a further sign of the DMC's torpor.

Crutchley continued to agonise over migrant farmers in Victoria and Western Australia. At worst, the latter story offered 'a tragic monument of stupidity', at best 'a scheme for the survival of the fittest'.[144] Bankes Amery, Crutchley, and Skevington all disputed Commissioner Mulvany's defence of the Victorian situation.[145] Crutchley's contacts with farmers there left him impressed with their stoic courage; 'there was very little bitterness except in regard to the false promises made in Australia House; ... a general air of cheerfulness and good humour ... no optimism, only a hope born of despair'.[146] He proposed a relief fund for those in distress, indicating that Skevington had seemed amenable to the idea when in Australia; but now that worthy vetoed such expenditure, although admitting it in Canada, so as to thwart French-Canadians from making capital out of British migrants' poverty.[147] The OSD continued to receive documentation of distress in rural Victoria, notably from one Charles Clarke:

> Will now the British Government stand by and turn a deaf ear to the truth known to them? To be quietened by what are no more than utterly false official statements, when the truth is that these men lay hopeless with their wives and children, nailed to the Southern Cross ...[148]

In September 1929 the Victorian government agreed to yet further enquiry.[149]

The DMC never abandoned all hope for progress. It attached some, for example, to forays into intensive farming, which the Empire Mission had endorsed, tentatively. Likewise the Commission approved when in January 1929 the Premiers advised amendment of the Agreement to allow funding of British experts and entrepreneurs who might lift Australian performance in both primary and secondary industry.[150] Writing to Christopher Turnor in mid-year, Gepp affirmed the 'practically unlimited' demand worldwide for foodstuffs; Australia should aim at 'proper processing' of germane exports, acting as 'a retail rather than a wholesale merchant'.[151] At a further Premiers' Conference in June, much paperwork came from the DMC, with stress on the need for the States to pursue the 'Business Stability' agenda.[152] Press releases from the Commission followed a hortatory, almost evangelical line, urging 'Live-Wire Citizenship' against pessimism and timidity.[153] In September–October 1929 the Commission, at Gepp's behest, publicised a consumptionist high-wage argument, drawn from Americans E. F. Gay and W. C. Mitchell, for economic recovery.[154] This clashed with many of Gepp's other pronouncements, yet it accords with the recollection of his secretary-aide that he urged the Prime Minister to attempt an heroic response to the country's economic troubles—but found Bruce 'too proud' to respond.[155]

Conceivably such an exchange lay behind Gepp's letter to McDougall (of all people!) which expressed his admiration for Philip Snowden's honesty in denouncing imperial preferences. 'I am sorry he is not in office out here', wrote he in whom Bruce had put such store; economic truths must prevail, now affirmed the Chairman, 'however the politicians may twist and turn'.[156] Writing to D. O. Malcolm, Gepp claimed good sense among Australians in accepting the Mission's *Report* and thinking. As for migration, 'the position ... has adjusted itself to economic conditions in this country as we have always said that it would; realities have to be faced however unpleasant and inconvenient they may be'.[157]

A passage in relations between the Commission and Whitehall ranked high among the strangenesses of 1929. Early that year Skevington reported on his Australian tour, to explosive effect. He spoke in true Treasury style:

> Australia has strayed so far from the path of economic sanity that she is not likely to get back without a good deal of pain. The Australian people, whilst they have some excellent qualities, are very conceited and ignorant; and their ignorance of economics is pathetic. They have a profound belief in the greatness of their country. Favoured with a warm and sunny climate, they are pleasure-loving and optimistic, living for the day and trusting to luck for the morrow. They are also strongly collectivist, and have learnt to rely on Governments to help them over difficulties and to make things easy for them.[158]

Class hostility, Skevington judged, traced back to convict settlement, and remained a heavy burden. Australia also suffered from its politicians and their populist ways. References to Bruce and Gepp were generous, but into the mouths of each Skevington put tendentious words. The Prime Minister, he said, had declared that dairy-farming did not offer scope for worthwhile development. Skevington used this datum to sustain Treasury opposition to amending the Agreement so as to enable subsidy for intensified farming. He also grudged allowing surpluses of migrant numbers in some States to balance debits in others. Furthermore:

> Mr Gepp told me *in confidence* that he was personally not anxious to see the Agreement amended at this stage because he believes (as I do) that no serious attempt will be made to increase efficiency in the secondary industries except through adversity and serious unemployment, and in order to help force the unemployment issue he does not want anything done that might induce the States to relax their efforts to find openings for migrants.

Skevington sent a confidential copy of all this to Gepp. A tremendous storm then broke, the latter deciding after much agony to break confidence and tell his Ministers of the contents.[159] Both he and Bruce denied Skevington's attributions. Did they lie? That Skevington sent his report to Gepp enhances its credibility. The Gepp attribution is astonishing, but Gepp could be astonishing, in a manic-depressive way. At his behest, Skevington retracted, in the most formal terms; Treasury agreed to cleanse the offending paragraph from the records, but there it stays.

All the while, the Commission pondered revision of the Agreement, along the lines that Skevington abhorred. But the DMC's wheels turned ever slower. 'It is the clumsiest machine I've ever met for getting things *done*', wrote Crutchley on 3 October.[160] Eight days later Gepp addressed Malcolm, as quoted above, and on the 12th Bruce's government suffered massive electoral defeat. The Prime Minister lost his own seat.

Issues central to this book helped vanquish Bruce.[161] Fundamentally, the Agreement had failed in upholding British-founded capitalism in Australia. This was so despite substantial and genuine effort by the Commission: notwithstanding all variations, its dominant message had been that by capitalism's own standards, Australia offered little scope for productive development. Critics had found more specific grounds for complaint against the DMC: in Parliamentary debate (in March) on the economic research bureau, Opposition speakers had alleged on one hand that the proposal showed Bruce's loss of faith in the Commission, on the other that it and the bureau might conspire to supplant Protection with ruthless *laissez-faire*.[162] Also espousing such views was the *Age* newspaper,[163] influential among such bourgeois moderates in Melbourne as rejected Bruce. The government's support, however modified, of assisted migration probably counted further against it; moreover W. M. Hughes especially had included charges of softness vis-à-vis Italian entry in the long crusade he maintained against the Prime Minister, itself crucial in the background to 12 October. Much more so, by general agreement, was Bruce's professed intent to cease federal involvement in wage arbitration. The Empire Mission's advice may have prompted that move. If so, Bruce was indeed hoist with his own petard. The Mission had destroyed, not saved him.

Thus to speak assumes that Bruce wanted to win. Some analysts have doubted that, but probably they underplay the man's will-to-power. His hope to save Austral–British capitalism may have been as desperate as any of the contemporary world, yet it was no less tenacious for that. This helps make the poll of 12 October 1929 one of the most decisive and dramatic in Australian history.

CHAPTER SEVEN

Nadir: 1929–1935

The accession in Australia of a Labor government under J. H. Scullin was followed within days by the Wall Street crash. Thereafter Australia and the world pitched into turmoil. Migration issues remained salient in Australian affairs, but in a negative way. Assistance virtually ended, as did the DMC and later, the Agreement. In several years more people left the country than entered it, a phenomenon unique in peace-time. Yet the 'nadir' had politics and drama at least as intense as earlier whirl, zenith, and confusion.

The supreme source for the immediate post-election time is E. T. Crutchley's diary. On the post-poll Monday it reported discussions with John Gunn, whom old gossip had declared to have joined the DMC after consulting with the now Prime Minister. True to that scenario, Gunn 'speaks well of Scullin and can't see how he can stop migration'. Next day the diarist told that campaign talk of abolishing the Commission seemed likely to evaporate into its reconstitution; then the probability appeared that the office would transfer to Canberra, shedding Gepp. Meanwhile, in Whitehall William Bankes Amery minuted that the new government was unlikely to make drastic moves.[1] Evidently HMG now cabled Scullin, protesting against any stop to migration.[2]

Gepp told Crutchley of this cable on 19 October, and also that the Commission would perhaps be absorbed into CSIR. Crutchley bemoaned this prospect, as did A. C. D. Rivett. Crutchley noted that Gepp had offered to resign, seemingly so that the Commission would lose odium in Labor nostrils, and its survival would be easier.[3] Gepp appeared quite buoyant in these days. A letter he now wrote to C. H. E. Manning declared that Australia was 'leading the world in many ways' in showing how a nation dependent on primary production could be as prosperous as industrial counterparts; true, migration was slackening but that recourse 'has never been suitable for failures', and the notion of steady inflow 'is an illusion born of Governmental routine'.[4] Gepp may have conceived a role as independent advisor to Scullin, with whom his recent relations had been amicable,[5] perhaps in step with distancing from Bruce. Still, the offer to forsake £5000 a year until August 1933 had some grandeur. One who saw it thus was G. A. Julius, a member of the CSIR executive.[6] Crutchley doubted whether Gepp's ploy would work. His warning to that effect depressed DMC Vice-Chairman Devereux, with whom the Representative had played many rubbers of bridge. Another ready to mourn the Commission was S. M. Bruce, who told Julius that his only sadness at defeat was the consequent likelihood of change to CSIR and of doom for the DMC. Decades later, Bruce repeated:

> My own deepest regret is that the day I went they kicked to death my Develop-
> ment and Migration Commission. Of course, people criticised the D. and M. idea,
> but every good idea is always damned. If it had gone on—and we gave it a good
> start with first class personnel and no colour of politics in it—you'd have had a
> clear-cut picture of the development of Australia and of necessary priorities.[7]

Rarely does a politician flatter others beyond their desserts.

The Minister currently involved with the DMC was Senator J. J. Daly. Gepp addressed him late in October, reiterating that the Commission had achieved much and promised more.[8] Daly inclined towards Gunn taking over the Commission's work, from a Canberra base. Crutchley urged Gunn to accede; 'he was the one man of the four who possessed *all* the requisite qualities'.[9]

On 4 November the Prime Minister delivered what Governor-General Stonehaven described to Crutchley as 'this bombshell'.[10] Citing unemployment, dire prices for wool, and a bad wheat season, Scullin told HMG of his decision to halt assisted migration 'except for dependants of people already in Australia'. He accepted that the Agreement revolved upon continuance of migration and so left it to HMG 'to decide upon the effects of this suspension' in relation to it. Scullin professed longer-term 'sympathy with the better distribution of the white population of the Empire' and looked to a future day of 'providing opportunities for suitable British Settlers'.

Stonehaven's was not the only critical voice in Australia. Migration, in a new variant, stayed contentious between States and Commonwealth. Rights were involved and funding too, for State development would suffer if Agreement moneys ceased. R. L. Butler and T. R. Bavin, non-Labor Premiers, quickly made the point; Queensland's Agent-General protested in London. Stonehaven's own first response was to hope that the States would now negotiate direct with Whitehall on migration.

Scullin's decision seems to have shocked Gepp, and depression befell him. Discussions with the government simmered, Crutchley writing of 12 November especially as 'a hectic day of intrigue'. During its course Gepp glimpsed a hope that the Commission would survive, but on the 20th Daly confirmed to Scullin his different view.[11] Daly criticised the DMC much as various Britons had, deprecating its acceptance of Agreement money without ensuring that, or even caring whether, expenditure resulted in absorption of new migrants on the agreed scale. (In his letter, Daly invoked some remarkable theorising by L. F. Giblin as to the 'multiplier' factor in growth.)[12] 'If an independent body were to review the Agreement the Commonwealth would stand in a very bad light from England's point of view', concluded Daly, shaking the kaleidoscope of imperial loyalties and nationalist sentiment. Yet he asserted the Agreement to be costing the Commonwealth more than it did HMG, evidently including in his arithmetic all expenses of the DMC. Daly nevertheless thought some shadow of the Commission should survive, to shelter any Minister from the 'direct responsibility' of supervising schemes under way: its membership might be three—a representative of HMG (Crutchley was the obvious contender), Gunn, and another. Gepp's resignation should be accepted and Devereux transferred, pending expiry of his contract in March 1934.

The matter came before Parliament in its new session. At the opening on 20 November, the Governor-General declared the government's intent to 'co-ordinate' the DMC's work with CSIR. The Address-in-Reply heard praise of Gepp and his fellows from various Opposition speakers, notably the new Leader, J. G. Latham. Senator E. B. Johnston of Western Australia criticised abandoning the Agreement, evidently still hoping for revival of the 3500-farm scheme. Beyond that, assisted migration found no supporters.

Back in London, bureaucracies adapted to new circumstances.[13] Immediately Scullin had dropped his bombshell, Crutchley argued for tact; in further cables he urged that HMG strive to keep the DMC alive, and reported Gepp's belief that pressure from London might yet modify the Australian stand against migration. Goodwill towards Australia had considerable play among OSD officials, as well as Under-Secretary Ponsonby and Secretary Passfield. Indeed, some concern prevailed lest Crutchley collude with Gepp against the government. Bankes Amery drafted a memorandum for Cabinet consideration which accepted responsibility for Agreement schemes already endorsed, and kept doors open for more. Commenting thereon, C. W. G. Eady argued that Australia should be pressured to accept some nominees. That would be for Australia's good, particularly because (as he, Eady, had told Gepp in 1926) potential investors saw readiness to accept migrants as showing a polity's confidence in its own future. Eady affirmed that HMG should foster Australia's standing in the finance market.

Treasury, eager to cancel the Agreement, snorted at Bankes Amery's memorandum: it was 'grossly misleading', in that it falsely imputed commitment on Scullin's part to the Agreement. Frank Skevington reiterated that Australia had failed to take migrants in such numbers as the Agreement had presupposed; 'serious malpractices' as to tariffs, wages, and borrowing had destroyed its capacity to do so. Bruce had lost office as soon as he attempted to expiate these sins. He had been replaced by a government bound to intensify them, and to abolish the DMC, the one hopeful gleam in the Australian pit. A paper from Chancellor Snowden developed these charges, which had more point in that increased tariffs had flowed from the Scullin government as soon as Parliament resumed.[14] Snowden remarked that 'in our time of need Australia shuts the door in our face'. On 3 December, Cabinet resolved that Passfield and Snowden achieve a compromise between their departments' views.[15]

A cable of the following day, answering Scullin's of 4 November, conveyed largely the OSD stance.[16] While regretting the migration decision, it promised continued funding of schemes in progress; others would be considered if approved by Crutchley and the DMC, and provided that they pointed towards 'early resumption of assisted migration to a corresponding extent'. Even in the short term, went HMG's hope, Australia ought maintain a skeletal migration bureaucracy, and receive household workers as well as allow family reunions. The cable also sought redress for the Victorian landsettlers. Crutchley elaborated these points, adding farmboys among those who might continue, and reminding Scullin of the Empire Mission's endorsement of intensive farming. When Daly read Whitehall's message to the Senate on 13 December, Sir George Pearce and Sir Harry Colebatch (former WA Agent-General) gloried in its goodwill. Of course, HMG's move echoed continuing belief that emigration could relieve British problems, yet it had acted with apparent generosity. Scullin stood to lose if he rebuffed that move, especially if thereby he denied the States their Agreement money. Until the end of his term in December 1931, the Prime Minister shadow-boxed this challenge. He much curtailed assisted migration, yet avoided closure of the Agreement.

Crutchley saw the cable of 4 December as requiring him 'to fight for scraps of concessions'. He spent many hours with Gepp on 9 and 10 December, one task being to help the Chairman compose a letter of resignation. To his diary Crutchley affirmed 'how D and M has failed us'[17] (presumably in finding migrant-absorbing projects and selling them to government and people). That judgment was as unreal as a bulletin, evidently one of a series, which Gepp sent at that time to the Prince of Wales's private secretary, predicating still greater imperial involvement in Australian growth.[18]

On 10 December Crutchley also saw Scullin, finding him 'a shaken man, very near a breakdown'. Stonehaven had reported similarly to Baldwin a fortnight earlier; possibly the Britons were revealing more of themselves than of their subject. Scullin thrice told the Representative that his wife had been besieged by job-seeking migrant domestics. 'He seemed to think this evidence quite conclusive.' Despite this, it appears that British pressures, which included official protest against escalating tariffs,[19] affected Scullin. Chances for the DMC's survival rose, and on 24 December Australia's reply to HMG's cable of the 4th accepted, if in the blandest terms, virtually all the points made in it. This included the promise of attending to the Victorian settlers; on 20 December Crutchley had again confronted bureaucrats of that State, when their leader, William McIver, 'fought like a rat'. Happier hours for the Representative came on Christmas Day, spent with Melbourne's uppermost crust:

> Driving back from Frankston along the coast one realised Australia's 'vulgar soul'. Common little flappers in pyjamas apeing the Lido. Flaunting fairs on picturesque headlands. Ti-tree scrub impregnated with tawdry mean bungalows. Pity. But they do enjoy themselves.

That was a fair epitaph for the decade.

Across the world, Treasury allowed no quarter to Australia's feckless hedonism.[20] Scullin might believe that tariffs would restore prosperity, thundered chieftain A. P. Waterfield on seeing the cable of 24 December; '*we* believe—to put it mildly—that until Australia adopts an entirely different economic policy, it is pure moonshine to visualise the resumption of assisted migration'. On 3 February another Treasury nabob, R. N. V. Hopkins, affirmed that HMG 'could certainly not' encourage the financial market to lend to Australia; the latter's cutting of migration ranked high among his charges. Next day the OSD broached with Treasury one Agreement 'undertaking' already approved from Australia, that for clearing land in Queensland, and three others in earlier process. The latter group soon aborted, but a predictable battle followed as to the first. Crutchley and the OSD pushed for a gesture of goodwill (or bribery?) to Scullin; Treasury stood against it, Snowden more adamant than his officials.

While paying lip-service to the Agreement, Scullin intensified his thrust against migration in the new year. Reductions at Australia House proceeded fast. Scullin even proposed that the OSD supervise approval of whomever might still offer for migration, and G. G. Whiskard agreed that 'knowledge of British character and physiognomy' might enable his staff to do the job well.[21] Manning and J. T. Barnes argued that such a change would fuel criticism from Australia, and so the OSD finally rejected the invitation. Manning took the occasion to hypothesise that under Australia's 'expressive' conditions there became manifest moral and physical flaws among migrants, hitherto disciplined by 'repressive' social and economic conditions in Britain.

All such talk became increasingly abstract after a Premiers' Conference of late February, where Scullin inveighed hard against migration.[22] The matter would henceforth be handled by the Department of Markets; Gunn was to head a 'Development Branch' within the Prime Minister's Department, while a Consultative Committee comprising Gepp, Gunn, and Rivett would overview continuing Agreement matters. (Gepp was to receive £1250 a year in lieu of salary; Gunn's salary fell from £3500 to £1800; Mulvany transferred to Markets; an aggrieved Devereux went to London on a still handsome salary, part paid by the Wool Council.) Most importantly, Scullin indicated that the Commonwealth would approve very few applications for fare-subsidy so long as unemployment prevailed anywhere in Australia. 'That means the total cessation of migration', protested Premier Bavin, and Scullin concurred. Bavin had some support from Butler and Philip Collier, but Scullin had his way. More even than W. M. Hughes, he asserted federal dominance in the issue. Crutchley saw this as reneging on the cable of 24 December, which had implied accepting all State requisitions for farmboys and domestics. Further angering the Representative was pusillanimity among the Premiers, five having promised him to sustain State rights. They wilted before the Prime Minister's fierce determination.[23]

Concurrently the OSD learned from Australia House that the Australian government was cancelling hundreds of already-approved nominations and intended a maximum annual intake of 500 boys and 500 domestics.[24] On 12 March a cable asked Scullin whether he was repudiating his policy of 24 December. He replied that present circumstances forbade satisfactory settlement as the Agreement required; for everyone's good, restriction must prevail. Crutchley advised approval of the Queensland land-clearance scheme to boost mutual confidence. The OSD agreed, but at April's end Treasury declared a veto. That was probably as much a relief to Crutchley as a disappointment, let alone a surprise. 'I am coming slowly but surely to the conclusion that Government assistance, I will not say is wholly wrong, but causes more trouble than it is worth', he meditated of migration on 18 February; while by 24 April, 'I sometimes feel a qualm of conscience in not having accepted Scullin's embargo on migration. It is really a very moot point as to whether we should help anybody to come to this country at the present time.' His own elder son was having troubles seeking a gentleman-jackeroo job.

The DMC had its final meeting on 27 March, urging the Minister to approve current Queensland nominations for domestics and farmboys. Already Daly had moved legislation for the Commission's abolition. The Bill's passage was desultory.[25] Scullin and·Daly made their usual points against the Agreement, and alleged the Commission to have had excessive autonomy. Daly allowed praise to its investigative activities, but cited the *Report* on business stability as a classic case where enlightened argument had failed to prompt governmental action. Scullin offered no great play against migration, using terms akin more to his cable of Christmas Eve than to his tougher actions since. E. C. G. Page, Pearce, and Latham spoke for the Commission, the last implying that government had compounded its churlish ignorance by casting aside this source of expert advice; privately he remarked to Bruce that the retention of Gepp showed 'some sense' in the ministry.[26] Migration as such won no support, wherever, and the Bill became law.

Perhaps Gepp now felt more relief than affront. On 11 January Crutchley had reported him as being 'V. pessimistic ... foretold much more unemployment. Bloodshed. No money obtainable. Australia in Profundis.' That day Gepp at last despatched his resignation to Scullin; its tone was elegiac, not apocalyptic.[27] Addressing fellow Rotarians later in the month he blended those qualities:

> If Australia is visualised as a vast laboratory, where one of the most virile races on earth is engaged in experimenting with almost unknown resources in an attempt to establish a new tradition of national prosperity and social freedom, then we are able to gain a clearer light on present difficulties ... Our effort is one of the most courageous spectacles in the modern world. I suspect that our failure has been to recognise the greatness of the task. Instead of all sections of the nation being drawn together in an indissoluble bond to give strength to a long drawn out national effort, we have blindly engaged in internecine conflicts concerning division of the spoils.[28]

*   *   *

For the rest of 1930, London more than Canberra was the focus of discussions about migration policy. The planning and actuality of a further Imperial Conference provided a major reason. Migration also had its place before the Economic Advisory Council, which HMG had appointed in hope of tempering the Depression.

The OSD continued to invest hope in migration. Passfield's advocacy of this cause was amplified by J. H. Thomas when he succeeded as Dominions Secretary in June. Both urged Treasury to reconsider its veto of the Queensland scheme, arguing that Australia could see rejection as betraying the cable of 4 December.[29] Crutchley reiterated that Daly might respond to Whitehall's goodwill. He applauded the Minister's concern for migrant after-care; he indicated that the new government was more polite to him than the old; and he cited J. B. Brigden to show that absorption of migrants had cost Australia much.[30] Snowden remained implacable. In a Parliamentary debate prompted by one of Stanley Baldwin's spasms for imperial integration, he sneered at Australia as showing that tariffs were no cure for unemployment.[31] Support for Baldwin came from organicists across party lines, Oswald Mosley and Robert Boothby to most effect.

Throughout much of 1930 the OSD, Whiskard leading, prepared materials for the Economic Advisory Council's committee on migration.[32] Vast in bulk, they were modest in message. Whiskard upheld the basic cause, computing that, by relieving unemployment, every migrant saved Britain £90. He urged that HMG should abandon the 50:50 principle of the Settlement Act, and fund fares unilaterally. Beyond that, Government involvement should be minimised. 'The great increase in Government intervention since the passing of the Empire Settlement Act has had no visible effect on the flow of migration'; it had moreover encouraged recipients of aid to look to government for continuing succour, and to cast blame thither for problems suffered. Yet Whiskard proposed that negotiations continue with 'large landowning corporations overseas' as part of a migration programme, noting that Empire marketing would be a necessary complement to any resulting development. As to female migration:

> The most satisfactory form of settlement for women is marriage; the difficulty is to bridge the gap between the arrival of women overseas and marriage. Domestic employment has hitherto been the only means of providing such a bridge; some alternative is desirable.

So others had been saying for years.

Treasury's response to these OSD submissions inevitably called for wariness in spending. At the most, it argued, there might be testing of Dominions' reaction to migration being managed by voluntary societies, with fares more heavily subsidised by HMG than at present. The Agreement should end; schemes approved by the DMC might have made economic sense, but that had encouraged rather than stopped the States borrowing and spending otherwise in disastrous way. Skevington berated expenditure even on Barnardo emigration. More than once the Australian Prime Minister's name appeared in Treasury papers as 'Scullion'.

Argument continued in verbal evidence to the Council committee, which sat from mid-1930 to mid-1931; members included historian G. D. H. Cole, demographer A. M. Carr-Saunders, and veteran migrationist Christopher Turnor.[33] Speaking for the Ministry of Labour, Eady urged that government underwrite an Australian fare of £12 to £15; indeed he would open such subsidy to returnees also, believing that ploy would ultimately assist migration. Beyond that and assistance to voluntary organisations, Eady too affirmed that official involvement should be minimal. He repeated that intense politicisation of migration had poisoned the cause both in Britain and the Dominions. Whiskard warned that subsidised return might lead to massive back-flow—nearly every emigrant had spasms of homesickness —but overall agreed with Eady. His minute as to female migration prompted Carr-Saunders to bemoan official dominance of policy:

on the question of women going to the Dominions and getting married, which is just what you would like to say to the women, you could not even say that in a government publication ... that was the kind of thing that could be done by the voluntary societies.

Treasury's Waterfield spoke against Agreement-like schemes, remarking (with sadness?) that 'you cannot go to war with a Dominion because it cannot carry out its share of a bargain'. Among other witnesses, Lord Lovat declared that while Australia 'talks very loudly about the Union Jack', it exploited boy migrants as cheap rural labour.

Its work for the Council left the OSD little need to prepare further for the Imperial Conference, and Dominions Office records offer only one other major file apropos that impending event.[34] Central was a report from Trade Commissioner Dalton which exulted in Australia's crisis and urged that HMG take this opportunity 'of securing for ourselves an entire change in Australian attitudes and practices'. One member of the department responded that the greed of British investors had contributed to Australian troubles, and that HMG had responsibility to assist Scullin. Whiskard inclined to the tougher line. Another indication of OSD attitudes was a proposal from G. F. Plant and Bankes Amery that State Premiers (and their Provincial counterparts from Canada) be invited to the Imperial Conference especially for direct discussion on migration.[35]

Australian preparations for the Conference were scant. Asking the Premiers for amendments which might revitalise the Agreement, Scullin implied sympathy for pertinent action, but nothing resulted.[36] A position paper detailed problems of the farm-settlement schemes, linking their sad story with that of ex-soldiers' experience on the land, and philosophising 'whether land settlement is capable of artificial orientation—whether, in fact, rural pursuits should not be left to self-appointed pioneers'.[37] On public works sponsored by the Agreement, the paper was more positive, and it suggested that Scullin might show readiness to extend such deals. Before Scullin left, Gepp urged him to maintain some migration machinery, invoking the need to uphold 'British stock' against southern Europeans, and pleading for orphan migration.[38] Crutchley pushed to like effect.[39] Gepp also tried to persuade Scullin to propose a body similar to the DMC for developing Empire trade.[40]

The Imperial Conference of 1930 met from 1 October to 14 November, lacklustre throughout.[41] Scullin's chief Australian associate was P. J. Moloney, who chaired the sub-committee on migration—a strange appointment, perhaps resulting from the OSD's still-flickering hope that Australia would take a more genial position on the matter. In the sub-committee, William Lunn, now Dominions Under-Secretary, urged overseas governments to offer Britain's commonalty the chance of migration.

There was some warmth in the response from New Zealand and Southern Rhodesia, but not from Australia. Moloney affirmed that Australia was ready to welcome Britons if jobs were available, and also that such was not currently the case. He abstained from a motion urging maintenance of current arrangements, but did allow a case for family reunion. His Prime Minister duly supported this policy, at least for the short term, and also orphan immigration.

Scullin's major discussions on the Agreement left little record. An opaque memorandum later prepared by Gunn indicates that some British pressure sought to have Scullin abandon the Agreement, save for the maintenance of schemes already in process, this cancellation to be accompanied by HMG taking a greater part in migrant after-care.[42] Scullin equivocated and 'for tactical reasons' the OSD decided to let the matter ride.[43] When challenged on Australia's policy of denying British ex-servicemen the same entitlements as their Australian counterparts, Scullin cited precedents established by Bruce.[44] The OSD hoped that Thomas would force the issue of the Victorian farmers' plight, but meeting the Secretary without bureaucrats attending, the Australian evaded that attack.[45] Thomas did write a consequent letter on the matter, arguing also for farmboy migration.[46] After Scullin had sailed, Crutchley sent news that both Victoria and New South Wales were further diminishing after-care, and consequently a stern cable followed the Australian to Port Said, seeking the Agreement's closure. It seems that Scullin ignored these missives.[47]

*   *   *

From his high post in the Bank of England, Sir Otto Niemeyer had taken the initiative early in 1930 in deciding that Australia needed an emissary thence to help maintain what little standing it had in the capitalist world. The role fell to himself. In Australia during July–September 1930 Niemeyer preached ultra-dry economics and was crucial in causing Scullin to uphold a programme of restrictive orthodoxy, thereby alienating radical elements in the Labor movement, led by J. T. Lang.[48] Australian historians have scarcely glimpsed how Niemeyer's thrust complemented the Treasury critique of Australia throughout the 1920s. That Scullin likewise had opposed aspects of Bruce's expansionism, migration among them, made it at once fitting and ironic that he should become both instrument and victim of Niemeyerism. Writing to Treasury from Australia, Sir Otto reiterated that Australia should be held to its war-debt obligations, and declared this to be 'an odd country full of odd people and odder theories'.[49] Crutchley told of Niemeyer remarking that 'he had had a lot to do with bankrupt countries but had never seen one more utterly impotent to help itself'. Niemeyer affirmed the Agreement to be dead; 'they wouldn't take migrants, they were over-populated already'.[50]

The Consultative Committee, appointed to continue some DMC functions, first met on 1 July.[51] Gepp pushed for it to take a positive role, but Minister Daly fended that. With the Agreement in limbo, this made the Committee vestigial indeed. The question of intensive farming remained one topic for debate, but in negative way: Murphy submitted a report on dairying, which government brushed aside.[52] Tobacco, fisheries, mining, beef cattle in northern Australia, paper in Tasmania: these and like issues had airing, also to scant effect. Mixed farming in the Murray valley, the citrus industry, and growing potatoes were subjects of *Reports* based on data earlier gathered.[53] Daly kept finances so tight that he refused Gepp a trip to Sydney to study a German ship which used pulverised coal.[54]

Gunn evidently retained standing with Cabinet as an advisor, while pursuing various other tasks. An application by the Australian Dried Fruits Association for underwriting of production costs he dismissed as threatening to sustain the inefficient;[55] as chairman of an enquiry into the sugar industry, he joined a minority criticising bounties long operative there.[56] The hop industry Gunn found in a pitiable mess, possibly necessitating government take-over.[57] Gepp's main consultancy probed chances for expanded goldmining. An echo of his Electrolytic Zinc heyday sounded when he persuaded miners at Mount Morgan to invest with their employer any wages they received beyond the arbitrated scale.[58] Now was published the *Report of the Royal Commission ... upon the Coal Industry of New South Wales*, upon which Gepp had spent many hours;[59] it lambasted bad management and class warfare as evils corrupting the industry.

Meanwhile, Gepp essayed a role in the socio-political turbulence gripping Australia. At its vortex was his old friend J. A. Lyons, currently in federal Cabinet and Acting Treasurer in Scullin's absence overseas. Presumably Lyons was the chief target of a memorandum prepared in September by Gepp, D. B. Copland, L. F. Giblin, and the Melbourne businessman-ideologue D. C. Dyason.[60] Warning of 'serious social disorder' if employment fell so far as threatened, the memorandum urged that creditor nations such as Britain and the USA must be generous to debtors like Australia, for whom the collapse in commodity prices had been horrendous. Accordingly, the memorandum hoped that some overseas loan moneys would be made available—'sympathetic assistance on extended terms'. Fatuous this might appear, but it confirmed Gepp's place among those who wanted some tempering of economic blasts. Other old DMC hands in like category were W. J. Rose, who urged subsidy of import-replacing manufactures, and G. F. Finlay, who advised massive removal of logs and rabbits to improve pasture lands.[61] Coincidentally Giblin nominated Gepp to Lyons for a committee to consider unemployment; this advanced sufficiently for Crutchley to remark 'rather a score for him after their vitriolic attack on him and his DMC',[62] but came to no effect. However, by late October Lyons was using

Gepp as an intermediary with Sir Robert Gibson,[63] chairman of the Commonwealth Bank, and a key figure in current political economy. Further in his formal consultative role, Gepp proposed first a 'Development Fund' of £1 million, citing his own recent goldfields studies as offering pointers for such investment, and secondly government subsidy of a steel-rolling mill which might employ 2000 men.[64]

All the while Lyons was suffering fire from radicals in caucus and Cabinet, his answers hinting readiness to leave the government and the Labor Party. That was to happen early in 1931, and in December Lyons was to be elected Prime Minister as head of the erstwhile Nationalists, revamped as the United Australia Party. Gepp may well have influenced Lyons's moves, and certainly in late 1930 he promoted schemes for new-style government.

> I believe there is a growing feeling that the best is unattainable from our present political representatives of all shades of opinion whilst party interests predominate, and that the modification or elimination of the Party system is worthy of all consideration,

declared Gepp in a contemporary speech that ranged from Russia's 'great experiment' to Gustav Le Bon's thoughts on popular mentalité.[65] He liaised with a group including Keith Officer (now intimate of Crutchley and R. G. Casey, and member of Australia's External Affairs branch), Keith Murdoch (Melbourne newspaper magnate), and the Baillieu interest.[66] Their pressure probably caused Opposition Leader Latham to assure Parliament on 9 December that party sniping would cease if government established a council of Parliamentarians and bankers to plan economic recovery. Gepp mobilised support; he hoped especially for that of Governor-General designate and current Chief Justice of the High Court of Australia, Sir Isaac Isaacs. Negotiations proceeded with Pearce, High Court judge Owen Dixon, and acting Governor-General Lord Somers. Lyons supported the notion in caucus, but it soon fizzled.

*   *   *

While Scullin made some small concessions on migration at the Imperial Conference, administrative policy continued very restrictive, impeding the few potential migrants still offering. Definition of 'family' for reunion purposes was narrow, and a maximum imposed of thirty such cases in any one State each month.[67] A characteristic rule required men betrothed to already-resident immigrants to pay their full fare in advance, the subsidy being supplied only after proof of marriage in Australia.[68] Some migrants very much resented curtailment on their nominating of relatives, insisting that such 'right' had been promised as an inducement to go to

Australia.[69] T. R. Bavin sustained protests against federal rigidity, but his electoral defeat by Lang in October 1930 told a message. Thereafter the senior State became ultra-exclusionist, even denying family reunions.[70] This outcome showed that the federal government allowed discretion to the States, so long as that increased restriction! Queensland, the only other State to propose 'selection' at the year's outset, also now repudiated migration, causing much distress at the OSD.[71] Western Australia still criticised federal policy, but to no effect.[72]

The High Commissioner reported that actual sailings in 1930 comprised 1434 nominees and 591 'selections'. Most would have been arranged before Scullin's policy prevailed. Self-subsidised migration evidently stayed quite high, doubtless fostered by denial of assistance to most aspirants. Less ambiguous is the estimated growth of return migration: 9516 in 1929; 12,808 in 1930; 11,747 in 1931.[73] Labor Parliamentarian P. E. C. Coleman went to London to report on the High Commission and Australia House, which he did with malicious gusto.[74] During 1930 migration staff fell from fifty-three to two. Manning and Barnes both lost their appointments, the latter suffering very abrupt treatment.[75]

The growth in the numbers of people returning underlined the distress and grievance suffered by many migrants. The figure could well have become greater, for Crutchley successfully protested against the readiness of Australian bureaucrats to allow return of many assisted migrants (some not even having repaid their loans) who had stayed in Australia less than the two years specified by rules prevailing since 1922.[76] Such loading of the employment market at home could not but perturb HMG. It resisted various calls from migrant groups for subsidised repatriation, although at least one provoked sympathy from the King.[77] Another, prepared in summer 1930 at an unemployment camp at Blackboy, Western Australia, also went to the King, via David Kirkwood, Clydeside socialist and Parliamentarian. Stressing their ex-service background, the 645 petitioners suggested that toughness of life in Australia, 'developing self-reliance and resource', might fit them for further service in the British Army. Their current plight they likened to that of Indians sent in earlier years to Fiji, whence many had enjoyed repatriation. Blackboy camp, they affirmed, dispensed not welfare but control. 'At the best the lot of the migrant is a hard one', went a covering letter to Kirkwood, 'but when his labour is not wanted and there is no work for him … it is difficult to find words which fittingly express his helpless condition.'

Another petition of 1930 had odder provenance.[78] Under the letterhead 'League of Englishmen', a group of migrants in the Dawson valley protested their lot. Evidently they had been recruited direct by the government of Queensland when it determined to settle the region despite the DMC's criticism. Now the Englishmen of Dawson cited the DMC report to show that they had been misled! The OSD expostulated that the protest was none of its concern. 'We seem to spend most of our time in trying to answer letters from anxious parents and discontented settlers', Plant wrote Crutchley.[79]

The Representative knew all about that. By November he believed that Australia's absorption in its own problems meant that 'neither press nor public cares a brass farthing for the British settler'.[80] Wrangling with Victoria as to the landsettlers continued its deadly grind. Yet that State offered a few gleams: some farmers (especially at Childers) seemed to be coping well, the current Minister of Lands was not too bad, and late in 1930 the State government at last agreed to appoint a Royal Commission into the migrant farmers' situation.[81] Now New South Wales was the bigger problem. Crutchley had become increasingly concerned at the fate of farmboys who faced destitution as they qualified for adult wages and so lost their appeal for employers in a tightening market; he floated the idea of an Agreement-funded scheme to assist them get their own farms, but to no effect.[82] In response to the worsening of migrant troubles, Crutchley established a new co-ordinating body, the British Settlers' Welfare Committee. It took much organising, being beset by 'cranks' among voluntary sympathisers and hostility from bureaucrats. The latter, according to Crutchley, persuaded Premier Lang to withdraw subsidy from the Welfare Committee.[83] This (and concern over farmboys in Victoria) had led to HMG sending the aforesaid 'stern cable' to Scullin at Port Said, and also to suspension of British payments for the Wyangala Dam until the NSW government resumed its subsidy.[84]

To chair the Welfare Committee, Crutchley enlisted P. H. M. ('Roger') Goldfinch, descended from P. G. King, Governor of New South Wales 1800–6.[85] Later in 1930 Goldfinch helped form a secret organisation intended to foil Lang-led moves towards republican socialism. Crutchley continued to socialise among the high bourgeoisie.[86] He noted their acerbity in turning on Bruce ('never did an idol fall with such a crash'), and readiness to believe that Reds were likely to upsurge, in arms. Camden Park, ancestral home of the Macarthur-Onslow family, supreme Australian type of landed gentility, Crutchley found enchanting; Geelong Grammar School, where new headmaster James Darling was cultivating an English public-school ethos, uplifting. (Darling had led a public-schoolboys' tour of New Zealand in 1928, and currently was organising yet another for Australia.)[87] Late in 1930 HMG considered appointing a High Commissioner to Australia. 'Must be a strong man and a diplomat and not a platitudinarian', wrote Crutchley.[88] Snowden's stringency modified the plan: Crutchley's title changed so as to omit specific reference to migration, and his location to Canberra.[89]

*   *   .   *

Economic despondency and socio-political tension remained strong in Australia during 1931. Newly labelled though he was, Crutchley had to sustain past struggles. The Settlers' Welfare Committee set to work, as did the Victorian Royal Commission on migrant land settlement. The great preponderance of evidence came from settlers, or otherwise affirmed their case.[90] Again and again they raised charges of deception practised by the Victorian government and its agents in Britain: witnesses detailed how utterly their experiences had contrasted with propagandist fantasy. Supporting testimony came from G. F. Finlay. His erstwhile DMC colleague, E. N. Robinson, currently was confirming that the NSW land-settlement scheme, while far smaller, told similar themes.[91]

Migrant repatriation stayed a major issue. In mid-May E. J. Hogan, still Victoria's Premier, said that only lack of funds inhibited him from subsidising return fares, as was urged upon him by a Parliamentarian, who claimed that South Australia was so doing in a thousand cases.[92] The WA Parliament longer debated the same issue. 'To where are we going to deport the Australians who are in need?' asked Philip Collier, now Leader of the Opposition, when a backbencher behind him upheld repatriation. 'They at least have friends', came the response. Some speakers invoked migrants' indolence and extravagance. Minister C. G. Latham declared that HMG had spoken against repatriation, with Scullin warning that Britain might counter any such move by curtailing payments under the Agreement. The repatriationists won, across party lines.[93] Presumably at this stage, the Western and South Australian governments urged Commonwealth funding of mass repatriation. Scullin still resisted, affirming Australia's contrary responsibilities under the Agreement.[94] He remarked too that the government had spent enough on migrants without repatriating them. In August–September the Premiers' Conference found the step 'not a practical one'.[95]

Crutchley had continued to argue this, citing the Agreement and Britain's own unemployment and massive outlays on the dole—which, he stressed, would not automatically be available to returnees.[96] Yet agitation persisted. 'Why, Sir, should we be kept here like convicts, nay worse than that', demanded a British Migrants' Association to Scullin.[97] Such episodes may have prompted Crutchley publicly to affirm:

> I am not a great believer in artificial Government control of plans of migration and settlement ... My experience has been that the most successful settler has been the one who has come out here on his own, possibly with some assistance for his passage'.[98]

(The assistor, presumably, would be friend or philanthropist.)

Notwithstanding the tactical strength it sometimes gained from the Agreement's existence, HMG pursued its closure. A cable of 20 May made that clear, meanwhile confirming suspension of the Wyangala Dam payments: while after-care had improved in New South Wales, it had worsened in Victoria, especially in that sustenance to migrant farmers in the Mallee district had been cut.[99] The Australian government replied with equal chill that there could be no preferential treatment for migrants, as against Australians; and that HMG should not punish one State for actions of another. In August–September the Premiers agreed that the Prime Minister should negotiate closure. As British bureaucrats entered upon that task, they met horrendously complex problems. William Bankes Amery sent Crutchley a massive report in October, 'in the intervals of administrative work connected with the destruction of most of our organisation'.[100] Relevant paperwork proceeded in Australia.[101]

Crutchley presented a kind account of Scullin, seeing him as upholder of virtue against Lang's extremism, and sympathising with his sense of having been betrayed by Lyons.[102] Yet Crutchley disliked the credit-inflation ideas of Theodore, who was now Treasurer, and upheld the Commonwealth Bank's resistance to them. Crutchley's style contrasted with that of R. W. Dalton, who repeated his old hopes:

> it might be that when the real crisis comes and complete incapacity to deal with it is revealed, any Government of whatever party might be tempted by hope of financial aid on a large scale to place such re-construction in the hands of an expert Financial Commission from the U.K.[103]

Further illustrating the ambiguity of current Australian affairs, Crutchley reported that the Governor of New South Wales, Sir Philip Game, judged Premier Lang likeable and his radical measures effective.[104]

For all his striving, Crutchley found scant reciprocal affection in the tedious Canberra of Depression days. 'The unity of the British Commonwealth of Nations!', he taunted, on learning from counterparts in Ottawa of 'the hatred the Canadians have for them'.[105] At the end of 1931 the Representative sailed homeward for a long spell, leaving in charge W. J. Garnett. In Perth James Mitchell, now again Premier, harangued Crutchley as to the virtues of development, while Collier, in drink, declared 'democracy a complete failure'.[106] By then, on 19 December, Lyons's United Australia Party had smashed Scullin at the polls. Rather contrarily, Crutchley found this 'wonderful',[107] while Dalton cabled that disaster now threatened to be all the more shattering.[108] Against this, the Dominions Office opined that Australia's 'heroic efforts' at budget-balancing should win international respect. Treasury agreed! That was rare but logical, for Scullin had stayed pretty true to Niemeyerism.

Erstwhile Development and Migration Commissioners found something to do in 1931. The Consultative Committee had occasional meetings, maintaining oversight of Agreement schemes and considering other possibilities for growth.[109] A report on paper-production in Tasmania, Gepp its mastermind, carried that long saga towards the reality achieved later in the decade.[110] It linked with Gepp's continuing interest in forestry. He now urged formation of a forestry service, which might pursue 'research, experimentation, reafforestation, the delineation of erosion in connection with national waterways'.[111] Gepp also kept continuing watch on goldmining, and this year appeared a book on geophysical prospecting arising from the DMC's sponsorship.[112] Conservationist sensitivity such as Gepp had shown apropos forestry further appeared in Murphy's work on Murray River irrigation.[113] In July 1931 the academic economist G. L. Wood urged reconstitution of such a body as the DMC, to prompt Keynesian policies of purposeful state action.[114] Perhaps inspired thereby, Murphy and Gunn wrote a paper calling upon government to boost employment: 'if the Premiers Conference can adopt a policy of justified optimism, and strike an appeal to "National Efficiency" as a slogan, much will have been done to counteract the feelings of despair and apathy which are at present overwhelming'.[115]

At their Conference the Premiers established a Secretariat, to continue long-term but at once to report on this document; members included Gepp, Murphy, Rivett, Giblin, Mulvany.[116] Gunn was elected to the chair, Rivett reporting this as an intended snub to Gepp. He also claimed that Gepp declared intent to have the Secretariat denounce Lang's extremism, and award-determined wages. Another to comment on the Secretariat was HMG's Assistant Trade Commissioner H. L. Setchell, who characterised it as a renewed DMC; criticism on that very point, he added, caused Scullin to specify limits on its operation.[117] Reporting on 3 September, to the reassembled Premiers' Conference, the Secretariat followed the Gunn–Murphy document and gave predictable favour to wheat-growing and dairying; forestry, fisheries and mining; paper, and iron and steel industries. 'There is some risk about all of them, but in this crisis some risk must be taken to avoid collapse or total default.'[118] Rivett scoffed at the inanity of the report, especially its proposal to spend non-existent moneys; he claimed that Scullin had warned Gunn not to tackle crucial issues concerning tariffs and wages, but that anyway the Prime Minister dismissed the outcome. Rivett also commented that Gunn ('a very straight fellow indeed') was annoying government by stressing the difficulties involved in developing such areas as fisheries and shale oil.[119] Gepp had written on the latter subject, and also addressed another ancient favourite, the alkali industry, before departing in October for a trade enquiry in Asia.[120] The Secretariat endured half-life through the rest of 1931.

That year's key event in Britain was the *Report* of the Economic Advisory Council on migration.[121] 'Nadir' was indeed its message. Life overseas offered the potential migrant little, went the argument, while Britain's declining birth-rate removed the 'push' from that quarter. There reappeared the theme that it was bad policy for the state to invest in children, and then let them spend their productive years abroad. Emigration accentuated the sex-imbalance within Britain and depleted precious agricultural labour. Furthermore:

> There is the self-selecting aspect of emigration. Whether assisted or unassisted, the emigrant tends in each category of the population to be the least ordinary surplus. Thus emigration takes the young rather than the old, the bright and ambitious rather than the dull and lethargic.

As had earlier anti-migrationists, the *Report* urged that Britain should encourage small-farm agriculture at home rather than rely on food imports. On another tack, the argument went (as it had with the ITB) that at one level the 1920s were conducive to migration, for then Britain slumped while Dominions boomed; the imputation was that sluggishness in despite of that showed migration to be obsolete and otiose. Mingled with this barrage went a half-admission of a contrary argument. Emigration *could* give some relief to Britain's economic distress; a few individuals *might* find such fulfilment abroad as they could not at home; Dominions *were* good trading partners. 'Migration from Great Britain to Australia may prove vital to the avoidance of serious international issues' ran allusion to Australia's defence vulnerability. Yet in its concluding survey the committee returned to negatives.

Imperialists and radicals joined in telling the House of Commons about the plight of Australian migrants.[122] Late in 1930 both groups affirmed that HMG should accept responsibility in the matter. Secretary Thomas warned against that 'very dangerous precedent', and later denied the policy or benevolence of granting homeward fares. Yet questions kept coming. On 1 December 1931 David Kirkwood, doubtless responding to that WA petition, threatened to raise a debate, but in fact did not.

On his homeward journey Crutchley wrote a survey of migration matters.[123] Many of his points have already appeared, and some better await later chapters, but a few have immediate relevance. He now espoused nomination, essentially as it had prevailed through the 1920s, while still yearning that there be more migrants of superior social type. Crutchley's critique of Australian bureaucrats remained sharp: McIver had been succeeded by someone worse! Politicians and public opinion were likewise slack. Australians paid little heed to their nation's dangerous isolation as against the world, yet simultaneously exaggerated its wealth which others might covet the more. T. G. Taylor, W. K. Hancock, and J. B. Brigden received Crutchley's plaudits, and so did the DMC's investigative work, in contrast to its disdain for migrant welfare. The Representative affirmed his anger that British ex-servicemen did not enjoy the same rights as Australian, and stressed that those who had proceeded under the post-1919 full-fare scheme were most insistent as to the responsibility still owed them by HMG. Among migrants generally, the disposition to return home ran strong, checked only by lack of means. Yet, Crutchley believed, many returnees would soon wish to go back to Australia, and he rebuked politicians there who had argued for mass repatriation.

That issue remained a cutting edge of more general migrant grievances and the Commons was a focus for the discontent. Giving it force was George Lansbury, patriarch of the Left and mindful of his own miserable venture to Queensland fifty years before. On 14 April 1932 Lansbury presented a petition from the British Migrants Association of Australia, which spoke of starvation, suicide, madness, prostitution. 'Propaganda ... extravagant, misleading, and in many cases undoubtedly false' had lured people to this fate. This petition activated the OSD. It investigated the petitioners' agent in Britain, Miss Kitty Bottoms, who had won much space in *Reynolds' News*, and summonsed a report from Australia. Written by W. C. Hankinson of the Representative's office, this presented an excessively cheerful scenario.[124] Governments did not discriminate against migrants in granting relief; voluntary organisations were striving so hard that some unemployed migrants were enjoying more succour than Australians; no case was known of eviction for default in rent-paying; charity workers told that prostitution did not rise with economic distress. Furthermore, the leader of the Migrants' Association in Melbourne worked with Communists.

Meanwhile, on 13 May, the migrants' plight had provoked more anger at Westminster. The most effective speaker was John McGovern, who told from his experience as a migrant 1923–5 of Australian hostility to Britons, especially miners. Thomas (still Secretary, although since August 1931 in Ramsay MacDonald's National government) again insisted that to repatriate migrants might entail 'the crime of bringing them home to something worse'. Truly, during 1932 many returned people confirmed Crutchley's thesis and sought advice from Australia House as to going south once more.[125] Yet this could scarcely have weighed with disconsolate emigrants. The women of Murrabit, Victoria, addressed the Queen:

We have worked in the byres and fields to help the men, this work being entirely new to us, and during the last five years many wives and mothers, some of whom employed domestic help themselves in the Old Country, have been obliged to enter Service in Melbourne, two hundred miles away, in order to buy clothes and boots so that their children might attend school decently clad.[126]

Her Majesty read this. Meanwhile Murrabit men were planning to impeach L. S. Amery. Angered by Scullin's assertion that they were Australian citizens since arrival, they claimed inalienable rights as Britons: the constitutional point was exquisite, but no-one pursued it.[127] This year yet another enquiry probed Western Australian group-settlement;[128] a minority report, reluctant to see all fault as lying with the scheme itself, bemoaned influence from 'a few settlers of the agitator type', and urged they be 'peremptorily dismissed'. Presumably these sinners were Britons.

Migrant welfare was the central issue for British bureaucrats as, month upon month, they pondered dissolving the Agreement.[129] The view resurfaced that its continuance was justified by the hold it gave HMG in urging Australia to provide due after-care. The decision went otherwise, but bureaucrats still found many problems. Continuing the flow of funds to yet-unfinished 'undertakings' was most obvious among these, but others were at least as complex. The Commonwealth's power, vis-à-vis the States, to negotiate as it had, came under renewed question. Provisions for 'satisfactory settlement' were more precisely formulated with regard to ordinary migrants, than to those settled on farms, yet the latter generally suffered more extreme trouble. Treasury and the OSD agreed that to make promiscuous claims for ordinary migrants was out of court. That decision must remain ultra-confidential, however: public opinion might dispute it. A threat of Western Australia reviving its 3500-farm scheme spurred the Britons to decision. Late in 1932 a draft closure went to the States.[130] On another front Treasury softened, accepting a plea from the Australian government that normally migrants be allowed to return within two years without demand for repayments of HMG's fare-subsidy.[131] Not that all the old feeling had gone. 'A scathing indictment of the working of a free democracy with triennial Parliaments', Skevington was to comment on Crutchley's shipboard essay.[132]

The great stage for imperial in-fighting in 1932 was the Trade Conference at Ottawa.[133] Migration played virtually no part there, but now Bruce (having become a Minister in the Lyons government) secured some such victory concerning markets as he had sought in 1923. Bruce's chief ministerial colleague was H. S. Gullett, and the pair proved tough bargainers. Among the British bureaucrats who were dismayed at the contrasting insipidity of their own leaders was Whiskard. The years seem to have diminished his sympathy for Australia; recalling T. C. Macnaghten, one might speculate that headship of the OSD inexorably had that effect.

Malcolm MacDonald, Dominions Under-Secretary in the National Government, was more dynamic than Whiskard's regrets might suggest. Late in 1932 he chaired another migration committee, nominally inter-departmental but dominated by old OSD hands: Whiskard, Plant, Bankes Amery, Pott. Perhaps the move responded to laments from some Tory-imperialists in the House of Commons late in 1932 as to migration's decline. The committee did not report until August 1934.

Gepp had coveted a post in the Ottawa delegation, Rivett told, interpreting the negative outcome as showing the Lyons government's refusal to accept the man at his self-value 'as the heaven-born'.[134] Gepp, Gunn, and Murphy were at odds, continued Rivett, himself barracking for the last. That the Public Service Board was considering dissolution of the Development Branch no doubt deepened stresses.[135] Gunn's major output for 1932 was a humdrum review of the superphosphate industry.[136] Gepp's report on his Asian voyaging had greater interest. He urged development of trade networks, and discussed *Realpolitik*. 'I venture no prophecy', Gepp said of China's future, 'except to say that communism is not out of the running'.[137]

*   *   *

During 1930–2 virtually all material relevant to our subject followed the 'nadir' theme. For the next triennium negativism remained ascendant, but against a counter-thrust. The remainder of this chapter continues with problems and negation, while the next will tell the other side of these especially ambiguous years.

Late in 1932 Representative Crutchley returned to Australia, aboard the same ship as D. R. Jardine and those other cricketers who were to make the summer of 1932–3 notorious in Austral–British relationships.[138] In Perth Crutchley heard yet more about group-settler troubles and the unpopularity of migrants ('even the Fairbridge child'). Back in eastern Australia, he learnt from Goldfinch of migrant-welfare work, and of secrets within recent NSW politics. Sydney's high bourgeoisie had been ruthless (the adverse value judgment seems to have been Goldfinch's as well as Crutchley's) in pressuring Philip Game to dismiss Premier Lang, well before that event occurred on 13 May 1932. During that crisis Goldfinch-style conservatives had been asked by the Commonwealth government to ready 2000 men; this 'old guard' looked askance at the provocative flamboyance of 'new guard' activists of the further Right.[139]

By now the cricket fields were providing drama.[140] Did Harold Larwood and Bill Voce seek to avenge the suffering of migrants, especially their fellow miners, as they hurled bodyline balls; did Australian barrackers vent anti-migrant spleen? Crutchley was central in the inter-governmental talks that were prompted by the commotion. His personal reaction at first ran true-blue British; barracking, he mused, ranked top among Australian defects, together with attitudes to women and to work. Late in February he reprobated 'a most blackguardly demonstration against Jardine when he was struck in the groin', but very soon after himself writhed when that worthy snubbed his invitation to dinner; the other gentlemen in the team did come, and told of their loathing for the captain and his tactics, and of his for Australians.

Another with whom Crutchley socialised that summer was Richard Linton, whose recent appointment as Victoria's Agent-General probably owed something to his pioneering the Big Brother idea. 'An appalling evening ... why *must* Australia always be represented by bounders—or worse. Rather sweeping remark but I was thinking of Shepherd and Jack Barnes'.[141] More happily for Crutchley, the Victorian Royal Commission now issued its *Report*.[142] It attended to each of the 311 settlers who had submitted a formal complaint. A handful of protests were found exaggerated, a few had been withdrawn, but the Commission endorsed 90 per cent. Training of settlers was almost always deficient, and most farms were incapable of providing both livelihood and a surplus for debt payment. Some of the migrants were too old, others incapable or cranky, but the overwhelming fault lay with Australian governments.

Financing of the Royal Commission was itself intricate—with HMG, the British Legion, and the National Relief Fund all contributing to the complainants' costs—and now compensation became far more so.[143] In mid-1933 discussions between Crutchley, the Commonwealth, and the Victorian government promised satisfaction. Then glitches arose, mostly because of the intricacy of Victorian politics and the machinations of Minister of Lands, A. A. Dunstan, 'a most objectionable little person' in Crutchley's generous words.[144] The Country Party, which Dunstan led, disparaged compensation for Britons, wanting rather to secure advantage for farmers generally. Seemingly, some of Lyons's own supporters questioned compensation.[145] After great pressuring, the two governments introduced legislation. Victoria would write off debt and offer resettlement, at an estimated cost of £350,000; the Commonwealth would provide £100,000 for compensation determined by an arbiter.[146] Consequent Parliamentary debates echoed wrangling about Commonwealth and State responsibilities, and all the ills of migration. Scullin alleged gross profiteering among those who had sold land to government for settler use. A Labor group inspired by Lang opposed the legislation, laying all fault with the Empire. A few days earlier Lyons had added to his Cabinet Senator Sir Harry Lawson, the ex-Premier responsible for the original scheme.

The Acts passed, but governments remained slow to move, enraging Crutchley.[147] Arbitration proved fearfully difficult.[148] In Britain sympathy for the settlers remained potent. Secretary Thomas agreed in November to see a delegation of concerned Parliamentarians. 'Whilst I have endeavoured in the House to make the best of the terms of settlement ... I have never been satisfied in my own mind that they were really fair', confided kind-heart Jimmy to Neville Chamberlain, now Chancellor of the Exchequer.[149] Accordingly, he intended to tell the deputation that HMG might give further aid, Treasury insisted that 'it is for the Australians to clear up the mess they made', and Chamberlain persuaded Thomas to avoid commitment. Yet very soon after, in response to Crutchley's pleas, Treasury agreed to advance £10,000 with which the Representative might defray the Victorian complainants' debts, so enabling a number to return home. When the first arrived, they activated more support from public, Parliamentarians, British Legion, and bureaucrats. Thomas sought funds to reimburse their fares. 'I do ask you to realise the strength of the feeling in the House and difficulty I have had in holding off a really serious attack upon the Government', he wrote Chamberlain on 6 July; 'the main strength of which comes not from the Opposition but from the Government's supporters'. Astonishingly, Treasury advanced another £20,000. Migrants who had stayed in Victoria showed interest and some jealousy as to these proceedings.[150] The Commons sustained pressure.[151] By July 1934 compensation had cost HMG £300,000. About a hundred of the farmers returned to Britain.

While itself financing repatriation in this instance, HMG continued to resist Australian governments that were doing so.[152] Talk much outweighed action; a NSW move to return unemployed miners was one scheme never to eventuate. Yet in October 1934 ten families repatriated from Western Australia arrived in Britain. Included were some militant protesters, notably John Bunce, a Communist. The Empire Migrants Protection League, which he now helped establish, aspired to combine all such in 'One Huge League'. Its President was Charles Clarke, long active among Victorian settlers. To Crutchley and the OSD the repatriation of Bunce was a classic case of State governments unloading a troublemaker. The Representative protested when further reports told of Western and South Australia subsidising returns without reference to himself or the Commonwealth. They were the two States granted more Agreement money than their migrant intake justified! Lyons responded to Crutchley's prodding, although his rebuke of the miscreant States was milder than Scullin's had been. Moreover, the (naive?) Representative reported, federal government's own Treasury had been conniving in the practice, unbeknown to Cabinet.

Militancy still sounded from Western Australia. The State had an active branch of the British Ex-Service Legion in Australia. In mid-1934 it petitioned HMG concerning its members' sufferings under group-settlement.[153] Names were cited of settlers and officials who had prepared misleading literature and film about Western Australia. Success had come to few, declared the petitioners, and they usually had private means or a family of full-grown workers. For the rest—

> We left our homes and kindred, and all that we held dear, came 10,000 miles on promise of being given the opportunity of making and owning our farms, and now because we cannot fulfil the impossible task imposed upon us, we

are to be cast adrift, hewers of wood and drawers of water, too old for a limited labour market, and no future for ourselves and children.

Although Western Australia had for years, and with some goodwill, engaged in such mitigation as Victoria was now pursuing, this plaint had much force. Endorsing it was a Royal Commission which in 1934 enquired into Western Australia's Agricultural Bank,[154] crucial in financing land settlement during the previous generation. This told of a massive lack of realism and competence. Criticism fell too on the DMC, for having encouraged the 3500-farm scheme, albeit finally spurning it; meanwhile the State had established 400 of the proposed farms, further disaster resulting.

Perhaps some old DMC hands noticed, perhaps not. For Gepp, nadir had passed. Knighted in 1933, he thereafter expanded his mining activities, and from 1934 chaired a Royal Commission on wheat, bread and flour, which surpassed even the best of DMC investigations.[155] The Development Branch sustained various old interests—tobacco, fisheries, paper, alkali, fuels.[156] Nemesis soon came, however, most grimly in the fate of John Gunn, who in mid-decade suffered disintegration of health, marriage, and personality.[157] The Branch virtually ceased in 1935. One of its final deeds, in association with the Representative's office, was to prepare yet another dossier on the Western Australian groups.[158] This estimated that some 4000 farms had been settled overall; migrants comprised about two-thirds, the maximum on farms at one time (January 1927) being 1525. Now there were 586. Most appeared secure, none was disposed to make any repayment, some were spendthrift. Altogether government expenditure had reached £4,848,000, of which £3,164,000 had been written off. That year, 1934, saw another statement about Victorian land-settlement too.[159] It concerned farms at Childers, where hope had survived quite long. Now soil deficiency had destroyed the pastures, and twenty-three of the original forty-five settlers had left. About eighteen others from the Maffra–Sale scheme, also in Gippsland, sold up in 1934.[160] Some of them had done quite well, but were tempted by the offer of the fare to return home. Treasury begrudged payment, but recognised the power of political feeling in the matter.

In October–November 1934 the Agreement concluded, in silence.[161] Most problems had exhausted themselves by then. The closure specified the continuing concern of both HMG and the Australian government with after-care, but even its agonies had passed the peak. Only a few 'undertakings' continued, and the governments agreed in subsidising their remaining span. Yet mysteries do pertain to the closure. It was backdated to May 1932, for no apparent reason. Western Australia was still making claims against HMG and the Commonwealth at the death knell, and their resolution is uncertain.[162] Nor are all other financial details clear.

Table 4 presents a survey of Agreement schemes prepared by G. F. Plant in early 1936. It indicated a total loan expenditure of £8,731,000, with HMG making 'actual payments' of £1,490,000. This excluded the 1932–3 State scheme in New South Wales. Founded in J. H. Carruthers's fantasies of 'A Million Farms' it had remained minuscule; thirty-five men had settled, twenty-three surviving in December 1934.[163] Evidently its accounting never came within the Agreement. It would have contributed little to filling the gap between the £8.7 million, of reality and the £34 million of promise. Plant commented on the various Agreement projects. He told that 741 people were selected for the old Victorian scheme, with 406 actually taking up farms; eighteen, he estimated, were currently viable. 'New' farm creations in Victoria numbered 92 at Maffra–Sale, 114 at Katandra; 46 at Childers. As to the Wyangala Dam, conclusion of which prompted Plant's exercise, he quoted Whiskard:

The New South Wales Government have spent £1½ million and we have spent £3¼ million on this project and during its completion the objects for which it was devised have disappeared.

I do not, however, regard the money as wasted. I have no doubt that the dam will eventually serve a very valuable purpose. But for the time being there is, and will be, no return for our expenditure.

Which was that.

Table 4   'Undertakings' and spending under the £34 Million Agreement

Scheme	Estimated cost	Loans issued by Commonwealth Government to 1934	Expenditure to 1935	Total liability (approx.) of HMG in the UK	Actual payments by HMG in the UK to 1935
	£	£	£	£	£
New South Wales:					
Lachlan River Development	1 521 600	1 434 807	1 382 700	304 320	219 671
Victoria:					
1. Maffra–Sale	541 000	325 000	321 008	41 258	41 258
2. Katandra	303 000	325 000	431 396	69 250	69 250
3. Childers	140 000	140 000	138 354	25 245	25 245
4. Old Land Settlement	291 518	291 518	unknown	43 569	43 569
5. Mallee Roads	90 000	nil	48 099	7 395	7 395
Total	1 465 518	1 081 518	938 857	186 717	186 717
South Australia:					
1. Tod River Water Supply	500 000	473 821	473 821	104 307	97 297
2. Water Conservation	80 000	36 114	36 114	16 000	7 421
3. Afforestation	358 250	315 014	304 404	71 650	57 869
Total	938 250	824 949	814 339	191 957	162 587

Western Australia:

1. Narembeen Water Supply	76 197	64 192	64 190	15 239	13 194
2. Norseman Water Supply	80 000	65 348	65 347	16 000	13 419
3. Barbalin Water Supply	264 437	239 305	239 419	52 887	49 085
4. Pemberton–Denmark Railway	475 500	475 500	500 928	95 100	97 679
5. Amery [Ejanding] Northwards Railway	400 000	356 524	356 906	80 000	73 087
6. Norseman Salmon Gums Railway	225 500	225 500	229 154	45 100	46 523
7. Busselton Railway	260 252	260 252	264 343	52 050	52 592
8. Old Land Settlement (Group Scheme)	2 031 000	2 031 000	5 902 670	406 200	410 392
9. New Farms Scheme	108 000	108 000	109 307	21 400	22 207
10. Preliminary Survey Wheat Farms	150 000	104 874	153 467	30 000	21 499
11. Busselton Drainage	205 000	187 267	188 657	41 000	38 492
12. Group Roads	500 000	401 087	392 961	100 000	82 362
Total	4 775 886	4 518 849	8 467 349	954 976	920 531
Queensland:					
Survey of Agricultural Lands	30 000	5 000	1 628	6 000	348
Total — Australia	8 731 254	7 865 123	11 604 873	1 643 970	1 489 854

Source: PRO: DO57/182.

Note: Figures are for the period to 31 December of the year named.

CHAPTER EIGHT

Toward the Wheel's Return: 1932–1940

The troubles and disasters that increasingly beset migration affected policies and debate throughout the 1930s. The dominant tenor always remained adverse, indeed hostile. Yet that was less the totality of the matter than logic might seem to warrant. Some people always clung to some part of the migrationist idea. The deepening crisis in world affairs strengthened this pattern, and by the decade's end the structures of the early 1920s were returning to place. So migration proved integral to Australian experience, and even to human disposition.

The earlier generalisation that 1932 was the 'nadir' of migration was qualified by the word 'virtual'. Creation of HMG's inter-departmental committee that year best made the point. As suggested, the move may have responded to a current wave of Tory imperialism. This peaked with a motion in the Commons on 7 December, urging that government 'secure the co-operation of the Dominions in comprehensive schemes for migration within the Empire'. A. A. Somerville wanted a five-man commission to be empowered for decisive action, and again exhorted Australians to remember 'that but for the British Navy, there would be no White Australia, that it would be yellow Australia'. F. E. Guest fantasised about a million people becoming involved in imperial ventures, modelled on war-time action. He won support from Lord Apsley, renowned for having gone to Australia in guise of a farmworker, about which adventure he wrote a ripping yarn. Now Apsley averred:

> I believe such a movement might spring from the youth of this country. It would have to be a movement similar to that of the young Communists in Russia, or the Nazis in Germany, or the Fascists in Italy—it does not matter what you call them ... it is exactly the same movement.

Whereas in this debate J. H. Thomas and William Lunn stressed the problems of the past, David Kirkwood complemented Apsley in calling for a socialist approach which might redeem migration from that legacy.

The imperialists' resolution passed and continued in early 1933 via a Home and Empire Settlement Bill. This moved to amend the Settlement Act by allowing its moneys to be spent on schemes within Britain; more importantly, it would abandon the requirement for 50:50 funding with Dominion governments on approved projects, and sought their direction by an expert commission. Again some Tories seemed ready to overlook the realities of imperial relations. Cabinet decided that its spokesmen 'should adopt a favourable attitude towards the Bill, but should not allow advance beyond Second Reading'.[1] The Bill's chief upholder was Mrs S. A. Ward, the sole woman Parliamentarian to prove an active migrationist.[2] Apsley and others warned that if Australia did not expand in population, there could be little answer were Germany, Italy, or Japan to ask by what right the land was held. The Bill, having passed the Second Reading, went to committee and silence.

E. T. Crutchley's diary for early 1933 showed that Australia retained its version of Tory imperialism.[3] T. W. White, politician and war-hero, espoused a 'big migration scheme', evidently to draw funding from HMG's unemployment relief funds. Keith Officer urged the Representative to gather '5 or 6 influential people' to push for migration revival. Possibly in aftermath of this, Crutchley cabled home early in March that some 'prominent businessmen' had approached him as to HMG backing land-settlement schemes, which should proceed free from Australian government control.[4] The OSD advised caution. It already had received from the Governor of Queensland (Sir Leslie Wilson, cast in classic Tory-imperial mould) a proposal as to HMG taking such initiative in that State's north;[5] Labor Premier William Forgan Smith condoned the letter. Late in 1933 the OSD heard afresh from James Connolly, who since ceasing to be Agent-General for Western Australia had remained in London as a business imperialist. Now he revived plans for developing the Kimberley region.[6] Almost simultaneously the Agent-General for South Australia—L. L. Hill, formerly Labor Premier—reported tentative plans whereby a chartered company financed in Britain might develop the south-east of his State, employing migrant labour.[7] Neither the OSD nor Hill personally were keen; debate about the proposal in South Australia's Parliament avoided reference to migration but still met opposition from Labor and, decisively, from local property-holders wary of compulsory acquisition of land at government-determined prices.[8]

HMG's inter-departmental committee worked away, surveying much documentation and by mid-1933 preparing a draft report.[9] Commenting on it, Crutchley stressed the duty of HMG to carry all burdens of after-care: 'however responsible you may make the overseas Government, bitter experience shows that it will not rise to that responsibility'.[10] Concurrently he disparaged a subsistence-level farm scheme for north Queensland, presumably related to Leslie Wilson's gambit. That arose again in further Commons debate early in 1934, when imperialists moved in support of redistribution of population and trade throughout the Empire.[11] They hailed a recent speech in such vein by S. M. Bruce, now High Commissioner for Australia in London. The fantasy was that these new migrants would be self-subsistent, therefore posing no competition to established farmers. It was hinted again that the requisite funds could come from unemployment relief. Now too the imperialists met little opposition: 312 members had called for this debate and Sir Henry Croft told of an active committee at work. Perhaps the government felt that the matter had been sufficiently aired, for a renewed Home and Empire Settlement Bill died stillborn this session.

Private enterprise complemented the Parliamentarians' rhetoric. The British Empire Settlement Organisation had on its executive the Australian pastoral tycoon J. B. Cramsie, and it backed grandiose schemes spun by L. S. Grondona, a veteran booster of Australian interests within the imperial setting.[12] Also concerned was W. S. Robinson—associate of W. M. Hughes, the Baillieus, and virtually every eminence in British–Australian high capitalism.[13] In January 1934 Robinson proposed that Australia lease the Northern Territory and an adjacent wedge of Western Australia to HMG. 'Great Britain's social and industrial position is much graver than is commonly believed in this country', wrote Robinson to John Gunn, implying that this offered the chance of a good bargain.[14]

In June 1934 the death occurred of Alice, widow of Baron Northcote, Governor-General of Australia 1904–8. During those years Lady Northcote had endowed Australian culture.[15] Now, herself childless, she bequeathed virtually all her estate, some £200,000, to the cause of child migration. In due course a farm on Fairbridge lines was established at Bacchus Marsh, Victoria.[16] That was in 1936, when further philanthropy triggered another Fairbridge farm, at Molong, New South Wales.[17] All the while Scullin's promises of 1930 as to orphan immigration had allowed a small but regular inflow of Fairbridge and Barnardo children.[18] No Australian government appears to have contributed to the costs. An informed and altruistic bureaucrat remarked that the local Barnardo committee was accepting children rejected for Fairbridge homes.

In August 1934 Crutchley reported that a recent trip to Queensland had indicated potential for boosting migration.[19] Canon D. J. Garland, long an enthusiast,[20] had influence with Premier Smith; farmers wanted cheap boy-labour; some ex-farmboys remained angry that the changes of 1930 denied them right to nominate relatives as migrants, and this feeling could assist a general push for Australia to subsidise family reunion. Yet the Representative stressed that migration remained a political anathema. There glimmered more hope of State than Commonwealth initiative.

Now at last appeared the *Report* of the inter-departmental committee. While claiming that migration of the 1920s had served both Britain and the places of reception, it echoed the disquiets of the ITB and the Economic Advisory Council. Very few people were equipped to become pioneer farmers; immigrants were a substantial cost to the receiving nation; attempts as in Australia to inject capital had led to 'artificial stimulation' and resulted in the production of goods for which no market offered. The *Report* questioned government direction and subsidy of migration. Clients of that system suffered a difficult status in their new country, went the argument, while encouraged in the vicious delusion that responsibility for their fates lay not with themselves but with governments. The future aim must be lower fares, not direct assistance. Migration of the Barnardo–Fairbridge type promised happier results than that of most adults. Training schemes had but limited value. 'Heroic' plans of mass, subsistence-style colonisation, funded from unemployment relief, offered little prospect of success. Encouragement of migration could easily become misleading propaganda. Voluntary societies had the potential to manage migration more effectively than did government, and should be so encouraged. Repeatedly the *Report* applauded 'spontaneous' migration, activated by 'pull' from the receiving country, rather than 'push' from Britain. 'The history of migration in modern times proves that migration is a symptom of prosperity and not a cure for depression' went an echo of earlier OSD arguments. In this context it seemed to confess that HMG's policy had often defied that truth, and so doom had befallen it. Yet the *Report* accepted that prosperity might come again, and with it the chance of spontaneous-pull migration. It recommended a new administrative structure. The OSC had not worked well, problems arising especially from vagueness as to its powers. It were better to have two bodies: an Overseas Settlement Board to decide policy, and a Central Committee to co-ordinate voluntary agencies active in migration.[21]

Hard on the *Report*'s publication, the chairman of the inter-departmental committee—Malcolm MacDonald, as Dominions Under-Secretary—came to Australia for Melbourne's Centenary celebrations.[22] In Western Australia he met many pre-1914 migrants who had achieved fair prosperity, contrasting with the lot of more recent group-settlers. Across the continent, Forgan Smith told MacDonald that farmboys had well served Queensland. Prime Minister Lyons confided as to having rebuilt some friendships with erstwhile Labor colleagues (a matter perhaps of interest to the MacDonald family), and that he would like to move on migration. The visitor saw that such action still threatened loss of votes. His subsequent memorandum on migration returned to that theme, but also stressed that defence considerations made population increase the more germane for Australia. Meanwhile press and Parliamentary comment probed MacDonald's interest in migration. Lyons affirmed that neither his government nor the Under-Secretary intended any policy move under present circumstances. 'But I hope that at some time in the future it will be possible, in the interests of Australia, to provide once again for migration by people from the other side of the world to Australia'.[23]

Early in 1935 Crutchley went to a dinner addressed by R. G. Menzies, who since October had been Lyons's Attorney-General and was already his likely successor. The speaker declared 'his intent to urge migration as part of a grand imperial plan' on a forthcoming trip to Britain.[24] Crutchley told his diary soon afterwards that 'there is no more real affection for England in Australia than there is for Australia in England', but Menzies's comment nicely demarcated the halfway point of the 1930s. The trip he cited, centring on the jubilee of George V's rule, was the first British venture for both himself and Lyons.

Before departing, the Prime Minister refused a nomination from Canon Garland for some farmboys and relatives of earlier migrants. Crutchley reported Lyons's insistence that one nation-wide policy should prevail.[25] Yet in London G. F. Plant ruminated whether the OSD might propose that Australian migration policy return to the States. Thomas told Cabinet that discussions begun by MacDonald in Australia could develop during Lyons's northern sojourn.[26] Some talk did occur then and it encouraged MacDonald (from November elevated to Dominions Secretaryship) to hope for a modest resumption in migration.[27] During mid-1935 approval of that idea came from non-Labor Premiers B. S. B. Stevens of New South Wales and R. L. Butler of South Australia. However, letters from HMG to Australia late in the year secured but temporising replies, while Lyons prevaricated to Australia's House of Representatives on 27 November when indicating that nothing relevant had happened in Britain.

Tory imperialists sustained their cause in the Commons. In mid-year one A. R. Wise, backed by Apsley, had warned of German plans for settlement in Australia and cited figures for recent non-British immigration thither, lamenting that the numbers of such immigrants had risen to a tenth of the total.[28] (In fact, the ratio was far higher.) Debate continued in December, the government defending itself by stressing reservations voiced by the inter-departmental *Report*, and by overseas governments in responding thereto.[29] Some Labour opinion supported the imperialist call, but radicals—notably John McGovern and Aneurin Bevan—remained resolute in hostility. The latter's brother-in-law had suffered defeat and debauch in Australia.[30]

Only now, in late 1935, did the government establish the Overseas Settlement Board. Treasury helped to select the members, showing itself wary of dangers. As to the eminent political theorist W. G. S. Adams, for example: 'I hear from two sources, both very good, that he is a man of somewhat sanguine temperament. To my mind this is a serious disadvantage. I need not emphasise what disastrous results optimism has produced in this field.' [31] Brigadier-General J. J. H. Nation was accepted as 'the best of a tiresome and noisy contingent', the ultra-imperialists; Nation's term proved short, so a successor was found in Lord Barnby, 'useless but innocuous'. The Department of Labour pushed for trade unionist George

Gibson, whom W. M. Citrine—supreme Labour moderate—had advanced. 'While he is of the bluff and burly type,' Treasury said of Gibson, 'he is not a bad fellow.' The new Board succeeded the OSC in February–March 1936.

Another breeze of change was felt when Crutchley was succeeded from March 1936 by Whiskard, now Sir Geoffrey and with the style High Commissioner. In charge during the interim was W. C. Hankinson, who told further of local politicians' reluctance to stand by migration; even Premiers Smith and Stevens failed that test.[32] However, the very day, 10 January 1936, on which Hankinson penned one such complaint, the federal government issued a statement, admittedly tentative, as to its interest in the matter.[33] Spokesman was that Thomas Paterson who had included migration within his portfolio 1926–8 and now was Minister for the Interior, consequent upon the inclusion of Country Party members in Lyons's government after 1934. Response to Paterson's statement was mixed, but some action proceeded. A. C. D. Rivett complained to F. L McDougall that Prime Ministerial memoranda were enjoining 'comprehensive investigation' of the issue.[34] While disdaining this task, Rivett backed McDougall's concurrent hopes for 'economic appeasement', which proposed burgeoning economic ties between Britaindom and Germany. Rivett remarked that Germans had proved much superior to Britons as Australian immigrants. McDougall's blueprint complemented the efforts of himself and Bruce to make the League of Nations more alert to socio-economic issues and also the diplomatic appeasement which Bruce approved vis-à-vis Axis powers.[35]

One enthusiast for migration was Sir Lennon Raws, director of many top-ranking Australian companies. Hankinson reported this, and also Lyons's assurance of commitment.[36] During 1936 at least two Governors avowed the cause, stressing defence considerations, which seemingly were topmost also in Lyons's mind.[37] His Department of Commerce floated a paper arguing for planned loans, development, and population increase, all highly reminiscent of DMC work.[38] The United Australia Party in New South Wales called for a successor to the Commission.[39] From 1936 the government received various statements on migration; most were in support, but still came to no great number and derived from altogether obvious sources—Chambers of Commerce, the Victoria Scottish Union, the Australian Development and Defence League.[40]

Late in February Lyons's two senior Ministers, Menzies and E. C. G. Page, embarked for Europe. From Aden, they reported having met many India-based officers keen for Australian retirement.[41] In Britain, the Ministers were more active on migration than Menzies and Lyons had been the previous year. They met the Overseas Settlement Board, Menzies philosophising:

Migration primarily depended on the building up of the economic, social, and political organisation of the Dominion concerned, and he, for his part, felt that it was more and more important to reproduce in the Dominion the political and social organisation of the British people and to establish a degree of economic independence which would render that Dominion a real asset to the Empire as a whole.[42]

He stressed that fear of Japanese aggression was affecting Australian attitudes; in contrast, Crutchley had discounted that factor when addressing the Board recently, albeit supporting renewed migration. The Australian duo echoed past concerns in calling for British receptivity to Australian exports, primary and industrial, and for more loans. The Board's officers embodied these points in an *aide-mémoire*, obviously hoping to impel Australia towards an affirmative policy. Meanwhile, Page had met a Jewish-refugee organisation and promised that some boys sponsored by it would be accepted into Australia as farmworkers.[43]

During spring 1936 the Board also interviewed Premiers Smith and Stevens. The former was wary as to migration, the latter forthright. At about this time Stevens included ideas for imperial development in an impressive programme of positive government.[44] His arguments received attention in and beyond Whitehall. Trade Commissioner Dalton was not enthusiastic, claiming that Australia's economic performance remained miserable. Stevens, Dalton said, was a tool of the Sydney banker A. C. Davidson, himself anxious to outpoint Commonwealth authorities, who clung more truly to economic orthodoxy. The Board of Trade followed Dalton's lead, and warned HMG against encouraging secondary industry in Australia, potentially competitive with that at home. Treasury deigned not to oppose renewed assistance for migration.[45]

On 6 May 1936 Paterson told Australia's Parliament of the government's decision to be more generous in admitting alien immigrants. Since about 1930 a tight rein had applied, especially as to southern Europeans, who were the only people applying in numbers. Paterson's announcement stirred some xenophobic antagonisms,[46] but fewer than past attitudes augured. In retrospect, his words seem to foreshadow Continental dominance in Australian immigration history.

In mid-year Menzies, back from Europe, declared his belief that Australia should expand migration so as to achieve a population of 20 million in the foreseeable future.[47] Lyons proposed such matters for the impending Premiers' Conference.[48] There they went to a sub-committee, but not quite to oblivion. In September Lyons wrote the Premiers, asking them to consider renewed assistance for some British migrants—family reunion cases, farmworkers, domestics, and anyone with moderate capital (£300 for families, £50 for singles). Annexed statistics showed that out-migration still prevailed among Britons, there being a net loss of 917 in 1935; but 'white aliens' were increasing, the 1935 figure being 2295. This sum is weightier in that government had been restraining entry of southern Europeans up to 1936. The current easing of those restrictions seems contrary to the tone of regret in Lyons's letter apropos rising alien numbers. Conceivably government hoped to generate a counter-response of popular support for Britons. Anyway the Premiers gave Lyons's letter a very cool reception, and he withdrew. In Tasmania at least the passage prompted thoughtful analysis of the 1920s experience, bureaucrats finding more cause for past lament than future hope, and one telling that even in the temperate island European migrants had proved more successful than Britons.

The OSD maintained its awareness of Australia's sensitivities. Proposals for renewed Maltese migration thither were suspended, lest they thwart wider resumption.[49] Plant queried the Jewish farmboys on like grounds. In September the current Dominions Under-Secretary, the Marquess of Hartington, set off for the antipodes; he had been advised to probe all migration possibilities and to discourage Australian repatriation of Britons, a matter of continuing tension.[50] The Department asked Whiskard whether Hartington might not liaise with Menzies, who had been 'very helpful about this when he was here'. The Commissioner affirmed that Menzies and Page were upholding the cause, in the face of much apathy and Labor opposition. Hartington found that analysis all too true. 'The People realised their need of population but did not want it', went his verdict.[51] Yet on 3 December Lyons told Parliament that the government had in view a comprehensive scheme of migration.

The following month beheld a conference on 'the future of immigration into Australia', sponsored by the Australian Institute of Political Science.[52] The Left-liberalism dominant there wanted that future to be minimal. H. C. Coombs, guru of such ideology through Australia's next half-century, argued that henceforth most employment would be in tertiary services; such development 'might therefore make it advantageous to Australia, and to the rest of the world, if there was a reversal of the stream of migration into Australia, and a net balance of people returned to Europe'. A British economist, W. B. Reddaway, minimised migration's capacity to diminish his homeland's troubles. Australia's strategic problems achieved some notice, but sheer population was not seen as their answer. Rather, the idea glinted that the world should learn how scant were Australian resources, and so have less reason to prize them. There were counter-views. Professor Adams offered Ameryesque doctrine as to migration helping effective distribution of imperial resources; Sir Philip Goldsmith echoed this faith. Gepp also spoke to the conference, stressing the DMC's erstwhile sensitivity to migration's problems, and calling for planned and purposeful government 'so that the active interest of the mass of the nation can be aroused and commanded'. Not for the first time, he urged appointment of an expert body to assist in this task, citing as a model not the DMC, but CSIR.

Another Australian to discuss migration at this time was R. B. Madgwick, as author of the impressive *Immigration into Eastern Australia, 1788–1851.* Madgwick noted various parallels between 'his' years and more recent times. The human quality of migrants in both of these periods he found wanting, contrasting them with the happier experience of the 1850s goldrush. While offering reasons for such variation, and chiding established Australians, of both centuries, for ignoring those reasons, Madgwick remained judgmental. 'During the twentieth century Australia has had many unfortunate experiences, with immigrants drawn from the wrong strata of the British and Irish populations.'

While Australia's savants were disparaging migration, HMG was renewing the Settlement Act.[53] The OSD used the occasion to advance the possibility of Britain giving aid under the Act to industrial enterprise overseas. Treasury, aligning with the Board of Trade, opposed this move. They failed, but the ceiling of annual expenditure under the Act now fell to £1.5 million, and large-scale land schemes would require separate statutory authorisation. Aid for approved migration projects, putatively those of voluntary societies, could rise to 75 per cent. There was a case for 100 per cent subsidy of after-care, bureaucrats agreed, but it were better that the world did not know that HMG believed Dominion governments capable of grossly neglecting immigrants.[54]

The renewal provoked interesting Parliamentary debate.[55] Malcolm MacDonald showed such deference to Dominion sensitivities that William Lunn jibed that he revealed underlying disbelief in migration. Not that Lunn now supported it. The radical voice of Labour came from Aneurin Bevan, who disparaged migration by recalling that many of Australia's first colonists were convicts. A Tory responded that 'fine men and women were sent out to Australia, although designated criminals', so expressing a view which within Australia has had support mainly from radicals. Bevan and another Labourite, F. J. Bellenger, offered their own style of appeasement, and contempt for Dominions' nationality, by suggesting that Britain should allow Germany, Italy, and Japan to share New World expansion; the alternative was war. Repudiation of that view came from a Rothschild in the House.

Coronation year brought Australian politicians and bureaucrats to London, several to converse with imperial authorities about migration.[56] Some remained negative—A. A. Dunstan, currently Premier of Victoria, for example, and V. H. Ryan, of the South Australian service. More effective were talks between MacDonald, Bruce, R. G. Casey (now federal Treasurer), R. A. Parkhill (Minister for Defence), and top-level advisors.[57] MacDonald pushed strategic issues hard, remaking the point that not all the world accepted Anglo-Australia's monopoly over the continent's resources. Potential British migrants were already few, MacDonald argued, and that would intensify. Bruce insisted that Australian strength could come only with more vigorous secondary industry, which Britain therefore must foster. MacDonald accepted that, but still stressed Australia's need for numbers. He proposed that the answer might lie with 'additional foreign settlers of the best type, such as Scandinavians and Germans': a stance akin to Bevan's, and even to McDougall's 'economic appeasement'. Casey thought such pondering should be kept secret.

Lyons's government continued its careful way. In July 1937 it declared its intent to join with Britain in subsidising the fares of those categories of migrants proposed to the Premiers months before. Ministers admitted that the States' response had been patchy, but the Commonwealth would ignore the dissentients and deal with the affirmers.[58] Whiskard declared apprehension at this tilt at the constitutional balance, 'in view of the weakening of Federal as against State loyalties'.[59] Parliamentary debate around this time bemoaned alien dominance among immigrants, and government backbenchers insisted that Britons be encouraged in counter-weight.[60] Lyons made some mention of migration plans in the election campaign which resulted in his return on 23 October, and so did the Governor-General's opening of the new Parliamentary session.

Early in 1938 Lyons veered towards a system of general fare subsidy rather than assistance to individuals, arguing to Whiskard that it would diminish migrants' disposition to rely overmuch on government support. The High Commissioner had been among those many who had supported this view in the past, but now told the Prime Minister of obstacles in that way.[61] Talks proceeded to a conclusion best summarised in a Parliamentary statement of 12 May, by Paterson's successor as Minister for the Interior, John McEwen.[62] In March, Australian and British governments had determined jointly to assist passage of relatives and friends nominated by Australian residents; nominees of schemes run by Fairbridge, Big Brothers, Salvation Army, YMCA, Boy Scouts and the churches; employment categories requisitioned by the States; and people with capital (as earlier proposed). Also the Australian government would grant half-fares for erstwhile servants of Empire in India. McEwen said that already the scheme was prompting response in all mainland States. The scale of assistance followed that of the late 1920s, save that domestics enjoyed no special terms. Loans did not prevail originally, but soon they were allowed to domestics and farmworkers, with voluntary societies acting as collectors. Another new flexibility was to allow a second round of assistance to migrants who had returned to Britain meanwhile.

The Commonwealth evidently intended that, while nominations would normally go through State offices, they were expected to approve them almost as a matter of course. Were rejection proposed in any case, it had to be submitted to the federal bureaucracy. Possibly some nominators dealt direct with the latter. Such developments were logical, and complemented Scullin's over-riding of those States who hankered to continue immigration in 1929–30, but still were forthright. They aroused only a little protest. South Australia queried the federal government's second look at rejections, while Tasmania nagged for restraints on employers' capacity to introduce workers and sought Commonwealth assistance with cost-causing migrants.[63] No change ensued. Whiskard now said that the States were happy with a decision in favour of migration for which they suffered no odium of responsibility.[64] States' rights did not arise in the debate following McEwen's statement. Opposition Leader John Curtin restated traditional Labor criticisms of migration, but even that in desultory way.[65]

This new-old move of government coincided with celebrations of the Sesquicentenary of British Australia, Hartington again visiting for the occasion. When he returned home, he prepared a Cabinet Paper which affirmed that 'largely for defence reasons, but partly also because of the return of prosperity, most Australians are anxious to see a revival of British migration in some form or other'.[66] Yet isolationism stayed strong, no less in the general community than in the Labor Party. Hartington proposed that Australia might help itself and the world by accepting not only Britons but Poles, Yugoslavs, and Austrians. He called for British industrialists to establish branch industries in Australia. Government Houses should cease to offer an 'island for an English clique', and instead relate with Australian democracy. Hartington spoke favourably of the Sesquicententary celebrations and pondered history:

> Australians have had a hard struggle. Unless they were of tough stock, they could never have prevailed over the conditions they have had to face. Their courage and vitality are wonderful. But both circumstances and the stock that was needed to meet those conditions have combined to produce a nation that lacks culture to an appalling degree.

The reception accorded musician Malcolm Sargent on a recent tour showed yearning for higher things. Hartington himself ascended to the Duchy of Devonshire in May.

In May also there appeared the first major *Report* of the Overseas Settlement Board.[67] It welcomed recent Australian migration initiatives while repeating the case for massive reductions in fares to facilitate non-government migration. Dominion reluctance to accept migrants on account of domestic unemployment made but limited sense, continued the *Report*. 'To wait until the unemployment level has been reduced to any arbitrary figure may well mean waiting until it is too late.' This hinted at the Board's concern with international tensions. Devonshire being the Board's chairman, it was natural that the *Report* should echo his urging of British support for Australian industrial growth, and of Australian acceptance of European migrants. Another thus to speak in mid-1938 was T. C. Macnaghten.[68]

This season saw Page, Menzies, and that other migrationist in Australia's Cabinet, T. W. White, forgather in London. Their particular hope was to renegotiate the Ottawa agreement so as further to reduce British duties on Australian products.[69] They had little effect, causing Page to remark that between the two governments lay 'utterly opposed views upon the commercial and industrial development of Australia as a British country'. There emerged a 'memorandum of conclusions', which mouthed shibboleths. They included recognition of a mutual interest in the expansion of Australia's population, and that this required development of secondary industry. Page and Menzies again liaised with the Overseas Settlement Board, Menzies applauding its advice as to European migration:

> Foreigners had played a large part in the development of Australia in the past, and he thought that Australia would be immensely strengthened, and in no way weakened, if there could be, during the next two decades, a considerable migration of aliens.[70]

Page had already travelled to the Netherlands and pursued the issue. The Board heard that Danes also won Australian favour, although there was no intent to subsidise fares for aliens. Menzies warned against pampering migrants ('the success of a migrant depended upon himself'), while denying that Australian social services were much inferior to Britain's.

The Board stimulated other migrationist thinking in these months. Ernest Bevin affirmed to it his hopes to foster sympathy among Australia's trade unionists on his visit thither in late 1938. (After returning, he stressed that new industries were necessary before mass migration would be welcome there, and that conditions were more favourable in New Zealand.) The Board's complementary talk with the Federation of British Industries also invoked rationalising of manufactures, Empire-wide. As well, the Board pursued the matter of reciprocity between social services in Britain and Australia. Early in 1938 the Australian Parliament had passed a National Insurance Act which promised to elevate Australian welfare towards that in Britain, thus giving sense to Menzies's pertinent comment. Whiskard's letters illuminate the further history of the issue, which deepened the crisis that was developing within the Lyons government. The Act was not proclaimed, business interests abhorring it, and both Menzies and Casey accordingly criticised the Prime Minister. At first Whiskard accepted their good faith, but spoke differently in March 1939 when Menzies resigned from Cabinet: 'Conscious as I am of Mr Menzies' many great qualities, I have never regarded him, and do not now regard him, as a man likely to sacrifice expediency to principle.'[71] As Whiskard further said, the episode showed the government's paralysis. A few weeks later Lyons died, and on 26 April Menzies became Prime Minister.

The House of Commons had its last substantial inter-war debate on migration on 21 December 1938. Tory imperialists made their eternal points, Canada bulking larger than Australia. MacDonald averred that the Overseas Settlement Board had impelled Australia's resumption of assistance. He spoke about industrial rationalisation as if he meant it, hitting at British interests being 'shocked and horrified' when confronted with such views. MacDonald reiterated the case for European migration to Australia. Yet he cited figures indicating that at last more Britons were going to Australia than returning; 1259 migrants had been assisted in 1938. (A few weeks later the Commons received data indicating that most of the puny expenditure under the renewed Settlement Act had arisen thus.)[72] MacDonald pondered how the flow might widen. 'From the highest Imperial reason, we have to see whether we can devise some policy of putting the birth rate up again.' Did honourable members have their giggle—before Christmas, before War, before Empire's End?

Australian Parliamentary debate gave an occasional gleam.[73] Labor suspicion of migration continued, Curtin jeering especially at Page's support of Scandinavian migrants and a target population of 30 million. H. S. Gullett upheld population growth, especially through Britons and babies, which latter source was much avowed in these years by his old antagonist, W. M. Hughes, as Minister for Health. 'We are, as a nation, doomed', said Gullett apropos demographic stagnation; 'we have no physical hold on Australia, and, what is worse, we have no moral claim upon all of it.' Response came from another veteran, Labor's Francis Brennan:

> We number nearly 7,000,000 people, and we claim some rights, not based upon conquest, but upon a tradition and history of unprecedented labour, development and expansion, intellectual and physical. The Australians owe nothing to anybody else for the development of their country ... When those convicts were placed upon British ships they were put there not for the purpose of establishing an Empire, but in order to get rid of the superfluous convicts, manufactured in too great numbers for the British Government to be able to cope with ... we owe nothing to the Imperial legislature or to the British taxpayer.

So persisted Irish-Australian radicalism.

Another venue of Australian debate in September 1938 was a conference on Empire relations, sponsored by the Royal Institute of International Affairs and its Australian counterpart. A preparatory book, *Australia's National Interest and National Policy*,[74] included a chapter on migration, remarkable for its indecision. A relevant paper was read at the conference by W. D. Forsyth, an able young Australian historian recently back from pertinent research in Britain. Entitled 'Dying Reservoirs of Migrants', Forsyth's address doubtless embodied the arguments that he developed in a learned article at the time and a book published in 1942.[75] These brilliantly explored issues which had burgeoned in the later 1930s, especially the reluctance of Britons to emigrate and the pertinence for Australia of Continental European migrants. 'The "New Immigration" in Australia' was one chapter title of the book, affirming European dominance among newcomers as an established phenomenon rather than a future possibility. Yet Forsyth believed that Continentals would prove no more fertile than established Australians, and as a result the country would remain dangerously under-populated. Another participant at the 1938 conference was W. K. Hancock, also soon to write of Empire migration, but in a much blander way than did Forsyth.[76] The conference could not have enthused any upholder of that cause. Ernest Bevin journeyed to Australia, in order to attend the conference; that he subsequently lost his migrationist zeal tells its own message.

Debate became even quieter in 1939. Australia's Parliament heard but one more pre-war passage—a member expostulating that Western Australian group-settlers were yet being pursued to pay outstanding loans, with government replying that those few remaining on their blocks were exempted.[77] On 6 September another backbencher asked about future migration policy. 'I have not at hand the full particulars,' replied Minister J. A. Perkins, 'but the war will certainly interfere with the arrival of migrants.' The Australian government declared itself ready to continue with current arrangements, but on 15 September Whiskard received instructions that henceforth HMG would allow only hardship cases.[78] Finance would continue for after-care, especially of children and as advised by the British Settlers' Welfare Committee. The wheel scarcely had completed one turn.

Emigration

Early in this book, migration is said to be fundamental in human experience. A historian who uses such terms must meet their challenges and delve that experience. The foregoing text has done so to the degree that its narrative purpose required. Such detail has been thickest for the years immediately after 1918 and, from a particular perspective, for the 1930s. Now 'experience' must become central, and the intervening period receive most attention (although even for the 1920s the effect often will be to look anew at material already noted). The exercise must first confront two related-but-opposed issues: obstacles retarding Austral migration, and dynamics impelling it. Both were important parts of the whole truth, and from different aspects each is the more important. Had a sizeable number of people not migrated, there would be so much the less validity in writing this book, and especially these last two chapters. Yet reluctance to migrate, inter-meshing with difficulties in doing so even where the will prevailed, was a larger part of British attitudes and life. Perhaps the best way to comprehend this dichotomy is by first further probing anti-migrationist themes, and so clearing the way for the positive story.

*   *   *

Big truths merit recapitulation. The 1920s never saw a repetition of the pre-1914 migrationist boom; even the early years of the decade showed that, and as it proceeded the lesson became more evident. This was one more expression of the isolationism and introspection which marked most European societies in these years (and which underlay much Australian hostility to immigration). Archetypal Britons had had their fill of excitement with the War, leaving little scope for the somewhat comparable experience of migration. Endemic hostility to the ruling class found easy vent in scorning its efforts to boost movement. That those rulers were simultaneously providing Everyperson with some social security and domestic comfort made anti-migrationism still more logical. Stories of migrant hardship in Australia, characteristically exaggerated but (as chapter 10 will confirm) not groundless, played their very important part. Some truth lay in the judgment of T. S. P. Pughe, an Anglican cleric, that migration to Australia had become 'the last throw—the last desperate chance. It is an expediency, not an expectancy. It is an act of despair, and not of hope ... we are trying to send the unwilling man to the unwilling land.'[1] Pughe himself twice visited Australia, hoping to alleviate the tragedy which he believed inseparable from migration.

News of the World, supreme populist voice, and Labour's *Daily Herald* were British-wide papers most active in telling migrant woes. They made a powerful pair, but it seems probable that local journals were yet more insistent and uniform in pursuing the theme. Likewise, while Parliament heard a deal on this subject, street talk rang louder. 'Local antagonism to migration is disturbingly widespread, finding its two chief centres in certain Labour organisations such as the Trades and Labour Councils and in the local press', ran a Ministry of Labour minute.[2] It pointed especially to Australia. As remarked, the ITB *Report* told to similar effect, and itself prompted further venting of popular anti-migrationism. 'Speeches about the need for migration rouse hostile complexes among the working classes here, especially the women', affirmed F. L. McDougall.[3]

The most able analyst of popular opposition to Britain's 1834 Poor Law has stressed how it drew strength from communal and familial emotion.[4] Animus against migration never achieved so much power, but parallels subsisted and historians should pursue them. Australia and Britain were antipodal, yet there prevailed an intense, specific, sensitive awareness in the homeland as to migrant experience down-under. Probably as important as the press in sustaining this, although still further beyond documentation, was the flow of information from migrant returnees. That number was always large, ranging from holiday-makers to those envenomed dissidents noticed especially in chapter 7. Political and class elements solidified anti-migration feeling. Labour in Britain was almost as hostile to emigration as its counterpart in Australia to immigration. Logically so, for the migrationists were seeking to save capitalism, and migrant sufferings resulted from that effort.

Writing in 1937, an emigrant of 1912 declared:

> In respectable working class England the member of the family who 'had to emigrate' was the blot on the escutcheon. You were rating yourself low if you imagined you could do better in any other country than your own. That, strangely enough, can march side by side with a smug satisfaction in Empire greatness, just as can pride in Britain's feats of arms and a contempt for the relative who 'had to enlist'.[5]

All this when emigration was booming! What happened after 1918 truly had deep roots. Yet the scribe, William Hatfield (author of several goodish travelogues and novels about Australia; a radical, interested in Communism and conservation), may have read the later situation into his memories. Anyway he underscored the idea of migration often being a matter of shame. So did those various official efforts to avoid the terms 'emigration' and 'immigration'.[6] One more variant on that theme merits note. A contributor to heated debate in Australia's Parliament in June 1921 was Joseph Cook—born in Staffordshire in 1860, a migrant of 1885, pioneer Labor Parliamentarian, but quick to leave that allegiance and in his new one to enjoy much success, even being Prime Minister 1913–14. 'I did not come as an immigrant', declared the older Cook in 1921; 'I paid my own way'.[7]

At least as salient as these socio-personal obstacles to emigration were sheer economic factors. David Pope has contributed much to the definition of these.[8] His analysis confirms that generally wage rates stayed higher in Australia than Britain through most of the 1920s, at least as much as during the buoyant migration years just before 1914. Any economic deterrent lay not in that quarter, Pope concludes, but rather in the escalating real costs of migration, especially the passage itself. Even for those receiving aid, outlays normally were higher than earlier. Yet, on Pope's own data, the favourable ratio of Australian wages might promise soon to cover that gap. Perhaps then one should emphasise, as has Pope himself, that Australian unemployment ran higher after the War than before.[9] Pertinent too is Pope's argument that 'pull' factors seem stronger than 'push' in determining British–Austral migration. That pattern is far from absolute—hope that Britain's new Labour government of 1929 might fulfil its promise to create jobs diminished interest in migration[10]—but it seems generally firm. A Board of Trade memorandum made the point:

> It is far nearer the truth to say that prosperous trade stimulates emigration than to say the opposite. The fact appears to be that it is the attraction presented by the prospects of life in the new country rather than disquiet with condition in the old, that is reflected in the mass figures of emigration.[11]

C. W. G. Eady led several others who argued to similar effect,[12] this context making sense of a remark that otherwise might appear vacuous: that the presence of welfare relief at home thwarted migration less than did its absence in Australia. Hereabouts too might lurk the germ of truth in OSD arguments about lack of Empire-wide prosperity being the great dampener. The period was not altogether grim in either hemisphere. Yet money ran not so free in Britain as to make fares easy, nor in Australia to sustain abundant jobs and/or unemployment relief. Migration, one can assert (but scarcely prove) requires the 'push' of a *big* disaster or the 'pull' of a *big* boom, and the 1920s saw neither. Pope makes the further point that Australian governments spent less in subsidising migration after the War than earlier, while talking louder; he suggests that 'money illusion', failure to accept the statistics of inflation, underlay this.[13] Perhaps Pope is himself a victim of illusion, not seeing that the rhetoric of Hughes and Bruce cloaked determination to spend only as much Australian money as lured more from Britain.

Both 'push' and 'pull' were especially weak in relation to 'selectees'. The point is already made that farmworkers and domestics were relatively in demand in Britain. One reason was widespread resistance to such employment. That applied toward the New World as the Old: 'there is a general feeling that neither the type of work offered … nor the wages promised offers very strong inducement', declared the Ministry of Labour about Australia. 'Dislike of country life with its isolation' applied on one hand, 'widespread and deeply rooted objection in the minds of women of the present generation' to domestic service, on the other.[14]

Are birth-rates a product more of economics or of attitudes? Most allusions to fertility so far have been apropos anti-migrationists' warnings that, because natural increase was falling, further population loss might endanger Britain. (There loomed the view of Australia as predator.) Another effect of the decline in the birth-rate presumably was to weaken the 'push' which might impel large families to migrate. C. H. E. Manning was one to make this point.[15] Malcolm MacDonald followed, when suggesting that imperial duty required busier procreation. However, duty ranks much less an incentive to that end than does pleasure, or prudential concerns for succour in old age. Pensions diminished the latter impulse, while improved contraception had a broader impact. The promise of Wakefield and other nineteenth-century migrationists that the New World offered sex without Malthusian doom lost its point. Yet low birthing in the 1920s probably was not the result of technology alone. Technology was no less efficient after 1945, but that period saw more babies, and more migration too. Those phenomena may have both derived from then-prevailing euphoria of spirit, whereas after 1918 there dominated wariness of commitment, a limiting of hope.

'War has produced a natural reaction, young men are not anxious to go off indefinitely from their own country, and parents are even more reluctant than usual to allow their boys to leave home.'[16] This was one of the most persuasive insights that Eady offered as to migration patterns, especially acute in stressing concern at loss of young men. That often reflected parental anger at removal of a migrant son's wage—the chief upholder of the YMCA's emigration programme, ascribed most opposition to his work to this factor.[17] Yet finer feeling had play also. One father wrote to Queensland authorities:

> I had a few lines from my boy, he doesn't seem to be satisfied with his wages …
> if he had taken my advice he would still have been at home, it breaks my heart
> to think of him being so far away and not happy … now that you have got

him away from home, you aught to look after him better. I am an old man myself, but will save every penny I can to get him home … I am going to Sunderland this week to Cooks Shipping Office. They told my boy such things about Australia …[18]

Here was one of the ways in which migration appeared to inflict ravages similar to those of War.

Of other evidence as to migration's unpopularity, the most forceful may lie in some accounts of recruiting campaigns. That their especial targets were those elusive 'selectable' groups made failure of these missions more logical, yet it remains stark. One report, October 1925, tells of M. L. Shepherd, key man at Australia House, back from scouring south-west England, declaring a drought of farmworkers. 'Adults … preferred the dole rather than risk the uncertainties of agriculture in Australia.' Almost simultaneously WA Agent-General H. P. Colebatch joined J. T. Barnes of the Migration Office in a similar (possibly the same) jaunt. Despite intensive advertising and vast unemployment in the region, only 169 people offered and 63 of them were not even worth a medical.[19] The following year Colebatch asked Barnes to find 50 group settlers. The latter sifted some 1700 applications and set off with a colleague to interview 70 possibilities. Five passed that test. 'In many cases, if the husband was suitable, the wife was unsuitable, and vice versa.'[20]

While class consciousness steeled proletarian hostility to migration, and most upholders of that cause were bourgeois, many among Britain's ruling class also were dubious. The black-hats of Treasury testified to that, as did L. S. Amery's failure to carry fellow Ministers. In February 1928 Montagu Norman of the Bank of England urged Stanley Baldwin to uphold migration in a forthcoming address to undergraduates at Cambridge. 'I know of no young men in the range of my acquaintance who think of settling in Australia,' went the response, 'and all those who have made money out there, like the Dalgetys, Gilchrists, Caldwells come back and live here.'[21] George V's early gestures in support of migration soon weakened, and in 1925 he declined to contribute to the Church of England's Council of Oversea Settlement.[22] Like so many parents, the King begrudged his sons' Empire travels, including the Duke of York's Australian tour of 1927.[23] (The duke was happy to go, while the Prince of Wales showed more interest in migration than in most public matters.) Occasional reports told of wealthy people enquiring about migration, and a few did venture, but most evidence confirms that Baldwin spoke for his England. The puny response to OSD organising of public-schoolboy tours of Empire, and failure of the Tasmanian elitist scheme, were two indicators already noticed. Similar doom befell Western Australia's Pioneer Memorial Association.[24] Its mastermind was General Sir J. J. T. Hobbs—orchestrator of much veneration for God, King, and Empire. That people at ease in their homeland should prefer to stay there is altogether logical, yet the exceptions to such a rule were now notably few.

*   *   *

Reinforcing these popular British suspicions of Austral migration, and intrinsically acting as a most formidable constrictor of that process, was Australian regulatory control, especially of those seeking subsidy. Every polity must proceed in some such way, and Australian sensitivities as to migration sharpened that rule in this case. However, such lofty truths had little play with those who wanted migration, for either themselves or others, as they saw the Australian machine at work. It angered those who were excluded and rejected, while badgering those it processed. To offer oneself was hazardous, repugnant, even humiliating. Many who were qualified to do so, went the claim, consequently did not. The ITB ground its axe when stressing popular British anger at Australia's restrictiveness, but did not invent. Barnes, overall more important than Shepherd, Manning, or anyone else in the implementation of policy, himself remarked that public meetings in support of recruitment could be counter-productive as some volunteers learned their ineligibility, while others who had reached first base and then suffered rejection declared their anger.[25] Yet again reared the image of Australia as greedy and arrogant—the more insufferable, many may have thought, in a place of convict origin.

Perhaps that generalisation is enough and the matter should end there. But conscience impels some attempt to map the intricacies of regulation—although nothing like comprehensiveness is possible, for there was little recording of variations, or even of all basic procedures, which prevailed from time to time and State to State. Nor does this account have much to say about the situation in 1920–1, likewise because documentation is slight until the Settlement Act brought HMG into active involvement.

All migrants had to undergo enquiry and form-filling, but this was vastly more true for those seeking assistance than for self-payers, and the following remarks apply to the former.[26] Everyone in Britain—shipping agents, bureaucrats, philanthropists—likely to be involved in encouraging migrants, received data as to Australia's rigorous selectivity. Physical and mental, even moral, health had large part in this prescription, which imposed a first sift. Next, the postulant had to supply particulars—skill, past employment, medical history, and so on. One rule denied aid to British residents who had formerly lived in Australia. Designed to kill any hemispheric jaunting at public expense, the proviso had remarkably strict application—for years, even against erstwhile Australian servicemen.

If preliminary scrutiny allowed, the applicant would be asked for two referees, and they would be contacted.

> Should any doubt arise with regard to these references, confidential inquiries are instituted through the British Ministry of Labour, or some social organisation such as the YMCA, who through their local representatives are often of the greatest value in establishing the true character of the prospective migrant.[27]

Barnes computed that the Ministry supplied 26,880 such reports by 1927.[28] Alternatively, or as well, the candidate would see an Australian official. A few consequent reports survive, usually of cases that did not proceed, as with these two:

> A poor family, the better half being the wife, despite her size (4'8" and 7st., 7lbs.). Husband an irregular worker unimpressive and of an unlikely temperament.
>   There are five children. The eldest boy aged 15 years is farming and can milk. He is also (like his father) on the small side. The balance of the children are still at school and will be some years before they will be of working age. The father advises me he has no money …[29]

To make such judgments was the bureaucratic task, but there appears some force in British complaints that Australian officials often become hypercritical, ready to view the potential migrant as adversary. This indeed seems to have been the attitude of an erstwhile staffer at Australia House, who argued to the WA Royal Commission on Group Settlement that HMG had played upon Australian sentiment to despatch many ex-servicemen of poor calibre, and alleged a similar motive behind the Settlement Act.[30] Another such—J. B. Greene, brother to Walter Massy-Greene, that major figure in Australian public life—spoke similarly, late in the decade.[31] Doubtless these two had reason to warn, but gratuitous malice wafts also.

Still, many applicants held good. Negotiations would begin as to financing their voyage, especially whether there should prevail supplementary loans. Now too loomed the formal medical examination. At least on paper, this was always comprehensive and demanding. Most people find such scrutiny repugnant. Moreover, a medical cost 10s. 6d. (for an adult), and until 1927 even the failures had to pay. That failures were many is the most obvious indicator of the test's severity, which tightened throughout the decade. Initially any practitioner was an acceptable referee, but from 1922 specified authorising prevailed. In 1924 N. R. Howse— physician of English birth, war-hero, and soon to join S. M. Bruce's Cabinet—investigated the system and urged stricter controls, warning of the high cost to Australia of every invalid in its population. H. W. Gepp pursued the matter in 1926, and two further medical officers joined the Australian payroll, their task being to travel around Britain and see as many applicants as possible. Psychological testing, using the Binet–Simon scale, came into play in 1927 or 1928.[32] Medical testing went on and on. Some Agents-General seem to have claimed a right of review. On board ship and at arrival, some surveillance continued.

However vigorous were efforts at rationalisation, there had to be variations of standard in the course of such a big programme and a fair span of time. No less inevitably, such variations and otherwise seemingly aberrant decisions provoked feeling from those, and their associates, who felt victimised or shamed by them. Australia House had a policy of not publicly defining its standards; this had its own sense, but gave a handle to criticism. Probably British bureaucrats were right in suggesting that 'selectees' were weeded more rigorously when requisition fell, so as to minimise the appearance of Australian bungling or ill faith.[33]

'Selectees' otherwise suffered particular subjection to regulatory processes. 'Selection' was not quite so narrow as earlier references might have implied. Up to 1924 at least, the Victorian and South Australian governments requisitioned for some skilled tradesmen, especially in the building trades; a handful of nurses and teachers were their female equivalent (although a few male teachers went too). There was also recruitment of farmers for those grim State schemes. Yet, farmworkers and domestics dominated requisitions—and these 'selected' categories dominated, and so distorted, discussion on migration matters overall. In turn this debate concentrated on men, an increasingly small proportion, within all 'selectees'. Of course it was because the requisitions in general and of men particularly, *were* small that British bureaucrats harped on them, seeing this as the area where Australia had most obviously failed its imperial obligations. And indeed State governments kept very tight rein in this matter, not only grudging requisitions, but imposing severe controls on those who did come, as will now begin to transpire, and be expanded in chapter 10.

All assisted migrants had to promise to remain in Australia for at least two years, but 'selectees' undertook as well to work at their calling for a specified term: normally for a year, boys usually more. The whole gamut of scrutinising and testing was tougher for 'selectees' than nominees. Age limits, too, were stricter—35 years for both men and domestics, down to 25 years for the latter 'without experience'. Even so, accepting girls 'without experience' was begrudged. Likewise, early in the decade Australian authorities insisted that the men have substantial and exclusive background in farming (and so be the less likely to evoke jealous hostility from Australia's trade unionists); later, when HMG's Ministry of Labour established training camps to convert industrials into farmworkers, the effect was to consign those recruits to a gaol-like experience.[34] For inmates with families, problems of maintenance arose. That number would have been small, however, for increasingly the norm was to 'select' single persons. Australia, like most migrant-receptors, wanted the maximum of health and energy, the minimum of 'encumbrances'. Sometimes wives were acceptable, so long as they undertook to work as domestics for the usual spell, if necessary separate from their spouses.[35] A high proportion of 'selectees' was unemployed (Albert Buckley's 1923 figure of 80 per cent probably would have risen thereafter, at least for adult males)[36] and/or in deep poverty. Thus, despite early Australian resistance, virtually all had to take government loans to cover the outstanding portion of their fares and landing money. The latter was usually £2 or £3, although occasionally the Australian States asked more. Migrants seem to have been more suspicious of loans as threatening to constrict their freedom in Australia, than of time-bonding.[37]

The Ministry of Labour had much to do with 'selectees' at every stage. Employment Exchanges, which had been involved in ex-service people's migration, thereafter became active in civilian schemes, and supremely in recruiting 'selectees' for Australia. Barnes boasted how he organised the Exchanges into thus becoming the instruments of Australian policy,[38] and truly British bureaucrats spent endless hours in this work, with the usual back-up resources of space, postage, paper, publicity. It was necessarily the unemployed whom the Exchanges addressed. Migration therefore became associated with agencies and policies of state relief, which often were repugnant not only to those who disliked such things on principle, but also to many who depended upon their bounty. Various commentators noticed and abhorred this tainting of migration. 'A good class migrant will not go there because his friends will think he is going for the dole', went such critique of the Exchanges.[39] While Blimpish, it was representative enough to force the question whether Exchanges did more to restrict migration by smirching it, than to boost it by recruiting migrants. Deepening the taint were repeated charges that Exchanges not only encouraged but coerced unemployed men to offer for migration.[40] Formal policy always denied that, but pressure mounted.[41] Geoffrey Whiskard told of up to six interviews occurring in such cases.[42]

Previous chapters have noted that various Britons deprecated emigration lest it weaken their patria. Such misgivings probably were most forceful in regard to Australian requisitions. British agriculture, the integrity and welfare of families, the servicing of bourgeois homes—the departure of farmworkers, boys, and domestics threatened each of these.

As already indicated, nominations had an easier ride with the bureaucrats than did 'selections'. J. B. Greene bemoaned that, up to mid-1927, 'an individual or family, had to be very bad indeed before the nomination, once established, could be squashed'. That meant that scrutiny, including the medical, was less intense. Others at Australia House might have shared Greene's acerbity; perhaps he found Gepp's ear during the latter's 1926–7 sojourn, and certainly strictness increased thereafter, despite HMG's wish for the opposite to prevail. Yet matters were never all that relaxed, and nominees had their particular problems. Some arose from being in families, as many were. For nominees, the age limit was 50 years (sometimes relaxed to 60 in the late 1920s), but that was enough to deny assistance to senior relatives. Again, while much logic advised that fathers should go ahead, such a move entailed financial problems, and worried bureaucrats, ever wary lest emigration assist family desertion and break-up. Even if the nominees' medical was easier, to get a whole family through obviously was fraught.

Greene spoke truly in suggesting that, at least before 1927, the major step with ordinary nominations was getting them 'established'.[43] The process required interchange between the two hemispheres which must have been at least tedious, often tortuous and wracking. Again family issues were dominant, for the overwhelming pattern was for fairly recent migrants to nominate relatives who might follow. Nominators had to affirm responsibility for their nominees' future welfare. While there was always an element of make-believe in this, State authorities checked that the nominators had some substance and respectability. If these were lacking, the nomination aborted. There is little documentation as to this process, or even debate upon it—extraordinarily, because State policies in this matter probably had more effect on migrant flow than did all the palaver on 'selection'. Obviously, State officials would look askance at nominators who were down-at-heel. Apart from that, the main pattern appears to be increasingly close restriction. New South Wales under Labor led in such matters, but not too far. In late 1929 E. J. Mulvany affirmed with characteristic approval:

> The States are now exercising a rigid control over nominations to the fact that too many nominators have, in the past, regarded their obligations too lightly. Quite recently I found in NSW that unemployed miners in the Newcastle district in receipt of food relief from the State government were seeking approval for the nomination of their friends.[44]

(By this time Labor had given way to T. R. Bavin's government in New South Wales.)

Provision of fare-loans to nominees was also contested. As remarked in chapter 2, although Australia itself gave loans before the Settlement Act, thereafter it disdained the OSD's enthusiasm for them. This reaffirmed the intent to check any migrant torrent, and perhaps also showed awareness of likely administrative troubles. Broadly, the upshot appears that, while 'selectees' came to receive loans virtually as a rule, nominees always enjoyed that dubious boon less, and even less as time passed. Often the nominators provided the cash necessary to make up fares. Some of them received Australian loans for the purpose; this practice too began before the Settlement Act, but in due course HMG went halves. Often when loans went to nominators, and sometimes when to nominees, there were also brought into play 'guarantors' who would vouch to reimburse the government should the other parties default. Whatever these particularities, one marvels at the load which nominators assumed.

> The worker must create 'capital' wherewith his worship the capitalist can exploit more workers; and at his own expense the worker must provide a 'substitute' in the labour market, one whom the government will ship across the sea for the advantage of his quondam master the capitalist.

In some respects this analysis was truer for the 1920s than for Britain's migration policy of the mid-nineteenth century which Karl Marx so characterised.[45] However, some nominators took no loans and protected themselves further by requiring that their nominees have a nest-egg of landing money. That some nominators showed reluctant to embrace large families was a matter for lament to the OSD,[46] but was altogether sensible.

Other sub-categories of nominees could suffer particular troubles. Group nomination, organised by either business entrepreneurs or philanthropists, evoked early damnation from New South Wales, and perhaps some other States felt similarly. Barnes required higher standards from group nominees than personal ones.[47] Large families were eschewed in such groups too. Those few assisted migrants of some wealth were subjected to the means test; if found above it, they received only Australia's contribution towards fares.

It was not only medical examinations that became stricter for nominees after 1926–7.[48] Henceforth a much higher proportion underwent interview by Australian officials in Britain. Nominators now had to be more specific about the jobs that might be available for the newcomers. All this points to the likelihood that an increasing number of nominations then suffered veto from Australia House, at the same time as State rigidity was growing. The extension of the age limit to 60 years scarcely denied this trend—it was to apply 'where the refusal of acceptances may lead to loss of other members of a family who are of useful age'.[49]

*   *   *

Despite all this and more anti-migrationism, there was another side of the story—that side of 'hope', upon which this book is predicated. As said many pages ago, between the Wars nearly half-a-million Britons came to Australia as intending long-term settlers. That fact is embellished by some comparative figures: average annual emigration for all Europe 1921–39 was barely one-third that of the previous generation,[50] while Britons also showed cool to other Dominions and left increasingly unfilled the quotas allowed them in the USA. Furthermore, there was that constant evidence, or at least intimation, that Australian restrictiveness rather than British apathy was the key factor throttling numbers. The Ministry of Labour offered striking figures as to volunteers for 'selection', as against consequent departures 1922–30: for men, 72,117 and 14,016; females, 4237 and 1512; boys, 7221 and 2421.[51] (Of course, not all 'selectees' went through the Ministry's Exchanges.) Australian authorities sometimes offered complementary figures. In 1921, the High Commissioner reported, Australia House (more specifically, the Migration and Settlement Office) received up to a thousand enquiries a day.[52] That indeed must have demanded 'patience and tact of a high degree', as many were told that they did not qualify for aid. Interest ran higher early in the 1920s than later, but a statement of 1925 still put applicants at five times the number of assisted migrants—without explanatory detail.[53] Notwithstanding his judgment as to the counter-migration effect of doles, M. L. Shepherd himself asserted that more generous assistance would much increase movement.[54]

How is one to reconcile such data with other evidence of apathy and resistance to migration? In part by repeating that Australia gave aid only after nomination or 'selection'. It wanted youngish and healthy people, and more especially agricultural workers and domestics, all of whom were in relative demand at home and so less likely to offer for migration, while those who did so were more often Britain's discards, and as such repugnant to Australia. But that does not cover the whole situation. Perhaps many people played with the idea of migration rather than confronted the reality: one recruiting officer said that a quarter of the people whom he interviewed won acceptance, and then only half of them went.[55] That enquiries at Australia House surged and waned randomly accords with this picture. But Australia House itself was sometimes bemused about relevant matters. One instance was Shepherd's self-contradiction noted above, while another occurred in November 1927. Then High Commissioner Granville Ryrie declared in *The Times* that Australia's current requisition for 250 boys a month was going unfilled, yet currently the OSD was hearing from Barnes that he had all he needed and from the Ministry of Labour that applications were being refused. The truth is undiscoverable, although soon afterwards Barnes declared a scarcity of boys.[56] Inefficiency and obfuscation among the bureaucrats; volatility, agonising, maybe deliberate cussedness among the clients: here were the major ingredients of this mess.

Some of its intricacies remain in murk. Again there is the remarkable lack of data as to specific requisition numbers. The broadest truth seems to be that quotas usually went short—not because gross applications were deficient, but because a sizeable number were found wanting. So ran the way to maximum all-round discontent! Other anomalies and oddities prevailed. For all the apparent apathy of many potential migrants, Barnes spent much of his time hearing appeals from applicants, especially as 'selectees', rejected during early process. Against the failure of the upper-class schemes mentioned above, one learns of young Patrick White working as a jackeroo in southern New South Wales in company with English gentlemen, recruited to give Australia some of the homeland's better blood.[57] Class-conscious radicals attacked emigration as a capitalist ploy, yet several themselves went to Australia.

The foregoing attempt to explain resistance to migration makes it all more necessary to ponder why counter-pressures often triumphed. Wage rates were better; the sun shone more strongly; family ties pulled; governments offered help. Migration could thus spell hope. While these are ultimate reasons for emigration, it remains important to pursue how such forces came into play. The obvious starting-point is with agencies of persuasion.

Delusive propaganda is likely whenever anything is being sold; it is close to inevitable when that something is beyond the seas, and the potential customer is anxious to hear good reports. Shipping agents at large had secured much ill-fame for using this situation to gross self-advantage. Perhaps their worst excesses before 1914 lay in cajoling European peasants to go to the USA, and there were occasional stories of the deception of such people with regard to Australia during the 1920s.[58] Britain was not free of similar skulduggery. To some extent, however, the agents were scapegoats, having to bear all blame for propaganda which was the work of governments, shipping companies, and other profit-seekers. HMG had addressed this situation immediately after the War, as noticed in chapter 1. The counter-feelings then aroused showed how sensitive were these issues.

While the government had then failed to carry its Act, shysters must have heard a warning. Yet migration remained a business, and agencies could not but speak with enthusiasm of places whither they were urging Britons to go. There never developed an easy balance within this situation. Related to it was another disparity. While some publicity glowed too rose-red, reasonable limits usually prevailed. Yet a frequent theme in subsequent migrant commentary is of the deep, even enchanting impact of propaganda.[59]

> The publicity showed what a home could be like after two or three years—a nice bungalow, a beautiful car and about two hundred sheep in very green grass ...

> Whenever and wherever my mother ventured on market day she seemed to be confronted with those banners saying 'Immigrant wanted for Australia—a land flowing with milk and honey there to gain an independence.'[60]

These two reminiscences stand for many. Sometimes they bolstered a critique of disillusion and protest, but not always. The will to believe, the yearning that the good life offered across the oceans made some migrants over-ready to glamorise the unknown.

This trend was reinforced because Britons of the 1920s heard, read, and saw many enthusing representations of the Empire. J. M. Mackenzie's *Propaganda and Empire* tells this story well. Especially remarkable was the publicity of the Empire Marketing Board. Its posters carried that art-form of the day to a peak, while John Grierson similarly embellished documentary film. Beaverbrook's papers had an enthusiasm for Empire which must have offset other journals' hostility to migration. Lord Northcliffe's similar feeling for Australia, generated during his tour of late 1921 and broadcast through press and pamphlet, would have been still more apropos, for he insisted on migration as necessary to Australia's viability as a British nation in the eastern hemisphere. The OSD had fed him much data.[61]

Other voices conveyed a similar message. Earlier chapters have said nearly enough about the Tory imperialists, but a further word should go to Lord Apsley and his ripping yarn, *The Amateur Settlers*. Apsley travelled to Australia in 1925 as a farmworker and laboured thus for a few weeks in Victoria, with a later sojourn among group settlers in Western Australia. *Amateur Settlers* is interesting and occasionally perceptive, but Apsley and his co-author wife remained aristocrats and their attempt to pretend otherwise sometimes rang absurd. Still, authorities in London arranged the publication of a shortened version, from which migrants may have learned something. Two further British Parliamentarians, likewise upholders of migration, wrote enthusiastic accounts of Australia. Anthony Eden did so following travels with the Press Union in 1925. His *Places in the Sun* extolled not only Australia's natural resources but its press, literature, and art. More ambitious was that Labour maverick, L. Haden Guest. The *London Weekly*, which he ran during early 1927, published Amery and Apsley, Gepp and McDougall. Most interesting in retrospect was the appearance of J. Boyd Orr, already renowned for his agricultural science, and moving towards an alliance with Bruce and McDougall which was to be crucial in shaping international nutrition policy through decades ahead.[62] In summer 1927–8 Guest travelled in Australia, seeing much of Gepp, and on his return he published *The New British Empire*.[63] 'Australia is a new adventure of man,' declared Guest; 'an adventure made possible of realisation in the twentieth century of applied science.' The DMC led this way, he enthused, presenting its work literally as an example to the world. Much of Guest's text was more restrained, recognising that Australia presented problems to the migrant, especially on the land. However, some final pages again ventured into Utopianism as—showing his theosophical beliefs—Guest argued that Australians were developing a biological identity: 'the honey-brown flapper' selected her like-toned mate, as they luxuriated in sun and sand. Having lost his Parliamentary seat, Guest proposed to Gepp in mid-1929 that he produce a film about Australia for the DMC, putting particular stress on Aboriginal society. The Chairman declined, remarking that 'as a general rule our Cinema Branch refrains from producing films or still photos of aboriginals (owing to the fact that such pictures might create a mistaken impression in some quarters that Australia is a land of blacks)'.[64]

Guest's concern with race, together with his sense of Australia as 'a strange, beautiful country' where mankind might grow anew, gave him affinity with another Briton to write of Australia, D. H. Lawrence. The latter's sojourn of 1922 was even briefer than Guest's. Yet it had elements of desperate hope and consequent disillusion, duly conveyed in *Kangaroo*. Fiction of greater contemporary impact would have been John Galsworthy's *Forsyte Saga*. Galsworthy had his idealistic Michael Mont first become engrossed in child migration and then assist a destitute Cockney pair escape to sun-bathed Australia.[65]

Academic scholarship did its mite to present Australia sympathetically. N. Skene Smith, *Economic Control. Australian Experiments in 'Rationalisation' and 'Safeguarding'* (1929) vied with Guest's *New Empire* in lauding Australian achievements; the DMC and CSIR, said Smith, promised to establish 'an Economic General Staff, such as has been suggested by Sir William Beveridge'.[66] Hugh Dalton, then reader in economics at the University of London, wrote a supervisorial introduction, lavishing more flattery on Australia and the Commission. (Gepp thought Smith over-optimistic as to governmental powers to create economic Utopia.)[67] Next year W. K. Hancock's *Australia* appeared in the Benn 'Modern World' series, adding its applause of Commission and Empire. Another young Melburnian, A. G. Scholes, published his Edinburgh doctorate as *Education for Empire Settlement. A Study of Juvenile Migration* (1932). It presented much useful information, not only about Australia, but had little or nothing to do with the migrant's idea-world, our subject at issue.

Considering its scepticism about migration, the Australian government played the propaganda game with surprising zeal. A future stalwart of the DMC, E. N. Robinson, wrote thus in 1921 for the Commonwealth Immigration Office:

> The story of Australia is largely a story of courageous men and women of British stock mainly who began life at the bottom of the ladder and climbed steadily upwards. The pioneers took up land as they found it, and handed on to their sons rolling wheat fields and well-stocked pastures. A runaway boy who became a cattle-drover is known as Australia's Cattle King. The farm labourer of today is the prosperous farmer of tomorrow.[68]

Reading the proofs, a bureaucrat advised deletion of 'runaway', perhaps out of deference to Sir Sidney Kidman to whom the passage pointed, but more likely to inhibit migrant lads from following that part of Kidman's example. The pamphlet floated a false notion that the 'Cattle King' was a migrant.[69] Other pamphlets of this provenance had similar euphoria.

Robinson was involved also with Australia's cinematographic publicity. Probably this medium did more than the written word to build exaggerated hopes, although the judgment is tortuous as virtually no film survives (and some publications have disappeared too).[70] Robinson directed a travelogue series—'Know Your Own Country'. While intended for domestic audiences, it duly went abroad, in consequence of a call from the OSD late in 1922.[71] By 1924, forty-one such films had shown throughout Britain via some 1650 outlets, usually at the instigation of Employment Exchanges. Contrarily, OSD bureaucrats found some of them too lush. Chief of the few films prepared directly for migration purposes was 'Australia Calls', presenting the story of Ernest Idiens, a Briton who prospered as a farmer in New South Wales. In 1923–4 Idiens himself spent three months in Britain speaking at showings of the film.[72] As earlier noticed, Raymond Longford, Lotte Lyell, and Arthur Higgins worked in behalf of migration around this time, and perhaps their skills added glamour to that message. Consequent films appeared at the Wembley Exhibition which in retrospect were seen— especially by Victoria's angry landsettlers—as purveyors of false notions.[73] To convey exciting images is the business of Exhibitions, but perhaps Australia did too well at Wembley. Schoolboys of that day remember the Australian pavilion still.[74] Murals by F. W. Leist throbbed with azure, gold, and sun.[75]

Yet much Australian publicity showed restraint. Even in 1921, a pamphlet titled *Australia's Offer to British Boys* stressed the rigours of country work.[76] A later variant likewise warned, 'don't run away with the impression that you are going to pick up a fortune in a few years, and if you are not prepared to take the rough with the smooth, don't come … Australia doesn't

Following pages: Australian publicity, 1921. (From pamphlets held by the Royal Commonwealth Society; reproduced by permission of the Syndics of the Cambridge University Library.)

ISSUED BY AUTHORITY OF THE PRIME MINISTER OF THE
COMMONWEALTH OF AUSTRALIA.

ISSUED BY AUTHORITY OF THE PRIME MINISTER OF TH
COMMONWEALTH OF AUSTRALIA.

want the groucher.' *Australia Invites the Domestic Girl* was open in its natalism:

> Australia, spacious sunny home of the sturdy, hearty Digger, is renewing her invitation to the people of the old Land to come out and help her realise her proud future as the Britain of the southern seas. Especially is there warmth and cordiality in this invitation to the healthy, wholesome British domestic girl—the girl who in some capacity, can help in the home as a first step towards entering into a home of her own. For Australia, above everything, is a land of home-making, and for the rapid multiplication of homes she needs more and more of the right type of girl, and there are not enough of the native-born to go around.

This belied A. M. Carr-Saunders's lament at the Economic Advisory Council committee that government propaganda could not spell out that migrants were wanted as wives.

Perhaps the best representative of Australia propaganda is *Australia: The Land of the Better Chance* (1926).[77] Most of this pamphlet is obvious and dull: statistics as to area, population, products; photographs of buildings and beauty-spots; advice as to banks' lending policy. Yet the title made its boast, amplified by an opening paragraph which spoke of 'infinite opportunity' in this 'rich and generous young country'. Such was enough to make *Better Chance* a prime target for attack by *News of the World*. Still more exaggeration may have come from agencies other than the Commonwealth of Australia, starting with the States. The official directing Victoria's desk at Wembley later admitted that literature distributed from it could have misled.[78] Probably his chief reference was to a pamphlet, *Speedway to Prosperity*, initially designed for consumption at home and perhaps tempered there by a scepticism not likely a hemisphere away. Tasmanian publicity suffered criticism too; an offending pamphlet seems innocuous, yet indeed it down-played rental costs—and for migrants one such error would pollute memory of the whole.[79]

British governmental agencies also issued migration publicity. Remembering the post-war Emigration Bill, with its restraints against double-crossing of HMG's subjects, one might expect this propaganda to be beyond reproach. Yet hope that emigration would relieve the nation's social problems impelled counter-pressures. Confusion resulted.

The OSD's chief publicity medium was the monthly paper, *Overseas Settler*, successor to the *Imperial Colonist*, and likewise balanced in depicting migrant life. Other propaganda from the OSD also stepped with care. Its *Handbook* of 1926 advised migrants to accept that Australia had its own way of doing things; they should not criticise, but persevere and save.[80] In affirming that most opportunities lay in rural work, the *Handbook* probably was guilty more of archaic Ameryism than conscious deceit. Its reservations as to tropical agriculture in Queensland evoked criticism from the State's

AUSTRALIA

THE LAND OF THE
BETTER CHANCE

An image of hope. Cover of migration pamphlet, 1926. (Mitchell Library;
reproduced by permission of the Library Council of New South Wales.)

Agent-General. The OSD withdrew a little, but insisted on being final
arbiter.[81] Such austerity sometimes faltered; we have seen that the OSD in
1928 rejected the DMC's advice to amend advertising which guaranteed
employment in Australia.[82] From April 1927 the OSD had its separate
Publicity Branch under Dame Meriel Talbot, doyenne of ladylike endeavours in the migrationist cause. However, boys and ex-servicemen as well
as women were targets her office sought. Dame Meriel intensified a long-
standing OSD policy of encouraging schools to teach more about the
Dominions' history and geography so that pupils might aspire to settle
there. Late in 1927 the OSD acted further, appointing an officer-and-
gentleman, W. C. H. Hudson, as Director of Voluntary Organisations.
Hudson's task was to establish yet another raft of local committees which
might boost emigration. Around 1928–9 some fifty such groups existed,
Newcastle the shining example. On Hudson's death his post went to
K. M. Lindsay, future internationalist, educator, and Parliamentarian.[83]

The Employment Exchanges' work for publicity went further than
distributing film. 'Free space is given both inside and outside all Exchange

buildings to all the posters which this Department issues', Barnes said in August 1927; 'the Exchanges arrange, where possible, for our posters and pamphlets to be on exhibition in public libraries, local institutes, club rooms etc. ... All this costs us nothing.'[84] For two years past, one hundred Exchanges had used 'illuminated signs' to attract migrant interest. However, Barnes overshot when implying full-bodied support from the 900 voluntary committees which assisted the Exchange bureaucrats in finding jobs. 'You have not yet had experience of the extraordinary views which our local committees produce for edification and guidance on matters of migration', snorted one veteran to a tyro.[85] The OSD's creation of new committees under Hudson almost certainly responded to anti-migrant feeling among the older bodies.

The shipping interest was always central in migration matters. An observer of 1924 noted that every railway station in the UK had its map of Australia, part of a promotion by the (Australian) Commonwealth Shipping Line.[86] Otherwise the interest was British, but all Lines worked through shipping agents. As remarked, agents have borne too much blame for deluding migrants; nevertheless they did advertise Australia, and the angry father intent on berating Thomas Cook's office in Sunderland signalled that agencies continued a prime source of (at least perceived) deception. 'The whole State has been grossly over-painted by these people', affirmed a knowledgeable Westralian.[87] Australia House, under pressure from White-hall, in 1921 stopped direct pay to agents for enlisting migrants, but it continued to subsidise their advertising.[88] Percy Hunter built close relations with his erstwhile trade. Early in the decade some agents were more favoured than others, perhaps via allocation of the advertising subsidy. Ridgways' chain seems to have been foremost. Then in early 1927 rumour broke of officers at Australia House receiving kickbacks from some agents.[89] One result was the charging of a well-known agent, S. M. Burton, with fraud; *inter alia*, Burton issued over-optimistic publicity. Meanwhile, the Australian government ruled that all agents must have equal treatment. Australia House was lukewarm about this.

Agents worked very hard. One result was acrid competition with the Employment Exchanges; the Ministry of Labour would have liked the Exchanges to have a monopoly over supplying 'selectees', but Australia House rebuffed that.[90] When Victoria sought farmers, it relied on agents for information as to whom among the enquirers justified further interview.[91] Most agents' business was with nominees. This went beyond helping with the paperwork, important though that must have been. Agents often stirred enquirers to seek nominators, and even did initial writing for them. At times this probably shaded into arranging nominations where the nominator had little or no acquaintance with the nominee, but got some pay-off for the trouble. No documents tell precisely that, although OSD did name an agent who sought to cajole nominations from Australian employers.[92] The agency business remained ultra-competitive, every adult fare winning some £1 13s. from the shipping companies.

Whereas agents worked for money, other migrationist interests and organisations dealt more in philanthropy. One of these was the Society for the Oversea Settlement of British Women, a hybrid of governmental and voluntary forces. It upheld the long-standing policy of expanding all female emigration, with the particular hope of facilitating that of women with skill and status. The SOSBW doubtless could claim some credit for the fact that Empire-wide female assisted migration exceeded that of males in 1929, even Australia going close.[93] Other news was less good. Almost all requisitions from Australia remained for menials. The Society responded by devising a superior genus of domestic, 'home helps' (or 'lady helps'). They were normally to be group-nominated—by Australian organisations (the Victoria League most actively) comprising the same kind of philanthropic women as upheld the SOSBW. However, the Society's largesse ranged wider, over other 'selectees', nominees, and self-payers. It mainly consisted of loans for outfit and fares. In 1925 the Society helped to Australia 57 ordinary domestics, 41 home helps, 21 teachers, 1 governess, 18 wives and fiancées, 44 other adults joining their families, 46 children, 2 clerical workers, and 4 'miscellaneous'. Such results seem small in relation to the Society's effort and structure. Of its potential clients who sought aid under the Settlement Act, a remarkably high proportion failed to meet the demands of Australia House, and generally its relations with Hunter and Barnes were chill.[94]

Another point at which bureaucracy and philanthropy fused was in emigration work by local government agencies, especially Poor Law Guardians. The Settlement Act obviously sustained British hopes that migration might diminish the demands on relief funds. Before 1922 Guardians had extensive powers to assist poor people (not necessarily on the rates) to migrate.[95] The power had little use: in 1921 only 354 people were assisted, mostly children to Canada. During 1922 Australian authorities showed surprising receptivity to extending these arrangements, with Australia sharing costs. Simultaneously the OSD became involved in Poor Law migration, jointly with the Ministry of Health. In July 1923 a circular prescribed new conditions under which Guardians could assist migration. A Treasury memorandum told the aftermath:

> The circular was widely commented on in the newspapers and the substance was cabled to Australia. The Australian public gathered the impression that an attempt was being made to indulge in 'pauper shovelling', and the Australian authorities became very nervous of accepting any immigrants, however deserving, if the Guardians were involved.

When matters quietened, the situation resumed whereby Guardians could help migrants equip themselves, the assumption being that fares came from Settlement Act provisions. Between January 1924 and April 1925, 41 children and 457 adults were thus assisted towards Australia. T. C. Macnaghten saw these figures as puny and sought Health's aid in lifting them. The Ministry retorted that it so encouraged matters, but

> in Unions in which the number of able-bodied persons or young persons in receipt of relief are large, political considerations are apt to be taken as a guide by the Board of Guardians with the result that they are unwilling to have recourse to this method of relieving distress. Moreover, the view adopted by the OSC that emigration cannot be regarded as a means for meeting unemployment in this country, has in its degree tended to discourage both Boards of Guardians and possible emigrants.[96]

If a fellow-bureaucrat could charge Macnaghten with double-speaking, one can imagine how public opinion in both hemispheres would see the matter. Nevertheless, sometimes Guardians gave more comprehensive help, even including full fares.[97] It seems that the OSD's 'voluntary' committees of 1928–9 also may have met migrants' incidental costs. Yet overall, there was only a little official 'pauper-shovelling' to Australia. Public antipathy was too strong, not least among potential victims.

Charity and philanthropy prompted various religious and secular bodies to migration work. While it could be claimed that this sought to widen opportunity for Britons at large, not merely those in immediate need, the OSD itself bemoaned that these agencies were likely to despatch 'classes which are not the most likely to prove successful overseas'.[98] Notwithstanding the OSD's own twists towards pauper-shovelling, such official argument persisted—being repeated, for example, to the Economic Advisory Council committee. All this was indicative: while the OSD subsidised voluntary work, and professed approval thereof, tensions always lurked. The Department saw threats of interference and competition from those quarters, and long resisted. In this stance, British and Australian officials cohered. Even the Royal Colonial Institute (later the Royal Empire Society) came under the OSD's fire.[99]

Some migrants, especially boys, sponsored by the voluntary societies went out as 'selectees'; that is, the societies recruited them, helping with outfit in the Old World and promising after-care in the New, but they went under requisition. A greater (but unspecifiable) part of the societies' people went as group nominees. Thereby each organisation's Australian agency gathered promises of employment and care for its British volunteers. As earlier intimated, Bruce boosted this scheme to his Premiers in May–June 1923. Evidently it had resulted from the recent Australian travels of J. H. Stanley and Cyril Bavin, enthusiasts respectively for the Church (of

England) Army and the YMCA.[100] Initially the nominees had to be specified by name, but from 1925 'open' nomination was allowed, with the organisation's British arm gathering recruits.

The scheme's heyday came in 1926–7, yet the OSD then affirmed 'that except for the Salvation Army whose methods were not wholly satisfactory, the voluntary societies were of little use'.[101] Sour grapes doubtless flavoured this verdict, without determining it. Truth certainly lay in putting the Salvation Army on a special plane. Salvationists showed ready to dominate the whole migration business. In January 1925 the Salvation Army chief, D. C. Lamb, advanced a critique which was to become widespread:

> A State-controlled movement is pre-destined to failure. In the United Kingdom no government is likely ever to come forward and openly advocate emigration! Overseas the question of immigration will tend more and more to become a party one. Hence the imperative need for a new effort on independent lines.[102]

The OSD's riposte that the Dominions would never accept such a move had sense: Gepp did not respond to similar proposals put to him by Lamb in 1926–7.[103] The Salvation Army always remained under much suspicion from the OSD, most interestingly when it moved towards alliance with the Colonial Institute.[104] The above reference to 'not wholly satisfactory' methods reflected the well-grounded suspicion that the Army wangled grants from both HMG and Australia for the same work, and exacted from its clients more than pay-back of loans.[105] That the Army—alone of all philanthropic societies—continued throughout the period to garner commission as a shipping agent intensified such odium.

Yet, as the OSD and everyone else recognised, the Salvation Army did the job. In Australia its work for farmboys mattered most, there being a special training camp for them in Queensland, but that was far from the whole story. The peak came in 1927 when the Army took a full ship-load to Australia. *'The New Exodus'* proclaimed a brochure.[106] Altogether that year some 2260 persons went to Australia under Army auspices.[107] After-care was thorough and effective.

The YMCA's major work probably was to assist Australia House in screening general applicants. However, its Cyril Bavin helped establish group nomination and this interest continued, in co-operation with Presbyterian and Methodist churches, most importantly in New South Wales. Despite the Y's altruist style (it had been the first among philanthropists to disclaim agent's commission),[108] Australian and New Zealand governments rebuffed its proposal to expand farmboy migration. In the late 1920s a Methodist YMCA activist, one Mr Coleman, beat up considerable business in New South Wales. Coleman's story had interesting sub-themes: William Bankes Amery did not know he existed; his other chief activity was to

Migration as salvation? This is a farewell photograph of a group recruited by the Salvation Army. (Australian Archives: B 4094; *Vedic*, 6 October 1928; reproduced by permission.)

confront Communism; and he procured some emigration outside the Settlement Act, presumably of people dependent on charity for all costs.[109] In Victoria Methodist YMCA work foundered on the antagonism of State officials, who blocked nominations.

The Church of England's Army, through J. H. Stanley, had begun work before the crystallising of group nomination. During 1921, it sponsored 174 persons to Australia, many of them ex-servicemen, and scores of boys soon followed.[110] Chief organiser was T. S. P. Pughe, whose perceptive fatalism (quoted above) contrasted with Stanley's hearty cheer. The Church maintained formal interest in migration, but when a Stanley-like enthusiast, A. G. B West, pushed for action in Britain late in the decade, he met resistance within the pertinent committees, and sought OSD help against them.[111] Australian churchmen followed a similar pattern. A. L. S. Wake, an Anglican organiser in Western Australia, had attitudes rather like Pughe's, making him a wise critic of migration's dilemma rather than an enthusiast.[112] Queensland's Canon D. J. Garland, by contrast, was always a super-boomer, running schemes for both boys and adults, meanwhile shaping his State's commemoration of Anzac Day. Yet in numbers New South Wales again won. An Anglican Council founded there in 1925 cherished about 700 migrants.[113]

Some Catholic voices opposed emigration. This correlated with the Protestant ascendance among migrationists in both Britain and Australia; with the converse Catholic strength in the Australian Labor movement; and with the policies of the Irish Free State, which in 1923 negated Australia's offer to subsidise fares jointly.[114] Yet some Catholics upheld the cause, most interestingly in Western Australia where the Knights of the Southern Cross sought to emulate the Fairbridge scheme with one of their own. Not until 1938 did this become reality, helped from Britain by Father C. C. Martindale, a disciple of social justice on the lines advocated by G. K. Chesterton and Hilaire Belloc.[115] For years past, Martindale had upheld the Catholic Emigration Society, evading the episcopal hostility which was strong throughout both British isles:

> The only way in one diocese in which he could introduce the subject was under the disguise of a lecture on I think Poland. He started off with a few sentences about Poland, and then compared Poland with Australia, and from that went on to deal with settlement possibilities there.[116]

This was in 1928–9 when an Australian priest proposed an advertising-lecture tour through Britain. C. H. E. Manning doused that with even colder water than he cast on migration generally.

The Fairbridge homes remained the chief example of secular charity. They and the Barnardo group in New South Wales alone received subsidy for organising orphan emigration to Australia, until the Catholic venture in

Western Australia of the 1930s. Such money went only for incidental and maintenance costs, and although Barnardo numbers rose above 150 a year, and hopes yet higher, child-centred migration to Australia remained but a small story.[117] Of some interest is Barnardo's support for 'plantation homes' in Tasmania. Percy Roberts, Barnardo's travelling agent, applauded that this scheme 'would not necessarily need the very flower of the flock'; that is, it might give work to youths otherwise unacceptable.[118]

Various secular groups added more machinery for migrating male youths, usually but not always farmboys.[119] Boy Scouts maintained a small group-nomination. 'Big Brothers' and their leader, Richard Linton, likewise persisted. In New South Wales an older organisation, the Dreadnought Trust, had a similar role, albeit more of after-care than attraction.[120] The Dreadnoughters dealt entirely with 'selectees', while the Brothers seen to have moved between that and group-nomination, often drawing on applicants recruited by Cyril Bavin.[121] Very similar to the Brothers was the WA Young Australia League, founded by one J. J. Simons, a panegyrist of God, Service, and Kingsley Fairbridge; Percy Hunter abhorred him.

A group of public-spirited students at Oxford University sponsored youths migrating to Australia; it centred on Balliol College, and was helped by the Rhodes Trust. Its secretary was Fred Alexander, like A. G. Scholes and W. K. Hancock a graduate from Melbourne.[122] In August 1922, about the time the Oxford venture began, one Dr F. C. Cossar launched Craigielinn Farm, outside Glasgow, to prepare boys for acceptance by Australia. Probably most inmates neared delinquence; one Hobart day, 1992, an intuitive student of Michael Roe's asked the elderly Scot beside her in the supermarket queue whether he was ever at Craigielinn; he gasped assent, and scarpered. Yet Cossar probably had something of Fred Alexander's philanthropy, and Craigielinn survived OSD scrutiny to retain its subsidy.[123] So, more modestly, did a few other such places, including a Catholic one.[124] At Wallingford, Berks, a Training Farm of the Colonisation Social Union did similar work for wards of Poor Law Guardians, who funded the migration of some of its graduates.[125] Possibly there were counterparts elsewhere.

In its 1926 *Handbook* on Australia the OSD listed organisations which advanced fares in necessitous cases: various Church of England bodies, the Salvation Army, SOSBW, Victoria League, the Board of Guardians for Relief of Jewish Poor, and the British Dominions Emigration Society. While not all their clients were destitute, the latter pair carry us further into charity work. The BDES grew from the Charity Organisation Society, and in 1921 it sponsored an agent to go to Australia and Canada, and report on migrant openings and needs.[126] During the decade the Society helped about a thousand people to go to Australia. Its reports lamented the decay of Empire migration, and specified how expensive the step had become. Other bodies probably were punier still, although quite numerous—one Agent-General spoke in 1928 of thirty or forty groups being interested in migration.[127] Probably more important was family or communal help with emigrants' costs. Such activity developed, for example, in the heyday of WA group-settlement, the notion prevailing that parties from particular localities in Britain might stay together on the frontier.[128] Another act of specialised philanthropy was that of the *Morning Post* in joining with the OSD to meet the supplementary costs of some miners who (in spite of general Australian policy) received assistance after the 1926 General Strike.[129]

Strongest among other pulses driving migration was industrial nomination, whereby employers secured workers with specific skills. Such action, while contested by labour interests, had a long history in Australia. Numbers are beyond gauge, although most passenger lists, more markedly in the early 1920s, have a sprinkling of such people: examples were two couples with whom D. H. and Frieda Lawrence formed shipboard ties.[130] The richest detail available concerns three Tasmanian operations: Cadburys' confectionery factory, Paton and Baldwin's knitting mill, and Rapson's tyre works. All nominated an elite of specialist workers: the first two asked for fifty or more apiece; Rapson's, about thirty. However, the bigger pair came to employ many more Britons—Cadburys' especially because other migrants felt attraction to a compatriot boss; Paton's through chain-nomination by the first-comers. The numbers could have risen further had not a Tasmanian bureaucrat pressured Paton's to employ locals (which, even so, went not so far that way as he wanted), while Cadburys' saw employment of Australians as necessary for selling its products.[131]

Chapter 7 remarked that the Queensland government settled migrant farmers. The Agent-General's reports regularly cited such a category; it comprised but a handful until it surged to 211 in 1930.[132] Possibly linked with this story was the Australian Farms Training College, Norfolk. Its prospectus claimed alliance with the Queensland government in preparing upper-class youths, who hopefully would form a 'College Guild' to uplift antipodean life.[133] A small but similar scheme had its brief span in Tasmania 1919–20, consequent upon an Anglican idealist persuading thirty-odd ex-officers there to establish an elitist farm-commune.[134] Despite the similarity of the names, the Norfolk venture had no tie with Australian Farms Limited which lured many ex-Indian Army officers to disaster. The sub-continent oft recurred in migrationist thought. In London in 1926–7, Gepp talked with the India Office about Australia taking ex-soldiers thence; 3000 a year was one suggested target, whereas in fact 36 came altogether.[135] As noted, the resumption of assistance in the late 1930s embraced Empire-builders retired from India. Fellowships endowed with Wembley profits assisted more than a hundred Britons to undergo relatively sophisticated agricultural training in Australia.[136] Similar were the schemes of J. J. T. Hobbs, Alexander Hay, and Patrick White's employer.

Industrial nominees. This photograph from the Launceston *Weekly Courier*,
21 June 1923, reports the coming of fifty-two industrial nominees to Paton and
Baldwin's knitting mill in that city. The be-hatted gentlemen are representatives
of the firm. Robert and Mary Snaddon stand to the left; Agnes and William Comrie
to the right; each couple had three children. Both families settled in Launceston.

Many others floated migrationist ideas. Arthur Rickard, an Australian
businessman otherwise shrewd, proposed in 1926 that the Co-operative
movement in Britain should spend the profits from the sale of Empire
produce to subsidise the fares of migrants, so avoiding the stringencies
applied to government-assisted people.[137] A gentle lady in Tasmania aspired
to set up an agricultural school for English gels.[138] There were at least two
vigorous proposals for the private organisation of migrant domestics in
Australia. One came from Ettie Rout, who was remarkable for her war-time
efforts to have Australasian authorities equip leave-going soldiers with
contraceptive gear. Rout urged that migrants build entirely new communities in Australia. Complementing her earlier interests, she also hoped
'to gather up the little children the Anzacs have left behind in England, and
arrange for their adoption'; meanwhile, migrant domestics could learn
mothercraft by tending them in special hostels.[139] Rout seems to have
belonged among those to whom W. M. Hughes once referred: 'there are
many cranks who flutter around the Migration Honey Pot'.[140] 'Cranks'
appeared to Percy Hunter as having undue influence on the OSD, while

Macnaghten himself said of a would-be agent of the Big Brothers, 'any crank—or more than crank—can put forward some beautiful paper idea. In fact they do—about two a week.'[141] This litany could continue, but Macnaghten's anguish advises a halt.

*   *   *

Virtually all migrants were ordinary, common people of their time and place. This generalisation is at once obvious, and profound. The present study has left all too much room for other scholars to enrich it. Some have already done so. Thus Geoffrey Sherington has mapped 'passengers to Australia by last address ... 1927'.[142] The heaviest inflow came from the quadrilateral bounded by Inverness, Glasgow, Hull, and Liverpool; next ranked London and the South-East; then the Midlands and Wales. That Northern Ireland scored low surprises a little. The clue might be that Treasury extended its anti-Hibernian animus northward, advising against advertisement of the subsidised-passage scheme there.[143] About a thousand people appear to have left the Irish Free State annually for Australia through the 1920s.[144] Presumably most would have enjoyed Australia's aid to non-UK nominees and have comprised by far the majority in that category.

Years ago Colin Forster computed that 15,682 breadwinners among nominees of the 1920s had skills in manufacturing industry, with engineering and clothing foremost.[145] One might suppose a tendency for chain-migration within trades: as noticed, its prevalence at Paton's provoked a Tasmanian bureaucrat. Many 'selectees' had industrial skills, disguised or denied though they might be to meet the Australian call for farmworkers. This might offset the calculation of skill indices by Glenn Withers which puts migrants of the 1920s well below those of the past, except for the immediate pre-war years.[146]

'Selectees', we have seen, were normally unemployed and impoverished. Despite regular Australian grouches to the contrary, medical testing must have meant that most had compensatory vigour. Nominees were less stringently tested and presumably had less consistent health, but a little more money. Perhaps the average capital among them was £20 to £30 a head, a few having substantially more, many less.[147] The rate of destitution probably rose over the period. Ex-servicepeople had on average still more money, but, as earlier intimated, poor health—'suffering from shell shock, the effect of poisonous gas, and all sorts of complaints'.[148]

Non-assisted migrants included a predictable elite: the series of the *Australian Dictionary of Biography* embracing 'floruits' 1891–1939 includes about twenty-five inter-war migrants, all but two or three being professional and/or bourgeois. The first volume (of four) to embrace the next generation presents about twenty-one such cases: several came as children, and the social pattern overall is only a little different. It is appropriate to repeat that, despite regular talk of wealthy applicants, only a few such ventured. Perhaps a handful had more class than money. Nomination was proposed for a young kinsman of Winston Churchill, although in the event the family coffers managed his fare.[149]

Guesswork must rule as to the mass of self-payers. The statistics indicate that they comprised one-third of all entrants, but perhaps some so described had first come to Australia as assistees and now were returning after a holiday sojourn in Britain. The paucity of comment on the self-payers is extraordinary. The Windham Delegation of 1923 hypothesised that, while some of them had failed Australia House testing or otherwise fell outside the Settlement Act provisions, others were simply too impatient to await bureaucracy's grind; necessarily, most had access to at least modest capital.[150] A further shard came from the bureaucrat who tabulated arrivals in Western Australia: 'these people had they so desired, could have taken advantage of the assisted passage scheme'.[151] Presumably the writer found minimal difference—as to age, health, wealth or occupation—between self-payers and assistees. His words have a hint, apparent in some British thinking too, that the former were more likely to be self-respecting and determined. Yet the category included some too sickly or aged to receive official help, and maybe others were shipped to Australia to avoid nuisance at home. That acerbic officer at Australia House, J. B. Greene, urged denial to self-payers of right to nominate others.

Self-payers, then, appear to have merged into the consummate ordinariness of migrants. The preceding paragraphs strengthen the rule that abstract generalisation about masses of humanity neither edifies nor satisfies. Such is scarcely a proper field for the historian. Only in concrete situations is analysis effective. Those conditions applied more in the aftermath of migration than its foreground. Between lay passage.

*   *   *

Materials offer for a whole book on the migrants' voyage. From 1923, and in some cases earlier, almost every ship taking assisted migrants carried its welfare officer—a policy fostered by the YMCA against the suspicions both of shipping companies and of Australian officials, hostile to such codd-ling.[152] After further discussions in 1926–7 as to improving migration's image, additional 'matrons' accompanied despatches of domestics. These ladies were in permanent employ, while welfare officers—often clergymen or school-teachers—received free passage. Australia House advised them to keep their charges' bowels open and purses shut; 'reserve towards the opposite sex, personal restraint, kindness, cleanliness, abstinence' should also prevail.[153] Most officers wrote reports. They often told more about the writer than the migrants, and betrayed antipathies to Britons, and/or to common people in mass. Historians who delight in finding 'moral panic' among the bourgeoisie might revel in these files. Yet some objective truths seem to emerge, even from the mere hundred or so scrutinised for present purposes.[154] A few published accounts add to the picture.

One of the latter was by Frederick Howard, destined to be a journalist in Australia for many years. His novel, *The Emigrant*, published by Longman in 1928, is fair as literature and good as history. Edgar, Howard's fictional self, suffered exclusion from university because of radical politicking. Poverty forced him to think of Australia, but 'pride crept in again, and told him that emigration was an admission of failure'.[155] Necessity conquered, and Edgar in mid-1924 waited at Tilbury:

> Crowds gazed about them with an interest which not even a three-hours' wait could tire. A middle-aged and surprisingly well-dressed lady talked with her son, a boy of fifteen or so. Several young women in what might be called 'sensible attire'—two of them wore breeches—kept up a flow of chatter which barely masked their hysterical excitement at the great adventure on which they were embarking.
>
> Edgar thought that many of the family groups were city folk, suburban people, clerks and their families. What in the world had brought them into the motley throng? Failure? Or that universal post-War discontent? There were dockers from Wapping, ex-soldiers from the Clyde—long out of work, and with their trade half forgotten through long months of dole-existence. There were tweed-capped and pimply boys from Lancashire mills; better-dressed men and women who had been the shopkeepers of suburbia; and, eating chocolates, that imperturbable product of the War, the London typist.
>
> Edgar remembered the pamphlets which filled his pockets. Where in this assembly were the farm hands, the labourers for whom such a golden opportunity was said to be waiting? Perhaps they were there, somewhere in the crowd, but he could not pick out any of this class amongst those immediately around him.
>
> Occasionally somebody would anticipate the opening of the gates, and the hum of many voices would rise on the hot June air; baskets and suit-cases would be raised, only to be put down again with a groan of disappointment. The crowd grew anxious; they wanted to be on their way, but they accepted the delay as a part of the congested conditions which were sending them forth.

The passage is incomparably rich.

Many migrants had never travelled beyond their home district and few had undergone shipboard life. For five or six weeks they were to move in a new realm. It had potential to liberate that expressiveness which Manning saw as transforming the Briton into a different and more difficult person in Australia. Aboard ship, desperation and hope both must have waxed hot.

Everyday conditions gave pleasure and pain, challenge and constraint, creating an almost existential mode.

In one post-war voyage, we have already remarked, 'a feeling of enmity and resentment' developed among passengers according to benefits they had or had not received, while other tensions caused officialdom to warn that 'third class passengers must realise that they will have to live ... at very close quarters with a number of fellow-travellers of very varied types'.[156] Here were intimations of constant troubles. All assistees travelled third-class: most cabins had six or eight berths, some twelve; a few smaller ones were available for an extra charge. Mothers and children were separated from men. While the intensity of the crowding varied, it was always high; cabins were kept empty when numbers were low rather than passengers being given more room. First- and second-class had most of the deck-space and amenities. In 1938 Oscar Thompson was to say that by then 'the standard of the cheapest class of accommodation was 100% better than in 1920'. His words were probably all too true.[157]

Conditions often became crude. 'The greater number of migrants are of a superior and most desirable type but there are some most ignorant and uncouth people'; 'before embarkation each migrant should be advised verbally or by printed instructions how to behave'; 'more shower accommodation is needed for passengers of both sexes who should be expected to use same and notices posted to that effect': such passages tell much.[158] Seasickness must have prevailed, yet—being taken for granted—vomiting has less place in the record than other bodily functions. Water closets were few, and sometimes used by children for play-cubbies and by graffitists for self-expression. Conversely, other places were used for excrement. Boys were promiscuous piddlers, and otherwise vented high and vulgar spirits. They might, for example, engage in cabin-gang jousting or pelt food at table. More horrific was to see adults gnawing and chomping, without recourse to cutlery. The quantity of food consumed was a frequent point of remark by welfare officers. T. E. Sedgwick, an enthusiast for boy-migration who made repeated trips, detailed what others hinted—that, having their first experience of leisure and supplied meals, many migrants ate to suffocation, and in the absence of exercise and work became constipated and liverish.[159]

Perhaps migrant poverty was the chief reason why drunkenness provoked less notice. Excess there sometimes was, however; allegedly £2000 went across the bar in a 1922 voyage which was uusually rumbustious and had as its scribe D. Hope Johnston, 'a member of Australia's oldest white family'.[160] Five of the passengers still had enough money left to get themselves drunk and disorderly at Fremantle, although Hope Johnston warned them against so smirching migration. Gambling also shocked welfare officers and some passengers. 'The bar and smoke room was the meeting place of the gamblers and "crooks" of both sexes, men and women drinking and gambling and girls smoking cigarettes, being an attraction for the lads who apparently had money to squander', wrote one officer.[161] Another spoke of a 'Gambling Gang' which caused some passengers 'to arrive penniless and in fact minus their clothes which I find some sell to secure money for the gambling craze'.[162] Sale of kit, sometimes by auction, was a matter for frequent criticism by the officers, although gambling would not always have been the cause. Theft seems to have been routine, but it rarely went beyond pettiness, if for no other reasons than that valuables were scant and privacy rare.

Quarrels had further sources. Welfare officers themselves were often the butt of suspicion, even hostility; there is a strong correlation between the extent of this dislike and the acerbity of their remarks. There was persistent, although not universal, tension between full-fare payers and assistees. This had most obvious play within third-class itself, but sometimes involved those further up the passenger hierarchy. Senior officers of the ship generally ignored all third-class passengers, whatever their status; some stewards, assessing likely tips as negligible, also were negligent. There is one report of stewards and migrants engaging in violent fisticuffs: perhaps the remarkable point is that there is only one.[163] Swearing, late-night talking, undisciplined children and so forth, although of great aggravation, were so inexorable as to merit little more notice than that.

While welfare officers contemned drinking, gambling, and general mayhem, such activities gave pleasure to many of their charges; that was the essential point at issue. This divide became yet more pronounced in regard to matters of sex. Sexual activity was inevitable: the liberating style of shipboard life reinforced biology. Some welfare officers recognised this inevitability, but other commentators sought to minimise it. Lady Mary Masson and Lady Eliza Mitchell, the two women of Melbourne's high society who worked hardest for migrant welfare, both spoke of the voyage as 'dangerous' for domestics, referring specifically to the girls' chastity but also to their general outlook—fearing, in effect, that assertion, independence, and hedonism might all grow too strong.[164] Lady Masson wanted matrons 'trained in welfare and in discipline'; single men and women should go in different ships, and male stewards never service women's cabins. Sexuality often dominated the accounts of migrant-ship shenanigans which became regular in the Australian press: 'The Women Seemed to Go to Hell' salivated one headline.[165]

Sex was a major ingredient in a fantastic voyage of S.S. *Ballarat* in mid-1925, and detail from it enriches the story better than does generalisation.[166] 'Oh, I would like to be wrecked on an island with a man and a cigarette', affirmed one girl at the initial boat-drill. She was among a handful who were allegedly promiscuous, although fornication went beyond them. Stewards were active, providing special cabins for their favourites. Officers too had fun, beguiled by a lady who dressed in nun's habit. At Cape Town *Ballarat* became entangled in a world-wide seamen's strike, which halted her there for seven weeks. The crew joined the strike, and received support from their sweethearts. Meanwhile, some of the girls befriended black Africans; such inter-racialism often rippled at both the Cape and Colombo, but rarely had such an opportunity to develop as in this instance. The efforts of the welfare officer, W. Curtis Atkinson, to impose rules on the girls increased the tensions. The captain gave little support and pursued his own seductions: 'surely you don't believe, Mrs So-and-so, that modern women are faithful to their husbands?' Sex-gossip was part of the information the captain gathered from various spies in order to indulge his salacity and to pull levers of informal power.

Other peccadillos, or fantasies, flavour the story of shipboard sex. Some stewards preferred boys to girls; some boys, masturbation to whatever. Ettie Rout could tell of scandals involving welfare officers, male and female.[167] Husbands and wives, their berths separate, might resort to other means of communion; the process amused Angela Thirkell as she went to Australia with fellow war-brides and their spouses.[168] Matrimonial impulses went further: marriage, like birth and death, was an occasional excitement of shipboard life. Betrothals doubtless were more frequent, sometimes defying circumstance. One swain who had nominated his lover and their child found on meeting the ship that during the passage she had switched her feelings to a Mr Shaw. 'To say the least Palfrey was very much concerned at receiving such news and immediately assaulted Shaw', but the new situation held, and Shaw paid Palfrey the nominator's part of the child's fare plus thirty (shilling) silver pieces for a wedding ring purchased in anticipation.[169]

Class-consciousness joined other human fundamentals in ocean life. On the aforesaid *Ballarat* voyage, the young women's support of their militant boyfriends merged with further radical influences aboard. Many passengers sympathised with the seamen's strike, a chorus singing 'The Red Flag' in defiance of welfare officer Atkinson's attempts to break it. His efforts at controlling the migrants surely shaped this scenario. It had more interest in that Atkinson came from the British working class and inclined to the political Left. No such qualifications prevailed as against welfare officer Hope Johnston, whose charges also sang 'The Red Flag' in descant to their non-conforming sexual and social mores. All this confirmed that, while British radicals opposed migration in theory, a fair number pursued it in practice. Various shipboard influences kept such mettle high. 'The consciousness of a class distinction, an inferiority, is made very real to one on boats such as the *Vespasian*', told Frederick Howard.[170]

Some radicalism had Australian sources. Aboard *Ballarat* in 1925 were seamen coming home after pay-off in Britain, and they stirred Atkinson's troubles. Another welfare officer had his affirmations about Australia challenged by a local fresh from Moscow, where he had met Trotsky.[171] Probably more effective counter-talk came from everyday third-classers returning to Australia. Many ships were met by Leftists on berthing. 'Loafers and ne'er-do-wells hanging around the docks at the Migration Bureau ... gave us most depressing stories of conditions in Australia', lamented Lord Apsley.[172]

Contested and not, the welfare officers' role as teachers about Australia was important. 'The intense desire of the migrants to learn as much as possible concerning the country of their destination' was as often noted, usually by the same individuals, as the profundity of ignorance on the subject.[173] Sometimes the officers' tone was disparaging, but more often sympathetic. Several urged Australia House to provide materials to meet this hunger. That does not seem to have happened, facilitating the continued dominance of over-optimistic gleanings from migration propaganda. Even well-meant officers' work may have tended likewise. 'Australia, in my opinion, is a land flowing with milk and honey, if one goes out with the idea of getting on and making it flow with milk and honey.' So wrote the winner of an essay competition conducted by one of them.[174] Such was many migrants' necessary faith, reinforced—as another officer remarked— by encouragement from nominator-friends already in Australia.[175]

The migrants' effort to learn was not the only point where, even by bourgeois standards, a voyage might see achievement and happiness. Welfare officers often affirmed that most migrants were decent, and a few moved towards enthusiasm. Frequently the seafarers helped keep their ship in good order, achieving reciprocal amity with stewards and crew. Some officers, even a captain or two, earned testimonials of appreciation. Ample food might constipate, but T. E. Sedgwick enthused that his boys literally outgrew their clothes (which created its own problems, but still ...). 'I have increased a lot and my wife is as fat as a bullock', said one migrant of a ship about which journalists told horror stories.[176]

Sometimes upper-class passengers swelled the prize-funds for the migrants' social activities. On the *Beltana* in late 1923, sub-committees attended to children, concerts, dances, deck games, whist, education, and finance. ' "The Captain's Birthday Tea Party" will live long in the memory of every kiddie on board', affirmed the officer in telling of this 'exceedingly happy' voyage.[177] Another listed a variety of games that were played— Darby and Joan; Apple Bobbing; Collar and Tie; Candle Lighting; O'Grady Drill; Snake Face; at night bright young things could dance in worship of 'jazz-music, their god'.[178] Apsley played 'a Swanee whistle' on his odyssey. Platonic as well as sexual friendships developed. The only social ties sustained by the D. H. Lawrences during their Australian sojourn were with those two artisan couples—the sort of people whom Lawrence spent most of his life hating. A. F. Ive, the DMC's photographic expert, met migrant ships and took group photographs which sold at ninepence: we know this since such a memento was sought avidly by a boy from a passage which had been 'two months' torture' for another migrant.[179] 'Could you tell me when the S.S. *Benalla* is due in at Outer Harbour', wrote a domestic to the South Australian bureaucracy in 1926; 'I would like to go down & see it again.'[180]

On balance, probably more migrants than not found their weeks aboard happier than the generality of life at home. The experience which awaited them was likely to enhance that image.

CHAPTER TEN

Immigration

In Australia most migrants continued a life of humdrum hardship. Often this shaded towards despair and tragedy, sometimes lightened towards pleasure and prosperity. Time heals all, goes the shibboleth, and thus ultimate truth tended to be. However, worsening economic conditions delayed even that process, which anyway might mean little more than that social-Darwinist severity left visible only those who had accommodated with Australia. Meanwhile, most deployed a stoic fatalism; it offers much for the historian to admire, but was less easy for those who had to fashion and wear the style. Always some Australian neighbours were welcoming, but others were hostile when not apathetic. Thus could deepen the migrants' feeling that not only bureaucracies but life itself had deluded them.

Perhaps this scenario is too gloomy. Dangers of academic fallacy abound. Humankind's normal life is short, mean, and brutish, it may well be said, and migrants merely followed that rule. This has truth, and furthermore is open to the codicil that humanity's resilience enables it to find more happiness within such confines than logic might promise. Many of our subjects were to display this resilience. There is point, too, in remarking the rigours many avoided by leaving Britain—life or death in World War II, rationing, austerity, post-imperial and post-industrial malaise. One must also allow that the archival bias is towards gloom. Most records result from and intensify a 'culture of complaint', being written by and about people who suffered or created problems. Politicising migration, which many people came to see as dooming the Settlement Act and its works, in very much the same way threatens the quest for the truth.

However ... It is the historian's task to slay such dragons once espied. While archives are strong in complaint, further migrant sadness welled from sources which have little documentation—alienation, homesickness, despair resulting from a life-decisive move that goes wrong. The calculus of pain must also embrace that suffered by the migrant's intimates at home. All this confirms T. S. P. Pughe's axiom as to the union of migration and tragedy. Such themes have sounded throughout this book. Now they become dominant, even repetitive. The following paragraphs attempt to deepen these generalisations by reference to sub-categories of migrants. They draw most importantly from archives in Adelaide, Brisbane, and Hobart, which retain files on every assistee to enter the respective States.[1]

'Selected' Men: Little More to Say

Western Australia and Victoria took by far the largest number of adult farm-workers, and the dearth of personal files from those States creates a void as to the category's experience. The norm seems to have been that State officials arranged an initial job, and that thereafter the men looked after themselves. Presumably some effort was made to keep them on rural work for at least a year, with fluctuating outcome. A few snippets enrich the story. 'There was a lot of personal contact with a lot of very personal stories and some of them were quite interesting', told a Westralian whose job had been to meet migrant arrivals.[2] The analysis of another man in the same office cut more sharply:

> A vast majority of farm workers arriving from overseas have no intention of permanently engaging in agriculture, and that number is increased after the first experience of farm work. The average 'rough neck' overseas youth has nothing to complain about. He starts off on his first job as a farm hand. Then as a rule he is attracted by the comparatively big moneys in Government constructional jobs. When those cease he turns again to farm work, leaving it again just as soon as the larger pay is available. His sole object is wages: he couldn't run a farm if he were given one: in fact it would embarrass him.[3]

The writer, H. M. Pullin, impresses as intelligent, well-disposed to migrants. His words show how behaviour which to critics appeared 'drifting' in fact might serve the migrant's aims and abilities.

Yet here, as everywhere, discontent sounded. 'If you don't call that slavely in this so-called Land of Freedom, I don't know what you would', affirmed a station hand to H. W. Gepp;

> They cannot get the Australian workers to do the work in the back blocks therefore they try the English, and when they complain, they know they can get more from the Company to which you are the high paid Commissioner, but this will not go on for ever, for the eyes of the blind shall be opened.[4]

Few of the writer's peers might have had his temerity, but many would have shared his views. Such treatment of farmworkers had disturbed William Bankes Amery's sleep.[5]

Perhaps the best evidence of discontent with these Britons was that, despite Australian xenophobic hostility to southern Europeans, the latter sometimes won favourable comparison. The point was made in both the Western and South Australian Parliaments.[6] More remarkable was that 1936 declaration of a Tasmanian bureaucrat:

> The Southern European migrant has been accustomed to hard work and hard conditions with scanty fare, also small wages … He is thrifty, industrious and is prepared to sacrifice personal comfort to attain his objectives. One has only to go into districts where they are settled to see the difference between them and the English emigrant.[7]

While Victorian and Western Australian farmworkers remain shadowy, the opposite applies to those States' migrant farmers. The tortured histories of the respective schemes have had so much notice in earlier chapters and (for Western Australia) in other writing that further comment is unnecessary. Even with regard to them, the danger looms of politicised problems seizing excessive historical space. Some migrant farmers did survive, a few throve. Such is one message to come from a surpassing study, J. P. Gabbedy's *Group Settlement*, which synthesises knowledge of Western Australian bureaucracy and farming, people and places. 'I have gained an unremitting respect for the qualities of most of the English migrants', concludes Gabbedy.[8] The Victorians endured less, complained more, won greater compensation. Still, most deserved it.

From the Victorians came one of the scant items of migration literature, R. A. Pepperall's *Emigrant to Australia* (1948). Pepperall gave a persuasive account of Australian farm life in general, and more particularly of privations suffered by fellow Britons. His most engaging pen-portrait is of a Mrs Bryn-Jones, who used her Welsh wit against various Australian antagonists. 'Yes, my dear, we may have received free passages, but at least we came out with our hands free, *not* in chains', she remarked; as Pepperall said, this broke the protocol against discussing this part of Australia's history.[9] Pepperall, compensated by the Victorian Royal Commission, returned to Britain and a satisfying career. His book aimed to prevent a re-run of such disasters as he had suffered.

Farmboys: A Surfeit of Documentation

Of all migrants, farmboys were kept under closest scrutiny. In South Australia from 1922 and in New South Wales 1924–5, the boys worked under terms akin to indentured apprenticeship, authorised by statute; Queensland had no Act, but boys and employers there were enmeshed in similar toils and forms. Tasmania offers the best records of a situation less formal yet of similar spirit: presumably similar patterns prevailed among larger numbers elsewhere. Geoffrey Sherington's splendid study of the New South Wales story points that way, although that State was distinctive in offering training to many of its boys, notably at Scheyville farm school.

The Queensland and South Australian schemes entailed supervision through the purported three years of the boys' apprenticeship (even longer if they had not reached the age of twenty-one at its end). Employment had to be approved, and wages managed so as to ensure speedy repayment of fare-loans and to force saving of the rest. This prompted much hege-monistic moralising. 'My advice to you is to pull yourself together and play the man', exhorted South Australia's bureaucrat, V. H. Ryan; '*Workers* are wanted out here, not *Shirkers*'.[10] He refused one boy release of savings to get a £10 suit, and several who wanted to purchase motor-bikes on lay-by. Ryan's Queensland counterpart, E. H. Abell, accompanied. 'These boys want to get away from us so that they may spend their earnings as they see fit', he told the parents of one troublesome lad;[11] another he warned against late-night revelry—'like a good chap, don't let the habit get a hold of you, and I think a fewer number of visits to the Billiard Saloon at Samford would be for your benefit'.[12] Police, bureaucrats engaged in rural work, clerical and lay philanthropists all kept eye on the situation. In 1924 Ryan affirmed that most of the 11,656 letters sent from his office over eight months dealt with the scheme.[13]

Boys (and bosses) bridled at such controls. 'I reckon I earned the money and I reckon I want it too', one of the thwarted motor-cyclists growled;[14] a fellow-spirit in Queensland was aggressive—'all I see is you try and hold a lad down, well, go your hardest, I'll fight you back'.[15] An Anglican cleric interested in migration noticed that 'by some peculiar psychology' boys refused to count board, or even earnings banked for them by the bureau-cracy, as part of their wage; they looked at the weekly 4s. 6d. in hand, and felt aggrieved.[16] When Labor (under John Gunn) came to South Australian office in April 1924, it modified the scheme, giving boys greater freedom of employment, which many were quick to take.

There always prevailed much cause of complaint. Ryan, an exemplary and circumspect bureaucrat, later spelled out that the restraints upon the boys, and their conditions of work, were such as Australians would not willingly accept.[17] The boys' basic wage was modest, usually about a pound a week, with board. Many employers had to be prodded into payment, and some defaulted—and/or dumped the boy when need or convenience pressed. Meanwhile, quarrels between master and hand were endemic, even trivial issues having corrosive effect. 'Sometimes we get on allright together and sometimes we don't so thats how it stands', wrote one boy in rejecting Ryan's advice that he go to church with his employers rather than spend Sundays with a mate.[18] Sleeping and smoking were further leisure activities which often stirred employer wrath. A Queenslander had another vice:

As soon as my back was turned he would sneak back to the house and read ... I took the whole of my books (a considerable number) and burnt them, thinking to give the lad his chance, by removing temptation ... I gave him lectures on the evils of 'Self Abuse' thinking that may have been the cause of the trouble.[19]

All went without avail.

As aboard ship, the farmboys' urine created more overt problems than their semen. Bed-wetting was 'the most serious complaint we have to deal with', averred Ryan in his role as employment-manager.[20] Enuresis surely resulted from anger and distress among the farmboys. These emotions prevailed widely. 'Many Australians do not feel bad language used towards them as Englishmen do', remarked a Minister in charge of the South Australian scheme,[21] and records include such complaints against masters as 'used to call me a Pommie B time out of number, he called me a FBLAPB'.[22] The bureaucrat most involved in the NSW scheme alleged that many boys were cheeky and lazy, insistent that government had to look after them until they turned twenty-one, while others broke all restraints (and were not prosecuted, lest that provide bullets for anti-migrationists).[23] Some South Australian boys felt much anger when after serving their terms they applied for a £300 loan to become independent farmers, apparently granted by statute, only to learn that financial stringency delayed honouring of that promise.[24] Everywhere many boys lost employment on reaching adult age, industrial awards prescribing relatively high wages thereafter.

Tasmania took most of its 80–90 boys in a single burst, 1923.[25] A bureaucrat later summarised:

The scheme for nominated boy farm labour was very far from satisfactory. In a large percentage of cases it was only used as a means to get cheap labour, the treatment that the boys received was regrettable. Many of them were required to work from daylight to dark seven days a week. The cash payment that was due in some cases was with-held, the boys were discouraged by their hopeless position, and at the first opportunity left the person who had nominated them, going to other employers, getting work on the roads, or coming to the cities for work in the factories.[26]

Many of these boys were from Dr Cossar's semi-reformatory at Craigielinn. In Tasmania they remained tight-knit, and aggressive. Their leader, one W. O. Leitch, denounced all involved with migrating them;[27] another told his employer that, should he write home of his experience, 'The English press will be full of it and it will cause war.'[28] Self-assertion took other forms. A letter to Leitch from one of his peers comprised little more than 'cunt' many times repeated. Leitch was to boast to the bureaucrats of his own infection with venereal disease. Another's affections were with a mate: 'I have never been happy since you went away ... I am just about broken-hearted with loneliness ... your old cobber'.[29]

Death had its impact on the farmboys. By 1930 twelve of the 1444 original South Australians had died; at least five had suicided by December 1924, that toll reverberating in the House of Commons and the Colonial Office.[30] Likewise, about thirty of the approximately 3000 Queensland boys had died by 1930; drowning was the dominant cause, murder and suicide contributing.[31] One Tasmanian died in a farm accident: 'he was my best chum', went a letter of mourning, 'he sailed from England with me and we became chums after a few days ... I was with him up to the moment of his Death.'[32] Another boy in the island spent four years dying of tuberculosis, without intimate or relation in Old World or New. His only request was for cigarettes.[33]

The schemes aroused much party-political feeling. G. W. Fuller instigated the NSW variant, which complemented his other migrationist work. Labor resistance was bitter: 'absolutely child slavery ... brought on for the purpose of breaking down the conditions and the pay awarded by the Federal Court ... a kidnapping bill'.[34] When Labor took office in mid-1925, an abolition Bill renewed battle. After long and acrimonious debate the shell of the system survived, but nothing like apprenticeship. Despite the milder quality of South Australian politics, the issue there was as divisive. The scheme was instituted by the non-Labor government of H. N. Barwell. Labor always opposed it, especially late in 1923 when a new Act refurbished the scheme, *inter alia* promising that £300 carrot for worthy graduates. Critics denounced this as giving preference to migrants, when local boys were yearning to become farmers. Even so, the Bill passed. Next year a Methodist clergyman, H. R. Cavalier, alleged grave ill-treatment of farmboys. The Legislative Council appointed a committee, intended to give Cavalier the lie. So it transpired, although party feeling divided the committee itself.[35]

The record of the happier side of farmboys' experience can begin with their own contemporary comment. Some of this, gathered most busily by the Big Brother movement, might appear compromised by its provenance. (In view of the later history of the phrase, it is interesting that the Brothers distributed such lore through a handsome magazine called *The New Australian*.)[36] More earthy and persuasive enthusiasm has its place in more impartial bureaucratic files:

> I have a good reputation and am noted as being the fastest sheep killer in the district my time for a sheep being three minutes. I am also known as one of the best riders in the district, I can ride buck jumping horses and have seldom been thrown.

> Tailing lambs today ... no knife is used—all teeth work. The taste is tasteless ... Mustering is good fun ... Last week I went down to Rockleigh to see some of my pommy friends. They are all getting on fine.

I am very please I have come to South Australia. I have found out what it is to work hard. I like the farm work. I have learned a lot ... and I have a very good and homely boss.

I have a very good job, and if it is possible I will be here for three year's ... I have been trying hard to get my brother out ... but Dad told me in his last letter he had not passed, worse luck, but I will just have to be contented and see what the future does for him and me.[37]

When the brother came, the pair angered their boss with eternal cigarette-smoking. Yet the letter stands as an example of a widespread farmboy readiness to encourage relatives to follow. Often their wages subsidised the move, a friendly boss sometimes helping. That was so even in the case of W. T. Balls, where the boy had shown self-assertion as an employee. Later he did so as a penman: 'Mum and Dad are settled down now and are quite content. Mum wants to go back to England to die. I reckon we can die just as easy out here.'[38]

The longer term had its brightnesses too. As of 1930, Ryan declared that two or three of his charges had entered the ministry, a few more had become teachers, policemen, motor mechanics—but the majority stayed on the land.[39] Perhaps the latter benefited especially from an Act of 1937 which provided that funds originally set aside for insurance should defray wages still owing to the boys (although even then a small deficit remained). One of the Tasmanian semi-delinquents already by 1928 had invented new types of safety lamp and rescue stretcher, both for use in mines. E. N. West had a tough spell as a Tasmanian farmboy, yet wrote an approving critique of immigration, and later became a Labor activist;[40] he served in Parliament 1941–6, alongside fellow immigrant, Edward Brooker. Of 1059 Little Brothers in Victoria, by 1932 twelve owned their own properties and eleven share-farmed, 827 had employment on farms and 45 elsewhere.[41] The British Settlers' Welfare Committee reported in 1935–6 that many NSW farmboys were doing quite well.[42]

Of complementary tone to the comments of West and W. T. Balls, was the 1931 soliloquy of G. E. Clarke, a former farmboy in New South Wales. He saw his peers' fate as sad, yet epic:

The fault is the combined scheme of English and Australian Governments who transported lads, all under age, to a country that was not prepared to assimilate them. They are not to be blamed for coming in their thousands. The promise that could not be fulfilled for three-quarters of them was a magnet which no healthy lad could resist. Take a gold rush, diamond find, a—yes, even a war—Hundreds of thousands of people rush to them with no thought of failure or Death. To them it is adventure, a chance to do something—be something. The aftermath—but these lads, poor devils, they know the track, want, starvation, all honour to them that they have remained law-abiding, with the exception of a small minority. I

Bernard Mills (32)

Mary Fairey (63)

Phyllis Bowerman (67)

Adam Duncan (29)

Robert Maxwell (28)

Jonah Pollard (39)

Faces in the crowd. These are official photographs held in the Archives Office of Tasmania. Names are followed by the numbers of the notes to chapter 10 which relate to each. (Reproduced by permission of the State Archivist of Tasmania.)

Ethel and Thomas Medford (96)   Flora Hood (48)

George Knight (32)   Ernest West (40)   Agnes McGee (48)

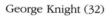

have heard them singing in the Club room, have sung with them. It has been raining outside and when the sing-song was over, out to a paper bed in the 'Dom' quite a few of our British lads went laughing and joking. Swearing too, telling the lowest of stories, this is fun to them, they have plumbed the uttermost depths, but the spirit of Old England, a tradition handed down for countless ages is theirs.[43]

Clarke himself had by then left Australia for beachcombing in Fiji. Further evidence confirms the commonsense assumption that many boys would depart the place. That was true for example of A. L. Lloyd. Born in 1908, Lloyd worked in outback New South Wales 1925–33. There he became interested in folklore, later claiming to have collected some 500 songs. Meanwhile, Lloyd borrowed books from the NSW Library service which taught him about art and music (Bach, Mozart, Bartok) and prepared him for his subsequent destiny as a folklorist of world eminence.[44] What he achieved in art, Tom Cole did in deed. Migrating to Queensland in 1923, Cole at once embarked on a life which came to transcend 'the Australian legend' as he worked as a master-stockman—and horse-breaker, and crocodile-hunter—in the far interior.[45] One doubts if any native Australian of this generation so enhanced outback experience. Yet some might judge the most remarkable farmboy to have been Harry Hooton (1908–61), seer of existential anarchism. For Hooton, the outback was resort and slogan of Australia's nay-sayers:

> Oh God, please do not let us evolve …
> Let us go back to the past, to death—
> Away from the tumult where the brain of a nation works out its destiny
> To the slothful inertia of its Bush.[46]

He had been there.

Domestics: A Gender Dimension

While domestics were among the 'selected' migrant categories, not all domestics were 'selected'. A fair number were nominated, often by prospective employees, sometimes in the usual friend-and-relative way. (However, it is not true, as sometimes said, that girls could receive aid, even as nominees, *only* if bonding themselves to such service.) Nearly all the following material depends upon 'selection' data, but most of the generalisations appear valid for nominees also. Specific documentation is lacking as to self-paying domestics, and likewise Barnardo girls, most of whom were intended for 'service'.

In some ways domestics' situation was easier than that of other migrants. At a pound or more weekly, plus board, they were in steady demand. One indication of this appeal was Australia's acceptance that all 'selected' women be granted free passage from late 1926. Marriage, even within the bond period, appears always to have released domestics from the obligation to work—and from 1927, to repay loans, as long as the couple were poor and the husband refused responsibility.[47] Thus was saluted that family-building role of the girls which we have seen at play in migrationist thinking and propaganda. Chivalric sexism prompted other gestures of respect, such as the refusal by the South Australian Parliament in 1923 to bring females within the apprenticeship prevailing for farmboys.

Domestics were just as ready as males to go from job to job, and the employment market eased their doing so. Hence arose hassles with the bureaucrats. As with other 'selected' labour, State officers arranged an initial job. Back in 1919–20 the Simm–Jones mission had clashed with Victoria's Samuel Whitehead, as he insisted that Australian-subsidised domestics must go whither he willed. That authoritarian style persisted. Practicality thwarted efforts to keep absolute control over girls' employment for the twelve months of their bond, but certainly they were pressured to stay that period in domestic service. Delinquents were punished by being compelled to repay the government grant towards their fare; among them were two Tasmanians who joined Paton's, while a South Australian was refused permission to transfer to nursing.[48] In similar way, a 1926–7 decision that any nominee who had worked as a domestic for a year should receive the further fare-rebate was made conditional upon the nomination having specified such service as her original intent, and the job not being in a hotel or such-like where Australians would have been happy to serve.[49]

Job mobility had a further nuance for domestics. As their supply fell below demand, the government spread them among States. Disposition to go to the bigger States may have been no greater among domestics than other migrants, but its frustration was. Many girls in the outlying States had this grievance, and often they proved it by walking. A variant of servant-stealing developed in Tasmania when holidaying mainlanders enticed girls to join their households.[50] The most sweeping bureaucratic denunciations of domestics came from outliers, Tasmania and Queensland.[51]

Other plaints sounded. Many Australian voices, and objective evidence too, affirmed that the girls often had little relevant experience: early on, many had a background of war-work, and shopgirls and mill workers continued numerous.[52] New World demands widened the gap between expectation and reality. 'May Swift did not know how to make a bed or sweep the house', went a complaint from Queensland, 'as for washing she simply could not do it. I must look out for a dark girl. These New Chums want too much.'[53] Mrs Matilda Armstrong spoke for hundreds, perhaps thousands.

' "Status" is only higher because most girls here will not submit', Mrs Simm remarked in 1920.[54] Many migrants upheld that tradition. The nicest glimpse of resistance comes from a soliloquy of E. W. M. Wood, administrative assistant to the British Representative. He and the Trade Commissioner, H. L. Setchell, had both engaged migrant domestics. Wood damned precisely as did Australians.[55] His employee lied and lazed, 'came out to Australia with the purpose of doing as little as possible, and getting out of domestic work as soon as possible'. Her boss pondered:

> It is really extraordinary how quickly the mental attitude changes. I suppose the girl which [!] we employed was quite a meek and mild type at home. I can imagine her environment and the struggle she had to live yet as soon as she reaches Australia and is ensconced in a comfortable home, she loses all sense of perspective. It is difficult to account for this quick change, but there is no doubt that some influence is assimilated which is not for the newcomer's good. I think the boat journey may be the cause of much of the trouble ...
>
> The girls were so obsessed with that much hackneyed phrase 'Australian conditions' that they lost all sense of proportion. Certainly there is a freer atmosphere in Australia and a girl is treated far more liberally—but because we endeavour to let them lead a freer and brighter life and pay them better, Australians are not disposed to relax the ordinary rules of mistress and maid.

Most obviously in his reference to the voyage, Wood endorsed the views of Lady Masson, Lady Mitchell, and others of like type, British and Australian. His words anticipated C. H. E. Manning's thesis as to Australian conditions having dangerously 'expressive' effect on hitherto controlled Britons.

Hostility to wearing uniform was a point remarked by Wood, and others. Victoria League ladies recognised that when girls—even SOSBW protégées—disdained the League's philanthropic embrace, they were showing a desire for independence.[56] Likewise, to the SOSBW's lament that many girls were working in hotels, Lady Mitchell replied that this was very much their positive choice.[57] The bureaucrats' surliness as to domestics partly derived from the girls' assertion. A Queenslander told of troubles with one group:

> When the ladies who required servants came to interview and the usual rate of wages was offered (25/- to 30/- with board) the four looked at each other, then broke into rude laughter, talking loudly that Australia House had told them nothing but lies; that it was disgraceful that girls should be brought out for such wages; that the other States offered them much more, etc. etc.
>
> During the following week certain positions were accepted and arrangements made for them to go to—but not one troubled to do so, nor cared what embarrassment was caused by their default.[58]

In counterpoint, a girl in Tasmania told of herself and friend meeting a Victoria League stalwart, 'a lady who was most rude and said we know nothing and wanted to send us off to the bush separated, so don't be surprised to see us again in Melbourne shortly'.[59]

Other domestics wrote not of affront, but distress. One from South Australia begged Ryan: 'It is so lonely—10 miles to go to Church. I shall never be able to go—before I go mad will you please get me another place?'[60] A Tasmanian wrote:

> There is nothing here for a girl. If you go to Swansea Thursday at 3 o'clock before the car comes and you are back at Riversdale at 5 o'c. So what is there for a Girl to live for—only bed & work—that is no good to any one young.[61]

The first girl seems tender: offered another job, she refused, with pathetic apologies to Ryan—'do not be cross with me—you are the only one I can come to if I want to know anything—will try not to upset you again—I thank you so much for troubling'. The second was tough: bureaucrats were happy at her move to Melbourne. Resentment had other sources, most frequently employer fraud or default. One nominee domestic claimed that she was receiving naught but board until the nominator's fare-loan was discharged.[62] Sometimes gross overwork was alleged: 'she does not give me the life of a dog', wrote a girl of her mistress at one of Tasmania's grand houses.[63]

To enquire into sexual matters risks both prurience and misapprehension. Many shipboard welfare officers strove to protect girls from adventure which, in fact, they were happy to accept and capable to manage. Likewise the one 'scandal' about sex ashore—the mid-1926 story of a group of girls just disembarked in Western Australia being exposed to insult and danger—derived from the (probably exaggerated) reports of a local philanthropist, not from any 'victims'. (Most distressed of all was T. C. Macnaghten, fearful lest 'infinite harm would be done' were Britain's press to use the story.)[64] Files sampled for this exercise have revealed not one complaint of harassment, further suggesting that the women saw such matters as their own business. Historians might take the hint.

Still, sex could be a problem. Perhaps the lack of complaints showed the domestics' belief that any reader would ignore or condemn, rather than help. The sample has revealed one story of abortion, the woman dying as a result.[65] Unwanted babies made their inevitable appearance. Sometimes they led to marriage, but it seems more often not. H. L. Setchell believed that, whereas Australian girls had sex only when they were sure that boyfriends would marry should conception occur, their British counterparts often had to face motherhood alone.[66] One girl knew her baby's father only as 'Dick'.[67] 'Most of the young men of Sydney are a disgrace', went another domestic's comment. 'They do not want our girls for any good, and if they cannot get what they want they ask them to fund the money they have spent on them.'[68]

'The doctor did not think me fit … so under the circumstances I got married as that was the only thing to do as I had no money of my own';[69] such remark confirms that not every marriage was an idyll. The woman conceived subsequently, to her husband's delight. Another South Australian, conversely, enthused at marriage and motherhood—her first baby 'weighed £7'—but soon cried, 'money matters worry me awfully … I want my Husband to go to England there would be no water-carting etc. or cattle & Horses to Water but of course it all takes money.'[70]

Less qualified accounts of domestics' happiness appear in the files, but not often. SOSBW materials offer more:

> I met my 'Fate' and got married early in 1922 … I married into the bush life and wherever we pitch our tents there is home, far from the 'madding crowd'. My husband is clearing by contract, he is a born bushman … The glorious sense of space and freedom in the bush districts of Western Australia can only be truly realised by those who have lived and worked in large cities and disliked them, all clatter and smoke.

> Since landing in Australia I have never looked back, I have been in the same position for *four* years to date. Since my arrival I have been joined by my two brothers and later by my parents, and quite recently by a married sister, her husband and three children … I am studying opera singing and may branch out as a professional before long.

> I was married in Sydney to my Aussie Boy and we are very happy. My luck in Australia has been the best thanks to the OSC. The life here is so free and easy. There is no mistress and maid (in the English meaning). Jack is as good as his master but when home people come out they must lose all their pride (as there is nothing that is honest living that is looked down on in this country). The best way is to be humble and start at the bottom of the tree. Just start life over again and kid you don't know anything not like the Americans they want to tell you there is nothing they don't know. But Aussie is a young country and we must all be beginners with it. It is really marvellous how quick the English get to the top although I mustn't give them too much praise before my Aussie husband no matter what I think.[71]

Deconstruct that third passage, and discover truth!

Among its nuances was stoicism, already suggested as a dominating theme in migrant adaptation. It is a keynote of *Chancy Times*, memoirs published in 1991 by Olga Wignall, who came as a toddler to Western Australia in 1925–6 with her unmarried mother, a domestic. Job followed job, usually so demanding that between them the mother would have to spend days of exhausted nullity. One spell was with railway tea-rooms, another with the 'Flying Domestics', providing emergency services. The woman married, happily enough, but that meant more children. Her life was that of the archetypal Australian battler.

Contemporary reports on the domestics are rich. Gladys Pott's position in the OSD generally, and above all her membership of the Windham Delegation of 1923, gave her unique status. In Queensland she fired at servants' presumption:

> The girl whose obvious object is to 'stand up for her rights' rather than assist in duties not actually specified in her contract of service is neither a credit to Britain nor to herself. Such an attitude has too often brought unpopularity on the British migrant.[72]

This comment bore especially on those who took false pride in being 'lady helps' rather than plain 'domestics'. However, as Pott toured Australia, her asperity increasingly bore on local employers and conditions. Rural life, she insisted, was very tough indeed, and even city houses often lacked the labour-saving devices that were becoming standard in Britain. Back home, Pott must have written, or at least approved, pertinent pages of the Windham *Report*. Like the whole, they were bland to the point of concealment: most girls were happy, some had saved 'an astonishing amount', lack of training and experience justified many employer complaints.[73] Yet late in 1925 Pott countered Bankes Amery's urging of domestics' emigration by reference to Australians' 'little consideration of the new-comer'.[74] Pott also upbraided well-meaning medicos for their easy endorsements of applicants' health. Migration, she stressed, demanded above-average physical and nervous health; to assist movement of people lacking them was to worsen their life chances.

Late in 1928 a Miss Cox from HMG's Ministry of Labour also studied domestics' experience in Australia. Her report was long and sensible:

> My enquiries did not reveal any sensational story of success. Frankly, this discovery disappointed me at first. Then I realised that my attitude ... was what propaganda had made it—an expectation of the 'extraordinary'. Gradually I realised that my sense of values was wrong and that in the scores of happy women whom I met I had far better testimony to the real advantage of life in Australia than in finding an odd woman who had made a brilliant marriage or who had some sensational stroke of good fortune.[75]

Cox told that whereas twelve of the 270 domestics going to South Australia, 1927–8, became unmarried mothers, only seven of 800 to New South Wales did so: her guess at explaining the difference was that Adelaide had no YWCA club. She remarked the meeting of migrant ships by Britons vociferous about 'promises unfulfilled'. The lady-help scheme failed because of its false assumption that such people could meld with employer families; anyway, the 'ladies' yearned for other work and often received less pay than workaday servants. The latter were not so ardent to move into factories as often alleged, said Cox, and generally enjoyed a better life than their counterparts in Britain.

E. T. Crutchley reminisced that domestic migration

> not only filled a need, because of the Australian's inherent objection to service of any kind and particularly to service which curtailed personal liberty, but it brought into the country a large number of young women, much more carefully selected than the male migrants, who married and brought to the upraising of the next generation a beneficial measure of English and Scottish blood and tradition'.[76]

The man's values shaped that verdict, but did not rob all its value. One supporting datum is that of a 1926 shipload of fifty-one girls, forty-eight 'had married and were doing well' by 1929; three Depression years later, only one was in distress and while others suffered wage-cuts, two had saved £400 apiece and seven had assisted relatives to migrate.[77]

One last report—by Edith Thompson, Pott's successor in the OSD, who visited Australia in 1939—had more restraint.[78] 'Too many' older, unmarried women still lived in hotels and boarding-houses, isolated from society; often they cherished hope of returning to Britain (although, Thompson remarked, many who had done so, now yearned for Australia, especially its climate). More generally, 'even those who were prosperous wives and mothers now, spoke bitterly of the "rough deals" they had had at the start'. Older migrants were happier, especially because their standard of comparison was with Britain of another day; newer-comers found 'conditions, even at their best, very little better than at home, and sometimes a good deal worse'. 'The "pommie" complex' continued to sour migrants' life. Australians still prized well-trained, subservient domestics, but resisted the lesson that 'if they want to attract a better type of migrant they must offer wider opportunities and a warmer welcome'. So Simm and Jones had argued two decades before.

What of the Less-Differentiated Majority?

The previous chapter presented ordinariness as the migrants' salient characteristic. Any large number of ordinary people will have failures and no-hopers among them. Many contemporaries alleged that the newcomers' faults exceeded such norms. Britons were among the critics. Kingsley Fairbridge affirmed that he would never employ a migrant; evidently several members of the Windham Delegation (most of all Major-General A. G. Wauchope, concerned with ex-servicepeople) felt that usually grievance-mongers had themselves to blame. Crutchley lamented of migrant compatriots, 'all the cases I take up specially seem to turn out badly'.[79]

Some figures put bounds to condemnation. Victorian bureaucrats, telling much about themselves and/or their masters, tallied migrants received each month in the State's gaols.[80] From a sample, the average was about eight—almost all of them assisted Britons, with a year's gaol the rare maximum sentence. The law allowed deportation of a migrant within three (after 1935, five) years of arrival for those sentenced to more than a year's gaol, living off prostitution, entering an insane asylum or charitable institution, or advocating forceful overthrow of government; and also of those found to be suffering physical or mental ill-health contracted before arrival. When the South Australian government in late 1929 asked the Commonwealth to establish special surveillance on assisted migrants, it was told that only sixty-one criminal deportations had occurred in the decade.[81] Between 1921 and 1929, a total of 453 people were returned on medical grounds; the lowest number for all deportations was nine in 1921 and the highest was 213 in 1930 (22 cases likely to be a public charge; 40, mental trouble; 89, physical ill-health; 30, criminal activity; 20, 'other').[82] In late 1928, only 30 of the 33,000 assistees who had arrived in New South Wales since 1925 were in lunatic asylums.[83] Such data probably ignored occasional cases where deportation was inappropriate, yet—usually in anticipation that the people concerned would become a public charge—the States funded repatriation.[84] However, after an initial burst of ex-servicepeople that number was modest, until the Depression. Of course, governments always had a vested interest in minimising such problems as culminated in repatriation, and still more in discouraging mass hopes of securing that bounty. There was early talk of a systematic funding policy to manage these problems; the failure to crystallise it marked another bureaucratic mess.[85]

The Victorian gaol figures endorse the notion that self-paying migrants had superior virtue. Yet suspicions about the quality of self-paying migrants, like those which J. B. Greene voiced in Britain, had their upholders in Australia, some remarking that unemployment was especially high among them.[86] Similarly, to most people nominees seemed to offer better hope than did 'selectees', but Lady Masson disagreed. She told Gepp that nominee families often included a member (for whom, presumably, full fare was paid) deficient in mind or body.[87] Furthermore, 'it does not seem desirable to accept as *nominators* people who are themselves precariously employed only in wage-earning work liable to seasonal or periodic interruptions'. Here obtruded the problems of nomination at which chapter 9 hinted. Masson presumably had some ideal of nominators being bourgeois Australians, serving national and imperial ends. As noticed, the usual reality was far different. Many nominators probably had but limited intent to succour their clients, and still more lacked means to do so. However careful the bureaucracy, it could not forestall such mishaps as Masson cited. Lord Gowrie, of South Australia, invoked these matters in 1928 when telling of 'constant letters' from recent arrivals seeking aid to return home.[88] Group nominees may have fared a little better, although some going to Tasmania under the aegis of the British Dominions Emigration Society had to contend with a local agent who cared little for them, while ready to mulct a fee.[89]

The State bureaucracies did little to help nominees, rarely providing even a night's lodging. Yet if loans had defrayed the newcomers' fares, and repayment was tardy, they were vulnerable to scrutiny as intrusive as that directed against 'selectees'. Thence must often have developed further tensions between nominee and nominator; the latter could be treated as responsible, even when not the actual borrower. Irrespective of that, dunning for repayment of fare-loans became the chief force in creating records which tell of migrant distress and anger. Obviously the danger of archival bias here reaches its extreme. Yet the files exist, and tell an inexorable part of the truth.

A sample might begin with W. C. Wood, one of those migrants sponsored by the British Dominions Emigration Society who tangled with their Hobart nominator. That the latter was Thomas Murdoch, a big figure in the small city's affairs, added its flavour. Arriving in April 1922, Wood soon warred with Murdoch, and then with established authority at large. Wood having found trouble in getting work, Murdoch negotiated with the authorities to have him offered a job in distant mines. 'He is only a disturbing element here and Lyell would be a good place for him to reside.' But the malcontent said rheumatism precluded that, and became more vehement. Placards that he paraded and posted through town, and his newspaper letters, denounced Murdoch and the authorities as 'liars and swindlers'. Allegedly labour radicals maintained Woods, as part of their war against immigration. When the Windham Delegation visited Hobart, Wood won an interview, and some sympathy; being a 'hero of Mons' helped that. Ultimately Wood was repatriated—which some critics said was always his aim and which certainly he did not oppose.

A South Australian case also involved deliberate protest against the system, if in vicarious way.[90] Annie Wesley suffered widowhood, illness, and trauma. Her case was taken up by another migrant who aspired to organise discontent among his peers. 'Remember a *human life* is at stake, but this is great *humour* to many, who brands us with the name of "Pommy" like the Italians is *Branded Dago*.' Yet the woman herself vented pathos rather than anger when her repatriation came through—'I Mrs Wesley does wish to thank you all for what you have done to help me since I have been out hear as I am very sorry that I have been such a lot of trouble to youse.'

Of other tragedies reported in the South Australian files, one will illustrate how crushing debt could be.[91] The father—boasting long service with police and army—and a son worked their passages in 1919. The father then nominated his wife and further six children. Even with some charitable help, a government loan of £104 was necessary. Before embarkation, illness struck the family, an augury of more to come. 'I am fully aware of the liability, and would be only too pleased to get it done with', wrote Emma Ferguson in November 1925;

> and if I had known what I do now I would never have come out here under those conditions as I could have paid it off better in the Old Country by instalments than I have had opportunity to do out here where we have met with nothing but reverses, insults, and looked upon with scorn by the average Australian because we have the misfortune to be POMMIES.

For years the file recorded constant troubles; only the husband's pension averted the shame of the dole, 'rations'. In the beautiful land of Australia, went Mrs Ferguson's repeated plaint, governments had denied 'chance to earn an honest living'.

Further South Australia quotations sounded that refrain:

> We arrived four years ago and find things entirely different as gazetted … a hopeless future lies before our children whose ages range from 19, 8, 5, 2 years.

> I am in receipt of your letter dated July 5th in which I learn of your intention to take proceedings against me for not paying my debt to you. Also, you do not want to embaress me, which by the way your department as done nothing else since I arrived in Australia … go ahead if that is your intention then the only thing left me to do will be to further embaress the Government by drawing rations.

> I am drawing relief and am forced to beg for a living which seems the proper thing to do in Australia.

> I came to this country in 1927 and like a good many others was thrown to the scrap heap when after the first four months of arrival in this country I was told to go to the bush and carry my swag and look after myself.

> Give me a chance to get myself a position to keep my wife and child and myself that is better than living in charity and also help me regain my manhood.[92]

South Australia offers the only example of a distressed migrant's child dying of malnutrition.[93]

A Queensland case gains remarkability from its span. 'I am full of worries … there is poverty here as well as at home', wrote Arthur Knibb in 1925. 'What a life farming is it is heart braking', his cry continued in 1937. Two years later, 'I am unable to carry on, I think it is terrible after 50 years of hard toil ... I have now got to depend on my children to find a home among them'.[94]

The files elaborate the tensions between nominator and nominee. One Queensland nominator in vain sought official help to get his nominees, now well-settled, to repay the fare-money he had advanced for them; another protested at his wife's committing him to maintenance of her kin.[95] In Tasmania a nominator denied her children food and Christmas presents so as to meet the fares of her sister, brother-in-law, and their four children.[96] Similar in essence, but extraordinary in detail, was another instance from the island. In 1924 or so a recent self-paying arrival, Mrs Jessie King, proposed to an old friend that she accept nomination; in mid-1927 the friend arrived, with husband, two children, a third gestating. The husband, Stanley Harper, was ill and generally hopeless, unable to keep his brood. The Kings did their best. Bureaucrats suggested that they subsidise the Harpers' return to Britain, which 'will relieve you of any further responsibility under your nomination agreement'! Harper grumbled along: 'I might just as well starve in my own country as out here.' After further agony, State and federal authorities secured the family's repatriation. Harper wrote back from Britain complaining that no-one had given him landing money and asking for help in finding a job there. But he was cheerful—'Tassy (the baby) is in trouble he has just been circumcised ... Here's Health and Prosperity to you.' What did Jessie King think?

That women had sizeable part in these miseries tells its own story. The 'gender dimension' of migration did not end with domestics: indeed its harsher aspect probably prevailed elsewhere. The near-certain fact that after 1921 migrant women reversed earlier patterns and became less fertile than settled-Australian counterparts hints at alienation.[97] For full-time housewives and mothers, the relative primitivism of Australian homes, especially kitchens, would be an even heavier burden than for domestics. In the isolation of such dwellings, nostalgia for home must often have overwhelmed. Senator E. D. Millen made these points in November 1921 when lamenting the many returnees aboard the vessel on which he had recently gone to England.[98] Angela Thirkell was one who suffered domestic drudgery, at least compared to her earlier life:

> When I think what I did in Australia between 1920 and 1930 ... I often wonder why I am alive. I might have been aliver had not all this happened, but anyway it did ... One gets through with courage and goodwill—but one leaves some of one's fleece in the hedge.[99]

For migrants of higher social class, Australia's lack of employment opportunities struck hard—factories, offices, shops offered diversity for domestics, but not for them. Not only Lady Masson and Lady Mitchell but Georgina Sweet (academic), Mildred Muscio (leader, National Council of Women), and Eleanor Hinder (welfare officer) brought this matter before the DMC.[100]

Upper-class sensitivity could find further affront in Australia. 'My relations in England raise the objection to the word immigrant being attached to them', wrote a posh Tasmanian to the bureaucracy concerning her nominees.[101] But a local newspaper used the dreaded term in reporting their arrival; matters never recovered, and the nominator had to pay more than £200 to speed her charges back to England. Similar consciousness pervades a further migrant narrative, R. W. Thompson's *Down Under*. Arriving in 1926, poor but polished, Thompson echoed the bourgeois criticisms of Australia that have rumbled throughout this book. He found Australia vastly different from Britain. Migration was not for decent chaps:

> In Australia it is impossible to get away from the mob; no one can be exclusive. On any beach, any resort or beauty spot, all classes are jumbled together in an unpleasant mass—unpleasant because they have few tastes in common, and therefore must clash. In England one need never go out of one's class; in Australia there are no classes—theoretically it is a democracy! And therefore there are more classes and more snobbery than anywhere else.[102]

Thompson was not always crabbed, yet at the Depression's onset he joined the 'literally thousands of people trying to leave the country by any means at all', and jobbed his homeward way. Thompson found 30 per cent of passengers on the ship to be returning migrants, their fares paid by friends or family; most of the rest were Australians, forever growling at 'Bloody Pommies, sending out their blasted emigrants' (but presumably spending years of savings on an overseas holiday centring on dear old England).[103] Thompson pitched his tales high, but nevertheless conveys a powerful sense of all-round disgust with emigration.

Returning migrants had always been many—probably almost as many during the 1920s as at the decade's turn. Some of the earlier returnees may have been nonchalant, having never committed themselves to Australia. Such is the normal way of migration. Nor must be forgotten that, once back in Britain, some wanted to retrace their way. Perhaps all these qualifications, atop statistics of great elasticity, obviate the need for further comment. Yet returns from Australia long bothered migrationists. J. T. Barnes travelled forth and back in 1924 to probe the matter.[104] He recognised that troubles were real (one recent shipload carried back seventy-one disconsolate families), and blamed deficient Australian after-care. Causes surely went deeper. The volume of returnees was indeed a black mark against migration, especially as many more would have joined them, had the chance offered. Unless repatriated, or able to work their passage, the poor could not move. During the 1920s bureaucrats were strict in refusing exit to assistees within two years of arrival, and to everyone owing fare-loans.

So, much hard fact carried towards despair and denied hope. Complementary to that, any summation as to the achievements of inter-war migrants must be modest, especially in relation to assisted civilian adults, the mainstream. As with Miss Cox's domestics, dramatic success scarcely existed. Ordinariness was supreme. Yet the register did have credits.

The previous chapter referred to that handful of migrants, usually bourgeois and professional, whom the *Australian Dictionary of Biography* esteems as having 'flourished' already by 1940. They all have interest: H. P. Brown, for example, genius of Australian telecommunications over decades; or P. R. Mountford and G. R. Hoff, sculptors whose work dominated the War memorials respectively of Melbourne and Sydney. As remarked, not quite all these 'flourishers' had had a favoured birth. Angela Thirkell is one of the two women among them; the other is Matilda Devine, also the wife of a soldier, and quick to become Sydney's surpassing prostitute and madam.

As exemplar of creativity there stands Roland Robinson. He was born in Ireland in 1912 of English parents. They migrated to Australia in 1921, and just got by. The parents warred:

> Once, before I had gone to bed, I heard them quarrelling behind the closed door of the living room. Mother was crying her voice rising, rising. I could not stand it. I ran out of the house and into the street. As I ran down the street, I heard mother scream. I ran as hard as I could, but the scream went through me as I ran. All the neighbourhood must have heard that scream and I know that I never stopped running away from it.[105]

The mother was suffering mortal illness. After her death, life became still harder. Young Roland scrambled for his first jobs, notably as a shearing-shed 'rouseabout'. He developed a love of the Australian land which has inspired his splendid poetry and prose. Robinson complements and even transcends A. L. Lloyd, Tom Cole, and Harry Hooton. When in 1943 two Australian littérateurs sought to hoax their modernist foes by creating 'Ern Malley', fount of sublime/ridiculous free-verse, by chance they gave him a background like Robinson's; born in Liverpool in 1918, Ern too was a young-child migrant.[106]

In workaday terms, the migrants' great contribution was just that—work. Farm labourers did it through very long days, under conditions which, indeed, few Australians would accept. They fulfilled the traditional role of coercible labour—not as well as most masters would have liked, yet still contributing to the economy. Something the same was true of domestics, more so if they served up-country. The story of migrant farming itself had some triumphs, as well as many tragedies; the former were perhaps in highest ratio in Queensland.[107] For the rest, chief emphasis must go whither Colin Forster has pointed. 'The critical importance of skilled migrants cannot be sufficiently emphasised', asserts his study of manufacturing in the 1920s; motor-vehicles, electricity, heavy industry, all showed that.[108] Forster tells too that the proportion of breadwinners was higher among migrants than among the settled population.

All this resounds more loudly if migration created, rather than merely redistributed, employment. Such is affirmed for this period by the most germane contribution to that debate.[109] Entwined also are still more protean issues as to whether population increase and capital investment benefited Australia during the inter-war years. The Depression seemed to confirm nay-sayers—yet nay-sayers then became expansionists after 1945, as H. C. Coombs most remarkably demonstrated. Migrants appear to have contributed to Australia's progress, as defined by traditional criteria. Those who deny legitimacy to such progress will see them as malign, albeit helpless and hopeless.

Migrants envigorated the politics of the period, most obviously from the Left. This continued not only a theme of migrant-ship life but a larger tradition whereby Australian radicalism and Labor parties derive markedly from British models.[110] Even local Laborites' vehemence against immigration complemented their British counterparts' hostility to emigration. This hostility might seem to make it paradoxical that British radicals should migrate, but that too followed tradition, as Henry Parkes's move of 1839 established.[111] Perhaps some pursued such hope of happiness as part of their radicalism. This seems apposite to what Olga Wignall writes about her mother, an active Leftist in Britain. It applied too to the protagonist of Frederick Howard's autobiographical novel, previously cited. Howard's 'Edgar' used his fists to reject 'pommie' insults from everyday Australians, but then worked alongside them happily enough, although baulking at ther values:

> They know no desire beyond uninterrupted accumulation of pianolas and clothes, pleasant week-ends and alluring betting tickets ... It seemed to him that the Labour movement, entrusted with a great mission, had failed. It had sold the people's birthright for a mess of pianolas.[112]

'Edgar' had a stint of radical journalism, itself barren.

The role of doctrinaire Leftists in migrant-protest movements in South and Western Australia around 1930 appeared in chapter 7. Jack Bunce of Western Australia organised all unemployed, not only migrants. One of his colleagues returned to England in 1934 and at once joined the Communist Party, remaining a member in 1972.[113] Very likely, Bunce led those to whom

Governor Campion referred, in January 1929—'rowdies ... undesirable who manage to come out here, and endeavour to make themselves a nuisance', wrecking meetings at recent federal elections.[114]

Governor-General Stonehaven likewise deplored the 'class hatred' spread nation-wide by migrants:

> I believe that when Australians realise they are being misled by imported protagonists of exploded fallacies they will provide and follow leaders who will be genuine Australians, and will give a new orientation to their policy and in effect lead them from the fool's paradise into which they have been inveigled.[115]

The coalfields of New South Wales saw migrant radicalism flourish. Among Marxist propagandists there was Charles Nelson, a Scottish migrant of 1914; his pupils included William Orr, a compatriot who came around 1920.[116] Tasmania offered its counterparts first in the aforesaid story of W. C. Wood, and later that of A. W. White.[117] A migrant of 1923, White seems to have been radicalised by Depression unemployment; in Launceston, his place of residence, migrants' anger waxed especially because Rapson's tyre-works had crashed with some employees still owing fares. Active in the Communist-led Unemployed Workers' Movement, White spent terms in gaol. The Movement resisted eviction of rent-defaulters from their homes, and when the Whites so suffered, demonstrations erupted. The family went on benefit, and 'as they displayed Communistic tendencies it was considered in the best interests of the State to pay their passage back to the United Kingdom'. White accepted, but this was probably as close to political deportation as any British migrant went. Comrades attended the family's sailing in early 1932, presenting Mrs White with red gladioli while her husband waved a red flag.

Other migrants served the Australian Communist Party. They included trade unionists of power and prowess—outstandingly James Healy (watersiders; migrated 1925), Ernest Thornton (ironworkers; c.1923), and James Coull (liquorworkers; 1922). Less able but very interesting was C. H. Sharpley, who in 1949 provided an Australian variant of Cold War confessions of Stalinist sin.[118] Of genteel birth, Sharpley came to Australia in 1928 as a Little Brother. His protector was Archdeacon William Hancock, father of the historian. The Hancocks' efforts failed to save Sharpley from four years' unemployment.

The outstanding migrant figure in mainstream Labor was J. J. Dedman.[119] Born in Scotland in 1896, Dedman secured officer rank during his army service in Europe and India. He migrated in 1922, maintaining a dairy farm until the Depression hit. Already interested in politics, he became a radical Keynesian during the 1930s. That heritage sustained him as a key member of the federal Cabinet 1941–9. Anyone involved with the Australian Labor Party up to 1960 or so would know modest counterparts of Dedman.

Some migrant politics veered Right. Crutchley reported tales of migrants being strong in a 'scab' watersiders' union in Melbourne.[120] Perhaps relevant too is evidence that a fair number became policemen[121]—including Sharpley's 'minder' during his post-confession trauma. More intriguing are putative ties between Britons and fascistic movements. The most famous episode concerns attempts to recruit D. H. Lawrence. Better grounded, and involving a genuine migrant, is R. A. Pepperall's account of being inducted into a force meant to save south-east Australia from red insurgency.[122] The son of an ex-officer migrant in Tasmania believes that his father had a similar involvement.[123]

A true account of the migrants' contribution must focus on local community rather than nation. That truism is enhanced by the 'ordinariness' of our people and their talents. Michael Roe knows only one community, Hobart, well enough to comprehend. He has already written of his

> links with various migrants of the 1920s: a student's father who came (with his two brothers) as a farm boy, and prospered in small business; a friend's aunt, resident here since 1925, rich in positive memories and in mid-1989 making her fourth trip 'home'; a retired upper public servant who writes regular newspaper letters full of shrewd and independent thought; above all, that beloved neighbour who has been our family's support through thirty years.[124]

To such data there can be added more public biographies. Three ex-officers had tough experience as farmers and left the island after a few years, yet there laid foundations for future distinction: N. W. Lamidey, who worked in the State bureaucracy, then with the DMC and later helped oversee Australia's post-1945 migration programme; A. G. Warner, who was outstanding as a Melbourne entrepreneur, politician, and yachtsman; George McGowan, who used Tasmanian knowledge of fruit-growing to develop a major cider industry in Victoria.[125] Youthful migrants included Dorothy Stoner, who for seventy years beautifully painted Tasmanian flora, landscape, and portraits; and S. W. T. Blythe, whose best architecture used contemporary idiom as did but little Australian work of mid-century.[126] Already adult when migrating, Helen George over decades opened a love of music to many Tasmanian children. Long the organising genius of local soccer football was Victor Tuting; that game has always depended in Tasmania upon imported interest, being played at Cadburys', for example—where British enthusiasm for structured recreation surprised natives.[127] The last two assisted migrants to enter Tasmania before World War II were north-of-England schoolteachers, Wilfred Asten and W. A. Townsley. The former became eminent in secondary education and the United Nations Association; the latter, foundation professor of political science at the University of Tasmania. Similar was the career of Winifred Curtis, the first woman to reach high academic rank at that university, and analyst of the island's botany. So mounts the migrant score in one place.

For an individual to contribute to Australia did not mean that his or her life there was joyous: McGowan and Lamidey have both written of their difficult times, while Tuting remembered pommy-taunting as having 'permeated into everyday life'.[128] Yet commonsense suggests that in the longer term the contribution often would prompt and reflect satisfaction. There is record, too, of shorter-term happiness among other everyday migrants, although it achieves little bulk. This is partly because such people had a full stint of hardship, and partly because there was no pressure-group with an interest in publicising laudatory material.

Let some cheerful voices speak. From Queensland a widow affirmed, 'I am very happy here, and thank you for helping me through. My little girl is very happy. This is beautiful country, all sunshine.'[129] Tasmania won similar praise from one pleased to 'have found a happy home in a land of sunshine. Last year I was enabled to retire from active work and to devote my energies to civic and local affairs.' Even loan-remitting could be positive: 'When I was paying back my passage it is nice to remember that not once was I pressed to pay any money, and now that I have paid in full the same if ever I want advice you may depend that I shall come to the Immigration Office of S. A. as one is always sure of a fair deal.'[130] The Victorian bureaucracy had a like supporter, who analysed local styles: 'Australian ladies as employers are generally very nice, thoughtless, selfish, and sociable, a strange mixture … What a pity the Aussies are such a slip-shod any-old-thing'll do type arising doubtless from their free and easy conditions.'[131] D. H. Lawrence would have agreed.

That recent migrants often nominated others in their wake counter-balanced those who returned homewards or yearned to do so. The vigour of industrial workers in nominating was stressed by Crutchley in the review he penned in early 1932.[132] While interesting, this document went little beyond the obvious—domestics had been of general benefit, farmers sometimes got by, few opportunities offered for farmboys as they got older, while nominees tended to merge in the general population. Crutchley argued against fare-loans, remarking that some who could pay evaded the law, while others beggared themselves to meet dues. Nevertheless, by 1939 nearly 75 per cent of such debt had been discharged; this seems further evidence that many migrants had come to terms with Australia.[133]

*   *   *

Australian attitudes to migration affected policy, influenced migrant experience, and revealed contemporary Australian society. Having such salience, they merit a final summation. It will stress popular attitudes, but first something more is due to the bureaucratic response.

The story is one of considerable shame to Australia. The Jones–Simm commission, the Windham Delegation, constant reports from Bankes Amery and Crutchley—all pointed thither, as did much migrant experience. To assess Australia's record, we begin with W. M. Hughes's promises, made about 1920, of secure jobs and general amenity for migrants. Hughes always ranted, but he probably did believe that newcomers should receive that bounty. A chasm lay between such notions and what government agencies later delivered. Deepening it further was dominance of nominees among migrants, whereas Hughes originally gave them small place. Subsequent Australian authority preferred nominees because the responsibility for their future fell upon the nominators.

The hostels which offered in most capitals forecast all too well the nature of government–migrant relations. Olga Wignall's recall of insects that tormented residents of 'Buggy House' at Fremantle makes for the liveliest passage of her autobiography, and Lord Apsley admitted the like desolation of Melbourne's quarters. A ship's matron reported on Brisbane:

> the most indescribable, unhospitable looking chamber I have ever seen in my life. One vast hall in which there must be nearly one hundred beds ranged close together. Some of the beds are made up and in the centre of the grey blanket the Government mark of the broad arrow is conspicuous and suggestive ...
>
> The crying and fretful children of which there were nearly a dozen besides mothers and girls, the moans and groans of the adults interspersed with curses of Australia and Australian to the accompaniment of resounding whacks on the floor—the slaughter of black beetles, was the ghastly entertainment which disturbed our much needed rest and sleep.[134]

The matron complained to E. W. Abell, who retorted that henceforth he would exclude her peers from the hostel. 'Mr Abell, whoever he is, is not in sympathy with migration or migrants.'

Much else added to that 'broad arrow' image of government. The control of farmboy apprentices saw the peak of authoritarian styles, but they prevailed generally. Police were used in pursuing repayment of fare-loans, as were various organs of both Commonwealth and State governments. Threats of legal action were made and, after much agonising, some proceedings began.[135] Were a debtor to die, enquiry might follow as to whether surviving assets would discharge the loan; dunning could continue back in England. Not only nominators and guarantors but employers too were mobilised to hunt repayment. Informers added venom by telling of alleged miscreants. Officials trod warily lest concessions to some provoke recalcitrance in others. Similar fears steeled the treatment of applications for repatriation or return within the two-year bond.

Bureaucratic aid to the migrants was scant at every level. Farmboys and domestics did get some job-help in return for bonding themselves into submission. But they were in relatively high demand. The more people needed help, broadly speaking, the less they received it. This would seem true nation-wide, although probably Victoria was worse than elsewhere. Certainly those evil spirits of land-settlement, McIver and Cattanach, were notably explicit in minimising responsibility to migrants generally.[136] So to speak is to allow that other officers had some virtue. In Tasmania, Burford Sampson—ex-officer, ardent imperialist, and embryonic Nationalist politician—cared with unusual warmth for migration and migrants. The perceptive sympathy of Western Australia's H. M. Pullin has already gained notice. South Australia's Ryan had something of Sampson's style, and within his office Jean Anderson excelled duty in caring for domestics.

The matter ranged beyond personality. Hughes moved towards involving federal bureaucrats with grassroots migration matters. The States' jealousy killed that, thereby diminishing the possibility that Australia would articulate machinery which might provide due care. State officials were everyday public servants, doing an onerous job with minimal aid. To their credit, they led in denouncing the fare-loan situation, whereby 'the honest man is penalised while a premium is placed on dishonesty', with themselves having to 'enforce harsh conditions' threatening especial danger to young women (presumably, by pushing them towards prostitution).[137] Rigid and autocratic as many bureaucratic decisions were, humanity also had its part. One day in mid-1924 Abell's office received a thank-you letter from a nominator. 'This is such a rare occurrence that a special note should be made of it', minuted the boss.[138] Perhaps he almost smiled.

Rarely did an Australian voice deplore the poverty of bureaucratic infrastructure. H. S. Gullett's when resigning in 1922 was by far the loudest. The echo of any note was feminine. Despite Jean Anderson and some counterparts elsewhere, men dominated migrant administration. Following the Jones–Simm *Report*, the OSC urged that this situation alter; the Windham Delegation followed,[139] likewise in vain. With establishment of the DMC, the point was pursued by the Australian Federation of Women's Societies for Equal Citizenship, led by Bessie M. Rischbeith. Lady Masson told Gepp that she and Lady Mitchell were 'steadfastly refusing' to join this dissent, but asked him to acknowledge the issue.[140] He did not.

Hughes's euphoria of 1920–1 had envisaged not only job security for migrants but longer-term care. With Gullett prodding, there resulted the New Settlers' League. 'The movement has been taken up by representative citizens all over Australia', the Prime Minister assured Parliament, on 24 November 1921. 'The object of the League is to prepare the way for settlers, to welcome them, to assure them they are not strangers in a strange land.' Governor-General Forster had already invoked the League when fending the OSC's call for women bureaucrats. Hughes evidently hoped that it might act as a nominator on considerable scale.[141] This never happened, but it did some work in all States except South Australia. By 1926 the Commonwealth was spending £4000 annually on the League, with States matching.[142]

The League was most active in Victoria, at one time claiming 247 branches there. It offered the same moralist exhortation to migrants as did Australia House. At Melbourne's Royal Agricultural Show in 1923 it exhibited 'makeshifts' which the ideal migrant farmer should create: 'Wardrobe, wash stand, settee, ottoman, sideboard, bookcase, writing desk, kitchen dresser and cupboard were constructed from kerosene cases, while kerosene tins had been turned into buckets, food bins, wash up dishes, shower bath and dust pan.'[143] While Lady Masson and Lady Mitchell endorsed the NSL and their sex sustained it, the professional organiser in Victoria was one Archibald Gilchrist. 'I am a migrationist second and a bad second', Gilchrist told the DMC. 'My first concern is the development of country districts. My aim is to capture the Progress Associations and link such bodies into a big forward drive for new industries, better farming and pleasanter living conditions.'[144] Only in that context, Gilchrist affirmed, could migrationist activity win popular support. He offered himself as nation-wide publicist for a League so revamped. It should work under the DMC, he said; currently migrants suspected the League as a tool of State government. Gilchrist doubtless wrote League pamphlets which exhorted *Keep Australia White. The Menace of an Empty Continent* and *Youth. The Invaluable Factor in Migration.*

Queensland also saw the League vigorous, D. J. Garland using it in his migrationist crusade.[145] As in Victoria, concern was much with improving country life. The salaried officers worked with State officials, long-term secretary Constance Clayton emulating Jean Anderson's devotion to migrant welfare. Yet nowhere did the League find a creative role. Its inherent position was difficult. Gilchrist told that migrants suspected it, yet so did bureaucrats. Both NSW and Victorian governments cut their subsidies in protest when Leaguers criticised the official treatment of migrants.[146] So recurred that tension between bureaucrat and volunteer enthusiast constant in both hemispheres: Bankes Amery reported that Percy Hunter and Senator Wilson spoke of Garland and his ilk as 'b——y pests wanting jobs'.[147]

Gepp heard much of British dissatisfaction with Australian after-care when in Britain 1926–7, and the DMC duly appointed one of its officers, T. H. Garrett, to pursue the matter. He found the League to have failed in its task, and called for the Commission to take other action to create a 'national consciousness ... favourable to migration'; currently there prevailed 'not only a spirit of apathy, but also hostility'.[148] That call too proved vain. In 1927 an Italian bureaucrat reported to Mussolini that Australia after-care arrangements 'are very meagre and economical, and appear to have for their object the limitation and not the increase of British migrants'.[149] In 1930 Crutchley affirmed the League's continuing inanition, save in providing a little oversight of farmboys and domestics.[150] In some places it struggled on a few years more.

One of the DMC's few initiatives as to welfare concerned the Country Women's Association—an archetypal element of the Australian 1920s, central in that move to improve rural life invoked by Archibald Gilchrist. In Victoria the Association's foundation awaited 1928, Governor Somers's consort and Lady Masson to the fore. On Masson's advice, Gepp attended the inaugural meeting and urged that the Association cherish migrant welfare.[151] The Association did move somewhat as Gepp hoped. The DMC gave it not a penny, let alone making headway with such issues as improvement of rural housing, which for years British authorities urged as a top priority.

The previous chapter referred to various groups—Salvation Army, YMCA, Victoria League, Boy Scouts, Church of England, Dreadnought Trust, Big Brothers —which promoted migration, and cared for those who consequently came. Much of this record was worthy; both Australian and British governments helped with modest subsidies.[152] Some of these, together with other established philanthropic bodies—the YMCA and YWCA most actively, and others such as Girls' Friendly Societies and Travellers' Aid groups—heeded more general migrant welfare. (The Returned Servicemen's League got money to do so too, albeit in Crutchley's opinion not earning it.)

Of these groups, only the Big Brothers were a creation of this period. It exhaled the bourgeois-Rotarian-'booster' spirit so strong in the 1920s. Such leaders as Richard Linton and Arthur Rickard embodied the style. That Crutchley found Linton a self-serving bounder echoed the tension between bureaucrats and volunteers. While Brothers spread from Victoria into New South Wales, the Dreadnought Trust retained eminence in the senior State, projecting a more patrician and established aura. New South Wales also had two female groups, the Anzac Fellowship of Australian Women and a Barnardo committee. The Fellowship cared for farmboys, providing club-rooms in Sydney and running a pleasant journal, *The Boy Settler*.[153] Serving the Fellowship outside her hours in the NSW Department of Labour was Mabelle Grant Cooper, supreme saint of migrant devotion. The chief of the Fellowship, Mary Booth, was different—aggressive and egotistic.[154] As well as the Fellowship, Booth launched the Women's Migration Council of New South Wales and an Empire Service Hostel, for migrants' use. She sought appointment to the DMC, with backing from the YWCA.[155]

The Barnardo committee had some notable members: (Cara) Lady

David, moral crusader and Girl Guide leader, and Ruth Beale, more in the style of Grant Cooper. Beale told of Lady David taking two Barnardo girls into her own home. 'She says that at present they are more work than help, but in a few months she expects them to be a real comfort.'[156] Was even David hoping to solve her servant problem?

Western Australia's story has particular interest. Chapter 9 introduced the Young Australia League, and other grassroots groups appeared there. The Women's Immigration Auxiliary Council was assiduous in welfare, Mrs C. H. E. Manning among its leaders. The New Settlers' League in the West coalesced with the Ugly Men's Association, an early exemplar of male, secular service-clubs in Australia. Some enthusiasm prevailed, but both the local H. M. Pullin and Garrett of the DMC criticised the situation. On one hand public money was going into private control (and successive secretaries of the League proved shonky), while migrants grumbled at the government off-loading its problems onto such a group. Pullin agreed that the government thus was seeking to avoid its due responsibility to migrants, the politicians being fearful of appearing to favour them over locals. Nemesis threatened:

> these bodies which have been financed and nurtured by the Government, will at the first instance of opposition or conflict with their ideas and wishes, scourge the Minister in no uncertain measure, and subsequent efforts made to discipline them will be regarded as an act of suppression.[157]

Pullin thought it impossible to sustain voluntary interest in migration. League officials were unpopular in country districts (presumably lest they criticise migrants' employment conditions), and were motivated by the perk of a free annual rail-pass to Perth.

Philanthropists opened themselves to further criticism. As Gladys Pott noticed in 1923, and later reports confirmed, various groups warred between and within themselves. That may have diminished the output of care, and suggests further that egotism often drove the protagonists. Reality moved far from the 1920–1 ideal of a puissant and comprehensive service. This dismal situation accorded with broader Australian attitudes to migration. Many earlier references have pointed towards that conclusion; now the issue requires final confrontation.

Generally, Australians were ready, even anxious, to exploit the newcomers. While that was most evident in relation to farmboys and domestics, there prevailed broader notions that migrants were acceptable only as subordinates or supplicants. 'An Australian will always employ an Australian unless he can get a Britisher to work for less', affirmed Arthur Crutchley, the Representative's son.[158] Outrage at Australian readiness to behave as a master-race could go further. 'Unfortunately it is the habit of most home people of influence to chuff the Aussie up and tell them what a damned fine fellow he is ... he has the cheek to return insolence for flattery':[159] for the ex-officer on a Victorian farm who wrote thus, the proper order of things had been inverted. Bankes Amery modified the theme in a newspaper article which beseeched Australians to give a fair go to migrants, attracted by promises and propaganda; 'they are not in all cases prepared, any more than all Australians are prepared, to abandon the standard of comfort which British people have achieved'.[160] The Marquess of Hartington's 1938 report likewise found repugnant, or at least obstructive, the average Australian's belief that he was doing a favour by accepting migrants.[161]

The Windham Delegation reprimanded 'the readiness with which the word "failure" is applied to those who, whether through their own fault or not, do not succeed at once in settling down at once in their new life', while another eminent Briton who visited Australia in 1922 noticed 'dislike and hostility towards the new settler—almost a wish that he should not succeed'.[162] This evidence suggests an Australian disposition to impose despair on the newcomers, and thus lower their self-esteem and status. Many newspapers were ever-ready to report migrant 'failure' and wrong-doing. Such became a near-staple of the yellower press—*Smith's Weekly, Truth*, the *Daily Guardian*, and such like: the very journals most brashly insistent on the richness of Australia and its vast potential. In creating as a stock-figure of fun the 'choom' farmboy, *Smith's* varied its mode of degradation.[163] All the while intensified the old Australian game of pommy-baiting. One last story can end that nasty record. A Sydney urchin, awakened to meet a just-arrived newcomer, responded with 'Fuckin' well go back there ya pommie bastard'.[164] Compare and contrast H. V. Evatt— already high among Australia's Labor intellectuals, destined to shape and lead the United Nations Organisation—who in 1926 at the International Labour Migration Conference resisted declarations upholding freedom of human mobility. Evatt's dominant concern was White Australia, but one of his tasks in Europe was to appear before the Privy Council for *Smith's Weekly*, with whose proprietor he was close.[165]

Jealousy and suspicion were constant. That was most obvious and logical among workingmen fearful for their jobs, but extended further. It found vent against British brides of Australian soldiers, against support of migrant farmers, against assisting farmboys acquire their own land, against migrants taking industrial jobs in Tasmania. A last example is the refusal of the South Australian Parliament to honour a governmental promise to subsidise migrant welfare work.[166]

As the Bishop of London remarked at the time, Australia's wealthier people—albeit less threatened by migration, more oriented towards Britain—gave but tepid support to migration.[167] There were Lady Masson,

Farmboy as fool. (*Smith's Weekly*, May Day, 1926.)

Linton, Rickard, but few more of such kind. Prime Minister Bruce, Chairman Gepp—they cared little for migration, less for migrants, as this text reveals. Their negativism derived from policy, while others responded to deeper calls:

> Our exclusiveness is not aimed only at the coloured races. We are bent on keeping our racial inheritance, but we are equally determined to import no 'poor whites' ... We have emerged into nationhood, and we want and will have only the best that Britain can send us. That I believe represents the average Australian's reaction towards the immigration question.[168]

So spoke Janet Mitchell, daughter of Knight and Lady so active for migration. The same case had strong support from Sydney's Racial Hygiene Centre, an upper-bourgeois body.[169] Fascistic styles of demographic exclusiveness and autarkic isolation spread wide. Whereas anti-migrationists in Britain accused Australia of stealing the old country's vigour and talent, their antipodean counterparts ever bewailed failure to find and deliver 'the right type of migrant'.

There is another facet to this story: resistance to migration and migrants had considerable logic. Autarkic fascism grew direct from the War and made some sense in the 1920s. Even before the Depression the Australian job-market was tight, and ordinary workers could scarcely philosophise as to the dynamic potential of immigration. Much academic opinion questioned expansive policies, especially demographic ones. Australia—a nation empowered and uplifted by its role in War—might naturally claim the right to subordinate migration issues to *sacro egoismo*. The normal, even universal, experience of migrants is to be bullied and exploited: Australia of the 1920s perhaps did no worse than conform to pattern. Such argument may further propose that as exploitation always threatens, migration should take place only under the most benign conditions, certainly not those of Bruce's domain. Still more certainly, British capitalism sought to use migration to solve its own problems. Australian capitalists profited too, especially by selling land for migrant schemes. The continuity between war and migration had pertinent meaning. Even G. M. Prendergast, at whom L. S. Amery scoffed for the crassness of his anti-migrationism, argued sensibly against immigration that it served the Empire's belligerent *Realpolitik*.[170]

Nor was Australian treatment of migrants all bad. Just as there were selfless bureaucrats and philanthropists, and some employers helpful to their domestics and farmboys, so everyday communities offered succour. A South Australian farmboy was found guilty of (consenting) sex with an under-age girl; 'do me the kind favour of not letting my parents know', he implored, 'as it will break my mother's heart ... I came out here to do good'; charges were not pressed and local people rallied to the boy's support,

Farmboy as fellow. (Mitchell Library; reproduced by permission of the Library Council of New South Wales.)

enabling him to work a passage home.[171] In Zeehan, Tasmania, an ex-serviceman succumbed to the aftermath of shell-shock; the district's Returned Servicemen's League led a move which eased repatriation of himself and family.[172] Such episodes offer a little credibility to the assertion of the OSD's McLeod in 1926 that Australians offered 'the utmost friendliness' to Britons.[173] Lord Salisbury spoke to similar effect. More persuasive, however, is the judgment of P. S. Cadbury, based on reports from his Hobart works, that Australia's response 'seems to be a matter of mass psychology and is full of contradictions'.[174]

Amelioration perhaps strengthened over time. T. S. P. Pughe affirmed that Australian antipathy to migrants was less in 1928 than in 1925,[175] and the ebb might have continued after the Depression halted the inflow. Consistent with this was Crutchley's action in mounting the British Settlers' Welfare Committee as an effective agency of after-care, and the granting of compensation to Victorian farmers. Even when discounted, W. C. Hankinson's euphoric report on migrant conditions in mid-1932 bears some weight.[176] Crutchley's declaration to the Overseas Settlement Board in early 1936 carried optimism further. While recalling 'many very bitter feelings' prevalent in the deep Depression years, and the sufferings of ex-servicemen, Crutchley continued:

> tales of the victimisation of other settlers had perhaps an exaggerated importance. Provided that migrants had attempted to adjust themselves to local social conditions, there was no doubt they were well received and there really was no hostility to the individual migrant as distinct from any general hostility to migration in principle.[177]

Crutchley would not have spoken thus a few years earlier, but his words attest the schizophrenic resilience of Austral–British ties. The near future told more about that. On 3 September 1939 Prime Minister Menzies announced that HMG had declared war on Germany; 'as a result, Australia is also at war'. Bruce's threat of 1923 went empty.

Heeding such evidence as Crutchley's dicta of 1936, the historian might conclude that while Australians' treatment of migrants was shabby, it stood small beside the many horrors of contemporary history. The broader issues of migrant suffering could bear like modification. Yet that suffering was real. One of its aftermaths and complements was that those who underwent the migration rarely celebrated it. Silence, even suppression, prevail instead. Australia's libraries hold few personal manuscripts telling of the experience. Perhaps the most substantial exception is a set of homeward letters by a woman full of virtue and courage. She died of terrible cancer in 1929.[178] Posterity has a duty to recognise the migrants' travail, and to see their story whole. Here indeed prevailed an exemplar of that desperate hope which is humankind's common lot.

A family snap. This photograph was sent homeward among the letters
mentioned on page 254. The correspondent was the woman on the right.
(Reproduced by permission of the State Library of Victoria.)

Afterword

From late 1942 HMG considered post-war migration. Treasury was dubious, fearing loss 'of the most active and enterprising people', and Prime Minister Churchill felt that way too. High Commissioner Bruce thought that, before committing themselves, 'Dominion Governments would wish to know what assumptions they could make regarding the world economic order in the post-war period.' The response from Australia spoke of the opinion that national security would require greater population, but also that Britons were thought unlikely to offer in numbers and so Europe might be the necessary source.[1]

All of this presupposed that life was going to continue much as it had been before 1939, whereas the reality often proved much different. A boom in Austral migration followed, or even led, that rule. Between 1947 and 1983 there was a net entry of nearly 3 million people, spread quite evenly over time. More than one-third came from the United Kingdom. Faces in that crowd included Harold Larwood and (for his second time) John McGovern, determined Parliamentary critic of migration in the 1930s. There could hardly be better exemplars of the general cheerfulness of the story in these days. The OSD's erstwhile argument that successful migration was a factor of prosperity thus won some proof. Overall, Australia and Britain jogged along more easily now, although and because each had increasingly less to offer the other.

One issue loomed large in fact and still larger in image: the derivation of most of the post-war migrants from places other than Britain—from a great range of Continental Europe and, since the late 1970s, perceptibly from Asia. This indeed marked extraordinary change in the whole nature of Australia as a community. Moreover, the 'multicultural' story witnessed the most remarkable successes of post-war migration. These successes were sometimes exaggerated by vested interests seeking advantage, and they require more critical analysis than they have yet been accorded; nevertheless, they were real and big. Many Continentals and Asians escaped death or cataclysm by coming to Australia. Their assimilation posed vast challenges, to themselves and to their precursors in the land. Many of those challenges have been met.

The historian of inter-war migration must not react to this scenario with any churlish denial of its import, but rather give high priority to the processes of change that so remarkably appear in and through these events. No less must a humanist be ready to stress and celebrate every victory for tolerance, survival, and happiness, which have all had their play in Australian ethnic history of the past fifty years. The human spirit has had victories in this field.

How, then, does the present study stand in relation to such subsequent events? One response is to stress how the earlier dialectic and difficulties of Britons' migration prepared the way for acceptance of others. Chapter 8 especially has pursued this story, giving appropriate notice to W. D. Forsyth's analysis of 'the new immigration'. Material from that chapter also allows for notice of historical ironies—with H. C. Coombs (guiding light of post-1945 expansionism) revealed as advocate of out-migration, and R. G. Menzies (vehement for Britishness throughout and beyond his Prime Ministerial term, 1949–65) receptive to Continentals. There were nice continuities too. H. W. Gepp remained active in public debate after 1940, especially via the Institute of Public Affairs, which in managerial mode upheld the active government which in different ways Coombs and Menzies (and many others) sustained through Australia's post-war years.[2] Lord Bruce and F. L. McDougall adapted their earlier ideas to help make the Food and Agriculture Organisation a force for the world's good. C. W. G. Eady found his somewhat similar destiny at Bretton Woods and beyond.

Yet the ultimate meaning of the data adduced in these pages lies not in relation to future events, but in their own essence and time. The historian must recognise change and be ready to celebrate success, yet a still higher priority is to find the truth about the period and places under study. That quest has made inevitable the domination of this book by stagnation and failure. Any humanist would prefer not to have these as his dominant themes, among other reasons lest he use others' misery for self-serving ends, and lest he fall into indulgent sentimentality. Indeed, the only justification for running such risks is that they are consequent upon the effort to imbue all experience with the dignity of revealing truths as to its provenance. Thus might be a little redeemed the fate of many who have appeared throughout this book.

Notes

In these Notes, authored items are normally cited by author and short-title; details appear in the Bibliography. However, notes do give full detail for some items, notably entries in dictionaries and government reports.

Manuscript material, archival and private, likewise is described more fully in the Bibliography. Notes citing archival material normally give first the repository, then more precise location; those to private material normally first name the collection.

Abbreviations used in Notes and Bibliography to identify repositories are:

AA	Australian Archives (Canberra), Commonwealth Record Series
AONSW	Archives Office of New South Wales
AOT	Archives Office of Tasmania
NLA	National Library of Australia
PRO	Public Record Office (of the United Kingdom)
PROV	Public Record Office of Victoria
QSA	Queensland State Archives
SAWA	State Archives of Western Australia
SRSA	State Records (South Australia)

The archival repositories are in the capital cities, or their suburbs, of the respective polities. The Battye Library is in Perth; the Mitchell in Sydney; the State Library of Victoria in Melbourne; the National Library of Australia in Canberra; the Royal Commonwealth Society Library now housed in the University of Cambridge Library. Much material from the PRO was seen, and/or checked, from microfilm held at NLA in consequence of the Joint Microfilm Copying Project.

INTRODUCTION

1 Beever, 'British Working Class Attitudes to Australia'.
2 Madgwick, *Immigration into Eastern Australia*, generally. Broader migration history is best presented in Jupp, *Australian People* and Sherrington, *Australia's Immigrants.*
3 Hayden, 'Anti-Immigration Movement'.
4 *Emergent Commonwealth*, chs. 2, 3.
5 La Nauze, *Deakin*, ch. 22 and generally; K. Williams in Constantine, *Emigrants and Empire*, pp. 28–29.
6 Pope, 'Assisted Immigration'; 'Report of the ... Interstate Conference', *NSW Parliamentary Papers*, 1911–12, joint volumes, vol. 2.

7 'Third Annual Report of the High Commissioner', *Commonwealth Parliamentary Papers*, 1913, vol. 2.
8 AA: A3934; sc23(1).

1 THE GREAT WAR'S IMPACT

1 Fedorowich, 'Foredoomed to Failure', pp. 48–9. I owe much to Fedorowich's writing and further help. See his chapters in Constantine, *Emigrants and Empire* and Bridge, *New Perspectives.*
2 AA: CP78/22; 15/95A.
3 K. Williams in Constantine, *Emigrants and Empire*, pp. 38–9; Pierce, 'Haggard in Australia'.
4 *Haggard Diaries*, pp. 60–1.
5 Bridge, *New Perspectives*, p. 133.
6 'Report of the ... Premiers' Conference ... May 1916', *NSW Parliamentary Papers*, 1916, joint volumes, vol. 1, p. 116 and generally.
7 Responses to letter from Colonial Office, 21 September 1916, AA: CP78/22; 15/95A.
8 Fitzhardinge, Hughes.
9 B. Attard in Bridge, *New Perspectives*, pp. 101–25.
10 'Report of the Premiers' Conference ... December 1916', *NSW Parliamentary Papers*, 1917, joint volumes, vol. 1, p. 24; the report of the January meeting is adjacent.
11 Bridge, *New Perspectives*, pp. 135–6.
12 *Report ... Settling within the Empire Ex-Service Men* (Command 8672); Gell's proposal is an Appendix; for him and his context, see Searle, *National Efficiency*, as indexed.
13 AA: CP314/3.
14 Memorandum, 16 January 1918, PRO: CO532/14.
15 Drummond, *Imperial Policy*, p. 52. I acknowledge my debt to this mighty book.
16 *Report of the Oversea Settlement Committee ... 1919* (Command 573), pp. 10–11.
17 M. Roe in Bridges, *New Perspectives*, pp. 150–1.
18 *Correspondence as to the Emigration Bill*, 1918 (Command 9173); A. Milner, memorandum, February 1919, PRO: CAB24/75.
19 W. E. Davidson, letter, 27 July 1918, PRO: CO886/7; print 60. Davidson was Governor of New South Wales; letters from those dignitaries were currently the normal route whereby governments expressed their opinion to HMG.
20 AA: A981; PRO: CO532/115.
21 AA: A3934; sc23(1).
22 PRO: CO721/1 has early files, but regular minutes of meetings do not survive.
23 Hynes, *War Imagined*, pp. 379–81.
24 PRO: CO721/2; 24.
25 Drummond, *Imperial Policy*, p. 60.
26 PRO: CAB24/75; Plant, *Oversea Settlement*, p. 69.
27 PRO: CO721/13.

28   Harrison, *Separate Spheres*, as indexed.
29   Meetings, esp. 21 July 1919, PRO: CO532/150.
30   25 July 1919, Hughes Papers: series 16.
31   G. C. Bolton, 'Connolly', *Australian Dictionary of Biography*, vol. 8 (1981), p. 90.
32   Fairbridge, *Pinjarra*, p. xiii.
33   SAWA hold letters from the Agent-General, those for 1919 being at PD134/19, for 1920 at PD85/20 and 379/20. Connolly's most immediately relevant letters were dated 10 May and 26 August 1919. PRO: CO721 holds very much material emanating from Connolly.
34   9 September 1920, SAWA: PD379/20.
35   10 December 1920, PRO: CO721/13.
36   26 August 1919.
37   PRO: CO721/13; 0580
38   Governor W. G. E. Macartney, letter, 23 June 1919, PRO: CO721/5; Bridge, *New Perspectives*, p. 137.
39   Letter, 16 May 1919, SAWA: PD134/19.
40   Letter, 16 October 1919, SAWA: PD134/19.
41   'Prospectus', Royal Commonwealth Society Library; Fedorowich, 'Fore-doomed to Failure', pp. 264–70; many files, PRO: CO721.
42   7 May 1920, PRO: CO721/16.
43   PRO: CO721/16.
44   Constantine, *Emigrants and Empire*, pp. 55–6; Macnaghten, memorandum, 24 October 1920, PRO: CAB27/115.
45   Correspondence, June–July 1919, QSA: PRE/100; letter, 29 October 1920, SRSA: GRG7; series 23; 135/1921.
46   Plant, *Oversea Settlement*, p. 74. Plant was a member of the OSD, and tends to optimise his story, but his facts seem reliable.
47   PRO: CO721/13; 3813–14. The reader might benefit by referring to 'Abbreviations and Usages', p. x.
48   'Report ... of the Conference of Commonwealth and State Ministers', *Commonwealth Parliamentary Papers*, 1917–19, vol. 4, p. 92.
49   10 September 1919, QSA: PRE/100.
50   House of Representatives, 13 August 1919.
51   AA: A461; 326/1/3.
52   'Report ... of the Premiers' Conference ... May 1920', *NSW Parliamentary Papers*, 1920 (second session), joint volumes, vol. 1, pp. vii, 44–5. The report of the July meeting is adjacent.
53   Undated memorandum, Hughes Papers: series 16.
54   *Commonwealth Year Book* 1922 (Melbourne, 1922), p. 1016.
55   *Fred John's Annual* (London, 1914), under name.
56   A. J. Hill, 'Gullett', *Australian Dictionary of Biography*, vol. 9 (1983), pp. 137–8.
57   Correspondence, early 1922, SAWA: PD474/21; H. N. Barwell, House of Assembly (of South Australia), 21 July 1921.
58   24 December 1920, SRSA: GRG 7; series 23; 150/1921.
59   SAWA: PD312/20.
60   AA: A461; X326/1/3.

61 AONSW: Premiers Special Bundle 4/6254.4.
62 15 January and 17 February 1920, QSA: PRE/100.
63 SRSA: GRG7; series 23; 88/1920.
64 House of Assembly, 9 November 1920.
65 AOT: SWD 4; M9/7,44,57,58,201.
66 SRSA: GRG 7; series 23; 150/1921.
67 Legislative Assembly, 12 August 1920.
68 PRO: CO721/10; 162.
69 Circular, 11 December 1920, PRO: CO721/15.
70 PRO: CO721/28; 1934.
71 Reported interestingly by Connolly, SAWA: PD379/20.
72 Memorandum, 10 March 1920, PRO: CO721/22.
73 Turnor, *Land Settlement*; C. S. Orwin, 'Turnor', *Dictionary of National Biography* 1931–1940 (1949), pp. 874–5; PRO: CO721/13; 3746.
74 Roe in Bridge, *New Perspectives*, pp. 151–2.
75 Various files, QSA: PRE/100 and 101.
76 PRO: CO721/23; 3819.
77 Memorandum, 13 December 1920, SAWA: AG1723.
78 Leicester committee, PRO: CO721/28.
79 J. M. Allen, 7 November 1920, PRO: CO721/33.
80 OSC, memorandum, 11 March 1921, SAWA: PD41/21.
81 Memorandum, 1 March 1921, SAWA: AG1723.
82 Command 1134, p. 3.
83 *Report ... as to the Openings in Australia for Women from the United Kingdom* (Command 745), p. 4; see also Davidson, letter, 24 November 1919, PRO: CO886/7; print 60.
84 27 November 1919, PRO: CO721/22.
85 *Report*, p. 5.
86 Letter, 27 November 1919, PRO: CO721/22.
87 *Report*, p. 5.
88 *Imperial Colonist*, vol. 24 (1926), pp. 160–2; see also vol. 18 (1920), pp. 91–4; vol. 19 (1921), pp. 39–42, 148–9.

2 THE WHIRL OF HUGHES: 1920–1923

1 M. Rutledge, 'Millen', *Australian Dictionary of Biography*, vol. 10 (1986), pp. 502–3.
2 AA: A458; G145/7.
3 Powell, *Historical Geography*, as indexed.
4 Drummond, *Imperial Policy*, pp. 62–74; K. Williams in Constantine, *Emigrants and Empire*, pp. 35–42. These are fundamental references throughout this chapter.
5 Minutes, PRO: CO721/17.
6 Barnes and Nicholson, *Amery Diaries*, p. 255.
7 PRO: CO721/30; 3839. Various files throughout CO721/23 show Treasury's resolution in monitoring the emergency grant.
8 Drummond, *Imperial Policy*, pp. 64–5.

9   Tsokhas, 'People or Money', pp. 2–6. AA: CP78/22; 1922/512 is generally important, and includes a report of the January–February conferences.
10   Correspondence, 13 January and 15 March 1921, SRSA: GRG 7; series 23; 135/1921.
11   4 November 1920, SAWA: PD37/20.
12   PRO: CO721/30; 2441.
13   Millen, letter, 27 April 1921, AA: CP103/12. PRO: T160/67/F2217/1.
14   24 May 1921, PRO: T161/110/S8787.
15   Letter, 23 March 1920, SAWA: PD85/20.
16   *Report*, July 1921, SAWA: PD396/21. PRO: T161/99/S7536.
17   22 April 1921, PRO: CO721/26. This piece includes many pertinent files.
18   PRO: T161/99/S7536.
19   Letter, 5 January 1921, Hughes Papers: series 16.
20   'Queensland Proposed Loan', *Commonwealth Parliamentary Papers*, 1920–1, vol. 4.
21   House of Representatives, 17 June 1921.
22   The most informative file is in QSA: IMM/175; Hughes, letter, 21 July 1922, AA: A457; P400/2.
23   Cable, 15 March 1922, and letter, 27 April 1921, AA: CP103/12; bundle 23.
24   AA: CP103/12; bundle 23.
25   PRO: CO721/31; 2441.
26   Fitzhardinge, *Hughes*, vol. 2, pp. 464–79.
27   Memorandum, PRO: CO721/31.
28   Drummond, *Imperial Policy*, pp. 78–83.
29   Tsokhas, 'People or Money', pp. 4–5.
30   Memorandum, 28 October 1921, PRO: CO721/32.
31   One rare weakness in Drummond, *Imperial Policy*, is failure to contextualise Hughes' actions at this time.
32   Memoranda, 14 July and 27 September 1921, Hughes Papers: series 16.
33   Enclosed by Connolly, SAWA: AG1813.
34   'Conference of Commonwealth and State Ministers … October–November 1921', *NSW Parliamentary Papers*, 1922, joint volumes, vol. 1.
35   Memoranda, 27 October and 23 November 1921, AA: A458; G154/7.
36   Drummond, *Imperial Policy*, pp. 76–7.
37   PRO: T161/111/S8787/01.
38   Letter, 14 December 1921, PRO: CO721/38. File 2449 in this piece is generally important, as too CO721/24; 2489.
39   OSC meeting, 7 December 1921, PRO: CO418/207.
40   Letter, 2 December 1921, Hughes Papers: series 16.
41   PRO: CAB24/131; CP3582.
42   PRO: BT65/11; PTE 2981.
43   Letter, 5 December 1921, Hughes Papers: series 16. Other responses are adjacent.
44   Correspondence, 2 November 1921 and 12 January 1922, SAWA: PD 399/21 and 60/22.
45   Lewis, 'Million Farms'; AA: A457; I400/5. PRO: CO721/26; 3707.
46   'Conference of Commonwealth and State Ministers … January 1922', *Commonwealth Parliamentary Papers*, 1922, vol. 2, esp. p. 34.

47 Much reported in the Australian press, 25 February to 3 March 1922.
48 Cables, 2 and 24 March, PRO: CO721/39.
49 Memorandum, 12 January 1922, PRO: CO721/51.
50 29 March 1922, PRO: T161/111/S8787/01; other Treasury data are adjacent.
51 Barnes and Nicholson, *Amery Diaries*, p. 284.
52 This complex story is documented in PRO: CO721/39; 2489. WA files generally, CO522/33. T161/1/S8787/03. AA: A461; 5349/1/5. Precise detail of the process of approval seems lacking.
53 R. R. Garran (Commonwealth Solicitor-General), 10 August 1922, AA: A432; 29/4140.
54 Gabbedy, *Group Settlement*, is the supreme work, although earlier historians contributed, notably Hunt, 'Group Settlement'.
55 Memorandum, 2 November 1922, PRO: CO721/60.
56 The Commonwealth–Victorian agreement was signed on 21 September 1922 and the consequent Commonwealth–HMG agreement on 29 November 1923; the respective NSW dates were 14 November 1922 and 1 June 1923. The major sources are (for Victoria) AA: A461; I349/1/5 and (for NSW) A461; D349/1/5 and A515; 26, and PRO: CO721/41 and T161/679/S8787/08.
57 Letter, 6 March 1923, PRO: CO721/62.
58 AA: A515; 26.
59 Letter, 16 October, 1922, AA: A461; D349/1/5.
60 Memorandum, 24 March 1923, PRO: CO721/62.
61 PRO: CO720/41 is largely concerned with relevant issues.
62 PRO: CO720/41; 2422.
63 'Report ... December 1922', pp. 15–16, SAWA: PD86/23.
64 PRO: CO721/40; 2442.
65 30 September 1922, AA: A461; I394/1/5.
66 PRO: CO721/40; 1851.
67 Esp. W. Windham, memorandum, 2 September 1922, PRO: CO721/45.
68 OSD, memorandum, 24 November 1922, PRO: CO721/43.
69 PRO: T161/111/S8787/02.
70 Skevington, letter, 31 May 1922, PRO: T161/111/S8787/02.
71 PRO: CO721/40; 2422.
72 Memorandum, 14 July 1922, PRO: T161/465/S16 395/1.
73 PRO: T161/111/S8787/010.
74 Esp. memorandum, 22 June 1922, PRO: CO721/47.
75 Memorandum on draft of letter to Governor-General of Canada, 22 June 1922, PRO: T161/111/S8787/04.
76 AOT: PD55/13/23. This is one of many cases where I cite a particular source, whence in fact my notes derive, while aware that the item must be available in many places.
77 Correspondence between Barnes, Shepherd, and Macnaghten, 7, 13, 16 and 27 October, PRO: CO721/43.
78 Minutes, PRO: CO721/41.
79 PRO: CO721/45.
80 PRO: CAB24/158; CP 35(23).
81 Cable, 3 February 1923, PRO: CO532/231.
82 Drummond, *Imperial Policy*, p. 90.

3 S. M. BRUCE AND EMPIRE: 1923–1925

1   Edwards, Bruce; H. Radi, 'Bruce', *Australian Dictionary of Biography*, vol. 7, (1979), pp. 453–61; Richmond, 'Bruce and Economic Policy'.
2   Edwards, *Bruce*, pp. 191–3.
3   13 February 1923, PRO: CO532/231.
4   House of Representatives, 22 November 1921.
5   Letters through Governor-General, 2 February, 5 March and 15 May 1923, PRO: CO532/231; Bruce, House of Representatives, 24 July 1923.
6   'Conference of Commonwealth and State Ministers ... June 1923', *Commonwealth Parliamentary Papers*, 1923–4, vol. 2, pp. 57–68.
7   14 June 1923, SAWA: PD287/23.
8   Constantine, *Colonial Development Policy*, pp. 101–14. Lloyd-Greame afterwards took the name Cunliffe-Lister and later still became Earl Swinton.
9   *Report on the Economic and Financial Situation of Australia Revised to October 1922.* This is one of an impressive series which Australian historians have ignored. It is not easily located; the Mitchell Library, for example, catalogues it only by reference to HMG/Board of Trade provenance. At PRO: CO721/66 this particular item sits with other items of interest, especially Macnaghten, memorandum, 14 June 1923.
10 Memorandum, 7 June 1923, PRO: CAB27/193.
11 Memoranda, 16 and 20 June 1923, PRO: CO721/66.
12 Macnaghten, memorandum, 16 July 1923, and Buckley, memorandum, 2 August 1923, PRO: CO721/63.
13 Documentation, 19 September 1923, AA: A461; A349/2/1. My reading of the situation differs slightly from Tsokhas, 'People or Money'.
14 Memorandum, 31 July 1923, PRO: T/161/216/S21713.
15 There are various relevant files through PRO: CO721/ 67, 68 and 76.
16 22 September 1923, PRO: CO721/68.
17 PRO: T176/11; the 'burglar' memorandum was dated 25 June 1923. See also Niemeyer's paper, 30 June 1923, Baldwin Papers: vol. 92.
18 7 September 1923, PRO: T161/216/S21713.
19 Hudson and Way, *'Secret Service Agent'*, introduction and generally.
20 Memorandum, 14 June 1923, PRO: CO721/61.
21 M. Saunders, 'Wilson', *Australian Dictionary of Biography*, vol. 12 (1990), pp. 530–1.
22 Letters, 4 and 19 September, 1924, McDougall Papers.
23 Edwards, Bruce, p. 100.
24 Barnes and Nicholson, *Amery Diaries*, as indexed.
25 AA: CP103/3; vol. 3. Here are transcripts of proceedings of the Imperial Conference, narrowly so called.
26 AA: CP103/3; vol. 6; *Imperial Economic Conference ... Proceedings and Documents* (Command 2009), esp. from p. 57.
27 Cabinet proceedings, 10 July 1923, AA: A2718. I owe this reference, and other help, to Dryden, 'Australian Immigration'.
28 Command 2009, from p. 174.
29 Constantine, *Colonial Development Policy*, pp. 106–7.

30 Command 2009, p. 151.
31 12 October 1923, AOT: CB19/1.
32 Command 2009, from p. 86.
33 Command 2009, from p. 136.
34 Edwards, *Bruce*, pp. 102–3; newspaper clippings at AA: A1486. The Beauchamp statement is from *Morning Post*, 17 January 1924.
35 Hudson and North, *Casey's Letters*, p. 109.
36 Letter, 20 December 1924, McDougall Papers.
37 AA: CP103/11; 5.
38 Letter, 22 February 1923, SAWA: PD63/23; OSC minutes, 6 February 1923, PRO: CO721/62.
39 Memorandum, 15 May 1923, PRO: CO721/62.
40 B. K. de Garis, 'Colebatch', *Australian Dictionary of Biography*, vol. 8 (1981), pp. 64–5.
41 Colebatch, letter, 28 December 1923, and Plant, minute thereon, PRO: CO721/62.
42 Letters through Governor-General, 7, 11 and 28 March 1924, PRO: CO532/271.
43 House of Commons, 17 and 19 June 1924.
44 J. H. Thomas, letter, 19 June 1924, PRO: CO721/94. The body did not begin functioning until early 1925 and never had such powers as Bruce had envisaged.
45 For text, see 'Development and Migration Commission. First Annual Report', *Commonwealth Parliamentary Papers*, 1926–8, vol. 5, pp. 58–60. The Agreement has had the benediction of study by both Drummond, *Imperial Policy*, and Tsokhas, 'People or Money'.
46 Passage Agreement file, PRO: CO721/79.
47 Memorandum, 6 August 1926, and associated papers, PRO: DO57/6.
48 Report of the meeting, 15 April 1924, with associated papers, PRO: CO721/96.
49 Memorandum, 28 April 1924, PRO: CO721/96.
50 Memorandum, 17 May 1924, PRO: CO721/96.
51 Memorandum, 24 November 1924, PRO: CO721/91.
52 Memoranda, May 1924, PRO: T161/231/S23957/1.
53 Drummond, *Imperial Policy*, p. 113.
54 The matter is best documented in Hunter's correspondence to Australia, AA: A461; B349/2/1, and PRO: T161/692/S22957/B10/1.
55 See his correspondence in PRO: CO532/306; CO721/67, 91, 95 and 104; LAB2/1233/EDO/309/1924.
56 AA: A461; B349/2/1.
57 Cable, 15 February 1925, PRO: CO721/104.
58 Memorandum, 12 March 1925, PRO: CO721/104.
59 Memorandum to Treasury, 12 March 1925, PRO: CO721/104. It is possible, but on balance unlikely, that the OSD was itself dissimulating vis-à-vis Treasury. Amery's attitude is likewise ambiguous, but see Barnes and Nicholson, *Amery's Diaries*, p. 395.
60 AA: A461; B349/2/1. SAWA: PD104/24.
61 File on renewal of Passage Agreement, PRO: CO721/104.

62   AA: A458; B156/1; part 1. A maximum of 100 passports per month was to be granted to Yugoslavs and Greeks; the governments of Italy, Malta, Greece, and Spain were to be approached so as to limit entry of anyone likely to become a charge upon Australia.

63   An historical sketch by L. J. Hurley dates Cabinet's decision to this effect at 6 July 1925, AA: CP211/2; bundle 2. Henceforth both nominators and nominees were to be British. Of course such citizenship could be achieved by naturalisation, and accordingly there continued assistance to some of non-British ethnicity, notably of wives (but not children! see memorandum, 18 February 1927, QSA: IMM/175) of ethnic Italians resident in Queensland. The most interesting debate on the 1925 Immigration Bill was in the House of Representatives, 25 June 1925. Even then Bruce disparaged Australian hostility to non-British migrants.

64   'British Settlement and Migration. Report of Discussions Held at the British Empire Exhibition Wembley', typescript, Battye Library.

65   Memorandum, 20 March 1924, PRO: CO721/95.

66   'Migration. *Oversea Settlement* Delegation to Australia. Report', *Commonwealth Parliamentary Papers*, 1923–4, vol. 2. The Report is further discussed below, esp. chapter 10.

67   PRO: LAB2/1233/EDO144/1924.

68   PRO: MH57/59.

69   House of Commons, 27 July 1925; Amery presented the figures as to spending, 20 April 1926.

4 THE MODEST ZENITH OF HOPE: 1925–1926

1   Currie and Graham, CSIRO.

2   Latham Papers: series 45.

3   Memorandum, April 1924, PRO: T161/231/S23957/1.

4   *West Australian*, 5 March 1925; R. B. Walker, 'Denison', *Australian Dictionary of Biography*, vol. 8 (1981), pp. 283–5.

5   Hudson and North, *Casey's Letters*, p. 59.

6   W. R. Maloney, House of Representatives, 23 September 1925.

7   Hudson and North, *Casey's Letters*, p. 56.

8   Macnaghten, memorandum and minutes thereon, 12 February 1925, PRO: CO721/108.

9   Memorandum, 13 May 1925, PRO: CO721/118.

10   PRO: CO721/104. The following passage draws on letters in the same location dated 8 and 30 September, 1 and 13 October. The impresarios were H. D. McIntosh and H. J. Ward. Note that there appears to be no compilation, or indeed any adequate record, of correspondence from the OSD to the Representative.

11   Appleyard and Schedvin, *Australian Financiers*, p. 201.

12   Minutes of meeting, 6 and 7 October 1925, PRO: CO721/105.

13   E. B. Histed, 'Mitchell', *Australian Dictionary of Biography*, vol. 10 (1986), pp. 526–8.

14 Memorandum, 8 March 1926, PRO: DO57/2.
15 Letter, 10 March 1926, PRO: DO57/2.
16 Cabinet proceedings, 25 February, 30 March, 19 April, and 4 May 1926, AA: A2718; vol. 2.
17 House of Representatives, 28 May 1926.
18 Gilbert, *Australian Loan Council.*
19 Memorandum, 24 June 1925, PRO: T176/17, which refers generally to the embargo.
20 Minute on Bankes Amery's letter, 23 December 1925, PRO: DO57/1.
21 D. C. McGrath, House of Representatives, 1 July 1926.
22 Roe, 'Gepp', esp. p. 97.
23 The daughter was Katherine; her autobiography is among the Gepp Family Papers.
24 In 1986 much valuable documentation was held by North Broken Hill Peko Ltd, Melbourne, which firm generously made them available to me. I believe they are no longer extant. Very extensive but less compelling material remains at AOT.
25 Letter, 26 September 1921, Robinson Papers.
26 House of Commons, 14 March 1929.
27 Clarke, 'The Argonauts'; D. Mossenson, 'Nathan', *Australian Dictionary of Biography*, vol. 10 (1986), pp. 666–7.
28 N. T. M. Wilsmore, letter, 3 May 1926, CSIRO Papers: series 578.
29 N. Blewett, 'Gunn', *Australian Dictionary of Biography*, vol. 9 (1983), pp. 141–2.
30 House of Assembly, 6 September 1921, 30 November 1923, and 30 September 1924.
31 G. G. Whiskard, memorandum, 13 November 1929, PRO: DO57/115.
32 'Development and Migration Commission. Second Annual Report', *Commonwealth Parliamentary Papers*, 1929, vol. 2.
33 Bankes Amery's letters for early 1926 consistently invoke this theme, PRO: DO57/2, 4 and 5. That of 12 May 1926 referred to the pamphlet, by one Shields, not located.
34 Authored by Wood, dated 24 June 1926, PRO: DO57/4; the embargo is the subject of many files, DO57/5.
35 Lake, *Limits of Hope.* The similarity of title between Lake's book and my own is indicative: still, I apologise for the plagiarism.
36 *Report on the Group Settlements in Western Australia* (Command 2673); compare 'Report of the Royal Commission on Group Settlement', *Western Australian Parliamentary Papers*, 1925.
37 Especially cable, 16 April 1926, and attached report, PRO: DO57/2.
38 Letter, 29–30 November 1925, PRO: CO721/105.
39 Cable, 18 January 1926, and minute thereon, PRO: DO57/2.
40 Letter, 18 June 1926, PRO: CO721/105.
41 Letters, 30 September and 13 October 1925, PRO: CO721/105, and 20 August 1926, DO57/5.
42 Letters, 10 and 27 February and 4 March 1926, PRO: DO57/2; an OSD minute on the first is important.

43   Letter, 20 August 1926, PRO: DO57/5.
44   Letter, 14 July 1926, PRO: DO57/5.
45   Letter, 27 February 1926, PRO: DO57/2.
46   Letter, 3 June 1926, and associated papers, PRO: DO57/4. The matter was commented upon in several letters.
47   Letter, 14 April 1926, PRO: DO57/4.
48   Letter, 26 July 1926, PRO: DO57/5.
49   Letter, 20 August 1926, PRO: DO57/5.
50   'Conference of Commonwealth and State Ministers ... May 1926', *Commonwealth Parliamentary Papers*, 1926–8, vol. 5, esp. p. 11; pertinent correspondence is available at AOT: PD55/26.
51   AA: CP211/2; bundle 2.
52   Minutes on Bankes Amery, letter, 23 December 1925, PRO: DO57/1.
53   E. T. Crutchley, memorandum 10 August 1925, and associated papers, PRO: CO721/104; Crutchley and Cuthbertson, correspondence, PRO: T161/465/S16395/3.
54   Hudson and North, *Casey's Letters*, p. 113; Bankes Amery, letters, 29 November 1925 and 19 May 1926, PRO: CO721/105 and DO57/4.
55   Letter, 5 September 1926, Amery Papers: not seen, but reported to me by K. Fedorowich.
56   Bankes Amery, letter, 13 July 1926, and associated documents, PRO: DO57/10; see further below, chapter 10.
57   Clarendon, letter, 6 January 1926, and Macnaghten, letter, 5 February 1926, PRO: CO721/105 and DO57/14.
58   PRO: DO57/6.
59   Letter, 3 March 1926, Amery Papers (see note 55); AA: AA1970/555.
60   Letter, 14 June 1926, PRO: DO57/6.
61   Memorandum, 25 January 1926, PRO: DO57/13.
62   House of Commons, 25 March, 29 April, 3 May, 29 July 1926.
63   Best exemplified at this time in his *Labour and Empire*.
64   Bruce, cable, 6 March 1926, PRO: DO35/1; further documentation is at PRO: CAB27/310 and Baldwin Papers: vol. 93. The best secondary account of the Board is by S. Constantine in Mackenzie, *Imperialism and Popular Culture*.
65   Barnes and Nicholson, *Amery Diaries*, p. 445.
66   The original memorandum is quoted in a further one (by Niemeyer), 9 May 1927, PRO: T161/278/S3238/1.
67   Niemeyer, memorandum, 28 May 1926, PRO: T176/25A.
68   PRO: T176/25A.
69   Command 2608, quotation from p. 23. The pertinent file at PRO: DO57/14 indicates that the first draft was yet more abrasive; see too T161/1098/S2938/1.
70   R. Armstrong, 'Eady', *Dictionary of National Biography 1961–70* (1981), pp. 319–20. Eady spoke at an OSC colloquium in June as reported at PRO: DO57/16, and wrote two important memoranda, 5 July and 5 August 1926, DO57/13.
71   PRO: LAB2/1223/EDO/197/1926.
72   AA: CP211/2; bundle 8.

73 Various memoranda pursued this subject, PRO: DO57/13 and 15.
74 *Imperial Conference, 1926* (Command 2769) presents much material, Bruce's speech running from p. 60, while a full account is at AA: CP103/3; vol. 10.
75 Command 2769, p. 288; complementary detail as to the sub-committee, PRO: CAB32/62.
76 Gepp, statement on his work in Britain, AA: CP211/2; bundle 96; a complementary memorandum of agreement between Australian representatives and the OSD is in the same series, bundle 2.
77 J. S. R. McLeod, memorandum, 19 March 1925, PRO: CO721/116.
78 Gepp, letter, 28 October 1926, AA: CP211/2; bundle 8.
79 'Notes on Career of Sir Herbert Gepp', Gepp Family Papers.
80 AA: AA1970; A555. This material documents this and the next paragraph but see also PRO: T160/67/F2217. On the War debts, see Tsokhas, ' "A Pound of Flesh" '.
81 PRO: T161/232/S23957/04, a file relating to the Conference generally.
82 Letter, 16 November 1927, PRO: DO35/22.

5 AMBIGUITIES: 1926–1927

1 Letter, 14 October 1926, PRO: DO57/5.
2 Memoranda, undated, PRO: DO57/43.
3 Paper, 11 January 1927, PRO: CAB24/184; CP7.
4 Notes and draft, AA: CP211/2; bundle 4.
5 Minutes, AA: CP211/1.
6 Diary, Nathan Papers. This is a crucial source for early DMC history.
7 See, for example, Bankes Amery's statement to DMC, 14 September 1926, AA: CP211/2; bundle 77.
8 Letter, 15 December 1926, PRO: T161/222/S23957/02.
9 Memorandum, 30 March 1927, PRO: T176/21.
10 Memorandum, 9 May 1927, PRO: T161/278/S3238/1. The file has general matter of importance, esp. Churchill, letter, 18 February 1927.
11 28 May 1927, AA: CP211/2; bundle 82.
12 Bankes Amery, letter, 16 February 1927, PRO: DO57/31.
13 Victorian settlers files, PRO: DO57/19; and AA: CP211/2; bundle 77. Bankes Amery, letter, 5 July 1927, PRO: DO57/31.
14 Bankes Amery, letter, 26 November 1928, PRO: T161/679/S8787/08/2.
15 Childers file, PRO: CO721/105.
16 Diary, 25–26 October 1926, Nathan Papers.
17 AA: CP211/2; bundle 77.
18 Letter, 10 February 1927, PRO: DO57/31.
19 AA: CP211/2; bundle 8.
20 Diary, esp. 11 June 1927, Nathan Papers.
21 Diary, esp. 27 August 1926, Nathan Papers; meeting with E. J. Hogan, 30 June 1927, AA: CP211/2; bundle 8.
22 Memorandum, 22 March 1927, PRO: T161/692/S2395/010/1. This responded to Bankes Amery, letter, 4 February 1927. The most pertinent DO file is at

57/31, but see too DO57/104 which includes a long retrospect by Bankes Amery.

23   Undated, PRO: DO57/47.

24   They connected Busselton, Flinders Bay, and Margaret River; PRO: T161/232/S2395/02.

25   Diary, 26 January 1927, Nathan Papers.

26   Letter, 12 January 1927, PRO: T161/232/S2395/02.

27   Letter, undated, AA: CP211/2; bundle 2.

28   Diary, 10–17 November, 1926, Nathan Papers.

29   PRO: T161/971/S23957/01.

30   Letters, 21 December 1926, 16 February, 4 March, 12 May and 21 June 1927, PRO: DO57/70.

31   Minutes, 6 January and 15–16 September 1927, AA: CP211/1.

32   'Development and Migration Commission. First Annual Report', *Commonwealth Parliamentary Papers*, 1926–8, vol. 5, pp. 65–6.

33   Correspondence, 4 and 11 October 1926, DMC file, AOT: CB19/1.

34   Respectively at AA: CP211/2; bundles 96 and 54; Rivett, letter, 25 July 1927, CSIRO Papers: series 9; M14/27/7.

35   DMC, *Interim Report on Investigation into Present Position of Tasmania*, Melbourne, 1927, pp. 6–7 and generally.

36   File on plant genetics, AA: CP211/2; bundle 33.

37   'Development and Migration Commission. First Annual Report', *Commonwealth Parliamentary Papers*, 1926–8, vol. 5, pp. 23–4.

38   Letter, 9 April 1927, AA: CP211/2; bundle 38. The matter receives frequent notice in Nathan's diary.

39   'Economic Situation in Australia'.

40   Cain, 'Economists and Population Strategy'.

41   Roe, 'Brigden', pp. 76–7.

42   Minutes, 19 August 1926, AA: CP211/1.

43   See esp. Gepp, letter to Wickens, AA: CP211/2; bundle 38.

44   Diary, 10 September 1926, Nathan Papers.

45   Minutes, 27 and 30 August, 1926, AA: CP211/1.

46   *Commonwealth Parliamentary Papers*, 1926–8, vol. 5, pp. 25–35.

47   For many references, see Hudson and Way, '*Secret Service Agent*', as indexed.

48   P. Adam-Smith, 'Clapp', *Australian Dictionary of Biography*, vol. 8 (1981), pp. 1–3.

49   AA: A458; B104/2. Film does not survive.

50   'Migration and Development Commission. Statement Showing Persons Employed ... August 1927', *Commonwealth Parliamentary Papers*, 1926–8, vol. 5. For the staff in 1929, AA: A786; A85/1.

51   Letter, 12 October 1926, AA: CP211/2; bundle 32.

52   All appear in Nathan's diary. Casey alone went on the payroll, but ill-health soon ended that; later he achieved standing as an archaeologist. Simpson became Bruce's secretary, Officer a member of the external affairs service.

53   At a public meeting, Brisbane, 15 July 1927, AA: CP211/2; bundle 47.

54   AA: CP211/2; bundles 46 (for Partridge and forestry references) and 47 (remainder).

55   Letter, 1 July 1927, AA: CP211/2; bundle 46.

56   Meeting with E. J. Hogan, AA: CP211/2; bundle 8.
57   Hudson and Way, *'Secret Service Agent'*, p. 262; following, pp. 376, 471, 491.
58   Letter, 19 July 1927, AA: CP211/2; bundle 11.
59   Diary, esp. 4 May 1927, Nathan Papers; following, 20 May, 11 and 13 July, and 17 June 1927.
60   AA: AA1970/555.
61   House of Representatives, 29 September 1927; following, J. E. West, 5 October; E. Findley, Senate, 30 November; Gullett, House of Representatives, 24 and 25 November; B. Sampson and W. Kingsmill, Senate, 30 November and 2 December.
62   Letter, 18 May 1927; AA: CP211/2; bundle 8.
63   Bankes Amery, letter, 19 March 1928, AA: A786; J22/2.
64   Report, AA: CP 211/2; bundle 103.
65   Memorandum, 1 October 1927, AA: CP211/2; bundle 29.
66   Report, late 1927, AA; CP211/2; bundle 46; also, PRO: T161/971/S23957/03/1.
67   SRSA: GRG7; series 76; 9.
68   Ms J. M. Keam, interview, November 1983.
69   Letter, 18 October 1927, AOT: PD22/10/27.
70   Correspondence, AOT: PD118/21/27.
71   Letter, 20 July 1927, QSA: IMM/171.
72   Marketing file, AA: CP211/2; bundle 54. Bundles 53 and 54 in this piece generally document the following Tasmanian material.
73   AOT: PD146/2/27.
74   Letter, 7 November 1927, AOT: PD22/2/27.
75   Letter, 28 Ocober 1927, AOT: PD22/2/27.
76   Ms M. Summerhayes-Garrett, interview, 30 March 1984.
77   Hobart *Mercury*, 7 and 8 June 1927.
78   The most comprehensive file is at PRO: DO57/10.
79   Memorandum, 18 January 1927, PRO: CO721/104.
80   AA: CP211/2; bundle 76.
81   AA: CP211/2; bundle 91.
82   AA: A458; O154/19.
83   Pearce Papers: part 1; series 15.
84   London publicity file, AA: CP211/2; bundle 82.
85   Diary, esp. 1 April 1927, Nathan Papers; meeting of Gepp, Thompson, and Bankes Amery, minutes, AA: CP211/2; bundle 8.
86   Letter, 8 May 1927, PRO: DO57/44.
87   Memorandum, 1 July 1927, PRO: DO57/32. Some hand has altered 'Australia House or in Australia' to 'here or overseas'.
88   Letter, 30 June 1927, AA: CP211/2; bundle 2; compare PRO: T161/278/S328/1.
89   PRO: T161/692/S2395/010/1.
90   O. Thompson, cable, 6 August 1927, AA: CP211/2; bundle 65. Presumably there was more official documentation, but it has not been located.
91   Letter, 17 August 1927, PRO: DO57/33.
92   6 September 1927, PRO: DO57/33.
93   Letters, 15–21 and 30 September PRO: DO57/33, and 19 September 1927, T161/971/S23957/03/1.
94   Hudson and Way, *'Secret Service Agent'*, p. 400.

95 Amery, *Political Life*, vol. 2; Huxley, *Both Hands* and his Papers; Whiskard, PRO: DO117/77.
96 L. Layman, 'Latham', *Australian Dictionary of Biography*, vol. 10 (1986), pp. 1–2.
97 Bankes Amery, letter, 25 January 1926, and associated papers, PRO: DO57/62.
98 AA: CP211/2; bundle 3.
99 AA: CP211/2; bundle 8.
100 19 November 1927, Baldwin Papers: vol. 96.
101 16 November 1927, PRO: DO35/22.
102 Whiskard, letter, 21 November 1927, PRO: DO57/62.
103 AA: CP211/2; bundle 2.
104 Memorandum, 6 January 1928, PRO: DO57/62.
105 Command 3088.
106 House of Commons, 23 March 1927.

6 THROUGH CONFUSION TO DOOM: 1928–1929

1   Barnes and Nicholson, *Amery Diaries*, p. 519.
2   House of Commons, 24 February 1928.
3   Memorandum for discussion, 22 February 1928, PRO: CAB23/57.
4   PRO: CAB24/193; CP95.
5   Memorandum, 22 March 1928, PRO: DO57/78.
6   Hudson and Way, '*Secret Service Agent*', pp. 611–12.
7   J. A. Schultz in Constantine, *Emigrants and Empire*, pp. 160–8; Drummond, *Imperial Policy*, pp. 99–108.
8   Letter, 16 February 1928, PRO: DO57/78.
9   Much relevant detail is at PRO: DO57/73.
10 Command 3156; following quotations, pp. 35, 44, 49 and 51.
11 First appearing in London's *Evening Standard*, Inge's remarks were published in Australia in mid-August 1928.
12 24 July and 2 August 1928.
13 Hudson and Way, '*Secret Service Agent*', p. 605; see also pp. 621 and 628.
14 Cable, 21 February 1928, AA: CP211/2; bundle 3.
15 So reported in DMC 'summaries for London office', AA: CP211/2; bundle 102; see also F. A. Bland in Campbell, Mills and Portus, *Australian Affairs*, pp. 60–2.
16 Hancock, *Australia*, p. 151; newspaper cuttings, SAWA: PD27/27.
17 File on Australian fares, PRO: DO57/99.
18 File on Passage Agreement, PRO: CO721/104.
19 PRO: T161/1098/S29398/1.
20 DMC Summary Report, 27 July 1928, AA: CP211/2; bundle 99.
21 See below, p. 119.
22 *Economic and Trade Conditions in Australia to August 1929*, see chapter 3, note 9.
23 Schedvin, *Australia and Depression*, p. 96; see also Hancock, *Australia*, pp. 162–3, and Gilbert, *Loan Council*, generally.
24 Letter, 18 July 1928, AA: A786; G106/3.

25   Melbourne *Herald*, 1 August 1928.
26   Letter, 14 October 1927, AA: CP211/2; bundle 96.
27   Edited respectively by Campbell et al., and Phillips and Wood.
28   Letter, 2 November 1928, AA: CP211/2; bundle 112.
29   AA: CP211/2; bundle 33.
30   QSA: IMM/171. DMC, 'Report Relating to the Dawson Valley Immigration Scheme' (roneoed, NLA).
31   AA: CP211/2; bundle 48.
32   PRO: T161/232/S23957/08. AA: CP211/2; bundle 47.
33   Hudson and North, *Casey's Letters*, pp. 393–4.
34   'Report ... on the Dawson Valley Irrigation Settlement', *Queensland Parliamentary Papers*, 1933, vol. 2.
35   *Australia*, pp. 163–4.
36   DMC, 'Report on Proposal to Construct a Railway from Nowingi to Millewa South' (roneoed, NLA), p. 34.
37   AA: CP211/2; bundle 63.
38   AA: CP211/2; bundle 51.
39   The clearest statements on this extremely complex matter are at AA: A786; D103/1. The major concentration of relevant data is at PRO: T/161/692/S23957/010/1 and 2, and DO57/64.
40   Minutes, 11 April 1928, AA: CP211/1. These minutes are a further source of data, sometimes helpful.
41   Letter, 24 April 1928, AA: CP211/2; bundle 3.
42   Letter, 9 July 1928, Pearce Papers: part 1; series 15. See also letter to Pearce, 17 June 1928.
43   'Development and Migration Commission. Second Annual Report ... 1928', *Commonwealth Parliamentary Papers*, 1929, vol. 2, pp. 33–5.
44   PRO: DO57/3.
45   As note 43, p. 46.
46   'Progress Report ... on the Tod River Waterworks', *South Australian Parliamentary Papers*, 1928, p. x.
47   AA: A786; A22/4.
48   PRO: T161/232/S23957/09.
49   Letter, 6 September 1927, PRO; DO57/33.
50   Devereux, memorandum, 12 June 1928, AA: CP211/2; bundle 3. This piece has much relevant documentation, but also see bundles 42 (Clarence River) and 99.
51   AA: CP211/2; bundle 96. Most of the following issues are noticed in 'Second Annual Report ... 1928', *Commonwealth Parliamentary Papers*, 1929, vol. 2.
52   AA: A786; V16/4.
53   'Development and Migration Commission. Report relating to the Canned Fruit Industries of Australia', *Commonwealth Parliamentary Papers*, 1929, vol. 2, esp. p. 15.
54   Committee's activities, AA: CP211/2; bundle 67. Gepp's awareness of irrigation-induced soil deficiency, A786; R22/7.
55   'Development and Migration Commission. Report relating to the Gold Mining Industry in Australia', *Commonwealth Parliamentary Papers*, 1926–8, vol. 5.

56   *Commonwealth Parliamentary Papers*, 1926–8, vol. 5; supplementary documentation, from which the following account draws, is at AA: CP211/2; bundle 39.

57   20 June 1928.

58   Minutes of meeting, 2 February 1929, AA: A786; E1/1.

59   Letter, 3 August 1928, AOT: PD19/31/28.

60   Letter, 16 January 1928, AA: CP820/1; bundle 1, which has much, although sometimes inchoate material on this tangled topic. The other most helpful source is CP211/2; bundle 95. A central issue was whether the Bureau should lodge with DMC, CSIR, or neither. Gepp argued for the last, seeing the Bureau as likely to give a political taint to any host. Rivett was prepared to embrace the Bureau. Bruce first agreed with Rivett, who noted the victory with satisfaction, but then the Prime Minister changed towards Gepp's position.

61   Roe, 'Brigden'.

62   'Report of the Premiers' Conference, June 1928', *New South Wales Parliamentary Papers*, 1928–9, joint volumes, vol. 1.

63   AONSW: Premier's Correspondence 9/2016; A31/26. The agreed annual ceilings evidently were 3000 for Italians (beyond which Italian authorities had undertaken to approve departure only of agricultural workers); 600 apiece for Greeks, Yugoslavs, and Albanians; 300 apiece for Czechoslovaks, Estonians and Poles. In November 1928 the quotas were refined on a State-by-State basis. Newspaper cuttings show Bruce still ready to confront critics of Italian entry. 'If we can't allow 5,000 of these to come in without saying they are undermining our constitution, then God help Australia' (Sydney *Sun*, 14 October 1928).

64   Letter, 13 October 1928, PRO: DO57/88.

65   AA: CP211/2; bundle 93.

66   Gepp, letter, 21 September 1928, AA: CP820/1; bundle 2.

67   Command 3308, esp. p. 7.

68   PRO: T161/232/S2395/07.

69   AA: CP211/2; bundle 9.

70   PRO: DO57/96.

71   Ellison, 'Immigration Issues in Tasmania 1919–36', ch. 4.

72   Letter, 1 December 1928, PRO: DO35/66.

73   AA: CP211/2; bundle 93.

74   Letter, 6 September 1927, PRO: DO57/33.

75   For this period continuing mainly at PRO: DO57/64; complementary material is at AA: A786; J22/2, K22/2, and P22/2.

76   Letter, 2 March 1928, PRO: DO57/64.

77   Letter, 7 and 12 February 1928, PRO: DO57/64.

78   Letter, 30 August 1928, PRO: DO57/64.

79   Bankes Amery, letters, esp. 18 and 23 July 1928, PRO: DO57/64.

80   M. T. Shaw, 'Currie', *Australian Dictionary of Biography*, vol. 8 (1981), 180–1.

81   Letter, 10 May 1928, PRO: DO57/64.

82   AA: CP211/2; bundle 63.

83   Autobiography, Crutchley Papers.

84 Diary, 2 October 1928, Crutchley Papers. I have not itemised obvious references to this source.
85 Letter, 3 October 1928, PRO: DO57/65.
86 Hudson and Way, '*Secret Service Agent*', p. 655.
87 Letter, 22 August 1928, AA: CP211/2; bundle 112.
88 PRO: T161/274/S1390/1, a file of general import.
89 Letter, 10 December 1926, AA: CP211/2; bundle 112.
90 9 February 1927, PRO: T161/274/S1390/1, a file of yet greater import, including Dalton's and Niemeyer's commentary.
91 Gilbert, *Loan Council*, p. 80.
92 House of Representatives, 21 March 1927.
93 Hudson and Way, '*Secret Service Agent*', generally, and Baldwin Papers: vol. 94. The latter includes the reference to Hirst.
94 Letters, 21 May 1927 and 14 April 1928, AA: M111.
95 Letter, 5 July 1928, AA: CP211/2; bundle 112.
96 3 September 1928, AA: AA1970/555.
97 Richmond, 'Bruce and Economic Policy'.
98 AA: CP211/2; bundle 102.
99 'Report of the British Economic Mission', *Commonwealth Parliamentary Papers*, 1929, vol. 2, esp. p. 17.
100 Devereux, letter, 23 October 1928, AA: CP211/2; bundle 112. Gepp, letter, 10 December 1928, CP820/1.
101 Hudson and Way, '*Secret Service Agent*', p. 708.
102 Crutchley, letter, 16 January 1929, PRO: DO57/95; report of discussions, AA: A786; K19/1.
103 Cable, 11 December 1928, PRO: DO57/95, a piece of general importance.
104 Letter, 11 December 1928, PRO: DO57/95.
105 PRO: DO57/95; T161/274/S21390/2.
106 Letter, 15 January 1929, PRO: T161/274/S21390/2.
107 30 April 1929, AA: M111.
108 February 1929, Baldwin Papers: vol. 94.
109 *Commonwealth Parliamentary Papers*, 1929, vol. 2, esp. pp. 5, 9, and 50–1.
110 The immense documentation is richest at AA: CP211/2; bundle 56, especially for the commentaries by P. E. Keam and W. J. Rose. AOT also holds much of value, outstandingly PD 95/28, while noteworthy too are letters of Nelson and K. Brodribb, CSIRO Papers: series 9; A12/20/77.
111 As well as the above, AOT: AD712.
112 Winspear, *Taking Stock*. See too his evidence, Royal Commission on Exporting Fruit, 1930, AOT: RC8/2.
113 DMC, *Third Interim Report on Tasmania*, Melbourne, 1928; G. J. Rodgers for DMC, *Report on Afforestation and Reforestation in Tasmania*, Canberra, 1929 (copy in AA: A786; H22/6); and AA: CP211/2; bundle 56.
114 AOT: PD68/29.
115 Rose, report, AA: A786; AA22/6.
116 DMC, *Investigation into Present Position of Tasmania … (Internal Transport)*, Melbourne, 1929. AOT: PD150/6/28. AA: A786; G22/6 and A100/2. AA: CP211/2; bundle 58.

117   There were published ... e Interim Reports on Tasmanian matters; the best consolidation is at AA: CP211/2; bundle 56.
118   E. T. Bieler, letter, 5 April 1929, AA: A786; E64/1. See Butcher, 'Science and Imperial Vision', which, however, ignores rich materials pertaining both to DMC and CSIR.
119   AA: CP211/2; bundle 57.
120   Rose, memorandum, 15 February 1928, AA: CP211/2; bundle 57. The inventor was one G. M. Walker.
121   *Mercury*, 5 June 1928; Keam, letter, 29 January 1929, AA: CP211/2; bundle 58.
122   *Mercury*, 29 August 1928.
123   AOT: PD25/10/29
124   AA: A786; K19/1.
125   AA: A786; B22/5. Teakle, *Teakle Saga*, esp. p. 207.
126   Report of Conference sponsored by Church of England, PRO: DO57/83.
127   Minutes, 22 March 1929, AA: CP211/1.
128   Crutchley, letter, 3 October 1929, PRO: DO57/118. The lack of a file of outward letters to the Representative remains galling.
129   Hudson and Way, '*Secret Service Agent*', p. 786.
130   PRO: BT56/45; CIA 1958.
131   Letter, 6 June 1929, PRO: T161/S31390/2.
132   25 June 1929, AA: A786; P31/1.
133   Memorandum, 29 August 1929, PRO: DO57/105.
134   Memorandum, 7 July 1929, PRO: T161/S31390/2.
135   G. F. Plant, memorandum, 6 June 1929, PRO: DO57/98.
136   10 April 1929, PRO: DO57/100. Macnaghten was referring not only to Australia.
137   AA: CP211/2; bundle 106. PRO: BT56/13 (Passmore and Drummond).
138   PRO: DO57/92 (Wedgwood and Mitchell).
139   Letter, 15 April 1929, AA: A786; W106/3.
140   PRO: DO57/104.
141   Letter, 11 October 1929, PRO: DO57/108.
142   Letter, 15 April 1929, Baldwin Papers: vol. 94; such activity receives frequent mention in Hudson and Way, '*Secret Service Agent*'.
143   Diary, 30 May 1929, Crutchley Papers.
144   Diary, 6 July 1929, Crutchley Papers; letter, 1 August 1929, PRO: DO57/98.
145   AA: A786; C61/1.
146   Letter, 12 September 1929, PRO: DO57/98.
147   Letter, 29 June 1929, PRO: DO57/98.
148   Letter, 9 May 1929, PRO: DO57/86. Other letters follow; Clarke lived at Willah in the State's far north-west.
149   Diary, 24 September 1929, Crutchley Papers.
150   'Development and Migration Commission. Report ... to 30th June 1930', *Commonwealth Parliamentary Papers*, 1929–31, vol. 2, pp. 6–7 and 31. AA: A786; G22/8 and I22/8, which documents following material.
151   10 July 1929, AA: A786; D4/1.
152   AA: A786; I19/1.
153   AA: A786; I76/1.

154 The above. AOT: PD25/40/28.
155 Interview, Ms M. Summerhayes-Garrett, 30 March 1984.
156 12 July 1929, AA: A786; B40/1.
157 11 October 1929, AA: A786; I22/8.
158 PRO: T161/692/S34376.
159 AA: A786; K19/1. Crutchley, letters, 28 September and 3 October 1929, PRO: DO57/118. Diary, Crutchley Papers.
160 Diary, Crutchley Papers.
161 Best analysed in Wildavsky and Carboch, *Australian Politics.*
162 House of Representatives, esp. 19 March 1929.
163 17 and 18 September 1929.

7 NADIR: 1929–1935

1 Memorandum, 15 October 1929, PRO: DO57/100.
2 My failure to locate a copy is disturbing, but its existence appears indubitable.
3 On this and the situation generally, much helpful data appears in the correspondence between Gepp and G. A. Julius, CSIRO Papers: series 67; vol. 3.
4 19 October 1929, AA: A786; C1/1.
5 See their interchange on industrial matters, July 1929, AA: A786; B43/1.
6 Julius, letter, 23 October 1929, CSIRO Papers: series 67; vol. 3.
7 Edwards, *Bruce,* pp. 400–1.
8 Letter, 26 October 1929, AA: CP211/2; bundle 84.
9 Diary, 30 October 1929, Crutchley Papers. (Henceforth 'Crutchley Papers' will be omitted from pertinent references in this chapter.)
10 Diary, 5 November 1929. The most pertinent file for the following sentences is at AA: A461; E349/2/1.
11 AA: CP367/20.
12 Cain, 'Recovery Policy', esp. note 4; Giblin's paper is itself at AA: CP103/11. Giblin was a Research Professor in Economics, University of Melbourne.
13 PRO: T161/232/S2395/013/1. DO57/115.
14 Robertson, *Scullin,* pp. 193–5. This is an essential source for the period.
15 PRO: CAB24/207; CP321 and CP347.
16 AA: A786; I73/2; complementary British documentation, including Australia's reply of 24 December, is at PRO: T161/232/S23957/013/2.
17 Diary, 29 November 1929.
18 25 November 1929, Baldwin Papers: vol. 97.
19 Cable, 14 December 1929, PRO: T160/807/F11935/1.
20 Memorandum, 4 January 1930, PRO: DO57/126. This piece and the Treasury file cited in note 19 sustain this account.
21 Scullin, cable, 20 January 1930, PRO: DO57/145. Manning's view is there too in a memorandum, 29 January; HMG's reply, 12 March, is at DO57/133.
22 'Conference of Commonwealth and State Ministers February 1930', *Commonwealth Parliamentary Papers,* 1929–31, vol. 2, esp. p. 13.
23 Cables, 24 February and 21 March 1930, PRO: DO57/126.
24 PRO: T161/232/S23957/013/2, and generally DO57/133.

25 Esp. Senate, 28 March 1930, and House of Representatives, 14 May 1930.
26 Letter, 7 February 1930, Latham Papers: series 1.
27 AA: CP367/2; bundle 1.
28 AA: A786; E76/1.
29 PRO: T161/232/S23957/013/2 and 3; T161/487/S34956/1.
30 Letter, 10 July 1930, PRO: DO57/145.
31 House of Commons, 16 July 1930.
32 Much material at PRO: DO57/147–8 joins the Treasury files cited in note 29 as the basic source.
33 PRO: CAB58/163–6.
34 PRO: DO35/219/9. Dalton's letter was dated 16 June; the sympathetic official was R. A. Wiseman, his minute dated 6 October 1930.
35 Undated minutes, PRO: DO57/105.
36 AOT: PD13/55/30.
37 AA: CP103/11.
38 This datum derives from AA reference kindly supplied me by Andrew Mack. His source reads 'PM & Cabinet; Secret Notes to PM. Undated—Probably 1930'.
39 Paper by Crutchley, 'Australian Migration', PRO: DO57/141.
40 K. Officer, letter , 15 August and 3 December 1930, Officer Papers: series 1.
41 A good recent discussion appears in Williamson, *National Crisis*, pp. 79–84. The densest files are at PRO: DO35/90, although apropos the OSD's hopes see Plant, memorandum, 8 October 1930, DO57/141. For proceedings of the migration sub-committee, *Imperial Conference 1930. Appendices* (Command 3718.)
42 AA: A786; M4/1.
43 Whiskard, memorandum, 5 November 1930, PRO: DO57/154.
44 Crutchley, letter 19 September 1930, and associated papers, PRO: DO57/138.
45 Crutchley, letter, 12 September 1930, and associated papers, PRO: DO57/153.
46 18 November 1930, PRO: DO57/154; further documentation, but little more clarification, is at AA: A461; B349/2/1.
47 Cable, 11 December 1930, PRO: DO57/142.
48 Attwood, 'Niemeyer Mission'; Love, 'Niemeyer's Diary'.
49 Letter, 1 September 1930, PRO: T160/67/S2217/5.
50 Diary, 14 August 1930.
51 Minutes, AA: A786; B1/1.
52 *A Survey of Dairy Farming in the Goulburn Valley, Victoria, and the Reclaimed Swamps, South Australia*, Canberra, 1930.
53 *Report on the Aspects of Mixed Farming in the Murray Valley*, Canberra, 1930; *Report on the Present Position and Future Prospects of the Citrus Industry in Australia*, Canberra, 1930; 'Notes on the Potato Industry' (roneoed, NLA).
54 AA: A786; P161/1.
55 'Dried Fruits Industry', *Commonwealth Parliamentary Papers*, 1929–31, vol. 2.
56 'Ministerial Statement with regard to the Australian Sugar Industry', *Commonwealth Parliamentary Papers*, 1929–31, vol. 3.
57 'Hop Industry in Australia', *Commonwealth Parliamentary Papers*, 1929–31, vol. 2.

58   AA: A786; J64/6.
59   *NSW Parliamentary Papers*, 1929–30, joint volumes, vol. 3.
60   A copy is held in the Bills and Papers Office, Parliament House, Canberra; it was presented to the House of Representatives, 19 March 1931.
61   Rose, memorandum, 21 September 1930, AA: A786; F43/1. Finlay, Report, A786; U7/1.
62   Diary, 11 September 1930.
63   Lyons, letter (to wife), 26 October 1930, Lyons Papers: 'miscellaneous'.
64   Memoranda, October–November 1930, AA: A786; Z31/1.
65   Delivered to the Engineering Society of the University of Sydney, this is among the H. W. Gepp Papers. The context is best developed in various papers in *Labour History*, no. 17 (1970), notably Hart, 'Lyons'; Loveday, 'Anti-Political Thought'; and Matthews, 'All for Australia League'.
66   Correspondence centring on Officer, October–December 1930, Officer Papers: series 1. Gepp, draft statement to Somers, 10 December 1930, Pearce Papers: part 1; series 5.
67   'Report of the High Commissioner for 1930', p. 69; copy seen in the Bills and Papers Office, Parliament House, Canberra; also thus located is 'Report' for 1929.
68   Memorandum, 11 June 1930, SRSA: GRG7; series 23; 20/1921.
69   Statement of immigration agent, 24 April 1930, QSA: IMM/172.
70   AA: A461; E349/1/2.
71   Queensland's earlier interest is documented at AA: A445; 124/6/45 (to be scrupulous, there is also reference to South Australia still requisitioning three domestics a month); the restriction and reaction thereto, PRO: T161/474/ S23957/015.
72   W. C. Angwin, statement, *West Australian*, 27 August 1930.
73   Thomas, House of Commons, 25 May 1932.
74   'Report upon the Organisation of the High Commissioner's Office', *Common-wealth Parliamentary Papers*, 1929–31, vol. 2.
75   AA: A32; 30/228.
76   Crutchley, letter, 4 March 1930, PRO: DO57/149.
77   For this and following, PRO: DO57/157; for WA context, Bolton, *Fine Country*.
78   Petition, 29 May 1930, PRO: DO57/153.
79   Letter, 31 May 1931, PRO: DO57/143.
80   Letter, 21 November 1930, PRO: DO57/156.
81   Letter, 12 September 1930, PRO: DO57/153. Diary, esp. 24 July, 11 September, and 10 December 1930.
82   Letter, 7 August 1930, PRO: DO57/142.
83   Diary, 24 December 1930.
84   Crutchley, cable, 12 August 1930, PRO: DO57/142. T161/474/S2395/015. AA: A786; S4/1.
85   A. Moore, 'Goldfinch', *Australian Dictionary of Biography*, vol. 9 (1983), pp. 39–40.
86   Diary, esp. 17 October (Camden), 19 (Bruce) and 26 (Geelong) November 1930.
87   Darling, *Richly Rewarding*; school tours, PRO: DO57/134 and 158.

88   Diary, 7 December 1930.
89   Diary, 20 January 1931. Various files, PRO: DO35/124. Crutchley, *A Printer*,
     p. 15. The last is by the Representative's son, who also compiled *Crutchley.*
     A Memoir.
90   PROV: VPRS2568.
91   AA: A786; T22/1.
92   Legislative Assembly, 12 May 1931.
93   Legislative Assembly, 19 and 20 May, 16 and 23 June, and 1 July 1931.
94   Crutchley, letter, 26 April 1935, PRO: DO57/182. Scullin, House of Repre-
     sentatives, 14 May 1931.
95   Record of the Conference of Commonwealth and State Ministers ... 1931',
     Commonwealth Parliamentary Papers, 1929–31, vol. 2, p. 7.
96   Letters, 31 July and 30 November 1931, AA: A458; Q154/19.
97   Letter, 26 April 1935, PRO: DO57/182. Presumably this was the same
     organisation as 'the British Migrants' Association of Australia' further noted
     below.
98   *Overseas Settler*, March 1931.
99   AA: A786; L4/1.
100 15 October 1931, PRO: DO57/164.
101 AA: A461; A349/2/1. A786; M4/1.
102 Diary, esp. 16 March 1931.
103 Letter, 20 May 1931, PRO: T160/807/F11935/1; adjacent is that of Crutchley,
     2 April 1931. Dalton was currently on home leave.
104 Diary, 4 October 1931.
105 Diary, 19 June 1931.
106 Diary, 22 December 1931.
107 Diary, 20 December 1931.
108 19 December 1931, PRO: DO35/220; associated papers document the
     following passage.
109 AA: A786; B1/1.
110 AA: A786; Q22/6.
111 AA: CP314/1; 15.
112 AA: A786; D64/2. Edge and Laby, *Geophysical Survey.*
113 Memorandum, 10 February 1931, AA: A786; G22/7.
114 AA: A786; D19/2.
115 AA: A786; T22/8.
116 The richest source is Rivett's correspondence (to McDougall) 21 September
     and 6 October, CSIRO Papers: series 30; bundle 2, and (to A. E. V. Richardson)
     12, 13, and 19 August 1931, series 67; vol. 4. There is also a file on the
     committee at series 9; M14/31/8.
117 Letter, 19 August 1931, PRO: T160/807/F1935/3.
118 AA: A786; G19/2.
119 Letter, 12 August 1931, CSIRO Papers: series 67; vol. 4.
120 Memorandum, 1 October 1931, AA: CP367/2; bundle 1.
121 Command 4075, esp. pp. 12 and 28–9.
122 18 November and 2 December 1930, 30 April, 30 June, 29 July and
     1 December 1931.

123 PRO: T161/531/S34376/02.
124 20 June 1932, PRO: DO57/166, which piece has other relevant files.
125 Report of the High Commissioner', *Commonwealth Parliamentary Papers*, 1932–4, vol. 4, p. 20.
126 Petition, 6 August 1932, PRO: DO57/131.
127 Murrabit file, PRO: DO57/66; see too AA: A786; I61/1.
128 'Report of the Royal Commission on Dairy-Farming in the South-West', *Western Australian Parliamentary Papers*, 1932, esp. p. 2.
129 There is much documentation through PRO: DO126/1 and DO57/164 and 169.
130 AOT: PD55/11/32.
131 H. C. Brown, letter, 9 May 1932, and associated papers, PRO: DO57/164. The practice had already applied, to some opaque extent; by obvious implication, the Australian government likewise waived its comparable claim.
132 Memorandum, 8 August 1933, PRO: T161/531/S34376/02.
133 The best overall account is Drummond, *Imperial Policy*, chs 5 and 6, well supplemented for Australia by O'Brien, 'Empire v. National Interests'. The latter cites Whiskard, p. 576.
134 Letter, 5 May 1932, McDougall Papers; complementary material, especially letter, 25 February 1932, CSIRO Papers: series 30; bundle 3.
135 AA: CP314/3; bundle 1.
136 *Commonwealth Parliamentary Papers*, 1932–4, vol. 4.
137 'Report on Trade between Australia and the Far East', *Commonwealth Parliamentary Papers*, 1932–4, vol. 4, esp. p. 67.
138 His diary continues invaluable.
139 Moore, *Secret Army*, notices both Goldfinch and Crutchley.
140 Sissons and Stoddart, *Cricket and Empire*.
141 Diary, 20 February 1933.
142 'Report of the Royal Commission on Migrant Land Settlement', *Victorian Parliamentary Papers*, 1933; McDonald, 'Victoria's Immigration Scandal'.
143 PRO: DO57/174–5. T161/679/S878/08/3.
144 Letter, 15 August 1933, PRO: DO57/175; this and the letter of following day are particularly important. See J. B. Paul, 'Dunstan', *Australian Dictionary of Biography*, vol. 8 (1981), pp. 376–9.
145 Lyons, letter (to Thomas), 2 November 1933, AA: A786; A64/2, a file of general importance. Lyons may have been dissimulating, to serve his own purposes.
146 House of Representatives, 28–29 November 1933; Legislative Assembly (of Victoria), 24 October and 9 November 1933.
147 Letter, 20 December 1933, PRO: DO57/178.
148 AA: CP103/11; 2.
149 Letter, 14 December 1933, PRO: T161/680/S878/08/4, which file documents the following passage.
150 Crutchley, letter, 25 July 1934, PRO: DO57/183.
151 22 and 29 March, 5 June, and 17 July 1934.
152 Crutchley, letter, 26 November 1934 and 26 April 1935, and W. J. Garnett, letters, 2 November 1934 and 14 June 1936, PRO: DO57/182, which piece is largely concerned with the matter.

153   Petition, 3 July 1934, PRO: T161/692/S23957/010/2.
154   'Agricultural Bank Royal Commission: Report', *Western Australian Parliamentary Papers*, 1934. The Bank's Trustees disputed these findings.
155   Dunsdorfs, *Wheat-Growing Industry*, p. 283.
156   AA: A458; AP154/24.
157   AA: CP268/3; bundle 2; 1/833. CP30/3; 49. Melbourne *Herald*, 12 July 1935. Rivett, letters (to McDougall) 6 September 1934 and 13 February 1935, CSIRO Papers: series 30; bundle 3. Andrew Mack much assisted me in this matter.
158   AA: A786; AG22/5. Garnett, report, PRO: DO57/186. Tsokhas, ' "Hard Times" ', pp. 88–9.
159   Memorandum, 16 August 1934, AA: A786; K22/2.
160   PRO: DO57/183.
161   Not without documentation, although less than might be expected. Most is at PRO: DO57/169, 172 and 182; also AA: A786; W4/1.
162   Crutchley, letter, 25 October 1934, PRO: DO57/182.
163   Garnett, letter, 11 December 1934, PRO: DO57/150.

8 TOWARD THE WHEEL'S RETURN: 1932–1940

 1   PRO: DO57/136.
 2   House of Commons, 24 February 1933.
 3   Diary, 18 January and 27–28 February 1933, Crutchley Papers.
 4   Cable, 2 March 1933, PRO: DO57/126.
 5   Letter, September 1932, PRO: DO57/126.
 6   Several letters, PRO: DO57/128.
 7   Correspondence, October 1933, PRO: DO57/175.
 8   House of Assembly, 1 November 1933; Legislative Council, 22–23 November.
 9   PRO: DO57/171.
10   Letter, 24 August 1933, PRO: DO57/171.
11   House of Commons, 20 March 1934.
12   PRO: DO57/171.
13   P. Richardson, 'Robinson', *Australian Dictionary of Biography*, vol. 11 (1988), pp. 428–33.
14   11 January 1934, AA: A786; O22/9.
15   Cunneen, *King's Men*, as indexed.
16   PRO: DO57/184.
17   The philanthropist was Scottish-born Andrew Reid, and the institution called Burnside, PRO: DO57/188.
18   PRO: DO57/168. The bureaucrat was Miss M. G. Cooper, noted further in chapter 10.
19   Letter, 21 August 1934, PRO: DO57/177.
20   W. M. Mansfield, 'Garland', *Australian Dictionary of Biography*, vol. 8 (1981), pp. 619–20.
21   Command 4689, esp. p. 72.
22   PRO: DO57/185 largely comprises documentation of this venture.
23   House of Representatives, 23 October 1934.
24   Diary, 21 January 1935, Crutchley Papers; following reference, 2 February.

25   Crutchley, letter, 29 April 1935, and associated documents, PRO: DO57/187.
26   PRO: CAB24/254; CP62.
27   Memorandum, 9 December 1935, PRO: T161/837/S80642, which piece documents the following passage.
28   20 June 1935. Wise's figure for alien entry in 1934 was 5390; of what that was one-tenth remains mysterious.
29   18 December 1935.
30   Lee, *Life with Nye*, pp. 283–4.
31   PRO: T161/837/S80642. The chief commentator was E. Hale.
32   Letters, 29 October 1935 and 10 January 1936, PRO: DO57/176.
33   W. J. Garnett, letters, 20 and 31 January 1936; Hankinson, letter, 18 February 1936, PRO: DO57/122.
34   Letters, esp. 29 February and 8 April 1936, CSIRO Papers: series 30; bundle 5.
35   Hudson, *Australia and League of Nations*, pp. 82–5, 169–80.
36   Letter, 10 April 1936, PRO: DO57/122.
37   A. G. B. Fisher in Duncan and Janes, Future of Immigration, p. 70.
38   AA: A601; 764/1/2.
39   AA: A461; I6/1/2.
40   AA: A436; 46/5/18.
41   Letter, 4 March 1936, AA: A436; 46/5/18.
42   Minutes, 21 April 1936, PRO: DO114/89. In contrast with the OSC, the Board's minutes are extant for this period here, together with associated papers which document the following passage.
43   PRO: DO57/175.
44   J. M. Ward, 'Stevens', *Australian Dictionary of Biography*, vol. 12 (1990), pp. 74–7.
45   Letter, 20 November 1936, PRO: BT60/50/4, where too is the Board of Trade statement, 9 April 1937.
46   AA: A367; C3075, and A458; S156/2. The restrictive policy had been declared by Scullin, House of Representatives, 12 March 1930.
47   Martin, Menzies, p. 193.
48   AA: A659; 41/1/173, which with AOT: PD55/8/36 documents the following passage.
49   PRO: DO57/153.
50   Memorandum, 8 August 1936, PRO: DO57/175; cable (to Whiskard), 15 September 1936, and Whiskard, letter, 16 September 1936, DO114/74.
51   Overseas Settlement Board, minutes, 17 February 1937, PRO: DO114/89.
52   Duncan and Janes, *Future of Immigration*, is a record thereof; Coombs, p. 44; Gepp, p. 136.
53   *Immigration*, p. 216.
54   Much material is at PRO: DO57/189 and T161/927/S41500.
55   House of Commons, 19 and 25 January 1937.
56   Overseas Settlement Board, minutes, 4 May and 6 July 1937, PRO: DO114/89.
57   Minutes, 28 May 1937, PRO: DO114/74.
58   G. F. Pearce, Senate, 1 July 1937.
59   Letter, 30 August 1937, PRO: DO114/74. Whiskard referred also to a statement by Paterson, 25 August, equally assertive of federal rights.

60   E. J. Harrison, House of Representatives, 7 September 1937; J. G. Duncan-Hughes, Senate, 9 September.
61   Whiskard, cable, 4 February 1938, PRO: DO114/74, which piece holds further memoranda of the period, crucial for this story.
62   Further documentation is at AA: A601; 764/1/2, and PRO: T161/1228/S33482.
63   SRSA: GRG7; series 24; 1932/96. AOT: PD55/5/38.
64   Overseas Settlement Board, minutes, 21 June 1938, PRO: DO114/90. Whiskard was briefly in Britain.
65   House of Representatives, 12 May 1938.
66   PRO: CAB24/276; CP 96.
67   Command 5766, esp. p. 15.
68   *Empire Opportunities*, p. 19.
69   O'Brien, 'Empire v. National Interests', esp. p. 586.
70   Minutes, 6 July 1938, PRO: DO114/90. Bevin also spoke that day, and again on 9 February 1939.
71   Letter, 15 March 1939, PRO: T161/1098/S2938/2, a most valuable piece.
72   6 March 1939; from 1 April 1937 to 31 December 1938 the expenditure was £54,757.
73   House of Representatives, 28, 29–30 June, and 30 September 1938; Gullett, Curtin, and Brennan respectively.
74   Harris, *Australia's National Interests*.
75   'British Migration' and *Myth of Open Spaces*; see too Melbourne *Herald*, 22 February 1938.
76   *Survey*, as indexed.
77   R. E. Clothier, Senate, 18 May 1939; response by H. S. Foll, 30 May.
78   Cable, PRO: T161/877/S2048/1.

On-going scholarship has affected the subject-matter of this chapter. P. R. Bartrop, *Australia and the Holocaust 1933–45* (Melbourne, 1994) illuminates not only its specific subject of Jewish immigration. At the Australian Historical Association conference, Perth 1994, I learned through R. F. Moore that in the late 1930s Australia entered formal migration agreements with the Netherlands, Scandinavian countries, and Switzerland. On this and other matters I had helpful conversation with Michele Langfield, author of ' "White Aliens": The Control of European Immigration to Australia, 1920–1930', *Journal of Intercultural Studies*, vol. 12, no. 2 (1991), pp. 1–14, and of an article (accepted by the *Australian Journal of Politics and History*), addressing much the same issues as does this chapter.

9 EMIGRATION

1   *Migration and Unemployment*, pp. 30–1; see also his letter, 30 November 1922, PRO: CO721/55.
2   January 1925, PRO: CO721/107.
3   Letter, 27 June 1929, AA: A786; B40/1.
4   Knott, *Popular Opposition to the 1834 Poor Law*, pp. 270–4.
5   Hatfield, *I Find Australia*, p. 1; see G. Serle, 'Hatfield', *Australian Dictionary of Biography*, vol. 9 (1983), pp. 227–8.

6   See above, esp. p. 24.
7   *House of Representatives*, 17 June 1921.
8   'Factors Inhibiting Australian Migration'.
9   'Empire Migration', p. 182.
10   Crutchley, cable, 19 July 1929, PRO: DO57/64.
11   By G. R. Hamilton, PRO: BT70/11/S1056.
12   His major pertinent statement, 5 July 1926, is at PRO: DO57/13; see also his evidence to Economic Advisory Council committee, PRO: CAB58/164.
13   'Factors Inhibiting Australian Immigration', esp. p. 50.
14   Memorandum, January 1925, PRO: CO721/107.
15   Pope, 'Factors Inhibiting Australian Migration', p. 41.
16   Memorandum, 5 July 1926, PRO: DO57/13.
17   C. Bavin, report, PRO: DO57/123.
18   J. Mole, 22 September 1925, QSA: IMM/65.
19   *West Australian*, 9 October 1925; Colebatch, letter, 17 September 1925, SAWA: PD104/24.
20   Barnes, letter, 14 August 1926, SAWA: PD340/26.
21   Jones, *Diary*, vol. 2, p. 132.
22   PRO: CO721/103.
23   Amery, letter, 30 March 1926, Baldwin Papers: vol. 96.
24   Best documented at PRO: DO57/23. See A. J. Hill, 'Hobbs', *Australian Dictionary of Biography*, vol. 9 (1983), pp. 315–17.
25   London advisory committee on migration, meeting, 23 August 1927, AA: CP211/2; bundle 87.
26   While this account synthesises very much data, there is one outstanding consolidated source: 'Migrants. Medical Examination … Report by Sir Neville Howse', *Commonwealth Parliamentary Papers*, 1923–4, vol. 2. The DMC's annual reports also are valuable in this way. For Howse, see A. J. Hill, *Australian Dictionary of Biography*, vol. 9 (1983), pp. 384–6.
27   Howse, *Report*, p. 5.
28   Memorandum, 11 August 1927, AA: CP211/2; bundle 82.
29   E. J. Little, QSA: IMM/N200, and J. H. Probert, QSA: IMM/N240.
30   E. Y. Taylor, evidence, *Western Australian Parliamentary Papers*, 1925.
31   Letter, December 1929, AA: A461; N348/1/8.
32   H. F. Farrands, letter, 9 March 1928, QSA: IMM/172.
33   Whiskard, evidence to Economic Advisory Council committee, PRO: CAB58/164; Gepp, report of activities and discussions, November–December 1926, AA: CP211/2; bundle 8.
34   These camps were at Brandon and Claydon (England), and Richill (Northern Ireland); the War Office had a similar camp at Catterick, which trained soldiers about to be demobilised.
35   Hunter, letter, 18 June 1924, PRO: CO721/91.
36   See above, p. 51.
37   Ministry of Labour, memorandum, January 1925, PRO: CO721/107.
38   'Outside Organisation', AA: A786; C75/3; also memorandum, 11 August 1927, AA: CP211/2; bundle 82.
39   Colonel Clegg, London advisory committee on migration, meeting, 23 August 1927, AA: CP211/2; bundle 82.

40   See chapter 1, note 69; subsequently the most persuasive statement to this effect was by A. L. S. Wake, organiser of a local Anglican Immigration Committee, to the Royal Commission on Group Settlement, *Western Australian Parliamentary Papers*, 1925.

41   Most specifically affirmed in Ministry of Labour evidence to the inter-departmental committee on social insurance, PRO: DO57/14.

42   Evidence to Economic Advisory Council committee, PRO: CAB58/164.

43   As elsewhere elaborated, the archives of Queensland, South Australia, and Tasmania retain files on all nominees. Much sparser, however, is documentation about nominations which aborted, Queensland alone retaining anything substantial in this regard.

44   Memorandum, 9 October 1929, AA: A786; D/1/1.

45   *Capital*, p. 857.

46   Most explicitly stated at PRO: DO57/28.

47   Hodgkiss case, PRO: DO57/34.

48   J. B. Greene, letter, AA: A461; N348/1/8. DMC, letters, June–July 1927, QSA: IMM/175.

49   DMC, letter, 11 February 1928, QSA: IMM/174.

50   Borrie, *World Population*, p. 88.

51   Submission to Economic Advisory Council committee, PRO: CAB58/164.

52   'Report of the Acting High Commissioner', *Commonwealth Parliamentary Papers*, 1922–3, vol. 2,p. 9.

53   R. V. Wilson, minute, 25 January 1926, AA: CP211/2; bundle 82.

54   Melbourne *Herald*, 29 April 1927.

55   T. E. Wyett to Royal Commission on Migrant Land Settlement, PROV: VPRS2568.

56   'Supply of boys for Australia', PRO: DO57/46.

57   Marr, *White*, p. 94.

58   R. C. Wallhead, House of Commons, 12 November 1928, said that Czecho-slovaks in Sydney were alleging that they had been told that the building of Canberra would supply employment for 20 years; PRO: CO721/104 has a file as to Cypriots having paid full fares on a ship that went only part way to Australia; SAWA: PD690/24 offers similar data re Yugoslavs.

59   On this, among other points, I am indebted to Yvonne Furneaux-Young, and her thesis.

60   Corbett, 'Battling', p. 44; Wignall, *Chancy Times*, p. 121.

61   Macnaghten, memorandum, 1 November 1921, PRO: CO721/26. See Northcliffe, *Empty Continent*.

62   K. L. Blaxter, 'Orr', *Dictionary of National Biography*, 1971–1980 (1986), pp. 644–5.

63   Quotations, pp. 146, 249, 143.

64   Guest, letter, 5 June 1929, and Gepp, 19 July 1929, AA: A786; G106/3.

65   *Silver Spoon*, part 2; *White Monkey*, generally.

66   P. 205.

67   Letter (to McDougall), 12 July 1929, AA: A786; K73/6.

68   *Australia's Minor Agricultural Industries*, unpaginated. This, with the comment, is at SRSA: GRG7; series 23; 1921/226. Here too is a copy of a

complementary handbook on *Fruit Growing in Australia*, while at the same
1921/397 is *Dairy Industry in Australia.*

69 R. Ward, 'Kidman', *Australian Dictionary of Biography*, vol. 9 (1983),
pp. 583–5.

70 The fullest listing seems to be that in *The Land of the Better Chance*, for which
see below.

71 Robinson's work is described in his application for appointment as a
Commissioner with the DMC, AA: A432; 29/2220. The National Film and
Sound Archive, Canberra, has an interesting file on the 'Know Your Own
Country' series. The cameraman was A. F. Ive. The call from the OSD, and
other pertinent data, is reported in documentation about a publicity sub-
committee of the OSC, PRO: DO57/15.

72 E. H. Farrer, letters and cables, early 1924, AONSW: Premier's Correspondence 9/4911B and 9/4914A; A24/1006 and 2665. 'Report of the High
Commissioner … 1923', *Commonwealth Parliamentary Papers*, 1923–4,
vol. 2, p. 12.

73 Much emphasised in evidence to the Royal Commission on Migrant Land
Settlement, PROV: VPRS2568

74 F. R. Chappell and C. J. Brackenbury, both of Hobart.

75 M. Rutledge, 'Leist', *Australian Dictionary of Biography*, vol. 10 (1986),
pp. 70–1.

76 Copies of this item and *Domestic Girl* seen in Royal Commonwealth Society
Library.

77 Mitchell Library.

78 AA: A786; J22/2. *Speedway to Prosperity* has not been seen.

79 Furneaux-Young, ' "The Right Stamp of Migrant" ', esp. p. 4.

80 PRO: DO57/19. This is one of the strikingly few issues of the *Handbook*
which remain extant.

81 PRO: DO57/59.

82 See above, p. 122-3.

83 These developments are noted in successive OSC *Reports*, notably for 1927
(Command 3085) and 1928 (3308); see also PRO: DO57/93.

84 AA: CP211/2; bundle 82.

85 W. Taylor, memorandum, late 1925, PRO: LAB2/1233/EDO/312/1925.

86 Farrer, report on migration, AONSW: Premier's Correspondence 9/4914A;
A24/2265.

87 Wake, evidence to the Royal Commission on Group Settlement, *Western
Australian Parliamentary Papers*, 1925.

88 R. V. Wilson, minute, 25 June 1926, AA: CP211/2; bundle 82.

89 The following complex story is best documented in a statement by
O. Thompson, 14 June 1927, AA: CP211/2, bundle 8; and complementary files
at PRO: DO57/35 and AA: A457; B/400/2. Perth *Daily News*, 7 December 1929
reported Burton's Western Australian origins.

90 Bankes Amery, letter, 9 December 1927, AA: CP211/2; bundle 76.

91 The process is best described by Wyatt, evidence, PROV: VPRS2568.

92 C. E. Youngson file, PRO: DO57/50.

93 OSC, *Report* … 1929 (Command 3589), p. 20.

94   The Society's papers are of major interest. The OSC *Reports* make consistent and substantial reference to its work. See also Monk, *New Horizons*, and J. Gothard in Constantine, *Emigrants and Empire*, pp. 72–95.

95   This account draws from files at PRO: T161/187/S17352/1 and 2, and CO721/97.

96   Letter, 8 October 1925, PRO: MH57/54.

97   Gibson file, PRO: MH52/340;; Knowles file, QSA: IMM/55.

98   *Report ...* 1923 (Command 2107), p. 17. This particular *Report* is outstandingly informative on relevant matters, but data appeared each year.

99   Most explicitly in file on migration conference, PRO: DO57/29.

100   OSC, *Report ... 1923* (Command 2107), p. 6; for Stanley, PRO: CO721/75.

101   Macnaghten (paraphrasing and approving O. Thompson), 5 November 1927, PRO: DO57/71.

102   Letter, 16 January 1925, PRO: CO721/117.

103   AA: CP211/2; bundle 6.

104   Institute file, PRO: DO57/28.

105   Of much comment to this effect, the most explicit is in the Army file, PRO: DO57/61.

106   SRSA: GRG7; series 76; 45.

107   AA: CP211/2; bundle 6 documents work of both Army and YMCA as follows; another useful file on the latter is at PRO: CO721/96.

108   Taylor, evidence to Royal Commission on Group Settlement, *Western Australia Parliamentary Papers*, 1925.

109   Plant, memorandum, 7 July 1929; PRO: DO57/91, and Crutchley, letter, 10 October 1929, DO57/118, the latter referring to both Coleman and Victoria.

110   PRO: CO721/75.

111   PRO: DO57/83.

112   Evidence, Royal Commission on Group Settlement, *Western Australian Parliamentary Papers*, 1925.

113   PRO: DO57/156.

114   Bruce, letter, February 1924, QSA: PRE96.

115   Coldrey, *Child Migration*. With shame, I admit to having discovered very belatedly indeed that Martindale visited Australia in 1928 and consequently wrote an interesting book—*The Risen Sun* (London, 1929). Its final pages affirm a continuing commitment to immigration, but Martindale recognises migrants' difficulties and Australians' suspicions. Martindale, I now learn, was a distinguished scholar and a man of general remarkability.

116   J. S. R. McLeod, memorandum, PRO: DO57/108, a piece of general importance. The Mitchell Library holds annual reports etc. relating to Barnardo work.

117   G. W. Fuller, letter (to Bruce), 3 December 1924, AONSW: Premier's Correspondence 9/1972; A28/1709.

118   PRO: CO721/53.

119   Readers are reminded of pertinent statistics given at pp. 4–5, above.

120   Sherington, *Dreadnought Boys*.

121   Bankes Amery, letter, 15 September 1927, PRO: DO57/33, and associated papers, which relate also to the Young Australia League (enclosing Simons's *Reflections*), as does his letter of 6 December 1925, DO57/1.

122   Of much documentation, the most informative is that at PRO: CO721/62.
123   Furneaux-Young, ' "The Right Stamp of Migrant" ', ch. 5; her richest source is PRO: CO721/100. Furneaux-Young was the specified 'intuitive student'.
124   PRO: DO57/85.
125   PRO: CO721/52.
126   The Society's papers give a little information, but only that.
127   'Report of the Agent-General for 1928', *Queensland Parliamentary Papers*, 1929, vol. 2.
128   PRO: CO721/57 documents the most vigorous example, Devon and Cornwall.
129   Perth *Daily News*, 9 October 1926, PRO: DO57/27.
130   Darroch, *Lawrence in Australia*, as indexed for Forresters and Marchbanks.
131   A. E. Weymouth, report, AOT: PD55/8/36. For Cadburys', see P. S. Cadbury, letters, PRO: DO57/108.
132   The Agent-General's Reports were published each year in *Queensland Parliamentary Papers*.
133   PRO: CO721/113.
134   Ellison, 'Immigration Issues in Tasmania', ch. 2.
135   PRO: DO57/141.
136   AA: CP211/2; bundles 105–6.
137   Rickard, letter, 24 June 1926, PRO: DO57/28.
138   Jessamine Green, for whom see AOT: PD55/16/28, and SOSBW Papers.
139   Letter, 1 January 1922, PRO: CO721/74, and considerable correspondence, SOSBW Papers. For the somewhat similar endeavours of Beatrice Mac-Donald, CO721/73, and also AONSW: Premier's Correspondence 9/1972; A28/1709.
140   Letter, 28 March 1923, AA: A1633.
141   Minute, 18 March 1925, PRO: CO721/103. For Hunter, see above p. 44.
142   In Jupp, *Australian People*, p. 93.
143   PRO: T161/184/S16952.
144   *Ministry of Labour Gazette*, a monthly publication, gives pertinent figures, e.g. in May 1926 specifying 1138 for total IFS emigration to Australia in 1924; 1076 in 1925. Even the British Library, London, appears to hold but limited files of the Gazette.
145   *Industrial Development*, p. 170.
146   *Immigration Contribution*, p. 10a. I thank the author for further help.
147   The Queensland Agent-General sometimes included relevant material in his *Reports*: see especially that for 1927 in *Parliamentary Papers*, 1928. There is a great deal more, but of dubious value, in the various series of migrant records. Perhaps least dubious are those in the shipping data described at note 154 below.
148   Cook, House of Representatives, 17 June 1929.
149   H. M. J. Frewen, SRSA: GRG7; series 10; 1579.
150   'Migration. British Oversea Settlement Delegation to Australia. Report. May 1924', *Commonwealth Parliamentary Papers*, 1923–4, vol. 2, p. 9.
151   'Report of the Under-Secretary for Lands and Immigration', *Western Australian Parliamentary Papers*, 1926, p. 5. The statement was repeated in succeeding years of this series.

152   Plant, memorandum, 27 August 1923, PRO: CO721/72.
153   *Notes for Welfare Superintendents on Ships Carrying Migrants to Australia*, SRSA: GRG7; series 76; 39.
154   Now comprising Commonwealth Record Series B4094, held at the Australian Archives, Melbourne. Future references will specify the particular sailing. The sample, as will become evident, did not probe far into the alphabet, but ranged fairly through the 1920s.
155   P. 41; following, p. 50.
156   See above, p. 27.
157   PRO: T161/871/S16053.
158   *Ballarat*, (sailing date) 17 June 1926; *Bendigo*, 17 December 1925; *Esperance Bay*, 21 September 1926.
159   *Benalla*, 21 June 1923.
160   *Borda*, 1 June 1922.
161   *Baradine*, 30 September 1926.
162   *Ballarat*, 1 November 1923.
163   *Ballarat*, 1 November 1923.
164   Masson, letter, 27 August 1927, AA: CP211/2, bundle 3. Mitchell, letter, 24 May 1926, PRO: DO57/28.
165   Sydney *Daily Guardian*, 24 July 1923, referring to Ballarat, 24 May 1923.
166   Roe, 'Strikebound in Cape Town'.
167   Report of interview, 17 February 1923, PRO: CO721/74.
168   *Trooper*, pp. 92–3.
169   AOT: SWD4; M9/795.
170   *Emigrant*, p. 53.
171   *West Australian*, 2 February 1925.
172   *Amateur Settlers*, p. 35.
173   *Benalla*, 2 April 1925.
174   *Borda*, 28 July 1927.
175   *Diogenes*, 4 December 1925.
176   *Benalla*, 21 June 1923.
177   20 September 1923.
178   *Borda*, 17 February 1927.
179   *Borda*, 1 June 1922.
180   M. E. Randle, letter, 26 September 1926, SRSA: GRG7; series 8; 597.

10 IMMIGRATION

1   Of course not every file has been scrutinised. Nor has the sampling been scientific. Rather I browsed through all the material, sensitive for general impressions and for enlightening detail.
2   J. Costello, oral history transcript, Battye Library.
3   SAWA: LSD2763/29; for Pullin, see Gabbedy, *Group Settlement*, as indexed.
4   T. Erswell, letter, 18 April 1927, AA: A786; K61/1. 'Slavely' is in original.
5   See above, p. 73.
6   L. L. Hill, House of Assembly (of South Australia), 9 May 1929; M. F. Troy, Legislative Assembly (of Western Australia), 16 August 1928. See also SAWA: PD690/24 and 498/28.

7   A. E. Weymouth, AOT: PD55/9/36.
8   Part 2, p. 143.
9   P. 127.
10 Letter, 24 November 1922, B. W. Hollins file, SRSA: GRG7; series 9; 5.
11 Letter, 21 June 1927, R. P. Hanlon file, QSA: IMM/N120.
12 Letter, 15 June 1926, S. W. Johnson file, QSA: IMM/N170.
13 Evidence, Select Committee on Boy Migration Scheme, *South Australia Parliamentary Papers*, 1924.
14 F. C. Derrick, letter, 11 February 1925, SRSA: GRG7; series 6; 985.
15 J. Kemp, letter, September 1931, QSA: IMM/N180.
16 N. Crawford, to Select Committee on Boy Migration Scheme.
17 Evidently 1930, SRSA: GRG7; series 80; 2.
18 J. F. English, letter, SRSA: GRG7; series 6; 987.
19 C. F. Denyer, letter (concerning R. Henderson), 28 March 1931, QSA: IMM/N130.
20 Evidence, Select Committee on Boy Migration Scheme.
21 G. R. Laffer, to Select Committee on Boy Migration Scheme.
22 G. N. MacCoy, letter, April 1929, SRSA: GRG7; series 7; 1516.
23 Bankes Amery, letter, 30 September 1925, PRO: CO721/105. The bureaucrat was F. W. Kitching. For Kitching's further views and other interesting matter see 'Report of the Select Committee on the Juvenile Migrants Apprenticeship (Repeal) Bill', *NSW Parliamentary Papers*, 1925–6, joint volumes, vol. 1.
24 Notably T. W. Blenkinsop, SRSA: GRG7; series 7; 1564.
25 Furneaux-Young, ' "The Right Stamp of Migrant" ', ch. 5.
26 Weymouth, AOT: PD55/9/36. The use of 'nominated' here is imprecise, Weymouth thus designating original seekers of boy-labour.
27 Leitch's file, including the obscene letter, is at AOT: SWD4; M1/507.
28 B. Thurstan, letter (concerning R. N. Maxwell, the boy), 26 November 1925, AOT: SWD4; M1/732.
29 A. Duncan, letter, 14 February 1926, AOT: SWD4; M1/733.
30 Plant, memorandum, 25 November 1925, PRO: CO721/105. Debate, House of Assembly (of South Australia), 2 December 1924. SRSA: GRG7; series 76; 25, and GRG7; series 80; 2.
31 QSA: PRE/118.
32 G. Knight, letter (concerning B. Mills), AOT: SWD4; M1/598.
33 J. Sutherland, AOT: SWD4; M1/544.
34 W. Davies, 18 December 1923, Legislative Assembly; generally Sherington, *Dreadnought Boys*, pp. 16–18.
35 'Report from the Select Committee of the Legislative Council on the Boy Migration Scheme', *South Australian Parliamentary Papers*, 1924.
36 The Mitchell Library holds the only recorded substantial file.
37 A. H. Hanson, letter, July 1930, QSA: IMM/N120. R. Y. Lee, letters 5 July and 30 September 1923, PRO: CO721/73. C. O. Jopson, letter, 24 September 1926, SRSA: GRG7; series 6; 999. N. U. Graham, letter, November 1926, QSA: IMM/N105.
38 Letter, 15 August 1926, SRSA: GRG7; series 6; 7.
39 J. Pollard, AOT: SWD4; M1/733.
40 Furneaux-Young, ' "The Right Stamp of Migrant" ', pp. 44–7.

41   Crutchley, report, January 1932, PRO: T161/531/S34376/02.

42   PRO: DO57/124.

43   Roe in Constantine, *Empire and Emigration*, p. 117. 'Dom' was the Sydney Domain, where many destitute people spent their nights, wrapped in newspapers. There is reference to the club established for these boys below.

44   'Lloyd', *The Oxford Companion to Australian Folklore* (1993), pp. 242–3; oral history collection, NLA.

45   Cole, *Wildman Plains*.

46   Soldatow, *Hooton*, p. 37.

47   Commonwealth Immigration Office, letter, 29 April 1928, SRSA: GRG; series 23. This piece is illuminating on various aspects of the domestics' treatment.

48   F. Hood, AOT: SWD4; M9/857, and A. Gee, M1/637. D. Fitchett, SRSA: GRG7; series 8; 133.

49   Commonwealth Immigration Office, letter, 19 March 1930, SRSA: GRG7; series 23.

50   G. S. Pott, report on Tasmania, PRO: CO721/74.

51   H. Reynolds, memorandum, 20 December 1923, AOT: SWD5; Abell, speech at 1924 New Settlers' League Conference, QSA: IMM/214.

52   B. Sampson, memorandum, 17 October 1924, AOT: SWD4; M1/708; this put sympathetically what angered many.

53   Letter, 14 January 1924, QSA: PRE/122.

54   See above, p. 28.

55   Letter, 23 May 1928, PRO: DO57/11.

56   Discussion of Australian sub-committee, early 1929, SOSBW Papers.

57   Letter, 24 May 1926, PRO: DO57/28.

58   Memorandum, 30 April 1924, QSA: PRE/122. The sign '/-' meant shillings (per week).

59   M. Redshaw, December 1923, AOT: SWD4; M1/621.

60   A. F. Abram, letter, April 1922, SRSA: GRG7; series 23; 89/1922.

61   A. Hall, letter, 28 August 1924 AOT: SWD4; M1/676.

62   E. K. Wilson, SRSA: GRG7; series 8; 90.

63   M. Fairey, letter, 19 September 1929, AOT: SWD4; M9/869. The house was Quorn Hall.

64   PRO: DO57/10 and 29. Macnaghten's comment is at latter.

65   M. Minnis, SRSA: GRG7; series 8; 440.

66   Diary, 28 November 1929, Crutchley Papers.

67   P. Bowerman, AOT: SWD4; M1/589.

68   *Imperial Colonist*, vol. 20 (1923), pp. 186–7. The writer's own, betrothed, Australian was different!

69   M. I. Hunt, letter, late 1929, SRSA: GRG7; series 8; 450.

70   M. Arzeian, letters, 20 July 1924, 11 February 1925, and 30 April 1928, SRSA: GRG7; series 8; 134.

71   These extracts come respectively from SOSBW, *Annual Reports* for 1923, 1924, and 1925. There is evidence that the SOSBW showed restraint and discrimination in its publicity.

72   Pott's reports are scattered through PRO: CO721/74.

73   'Migration. British Overseas Delegation to Australia. Report', *Commonwealth Parliamentary Papers*, 1923–4, vol. 2, esp. p. 39.

74 Memorandum, 19 November 1925, PRO: CO721/104.
75 PRO: DO57/101.
76 Autobiography, Crutchley Papers.
77 Memorandum concerning a Ms Robins, reporting on a group of domestics for whom she had been shipboard matron, PRO: DO57/126.
78 PRO: DO57/125.
79 Fairbridge, letter, 6 July 1922, PRO: CO721/56. Wauchope, report, CO721/98. Diary, 8 May 1931, Crutchley Papers.
80 PROV: Chief Secretary's Department 1927; VPRS 3992; R1858.
81 J. J. Daly, letter, 19 December 1929, AA: A1; 1932/7598.
82 AA: A445; 124/6/45. PRO: DO57/173.
83 Bavin, Legislative Assembly, 5 December 1928.
84 For an analysis of one State's deportations see Ellison, 'Immigration Issues in Tasmania', ch. 3.
85 Papers associated with Governor-General Stonehaven, letter, 7 December 1925, PRO: DO35/1.
86 Esp. Hurley at conference, 17 August 1926, AA: CP211/2; bundle 2.
87 Letter, 27 August 1926, AA: CP211/2; bundle 4.
88 Letter, 1 December 1928, PRO: DO35/66.
89 Furneaux-Young, ' "The Right Stamp of Migrant" ', ch. 4. The following story of W. C. Wood is told here; I draw from that and the crucial file, AOT: SWD4; M9/188.
90 SRSA: GRG7; series 8; 128.
91 SRSA: GRG7; series 8; 16.
92 Roe in Constantine, *Emigrants and Empire*, p. 116.
93 I. R. Bavin file, SRSA: GRG7; series 9; 1433.
94 Roe in Constantine, *Emigrants and Empire*, p. 115.
95 C. B. S. Davies, letter, 18 April 1934, QSA: IMM/N65; T. J. Green file, IMM/N110.
96 AOT: SWD4; M9/799, and following, SWD4; M9/529.
97 Jupp, 'Factors affecting … Australian Population', p. 227.
98 Senate, 25 November 1921.
99 Strickland, *Thirkell*, p. 160.
100 AA: A786; D43/1.
101 Stevaton file, AOT: SWD4; M9/400.
102 P. 293; I thank Simon Harris especially for bringing this book and its author to my attention.
103 *Glory Hole*, esp. p. 155.
104 Report, and associated papers, April 1924, PRO: CO721/97.
105 *Drift of Things*, p. 35.
106 Heyward, *Malley Affair*.
107 Abell, letter, 2 June 1927, QSA: IMM/175 is interesting and persuasive as to this. For a fine case study from Tasmania, Furneaux-Young, ' "The Right Stamp of Migrant" ', ch. 6.
108 *Industrial Development*, pp. 193–4.
109 Pope and Withers, *Immigration and Unemployment*.
110 For a recent exemplification, see Macintyre, 'Communist Party of Australia'.
111 See above, pp. 5–6.
112 *Emigrant*, pp. 170–1.

113   Corbett, 'Battling'.
114   Letter, 20 January 1929, PRO: DO35/66.
115   Letter, 16 November 1927, PRO: DO35/27.
116   D. Dingsdag, 'Nelson', *Australian Dictionary of Biography*, vol. 10 (1986), pp. 675–6, and G. Browne, 'Orr', vol. 11 (1988), pp. 97–8. I thank Christopher Cunneen, of the *Dictionary* staff, for his help.
117   Ellison, 'Immigration Issues in Tamania', pp. 89–91; for militance at Rapson's, AOT: SWD4; M9/830.
118   Sharpley, *Great Delusion*.
119   A. Spaull, 'Dedman', *Australian Dictionary of Biography*, vol. 13 (1993), pp. 606–7; like Spaull, I have enjoyed the help of Ms Ruth Rodgers.
120   Letter, 22 June 1931, PRO: DO57/138.
121   W. C. Brown, report, 1929, PRO: DO57/119. Brown was an Anglican clergyman who went to Australia as a welfare officer and then travelled around. His report endorses the generally drear picture of migrant experience.
122   *Emigrant to Australia*, pp. 174–6.
123   W. E. Kallend.
124   Constantine, *Emigrants and Empire*, pp. 117–18.
125   For Lamidey, see his *Political Success*; for McGowan and Warner, the former's *Core of the Apple* and Ellison, 'Immigration Issues in Tasmania', pp. 46–7.
126   While this passage depends on personal knowledge, there is more formal pertinent record in the Tasmaniana Index, State Library of Tasmania.
127   P. S. Cadbury, letter, 29 June 1929, PRO: DO57/108.
128   Walter Pless has kindly made available to me a tape-recorded interview with Tuting.
129   Roe in Constantine, *Emigrants and Empire*, p. 114; following, ditto.
130   W. M. Uren file, SRSA: GRG7; series 9; 180.
131   F. Dodd, letter, 22 December 1924, PRO: CO721/115.
132   See above, p. 156.
133   PRO: T161/531/S34376/02.
134   H. E. Jones, letter, 1926, QSA: PRE/122.
135   AA: A432; 29/2220.
136   Conference, 17 August 1926, AA: CP211/2; bundle 2.
137   Conference, 7–9 October 1924, QSA: IMM/175.
138   R. Martin file, QSA: IMM/N200.
139   See esp. Forster, letter, 27 April 1921, and associated papers, PRO: CO418/205.
140   Letters of 6 October 1926 (Rischbeith) and 27 October 1927 (Masson), AA: CP211/2; bundle 4.
141   Letter, 7 March 1922, SAWA: PD474/21.
142   L. J. Hurley, historical account, AA: CP211/2; bundle 2.
143   *New Settlers' Handbook to Victoria* (Melbourne), p. 131. This is held at the State Library of Victoria, where too are the pamphlets attributed to Gilchrist, while other League offerings (*Makeshift Home Made Furniture from Kerosene Cases; Outback Homes and How to Build Them*) are at SRSA: GRG7; series 76; 39.
144   Letters, 14 and 28 April 1927, AA: CP211/2; bundle 4. Gilchrist merits honour among historians especially for his compilation of comprehensive materials concerning John Dunmore Lang, for whom see p. 6 above.

145 There is much documentation at QSA, notably at IMM/214 and 217.
146 Bankes Amery, letter, 10 October 1926, PRO: DO57/5.
147 Letter, 29 September 1925, PRO: CO721/105.
148· Report, AA: CP211/2; bundle 98. This concentrated on Victoria and Queensland.
149 *Sydney Morning Herald*, 3 September 1927.
150 Letter, 7 May 1930, PRO: DO 57/149.
151 AA: CP211/2; bundle 5.
152 The best general account is in 'Migration. British Overseas Delegation to Australia. Report', *Commonwealth Parliamentary Papers*, 1923–4, vol. 2, pp. 38–40; and Garrett's report as referred in note 148 above and as supplemented by that of June 1932, PRO: T161/531/S34376/02. The latter dealt especially with Western Australia.
153 The Mitchell Library holds the fullest file. The best archival material is at PRO: DO57/145.
154 J. I. Roe, 'Booth', *Australian Dictionary of Biography*, vol. 7 (1979), pp. 345–6.
155 AA: A432; 29/2220.
156 PRO: CO721/96 has relevant documentation.
157 Report, 1928, AA: CP211/2; bundle 5.
158 Letter, 28 December 1929, PRO: DO57/117.
159 B. Godly, PRO: DO57/50.
160 Enclosure in letter, 6 February 1929, PRO: DO 57/98.
161 PRO: CAB24/276; CP96.
162 *Commonwealth Parliamentary Papers*, 1923–4, vol. 2, p. 12; Sir Arthur Stanley, report of conversations, 7 February 1923, PRO: CO721/67.
163 Blaikie, *Smith's Weekly*, pp. 104–6.
164 Kirkpatrick, *Sea Coast of Bohemia*, p. 284.
165 Tennant, *Evatt*, pp. 57–60.
166 House of Assembly, 1 and 6 November 1923.
167 A. F. Winnington Ingram, note of statement, 25 March 1927, AA: CP211/2; bundle 111.
168 *Spoils of Opportunity*, pp. 62–3.
169 Best documented at AA: CP211/2; bundle 74.
170 Legislative Assembly (of Victoria), 31 July 1923; see above, p. 103.
171 Roe in Constantine, *Emigrants and Empire*, p. 115.
172 AOT: SWD4; M9/655.
173 Notes on visit, 1926, PRO: DO57/43; for Salisbury, see above, p. 85.
174 Letter, 26 September 1929, PRO: DO57/108.
175 *Migration and Unemployment*, p. 18.
176 See above, p. 157.
177 6 April 1936, PRO: DO114/89.
178 Nicholls Papers.

AFTERWORD

1 PRO: T161/1412/S50896/1.
2 Hay, 'Institute of Public Affairs'.

Bibliography

ARCHIVAL MATERIAL

Australian Archives, Canberra

AA1970/555: S. M. Bruce; Further papers 1918–29.

A1: Home and Territories Department; Correspondence.

A32: External Affairs Department; Correspondence with the Governor-General.

A367: Investigation Branch; Correspondence.

A432: Attorney-General's Department; Correspondence.

A436: Department of the Interior; Correspondence: British Migrants.

A445: Department of Immigration; Correspondence; policy.

A457: Prime Minister's Department; Correspondence.

A458: Prime Minister's Department; Correspondence.

A461: Prime Minister's Department; Correspondence.

A515: Department of Markets and Migration; Correspondence.

A601: Department of Commerce; Correspondence.

A659: Department of the Interior; Correspondence; general, passports.

A786: Prime Minister's Department, Development Branch; Correspondence.

A981: Department of External Affairs; Correspondence.

A1486: S. M. Bruce; Press cuttings re Imperial Conference 1923.

A1633: M. L. Shepherd; Correspondence with W. M. Hughes.

A2718: Secretary to Cabinet; Bruce–Page ministry, minutes, submissions.

A3934: Prime Minister's Department; Secret and confidential correspondence.

B4094: Commonwealth Immigration Office; Ships' Files relating to the Assisted Passage Scheme. (Note: as remarked, this series is held in the Melbourne repository.)

CP30/3: J. A. Lyons; Correspondence 1931–7, mainly personal representations.

CP78/22: Governor-General; Correspondence.

CP103/3: Prime Minister's Department; Correspondence and papers regarding Imperial Conferences.

CP103/11: Department of Prime Minister and Cabinet; Correspondence.

CP103/12: Prime Minister's Department; Records of Imperial Conferences.

CP211/1: Development and Migration Commission; Minutes.

CP211/2: Development and Migration Commission; Correspondence.

CP268/3: Prime Minister's Department; Various personal files.

CP314/1: Development and Migration Commission, and Development Branch; Correspondence and reports.

CP314/3: J. Gunn: Personal papers.

CP367/2: Development and Migration Commission and Development Branch; Papers and reports, especially as to consultative committee on science and development.

CP820/1: G. F. Pearce; Personal papers 1926–31.

M111: S. M. Bruce; Correspondence with F. L. McDougall.

Archives Office of Tasmania

AD: Agriculture Department.

CB: Committees and Boards.

PD: Premier's Department.

RC: Royal Commission.

SWD: Social Welfare Department. Series 4 holds basic correspondence with migrants, series 5 further 'unregistered' material.

Public Record Office, UK

BT56: Board of Trade; Chief Industrial Advisor.

BT60: Board of Trade; Department of Overseas Trade.

BT65: Board of Trade; Power, Transport and Economic Department.

BT70: Board of Trade; Statistical Department.

CAB23: Cabinet; War Cabinet, Minutes.

CAB24: Cabinet; Memoranda, including Cabinet Papers.

CAB27: Cabinet; Committees.

CAB32: Cabinet; Imperial Conferences to 1939.

CAB58: Cabinet; Economic Advisory Council.

CO418: Australia (General); Original Correspondence.

CO532: Colonial Office; Dominions. Overseas Correspondence.

CO721: Colonial Office; Overseas Settlement. Original Correspondence.

CO886: Colonial Office; Confidential Prints.

DO35: Dominions Office; Dominions. Original Correspondence.

DO57: Dominions Office; Overseas Settlement. Original Correspondence.

DO114: Dominions Office; Confidential Prints.

DO117: Dominions Office; Supplementary Original Correspondence, 1926–9.

DO126: Dominions Office; High Commission and Consular Archives Australia; Correspondence, 1931–41.

LAB2: Ministry of Labour; Correspondence.

MH: Ministry of Health; Public Assistance.

T160: Treasury; Finance Files.

T161: Treasury; Supply Files.

T176: Treasury; Niemeyer Papers.

Queensland State Archives

PRE: Premier's Department. Series 100–1 have correspondence about assisted migration schemes 1919–23.

IMM: Immigration (with following N: Nomination Cases). IMM 5–107 and IMM N/1–309 hold individual files. IMM/171 has further correspondence re schemes;

172: miscellaneous correspondences, 175: general correspondence on migration policy.

State Archives of Western Australia
AG: Agent–General's.
LSD: Lands and Survey Department.
PD: Premier's Department.

State Records of South Australia
GRG: Government Record Group. Group 7 pertains to migration, and all the following series belong there. Series 6: applications for farm apprenticeship and consequent correspondence, 1922–4. Series 7: similar, 1927–9. Series 8: equivalent for domestics. Series 9: correspondence as to male 'selectees' from other States. Series 10: nominations. Series 23: items of general correspondence from pertinent departments. Series 24: pertinent correspondence from Intelligence and Tourist Bureau. Series 76: miscellaneous material re miscellaneous schemes. Series 80: miscellaneous items, notably (item 8) a paper by V. H. Ryan on boy migration.

PRIVATE MANUSCRIPT MATERIAL: 'PAPERS'

S. Baldwin: Churchill College, Cambridge.
British Dominions Emigration Society: Greater London Record Office.
E. T. Crutchley: Microfilm collection, NLA, M1829–30.
CSIRO: retained by the Organisation, Canberra.
H. W. Gepp: NLA, MS1949; 'Addresses'.
Gepp Family: NLA, MS2052.
W. M. Hughes: NLA, MS1538; Series 16, 'Prime Minister, 1915–23'.
G. Huxley: NLA, MS7413; 'Autobiography. Extracts 1928'.
J. G. Latham: NLA, MS1009; Series 1, 'General Correspondence'.
J. A. Lyons: NLA, MS4851.
F. L. McDougall: NLA, MS6890.
S. M. Nicholls: La Trobe Library, State Library of Victoria, Box 2604.
C. S. Nathan: SAWA, MN297.
F. K. Officer: NLA, MS2629; Series 1, 'Correspondence'.
G. F. Pearce: NLA, part 1 = MS213; Series 5, 'Miscellaneous ... Correspondence' and
    Series 15, 'Papers relating to the Development and Migration Commission'.
W. S. Robinson: University of Melbourne Archives.
Society for the Oversea Settlement of British Women: Fawcett Library, City of
    London Polytechnic.

ORAL MATERIAL

As noticed at chapter 10, note 2, I found one helpful item in the oral history transcripts at the Battye Library. More substantial were pertinent offerings from the New South Wales Bicentennial Oral History Project, among the 200 contributors to which were eight farmboys and a sizeable number of other migrants. I read this material at the Oral History room, NLA. There too is held the recording of an interview with A. L. Lloyd (identified as TRC2949), which is of supreme interest. My own oral work is further remarked in notes.

SECONDARY SOURCES

Amery, L. S., *My Political Life*, 3 vols, London, 1953–5.

—— see Barnes, J. and Nicholson, D.

Andrews, E. M., *The Anzac Illusion. Anglo-Australian Relations during World War I*, Melbourne, 1993.

Appleyard, R. T. and Schedvin, C. B. (editors), *Australian Financiers. Biographical Essays*, Melbourne, 1988.

Apsley, A. A. B., *Why and How I Went to Australia as a Settler*, London, 1926.

—— and V. M. B., *The Amateur Settlers*, London, 1926.

Attwood, B., 'The Bank of England and the Origins of the Niemeyer Mission 1921–1930', *Australian Economic History Review*, vol. 22 (1992), pp. 66–83.

Barnes, J., and Nicholson, D. (editors), *The Leo Amery Diaries … 1896–1929*, London, 1980.

Beever, A., 'From a Place of "Horrible Destitution", to a Paradise of the Working Class. The Transformation of British Working Class Attitudes to Australia, 1841–1851', *Labour History*, no. 40 (1981), pp. 1–15.

Blaikie, G., *Remember Smith's Weekly. A Biography of an Uninhibited National Australian Newspaper*, Adelaide, 1975.

Bolton, G. C., *A Fine Country To Starve In*, Perth, 1972.

Borrie, W. D., *The Growth and Control of World Population*, London, 1970.

Bridge, C. (editor), *New Perspectives in Australian History*, London, 1990.

Broome, R., *The Victorians. Arriving*, Sydney, 1984.

Butcher, B. W., 'Science and the Imperial Vision. The Imperial Geophysical Survey of 1928–30', *Historical Records of Australian Science*, vol. 6 (1984), pp. 31–43.

Cain, N., 'The Economists and Australian Population Strategy in the Twenties', *Australian Journal of Politics and History*, vol. 20 (1974), pp. 346–59.

——, 'Recovery Policy in Australia 1930–3', *Australian Economic History Review*, vol. 23 (1983), pp. 193–218.

Campbell, P., Mills, R. C., and Portus, G. V. (editors), *Studies in Australian Affairs*, Melbourne, 1928.

Clarke, F. G., 'The Argonauts Civil and Political Club … ', *Labour History*, no. 18 (1970), pp. 32–9.

Coldrey, B. M., *Child Migration, the Australian Government, and the Catholic Church, 1926–1966*, Melbourne, 1992. This is now largely incorporated into the author's *The Scheme. The Christian Brothers and Children in Western Australia*, Perth, 1993.

Cole, T., *Riding the Wildman Plains. The Letters and Diaries … 1923–1943*, Melbourne, 1992.

Constantine, S., *The Making of British Colonial Development Policy, 1910–1940*, London, 1984.

—— (editor), *Emigrants and Empire. British Settlement in the Dominions between the Wars*, Manchester, 1990.

Copland, D. B., 'The Economic Situation in Australia 1918–23', *Economic Journal*, vol. 34 (1924), pp. 32–51.

Corbett, T. W., 'Battling in Australia', *Overland*, no. 53 (1972), pp. 42–4.

Crutchley, B., *Ernest Tristram Crutchley. A Memoir*, Cambridge, 1941.

——, *To be a Printer*, London, 1980.

Cunneen, C., *King's Men. Australia's Governor-Generals from Hopetoun to Isaacs*, Sydney, 1983.

Currie, G. and Graham, J., *The Origins of CSIRO. Science and the Commonwealth Government 1901–1926*, Melbourne, 1966.

Darling, J. R., *Richly Rewarding*, Melbourne, 1978.

Darroch, R., *D. H. Lawrence in Australia*, Melbourne, 1981.

Drummond, I. M., *Imperial Economic Policy 1917–1939. Studies in Expansion and Protection*, London, 1974.

Dryden, P., 'Australian Immigration from World War I to the Depression', Master's thesis, University of Sydney, 1978.

Duncan, W. G. K. and Janes, C. V. (editors), *The Future of Immigration in Australia and New Zealand*, Sydney, 1937.

Dunsdorfs, E., *The Australian Wheat-growing Industry 1788–1948*, Melbourne, 1958.

Eden, A., *Places in the Sun*, London, 1926.

Edge, A. B. B., and Laby, T. H., *Imperial Geophysical Experimental Survey*, Cambridge, 1931.

Edwards, C., *Bruce of Melbourne. Man of Two Worlds*, London, 1965.

Ellison, M., 'A Study of Administrative Policy and Practice. Immigration Issues in Tasmania 1919–36', Master's thesis, University of Tasmania, 1992.

Fairbridge, R., *Pinjarra. The Building of a Farm School*, London, 1937.

Fedorowich, K., 'Foredoomed to Failure. The Re-Settlement of British ex-Servicemen in the Dominions, 1914–1929', Doctoral thesis, London, 1990.

Fitzhardinge, L. F., *William Morris Hughes. A Political Biography*, 2 vols, Sydney, 1964 and 1979.

Forster, C., *Industrial Development in Australia 1920–1930*, Canberra, 1964.

Forsyth, W. D., 'British Migration to Australia. Demographic and Social Aspects', *Economic Record*, vol. 14 (1938), pp. 39–47.

——, *The Myth of Open Spaces. Australian, British and World Trends of Population and Migration*, Melbourne, 1942.

Furneaux-Young, Y., ' "The Right Stamp of Migrant" ', Master's thesis, University of Tasmania, 1992.

Gabbedy, J. P., *Group Settlement*, 2 vols, Perth, 1988.

Galsworthy, J., *The White Monkey*, London, 1924.

——, *The Silver Spoon*, London, 1926.

Gilbert, R. S., *The Australian Loan Council in Federal Fiscal Adjustments 1890–1965*, Canberra, 1973.

Gilchrist, A., *John Dunmore Lang. Chiefly Autobiographical ... Contemporary Documents*, Melbourne, 1952.

Guest, L. H., *The Labour Party and the Empire*, London, 1926.

——, *The New British Empire*, London, 1926.

Gullett, H. S., *The Opportunity in Australia*, London, 1914.

Haggard, H. R., *The Private Diaries ... 1914–1925* (D. S. Higgins, editor), London, 1980.

Hancock, W. K., *Australia*, London, 1930.

——, *Survey of British Commonwealth Affairs: Problems of Economic Policy, 1918–1939*, London, 1942.

Harris, H. L. (editor), *Australia's National Interests and National Policy*, Melbourne, 1938.

Harrison, B., *Separate Spheres. The Opposition to Women's Suffrage in Britain*, London, 1978.

Hart, P. R., 'Lyons: Labour Minister — Leader of the U.A.P.', *Labour History*, no. 17 (1970), pp. 37–51.

Hatfield, W., *I Find Australia*, London, 1937.

Hay, J. R., 'The Institute of Public Affairs and Social Policy in World War II', *Historical Studies*, vol. 20 (1982), pp. 198–216.

Hayden, A., 'The Anti-Immigration Movement 1877–1893', *Royal Australian Historical Society Journal*, vol. 48 (1962), pp. 25–43.

Heyward, M., *The Ern Malley Affair*, Brisbane, 1993.

Hooton, H., see Soldatow.

Howard, F., *The Emigrant*, London, 1928.

Hudson, W. J., *Australia and the League of Nations*, Sydney, 1980.

——, and North, J. (editors), *My Dear P.M. R. G. Casey's Letters to S. M. Bruce, 1924–1929*, Canberra, 1980.

——, and Way, W. (editors), *Letters from a 'Secret Service Agent'. F. L. McDougall to S. M. Bruce, 1924–1929*, Canberra, 1986.

Hunt, I. L., 'Group Settlement in Western Australia', *University Studies in Western Australian History*, vol. 3 (1958), pp. 5–42.

Huxley, G., *Both Hands. An Autobiography*, London, 1970.

Hynes, S., *A War Imagined. The First World War and English Culture*, London, 1990.

Jones, T., *Whitehall Diary* (K. Middlemas, editor), 3 vols, London, 1969–71.

Jupp, J. (editor), *The Australian People. An Encyclopaedia of the Nation, its People and their Origins*, Sydney, 1988.

Jupp, K. M., 'Factors Affecting the Structure of the Australian Population ... 1921–1933', Master's thesis, Australian National University, 1958.

Kirkpatrick, P., *The Sea Coast of Bohemia. Literary Life in Sydney's Roaring Twenties*, Brisbane, 1992.

Knott, J., *Popular Opposition to the 1834 Poor Law*, London, 1986.

Lake, M., *The Limits of Hope. Soldier Settlement in Victoria, 1915–38*, Melbourne, 1987.

Lamidey, N. W., *Partial Success. My Years as a Public Servant*, Sydney, 1970.

La Nauze, J. A., *Alfred Deakin. A Biography*, 2 vols, Melbourne, 1965.

——, *The Making of the Australian Constitution*, Melbourne, 1972.

Lawrence, D. H., *Kangaroo*, London, 1923.

Lee, J., *My Life with Nye*, London, 1980.

Lewis, G., ' "Million Farms" Campaign, NSW 1919–25', *Labour History*, no. 47 (1984), pp. 55–72.

Love, P., 'Niemeyer's Australian Diary ... ', *Historical Studies*, vol. 20 (1982), pp. 261–77.

Loveday, P., 'Anti-Political Political Thought', *Labour History*, no. 17 (1970), pp. 121–35.

Macgregor, L. R., *British Imperialism. Memories and Reflections*, New York, 1968.

Macintyre, S., 'Foundation. The Communist Party of Australia', *Overland*, no. 132 (1993), pp. 6–12.

Mackenzie, J. M., *Propaganda and Empire. The Manipulation of British Public Opinion, 1880–1960*, Manchester, 1984.

—— (editor), *Imperialism and Popular Culture*, Manchester, 1986.

Macnaghten, T. C. (editor), *Empire Opportunities, A Survey of the Possibilities of Overseas Settlement*, London, 1938.

Madgwick, R. B., *Immigration into Eastern Australia 1788–1851*, London, 1937.

Marr, D., *Patrick White. A Life*, Sydney, 1992.

Martin, A. W., *Robert Menzies ... 1894–1943*, Melbourne, 1993.

Marx, K., *Capital*, London, 1946 (Everyman Edition).

Matthews, T., 'The All for Australia League', *Labour History*, no. 17 (1970), pp. 136–47.

McDonald, S. R., 'Victoria's Immigration Scandal of the Thirties', *Victorian Historical Journal*, vol. 49 (1978), pp. 228–37.

McGowan, G., *The Core of the Apple. The Memoirs ...* (F. Strahan, editor), Melbourne, 1982.

Mitchell, J., *Spoils of Opportunity, An Autobiography*, London, 1938.

Monk, U., *New Horizons. A Hundred Years of Women's Migration*, London, 1963.

Moore, A., *The Secret Army and the Premier. Conservative Paramilitary Organisations in New South Wales 1930–32*, Sydney, 1989.

Norris, R., *The Emergent Commonwealth. Australian Federation, Expectation and Fulfilment 1889–1910*, Melbourne, 1975.

Northcliffe, A. H., *The Empty Continent. Australia and its Needs*, London, 1921.

O'Brien, J. B., 'Empire v. National Interests in Australian-British Relations during the 1930s', *Historical Studies*, vol. 22 (1987), pp. 569–86.

Pepperall, R. A., *Emigrant to Australia*, London, 1948.

Phillips, P. D., and Wood, G. L. (editors), *The Peopling of Australia*, Melbourne, 1928.

Pierce, P., 'Rider Haggard in Australia', *Meanjin*, vol. 36 (1977), pp. 200–7.

Plant, G. F., *Oversea Settlement. Migration from the United Kingdom to the Dominions*, London, 1951.

Pope, D., 'Empire Migration to Canada, Australia, and New Zealand, 1910–1929', *Australian Economic Papers*, vol. 7 (1968), pp. 167–88.

——, 'The Contributon of United Kingdom Migrants to Australia's Population, Employment and Economic Growth; Federation to the Depression', *Australian Economic Papers*, vol. 16 (1977), pp. 194–209.

——, 'Assisted Immigration and Federal-State Relations 1901–30', *Australian Journal of Politics and History*, vol. 28 (1982), pp. 23–50.

——, 'Some Factors Inhibiting Australian Immigration in the 1920s', *Australian Economic History Review*, vol. 24 (1984), pp. 34–52.

——, and Withers, G., *Immigration and Unemployment. A Long Term Perspective*, Canberra, 1985.

Powell, J. M., *An Historical Geography of Modern Australia. The Restive Fringe*, Cambridge, 1988.

Pughe, T. S. P., *The Problem of Migration and Unemployment*, London, 1928.

Richmond, W. H., 'S. M. Bruce and Australian Economic Policy 1923–9', *Australian Economic History Review*, vol. 23 (1983), pp. 238–57.

Robertson, J., *J. H. Scullin. A Political Biography*, Perth, 1974.

Robinson, R., *The Drift of the Things*, Melbourne, 1973.

Roe, M., 'H. W. Gepp. His Qualification as Chairman of the Development and Migration Commission', *Tasmanian Historical Research Association Papers and Proceedings*, vol. 32 (1985), pp. 95–110.

——, 'Strikebound in Cape Town, 1925; Responses aboard an Australian Migrant Ship', *Labour History*, no. 53 (1987), pp. 73–85.

——, ' "The Best and Most Practical Mind": J. B. Brigden ... 1921–30', *Journal of Australian Studies*, no. 30 (1991), pp. 72–84.

Schedvin, C. B., *Australia and the Great Depression. A Study of Economic Development and Policy in the 1920s and 1930s*, Sydney, 1970.

Scholes, A. G., *Education for Empire Settlement. A Study of Juvenile Migration*, London, 1932.

Searle, G. R., *The Quest for National Efficiency*, Oxford, 1971.

Sharpley, C. H., *The Great Delusion. The Autobiography of an ex-Communist Leader*, London, 1952.

Sherington, G., *Australia's Immigrants 1788–1978*, Sydney, 1980.

——, *The Dreadnought Boys*, privately printed.

Simons, J. J., *Reflections*, Perth, 1926.

Sissons, R. and Stoddart, B., *Cricket and Empire. The 1932–33 Bodyline Tour of Australia*, Sydney, 1984.

Smith, N. S., *Economic Control. Australian Experiments in 'Rationalisation' and 'Safeguarding'*, London, 1929.

Soldatow, S., *Poet of the 21st Century. Harry Hooton. Collected Poems*, Sydney, 1990.

Strickland, M., *Angela Thirkell. Portrait of a Lady Novelist*, London, 1977.

Swann, B., and Turnbull, M., *Records of Interest to Social Scientists 1919 to 1939. Employment and Unemployment*, Public Record Office Handbooks no. 18, London, 1978.

Teakle, L. J. H., *The David Teakle Saga*, Brisbane, 1979.

Tennant, K., *Evatt. Politics and Justice*, Sydney, 1970.

Thirkell, A., *Trooper to the Southern Cross*, Melbourne, 1966 (first published, 1934).

Thompson, R. W., *Down Under. An Australian Odyssey*, London, 1932.

——, *Glory Hole*, London, 1933.

Tsokhas, K., *Markets, Money, and Empire. The Political Economy of the Australian Wool Industry*, Melbourne, 1990.

——, 'People or Money? Empire Settlement and British Emigration to Australia, 1919–34', *Immigration & Minorities*, vol. 9 (1990), pp. 1–20.

——, ' "A Pound of Flesh"; War Debts and Anglo-Australian Relations, 1919–1932', *Australian Journal of Politics and History*, vol. 38 (1992), pp. 12–26.

——, ' "Hard Times": British Emigration to Western Australia 1919–1934', *Journal of the Royal Australian Historical Society*, vol. 78 (1992), pp. 69–91,

Turnor, C. H., *Land Settlement for Ex-Servicemen in the Oversea Dominions*, London, 1920.

Wade, C. G., *Australia. Problems and Prospects*, Oxford, 1919.

Wignall, O., *Chancy Times*, Mundaring, 1991.

Wildavsky, A, and Carboch, D., *Studies in Australian Politics*, Melbourne, 1958.

Williamson, P., *National Crisis and National Government. British Politics, the Economy and Empire, 1926–1932*, Cambridge, 1992.

Winspear, R. W., *Taking Stock. A Tasmanian Viewpoint*, Launceston,1935.

Withers, G., *The Immigration Contribution to Human Capital Formation*, Canberra, 1987.

Index